LET THEM TREMBLE

LET THEM TREMBLE

Biographical Interventions Marking 100 Years of the Communist Party, USA

TONY PECINOVSKY

With a foreword by
GERALD HORNE

INTERNATIONAL PUBLISHERS, New York

First Edition, 2019 by International Publisher's Co., Inc. / NY
With Foreword by Gerald Horne, © 2019

Printed in the United States of America

This Printing, 2021

ISBN-10 0-7178-0769-X   ISBN-13 978-0-7178-0769-7
Typeset by Amnet Systems, Chennai, India

Contents

Foreword by Gerald Horne

This book is a worthy exploration of one of the more important developments in recent times: the rise of an organized force designed to bring about socialism in the long term and, in the short term, to struggle relentlessly against all forms of bigotry – class bias, white supremacy, male supremacy and homophobia not least. Moreover, this organized force is sworn to build what I call the "class project," i.e. unions at the workplace and, more to the point: a political party designed to contest for political power.

In order to grasp fully the remarkable nature of this phenomenon, it is important to take a brief stroll down memory lane. In the early stages of the European invasion of the Americas, post-1492, religion was an animating factor in society. Indeed, saving souls was – ostensibly – a reason for obtaining enslaved labor from Africa or proselytizing among the indigenous of the Americas (the latter too were enslaved, of course).

Like day following night, this led ineluctably to the development of an "abolitionist" movement – among the enslaved in the first instance, then joined by their allies. Abolishing slavery became a holy crusade, that led directly to the Haitian Revolution, 1791-1804, which contributed to a general crisis of the entire system of slavery, that could only be resolved by its collapse. That is to say, Haitian revolutionaries, like their counterparts before and since, not only provided a "dangerous" example for slaveholders but, as well, were interested in spreading their abolitionist gospel far and wide,[1] which then impelled London to seek to abolish the Trans-Atlantic traffic in the enslaved by 1807, then abolish slavery altogether by the 1830s. This contributed to enormous pressure on the slaveholders' republic based in Washington, D.C., leading to a Civil War, which at a bloody cost led to the abolition of slavery by 1865 in the U.S. itself.

However, this immense development fed a counter-revolution in the form of the rise of the Ku Klux Klan and the effective nullification of the rights of the newly freed enslaved population, as had been embodied in constitutional amendments, especially (male) suffrage and putatively guaranteeing "equal protection under the law."

Still, the post-1865 era also featured the acceleration of another potent trend that had arisen in the antebellum era: the organizing of trade unions, e.g. the Knights of Labor and the American Federation of Labor.

This earlier "class project" received added impetus in 1917 with the Bolshevik Revolution, which led in turn to the subject of the book at hand: the organizing of the Communist Party, USA. Just as 1865 signified the uncompensated expropriation of private property, generating a tidal wave of fury fueling the rise of the KKK, 1917 also involved the battering of economic royals and their subsequent unremitting rancor.

Yet as this book indicates, this latter force was met by a countervailing force, that advanced the "class project" in the 1930s by dint of organizing of industrial unions, the Congress of Industrial Organizations, targeting steel and automobile plants in particular, leading to a rise in wages and improvement of working conditions. This herculean effort was spearheaded by the CPUSA.

As detailed in these stimulating pages, among those who joined the ranks of the vanguard was the lanky intellectual, W. Alphaeus Hunton. From his perch as a teacher at Howard University in Washington, D.C. – the capstone of Negro Education, as it was then termed – he not only instructed in the classroom but led on the picket-lines as a premier official of the American Federation of Teachers.

Hunton was blessed to possess a lengthy lineage of abolitionism. Canada, then a British possession, was a bulwark of abolitionism – especially after the 1830s – and was the home of the Hunton family. Hunton's ancestors worked alongside the heroic John Brown, who led a revolt against slavery in 1859 that set the stage for the onset of the U.S. Civil War, a few years later.

Hunton's father was a religious missionary, just as the younger was a kind of political missionary. By 1906 the Huntons were residing in Atlanta, on Houston Street, not far distant from the flashpoint of a pogrom that notoriously targeted African Americans. By 1907 the family had fled to Brooklyn and by 1910 Hunton the younger accompanied his mother to Germany where there was an acceptance of socialism and socialist parties, assuredly unlike what they had experienced in Georgia. Hunton's father died prematurely and his mother's influence on him grew accordingly. Addie Hunton was a primary force in favor of peace and Pan-Africanism, where she toiled selflessly alongside W.E.B. DuBois – and was monitored and surveilled relentlessly by Washington.

Her son continued the tradition from his post at Howard University in the 1930s, where he helped to organize domestic workers, a job held disproportionately by African American women. He fought for the appointment of African Americans to the local Unemployment Compensation Committee and successfully insisted upon the right of unemployed African Americans to register for jobs in the Works Progress Administration. With Hunton serving as Chairman of the Labor Committee of the Washington branch of the National Negro Congress, a vigorous campaign was mounted to ensure a decent wage for laundry workers, who were also disproportionately African American. It was Hunton who led the organizing of mass protests of the right of African Americans to obtain employment in the city's public transit system and to be hired at the Glenn L. Martin aircraft factory in Baltimore. During the course of this campaign, he led delegations to meet with – and pressure – government officials.

In the midst of the anti-fascist war in the 1940s, Hunton moved to New York City to work beside Paul

Robeson in the Council on African Affairs, which had been organized to push aggressively for decolonization of Africa and the Caribbean. The end of the anti-fascist war in 1945 led to an acceleration of what had been commenced in 1917 and receded somewhat because of the press of defeating Hitler and the Axis powers: The Cold War, i.e. the ongoing effort to destabilize then existing socialism.

Like so many of his comrades, Ben Davis, Jr., and William L. Patterson most notably, Hunton too served time in prison because of his political beliefs, a rite of passage for too many Communists then. By 1960 Hunton and his equally valiant spouse, Dorothy Hunton, moved to Africa – Conarky, Guinea at first then to Accra, Ghana where he reunited with DuBois. It was there in August 1963 that he led a group of expatriates protesting U.S. Jim Crow at the time when Dr. Martin Luther King, Jr., was leading hundreds of thousands in a March on Washington with the same goal at mind. However, yet another counter-reaction ensued, in the form of a CIA aided coup there overthrowing Kwame Nkrumah's government in Accra. It was at that juncture that the Huntons moved further south to recently independent Zambia, where Hunton passed away in 1970, as Founding Father, Kenneth Kaunda, wept at his graveside.[2]

Hunton and the other stalwarts sketched in these riveting pages are beacons lighting the path to a complex future. As such, studying their lives – and emulating their examples – has to be seen as a priority for the 21st century and beyond.

Gerald Horne, May 2019

Acknowledgements

The book at hand is a modest attempt to tell a story, or to at least tell part of a story. As such, I am deeply indebted to the comrades who continued to organize, fight for and popularize the perspectives of the Communist Party, USA, especially in the post-1956 period. Your determination and tenacity is worth emulating. Your story is worth being told. To not tell your story is to not fully comprehend and understand the second half of 20th century U.S. history. It is to deny your existence.

I am lucky to have support and encouragement from a number of individuals and institutions. Communist Party leaders Joe Sims, Roberta Wood, John Bachtell, C.J. Atkins and Chauncey Robinson among others, offered encouragement and insight. Tim Johnson, director of Tamiment Library and editor of the journal *American Communist History*, offered feedback on various chapters as they were developed, and happily accommodated my research schedule at NYU. Gary Bono, at International Publishers, saw early potential in the project. Don Giljum and Al Neal also read chapters and offered feedback. Andrew Zimmerman, at George Washington University, was always positive and encouraging. Gerald Horne, at the University of Houston, not only inspires me with his prolific research, but also encouraged my work on this project. Zimmerman and Horne, among others, indulged my excitement at creating a panel for the 2019 Organization of American Historians Annual Conference on the 100th Anniversary of the CPUSA, where some of my research on party activism during the 1960s youth and student upsurge was presented. Joel Wendland, at Grand Valley State University, was an early supporter as well. Jimmy Lappe also offered constructive criticism and encouragement. Without the generous support of Long View Publishing, the Chelsea Fund for Education, and the *St. Louis Workers' Education Society* this project would not have been possible.

It is impossible to list everybody who supported this project and saw this book through to completion. Know that I appreciate all of you!

This book is dedicated to my daughter, Ida. Perhaps the lives outlined in these pages will be an inspiration to you and your generation as you chart your own path towards a better and brighter future.

Throughout the process of researching and writing this book, I have remained unapologetically partisan. Historical objectivity is a ridiculous concept. All errors are mine and mine alone.

Abbreviations and Acronyms

American Federation of Labor - AFL
American Indian Movement - AIM
African National Congress - ANC
Civil Rights Congress - CRC
Communist Party, USA - CPUSA
Congress of Industrial Organizations - CIO
Council on African Affairs - CAA
Free Speech Movement - FSM
House Un-American Activities Committee - HUAC
International Publishers - IP
International Labor Defense - ILD
Labor Youth League - LYL
National Alliance Against Racist and Political Repression - NAARPR, or National Alliance
National Negro Congress - NNC
National Anti-Imperialist Movement In Solidarity with African Liberation - NAIMSAL
National Student Association - NSA
People's Coalition for Peace and Justice - PCPJ
Progressive Youth Organizing Committee - PYOC
Native Organizers Alliance - NOA
National Youth and Student Peace Coalition - NYSPC
South African Communist Party - SACP
Southern Christian Leadership Conference - SCLC
Southern Negro Youth Congress - SNYC
Steel Workers Organizing Committee - SWOC
Students for a Democratic Society – SDS
Student Nonviolent Coordinating Committee - SNCC
Trade Union Unity League - TUUL
United States Student Association - USSA
W.E.B. DuBois Clubs - DBC
Young Communist League - YCL
Young Workers Liberation League - YWLL

LET THEM TREMBLE

Author Introduction: A familiar tremble

More than 170 years ago Karl Marx and Friedrich Engels in the *Communist Manifesto* wrote, "Let the ruling classes tremble at a communist revolution. The proletarians have nothing to lose but their chains. They have a world to win. Workingmen of all countries, unite!"[1] With the triumph of the Bolshevik Revolution in 1917, the formation of the Soviet Union and the corresponding emergence of Communist Parties throughout the world, the objective conditions were ripe for the working class to take full advantage of the "general crisis of the capitalist system," as historian Gerald Horne noted in 2017,[2] the centennial year of that historic revolution. For a brief moment in world history the ruling class did in fact tremble. The end was nigh – in possession, if not also in person. Though it may be difficult to imagine today, ascendant socialism compelled a retreat away from the most egregious aspects of capitalism and imperialism. Regardless of conditions within the geographical borders of the Soviet Union and later the Eastern European states, for more than 70 years this experiment in socialism projected a democratic, anti-racist, anti-sexist, pro-worker, egalitarian vision externally – a vision those professing allegiance to liberal, Western democracy, especially in the United States, were compelled to compare themselves to and compete against. Kristen Ghodsee notes, "the Soviet Union and its allies often accused the capitalist West of failing to improve the lives of women, youth, workers, and racial minorities." These "accusations...forced attention to marginalized groups and proved productive" in the struggles for economic and social justice. Additionally, "coalitions between the Eastern Bloc countries and nations in the developing world forced concessions from the advanced capitalist countries." Ultimately, she concludes, "the world's workers benefited from the ideological tensions that manifested themselves" between the capitalist West and the socialist East.[3] It was, in part, these "ideological tensions" that forced a reappraisal away from the ugliest, most vile aspects of U.S. domestic and foreign policy, and toward concessions. Further, the damage sustained by American democratic institutions due to the ongoing violation of African American civil liberties, for example, not only called into question the intent of U.S. transnational politics in the contest for hearts and minds during the Cold War,[4] it also provided fodder for the socialism's external projection, a fact not lost on astute members of the Communist Party, USA.

In 1966, the African American revolutionary, Henry Winston, told his comrade and friend, James E. Jackson, "U.S. imperialism had to take...into account" Soviet aid to national liberation movements. "It had to make concessions on the home front as a condition for the pursuance of its neo-colonialist policies" abroad.[5] In other words, the soft the under belly of U.S. imperialism was vulnerable. That the then "growing strength of the socialist world has weakened the hold of the imperialist powers on Africa and Asia,"[6] as the one-time Communist councilman from Harlem, Benjamin Davis, Jr., noted, wasn't lost on reds. That African Americans and Africans both looked East in their search for allies[7] served to bolster what I call a Red-Black alliance[8] that would span decades and continents. In 1960, William L. Patterson, head of the party-led Civil Rights Congress often referred to as "Mr. Civil Rights,"[9] told 500 students at Simmons College, the developing nations of Africa and Asia "get loans [from the Soviet Union] without entangling political conditions." Ascendant socialism, he continued, was "prepared to negotiate on terms of full equality without condescension, free from arrogance or an air of white superiority."[10] This reality forced U.S. imperialism to rethink its commitment to domestic Jim Crow and support of Europe's fading colonial empires. W. Alphaeus

Hunton, mainstay of the Council on African Affairs, reinforced Winston, Davis and Patterson's comments with exhaustive documentation in his book *Decision in Africa.* He argued, "the peoples of Asia, the Middle East and Africa" were no-longer forced to "bend the knee," as he put it. For "they now have an alternative to Western markets in the socialist sector of the world...The *kind* of assistance given is of more significance than the quantity," [*italic* in original] as the socialist states assisted "poorer countries" with "barter transactions that will enable the countries to industrialize themselves"[11] free from debilitating interest rates or austerity conditions. The young Communist Bettina Aptheker noted a similar political shift in her spring 1969 *Political Affairs* article. "One-third of the world is socialist. One-third of the world is in the throes of revolution to achieve national liberation...While the *will* of imperialism to crush revolutions has not altered, its *power* to execute counter-revolution is not unlimited. It no longer enjoys hegemony in the world" [*italic* in original].[12] Chicago-area party leader Claude Lightfoot echoed these comments at a 1979 conference sponsored by the National Black United Fund. "The balance of forces in the world has changed," he said. "The system of capitalism is no longer the dominant force." Further, the "advancement of black people in this country is not in isolation from what is happening in the rest of the world. We are part of a world-wide revolutionary process," he argued, a process "assisted by the Soviet Union and other socialist countries." To the 800 conference attendees, it probably came as somewhat of a surprise to learn that the Soviet Union made "a tremendous contribution in terms of money, material and education" to the struggle for African American equality and national liberation,[13] a reality likely surprising to most Americans today nearly 30 years after the USSR's collapse.

While illuminating the support given by the Soviet Union to the struggle for African American equality and national liberation, for example, adds nuance and complexity to our understanding of both Marxist internationalism and the strategic utilization of *realpolitk*, it is equally important to highlight Moscow's support of individual Communists and Communist Parties – tangible, demonstrative support. For example, in spring 1990, William Pomeroy, the former Philippine Huk guerilla and political prisoner,[14] candidly wrote to his friend and comrade, Marilyn Bechtel; he was lamenting the slow-motion collapse of "Real Socialism."[15] While he and his wife were busily making plans to visit the Soviet Union, Pomeroy wrote, "As the CPSU [Communist Party of the Soviet Union] loses its leading status, the hospitality facilities for brother parties may dwindle away." Begrudgingly, he added, "quotas for rest are [already] nearly cut in half," while free transportation to some Soviet Republics had been eliminated altogether. "We expect that facilities like party hotels may have to be dispensed with," a modest perk for aging revolutionary. "Well, we've been there 20 times or more," he told Bechtel, "and knew it in its better days and the memories are good to live with." Pomeroy, a member of both the Philippine Communist Party and the CPUSA, was making this trip as part of the PKP annual "rest quota."[16] By simply providing travel, leisure and rest, a reprieve from the often harsh conditions of revolutionary life, the Soviet Union aided Marxist movements throughout the world.

Historian Julia Mickenberg noted, the Soviet Union articulated *and* reinforced "networks of hope" with material aid. It was the "fact of Soviet Russia's existence,"[17] its willingness to subsidize peace conferences, world youth festivals, training schools, international trade union confederations, women's congresses, educational seminars, friendship tours, cultural exchanges, travel and rest, as well as countless Marxist journals, newspapers and books (through subscriptions and royalty payments) in multiple languages that nurtured the rise of the global left for much of the 20th century. Direct military and technical aid to decolonizing nations and financial assistance to sister parties only partially captures the varied ways in which the USSR practiced international solidarity. This interconnected, mutually beneficial global network of hope should not be in dispute and is the foundation stone on which my analysis of the Communist in this study rests – and partly explains the then trembling within the U.S. ruling class.

That the CPUSA had links to and support from the Soviet Union is not in dispute.[18] Further, this support is best understood, acknowledged and studied as a by-product of a prolonged international contest between two competing ideological and economic rivals – rivals that viewed the struggles for African American equality,[19] national liberation and women's rights[20] through very different lenses. Acknowledging that Communists and their allies were inspired by the birth of the first socialist state[21] is not an admission of guilt; domestic Communists were not Soviet puppets. They initiated and led many of the most important struggles in 20th century U.S. history, especially among African Americans,[22] hardly because of Moscow's dictates. They fought and struggled, organized and mobilized, because they sincerely believed in creating a better, more egalitarian world right here, in the United States – where they lived. That workers everywhere have, "shall we say, a portion [an interest] in Marxism has something to do with bread and housing, with wages and working conditions, with the fight against fascism, with the struggle [for] revolution and socialism," party cultural writer, V.J. Jerome, noted in a 1937 issue of *The Communist.* This reality, he added, "is, on the whole, an unpleasant intrusion," an all-together series of "constant rude interruptions"[23] that ruling elites lazily blamed on rising Bolshevism rather than poverty, poor working conditions, exploitation and oppression generally.

While some domestic reds had their gaze fixed abroad,[24] most did not. Instead, they looked to domestic radical traditions for inspiration.[25] Harlem's Communist councilman, Benjamin Davis, Jr., summed up the dominant sentiment among party members when he told students at Brown University, "I joined the Communist Party as a result of my experience as a Negro." He said that he was "looking for freedom and first-class citizenship," that his Communist beliefs were "made in the U.S.A."[26] George Meyers, Baltimore party leader and long-time CPUSA labor commission chair, made a similar comment regarding the 1956 Khrushchev revelations revealing Stalin's crimes: "I joined the Communist Party because of the class struggle in the United States... That's why I never had any problems about all these foreign ups and downs."[27] Others, like Anne Burlak, who in the 1930s was labeled a red, and so figured, "I might as well join the Communist Party and learn more about it," refused to fall into the anticommunist trap. Burlak, known as the 'Red Flame,' energetically embraced the presumption of membership and became one of the most well-known organizers of the Communist-led National Textile Workers' Union and remained a party member the rest of her life. "My class struggle education developed rapidly," Burlak recalled. "Daily experience in the mill taught me that my boss and I had nothing in common. He was looking out for ever more profits, which he could only achieve at his workers' expense. We were anxious to increase our wages, which we could accomplish only if our boss would part with a bit of his profits."[28] As Charlene Mitchell, the first African American woman to run for president of the United States, said, people of color joined the party, "not out of love for the Soviet Union but because they believed socialism to be the necessary response to capitalism and oppression."[29] Of course, the party's stellar reputation fighting for African American equality figured into this political equation. Mexican American party leader Ralph Cuaron would note in retrospect, "I don't remember ever thinking of accepting some doctrine or some order [from abroad]. Of course, I was a very ardent reader. I read the science of Marxism. I didn't consider that as an order from Moscow."[30] Tim Wheeler, a *Worker* reporter, added, "The Soviet Union was never the main thing for me. We were always so involved, so deeply immersed in local struggles, it was almost an afterthought." For Wheeler, party membership was "about the personal connections with people. It's all about the people."[31] The *Daily World* editorialized during the party's 50th Anniversary in 1969, "The U.S.A., beginning with 1776, has been the battle ground for many parties and movements in the search for freedom...The Communist party grew out of these gallant struggles and native movements."[32] Gus Hall, the party's general secretary, addressed the claim that Communists were nothing more than Soviet agents too. He turned the slander on its head. The CPUSA is "an indigenous Party, native in our roots and form," he said. "Capitalism is the foreign transplant from Europe," he added. "Our roots [are] Native Indian communialism [sic]...truly American...[a] unique but integral part of the life of this country."[33] Like his comrades, Hall associated the CPUSA with domestic radical democratic traditions. The class struggle, not Moscow, inspired party membership.

Though solidarity with and affinity for the Soviet Union put some Communists in a morally precarious situation – especially, after 1956 with the Khrushchev revelations and the suppression of the Hungarian Revolution – it did not make them bad organizers or any less committed to the struggles for democracy, workers' rights, African American equality, and socialism domestically.[34] Rather, the loss of Communists – and the organizations they led – proved to be a major setback for the domestic movement for social and economic justice.[35]

Deeply held convictions rooted in the American radical tradition, however, did not save Communists from the ongoing and prolonged violation of their civil liberties. Throughout the 20th century, CPUSA members were often targets of political repression. They were labeled agents of a foreign power and "denied every shred of justice in the courts."[36] For much of its 100 year existence the CPUSA has been hounded, harassed, infiltrated and spied on. As a result, civil liberties for all Americans have suffered. Party leaders were even harassed in death; at William Z. Foster's memorial, for example, pickets declared "We Hate Reds" and "One Less Red Pest."[37] The lawyer John Abt noted in his memoirs, "After more than three decades as general counsel of the Communist party, I know as well as anyone the extent and extremes of repression to which this mightiest of all governments in history has gone to destroy a small Party of modest means because it sought to fundamentally alter the existing relations of economic and political power... Its leaders have repeatedly been imprisoned, often for years, without having committed a criminal act."[38] Party leader Henry Winston, lost his eye sight due to prison negligence[39] ; Robert Thompson - a World War II veteran awarded the Distinguished Service Cross - was nearly beaten to death (Thompson and other Communists would later be denied their veterans' pensions, as well)[40] ; still others, like Ella Mae Wiggins (Gastonia Strike),[41] Joseph Rothmund (Little Steel Strike),[42] Joe York (Ford Hunger March)[43] and Oliver Law (Spanish Civil War),[44] gave their lives fighting for workers' rights, African American equality and the struggle against fascism abroad. Communists organized 3,000 volunteers to serve with the Abraham Lincoln Brigade and fight fascism in Spain,[45] while an estimated 15,000 Communists served with honor in the armed forces during WWII,[46] including two of the Communists discussed in this book, namely, Hall and Winston.

Fred Graham, Supreme Court correspondent for *The New York Times* and former special assistant to the secretary of labor, wasn't wrong when in fall 1965 he postulated, "Its [the CPUSA's] funds and energies have been depleted by the constant litigation. As an instrument of harassment, the law [the Smith Act] has been a success."[47] It failed miserably at its stated purpose, though, of forcing reds to register - a classic political bait-and-switch. Conservative political leaders knew reds would refuse to register on constitutional grounds.

Communists likened registration to political "suicide,"[48] as was well known. To register would be to acquiesce to two equally dangerous and demonstratively false claims. First, that Communists by their membership in the CPUSA advocated for the overthrow of the U.S. government through "force and violence." Second, that they were nothing more than agents of a foreign power, namely the Soviet Union. The Red Scare was a pretext for political repression. The real goal was to harass, demonize, isolate, and bankrupt Communists and the organizations they led, to destroy what was – for a brief moment in history – a vibrant and expansive culture of working class militancy. Fearful that Communists might succeed in shifting domestic political discourse dramatically to the left, ruling elites set out to destroy its ability to function as a legal entity. A more complex political framework emerges when registration is viewed in this context. Instead, it was the party's ideological commitment to democracy and its members' unique working class approach to protecting the Bill of Rights,[49] rather than a presumed conspiracy to use "force and violence," that caused increased fear among ruling elites and political charlatans who used redbaiting scare tactics to justify their civil liberties assault. They hoped to confine domestic political discourse safely within the bounds of liberal capitalism. The Communist Party was their boogey man, the monster in the closet.

Fortunately, as party leader Elizabeth Gurley Flynn put it, "the Communist Party has been compelled to fight for its own existence. In so doing it has spearheaded the fight for the rights of others,"[50] especially African Americans. As Horne notes, "despite its flaws, the party was probably unparalleled in not just fighting racism in society but within the ranks as well,"[51] the Yokinen Trail[52] being but one example. The party's struggle against racism "redefined the debate over white supremacy and hastened its end," as Glenda Gilmore argued. The "very existence" of the CPUSA constituted "a threat" to racism, she added, as Communists "stood up to say that black and white people should organize together, eat together, go to school together, and marry each other if they choose."[53] African American party leader James W. Ford noted in 1939, Communists "through their pioneering work in the South, may justly claim to have laid the foundation for these great social movements," namely the National Negro Congress and the Southern Negro Youth Congress – organizations that built the architectural framework for the modern civil rights movement. This "new phase of struggle" also "marked the transition of the Communist Party from a minority, fighting almost alone on this issue [of African American equality], into a definite part of the democratic majority" thereby winning the "respect and confidence of the Negro people."[54] It is little wonder then that even moderate African Americans in the heartland, like Chester Arthur Franklin of the *Kansas City Call*, opined to the FBI: "my people are interested in Communistic views or are members of the Communist Party" due to white people "continually suppressing and oppressing the Negroes. At least in Russia everyone is equal according to their philosophy."[55] Long time party stalwart Arnold Johnson, like many of his comrades, echoed Franklin's remarks, while highlighting the centrality of African American equality to the struggle for democracy. During this time, Communists began to shift away from the Black Belt thesis and self-determination.[56] To Johnson, the centrality of the struggle for African American equality wasn't just about expanding democracy. It was also about stunting the post-war conservative backlash as returning veterans, particularly Black veterans, fought against white supremacists determined to reassert the pre-war racial order. As Johnson wrote, "It is, therefore, no accident that the Negro people are most alert as a people to the need of fighting for the rights of Communists" and "see the meaning of this struggle in terms of bitter experience of brutality and oppression." He also wrote with pride, "They [African Americans] see the common enemy. Ever greater numbers among them also see in the Communist Party the champion of their struggle,"[57] which partly explains why Black luminaries like Paul Robeson and W.E.B. DuBois – among others – threw their lot in with Communists. At a June 19, 1949, Welcome Home rally in Harlem the athlete, actor, artist, and secret party member Paul Robeson[58] told a crowd of 5,000, "I'm not afraid of Communists; no, far from that. I will defend them as they defended us, the Negro people." "Their struggle is our struggle," he added.[59] That the Communist Party had "unquestionably been a powerful factor" in the advancement of African American equality, as William Z. Foster noted,[60] made Blacks less susceptible to anticommunism generally, and helps to explain why white Communists, like Lee Lorch[61] – who, along with his wife, in September 1957 accompanied the Little Rock Nine as they attempted entry into that city's Central High School amid threats by white supremacists, segregationists and KKK members[62] – are still remembered fondly today. Perhaps, this sentiment coupled with a robust international coalition building strategy also explains the support awarded Angela Davis, domestically and internationally, during her frame-up trial. If hindsight is 20/20, then the domestic post-war anticommunist hysteria *and* the growing right-wing fear of an emerging Black militancy comfortable with red allies, can be considered symptoms emanating from a general crisis of capitalism, a crisis spurred by socialism's advances around the world.

This crisis was a manifestation born of fear and weakness, which may also come as a surprise to some. African American party leader William L. Patterson told 5,000 demonstrators at a 1963 May Day rally in New York's Union Square, "in Africa, Asia, Europe and Latin America more than a hundred million people are marching in cities where they hold the destinies in their hands." The ruling class, he added, is "haunted by fear of those free peoples, fears of our class." They are "haunted by [a] greater fear of unity,"[63] he concluded, particularly the still potent Red-Black alliance – something Patterson had been instrumental in building as lead council for the Scottsboro Nine and as head of the CRC.[64] The Marxist historian and Communist Herbert Aptheker articulated a similar theme. He told 4,000 people at the National Conference for a United Front Against Fascism sponsored by the Black Panther Party in July 1969, "Two basic things must be kept in mind as one considers ruling class movements towards fascism. One," he said, "is that such a tendency reflects *weakness* on the part of that class; its leading elements are tending to believe that it is not possible to rule in the old, legal way; that parliamentary methods and bourgeois-democratic forms are increasingly unmanageable and dangerous to their interests. And second, [that] fascism is not fated to win – even temporarily – anywhere and it never does win *unless its opponents are divided*" [*italic* in original],[65] hence the CPUSA's emphasis on multi-racial unity. Five years later, on July 4, 1974, nearly 10,000 people rallied with the party-led National Alliance Against Racist and Political Repression in Raleigh, North Carolina. Communist Angela Davis was the main speaker. Unity was the theme as the crowd drew attention to the state's disproportionate incarceration rates among people of color. Davis argued, we must lay "to rest the myth that the oppressed people of this land – Black, Brown, Red, Yellow, and white, and people of varied political and religious beliefs – cannot work together." Speaking alongside Davis was the Rev. Ralph D. Abernathy, head of the Southern Christian Leadership Conference. The heir to Dr. Martin Luther King, Jr.'s, SCLC was proud to publicly work with Communists. Ruling class efforts to isolate reds after decades of political repression was not entirely successful. "They must be trembling in Washington to see us holding hands today," Davis said as she put her arm around Abernathy. "Because...here is a minister, and here," she continued, tapping her chest, "is a Communist." Abernathy addressed the crowd, saying in part, "my Communist brothers and sisters" if President Nixon, "that trickster in Washington can go to Russia and sit down with the head of the Communist party, it is with pride and honor that I march with Angela Davis." The Red-Black alliance Communists had spent decades building still posed a formidable challenge. "Now we must consolidate our unity, make it firm as a rock," Davis added.[66] That ruling elites continued to fear such an alliance is easy to see in hindsight. That Communists, like Patterson, Aptheker and Davis, among others, continued to play a decisive role throughout much of the second-half of the 20th century is, however, unfortunately obscured by an ongoing insistence of the CPUSA's demise post-1956.

Though she was not part of the party's organizational apparatus, the folk revivalist Agnes 'Sis' Cunningham saw the CPUSA as her "political home."[67] This sentiment was shared by hundreds of thousands of activists throughout the party's 100 year history. Of course, some Communists found the burdens, contradictions and the ongoing harassment too much to bear, and like members of all political organizations, decided to move on. The fact that so many stayed despite repression is worthy of more analysis. One 1956 *New York Times* editorial commented, due to the wide array of oppressive legal measurers directed towards party members, as well as the recent Khrushchev revelations, "It is probably safe to say that none but the dedicated or the foolhardy would risk continued membership in the Communist party under such circumstances."[68] For example, Claude Lightfoot was spied on while serving in the U.S. military during WWII, was forced underground during the McCarthy period and had paid informants reporting his every move to the FBI. In what was surely a heart wrenching experience, the informants proved to be some of his "closest associates." That they were handsomely paid for their services added insult to injury.[69] Lightfoot's case is hardly unique. The climate of political repression sent a cold chill down the spine of sincere progressives, especially those exploring socialism. If, as some have argued, the CPUSA was a "shattered organization" "afflicted with a mortal illness" and played a negligible role after 1956 as its "membership plummeted,"[70] it seems odd that hundreds – if not thousands – of FBI personnel and informants [71] continued to harass the embattled and besieged organization. One FBI agent bragged, "'We'd have to back up a truck to the FBI office to load up all the wire-tap material we had on Arnold Johnson,'" then head of the party's Peace Commission. That the wiretap was conducted without a warrant[72] was just another example of the decades long assault on the Bill of Rights, the Communist Party and its leaders. It is partly due to the insistence of the CPUSA's decline post-1956 that this study places special emphasis on the 1960s, 1970s, 1980s, and on into the 2000s.

Though weakened, Communists played a vital role in many of the social and economic justice movements of the second half of the 20th century. It is estimated that reds spoke with at least 100,000 students on college and university campuses in the early 1960s as the student free speech movement emerged.[73] In the mid-1960s, Communists initiated the first call for an "international student [peace] strike"[74] against the war in Vietnam; and it was Communists – two of the Fort Hood Three[75] – who as soldiers, refused to deploy to that war-torn country, thereby marking "the genesis of the organized GI [anti-war] movement."[76] Additionally, it was Communists in the early and mid-1970s who founded and led Trade Unionists for Action and Democracy,[77] the National Anti-Imperialist Movement in Solidarity with African Liberation[78] and the National Alliance Against Racist and Political Repression,[79] which, respectively, helped initiate rank-and-file movements against labor's conservative – perhaps, reactionary – old guard, led the domestic divestment movement against apartheid South Africa and helped make legal history with the defense of Joanne Little, a North Carolina Black woman charged with murder while defending herself against sexual assault from a white prison guard, among other cases.[80] And it was Communists in the early 1980s who initiated and led the National Congress of the Unemployed.[81] Frank Lumpkin, chairman of the Wisconsin Steel Save Our Jobs Committee, which would later win multiple lawsuits against Wisconsin Steel totaling $14.5 million in back pay, pensions, and benefits,[82] keynoted the congress' founding convention. He and Scott Marshall, the congress' national organizing director, would move to posthumously elect Rudy Lozano, the Midwest director of organizing for the International Ladies Garment Workers' Union who had been assassinated in his home in June 1983, as chairman emeritus; Lozano was considered Harold Washington's right-hand man among Latino voters in his bid to become Chicago's first Black mayor.[83] That Lumpkin, Marshall, and Lozano were all also Communists[84] likely caused a familiar tremble among ruling elites in the Windy City, the birth place of the CPUSA. Other Communists were simultaneously registering impressive electoral results, not least of which was the independent candidate, St. Louis Alderman (22nd Ward) Kenny Jones. Jones, an iron-worker by trade, was elected in 1983 and was known for leaving copies of the *Daily World*, the party's newspaper, in Aldermanic chambers. In 2005, he would nearly come to blows with St. Louis' then mayor over a dispute regarding Jones' support for fellow red and Coalition of Black Trade Unionists leader, James 'Jay' Ozier – Jones' longtime Ward Committeeman, confidant and friend.[85] Further, it was Communists in the 2000s who would help lead United For Peace & Justice and the National Youth and Student Peace Coalition,[86] as they organized hundreds of thousands to take to the streets against the wars in Iraq and Afghanistan. NYSPC also organized an estimated "30,000 to 50,000 students at 400 to 500 colleges" to walk out demanding Books Not Bombs.[87] More recently, it would be a Communist, Rasheen Aldridge, who would be part of a meeting in December 2014 – 115 days after the killing of Michael Brown in Ferguson, Missouri – with then President Barrack Obama[88] to discuss race relations and police violence directed against people of color. Aldridge cut his political teeth as a fast food worker striking a local *Jimmy Johns* restaurant, and it was this activism – through the fast-food workers' local organizing committee – that Aldridge met Al Neal, the then Midwest coordinator of the Fight for $15, Nicholas James, an organizer with the Service Employees International Union-Health Care, and Mark Esters, an organizer with the Missouri State Workers' Union-CWA 6355, all Communists. Aldridge would soon officially join the Communist Party, USA at the party's 30th National Convention in June 2014,[89] roughly six months prior to his meeting with President Obama, who also welcomed the counsel of Communist, Frank Marshall Davis, while still a young man.[90] Obama would in 2018 also send congratulatory remarks to Beatrice Lumpkin for her 100th birthday celebration, an event at which hundreds of union organizers, activists, and elected officials, including Congresswoman Janice Schakowsky, packed the Chicago Federation of Teachers' Hall to celebrate the long life of a Communist.[91]

Perhaps, the recent upsurge and interest in socialism[92] is indicative of a larger trend, one that seems perfectly timed to correspond with the centennial of the Communist Party's birth. Perhaps, it is precisely these aftershocks, the waves of revolt that gained organizational form after the cataclysmic initial quake that was the Bolshevik Revolution and became ascendant world socialism, that the ruling class continues to fear. Perhaps, CPUSA general secretary, Gus Hall, was right when in 1961 he told reporters, "The attempt to jail ideas cannot succeed...Thought cannot be outlawed,"[93] a lesson right-wing demagogues seem painfully slow to learn, a lesson that continues to resonate today a century after the birth of the Communist Party, USA!

* * *

Let Them Tremble: Biographical Interventions Marking 100 Years of the Communist Party, USA is a collection of six biographies exploring unique and often neglected aspects of the CPUSA and its 100 year history. Each intervention explores a specific CPUSA leader's life, work and times – and situates them in political and historical context. The goal of these interventions is not to tell a complete story, to paint a complete picture; intimate knowledge of personal lives and relationships is not the goal and is largely absent from this text. Rather, the goal is to let each biography tell a *partial political story*, a story that emphasizes topical aspects of the party's ongoing work, especially in the post-1956 period. This project is not a complete history of the CPUSA. It is a series of thematic narratives. My hope is that each individual story helps build on and adds to a more complete history of the CPUSA, thereby helping to create a larger organizational narrative more easily digested and discussed.

The interventions collectively span the party's century-long history, not just the Hey Day, Popular Front, McCarthy, or Old Left periods. Special emphasis is placed on party activity and analysis in the 1960s, 1970s, and 1980s, and on into the 2000s. Comprehensive histories of party activity during the second half of the 20th century and early 21st century written by more competent authors is desperately needed. Unfortunately, due to a lingering Red Taboo [94] in much of U.S. historiography considerably less has been written about this period. Sadly, the prospects for a course correction are not promising. The biographies included herein should be considered a sincere attempt to modestly add some nuance and complexity, to explore a largely neglected period of Communist activity in U.S. history, and to add knowledge, breadth and depth to the study of U.S. radicalism in the post-1956 period while marking the 100th anniversary of the CPUSA.

Each biography consists of two or three overarching themes; the individual narratives largely focus on aspects of party work as they relate to these themes. Often party leaders held numerous positions within the organization and took on multiple assignments, which could easily constitute larger projects. However, the intent here is not to cover the waterfront. The Communists in this study spent most of their adult lives as party leaders, in one form or another. Some spent their lives as fulltime revolutionaries. Others never held an official party position and were never on party pay roll. Still others, served as fulltime party staff – in different capacities – but also led mass movements where their party membership was known, but not necessarily advertised. I have avoided party leaders who have already been given considerable biographical attention by other authors, such as William Z. Foster,[95] Earl Browder,[96] Claudia Jones,[97] Benjamin Davis, Jr.,[98] Elizabeth Gurley Flynn,[99] James and Esther Cooper Jackson,[100] William L. Patterson,[101] Herbert Aptheker,[102] and Angela Davis,[103] among others. Where significant accounts, for example from Henry Winston[104] and Claude Lightfoot,[105] are available, I have summarized and condensed, while attempting to highlight neglected or unique aspects.

Readers will no doubt note that only two women are included in this study. There are numerous reasons for this omission. The party made great strides to challenge sexism internally and externally with prominent women providing decisive leadership throughout its history. Of note are Ella Reeve 'Mother' Bloor, Elizabeth Gurley Flynn, Betty Millard, Claudia Jones, Moranda Smith, Emma Tenayuca, Shirley Graham DuBois, Esther Cooper Jackson, Dorothy Healy, Kendra Alexander and Angela Davis, among many others. However, it nonetheless remains a male dominated organization with a largely masculine persona. This project reflects those organizational shortcomings and weaknesses.

The party's substantial role building the U.S. labor movement, especially prior to the 1949 purge of Communist-led unions in the Congress of Industrial Organizations,[106] is well known. This study, however, does not place that role front and center. Instead, the focus here can primarily be divided into a number of overlapping thematic categories: the struggle for African American equality and Indigenous rights; Marxist internationalism, the anti-Vietnam War movement and peace; the youth and student upsurge of the 1960s and 1970s, free speech and the Bill of Rights; and the party's efforts at public access television in the late 1990s and early 2000s, for example. Of course, other, less pronounced topics are also discussed. This project hopes to add to our understanding of 20th century U.S. Communist activity and fill the gap in the historiography of U.S. radicalism in the post-1956 period.

The Communists in this study – as well as others – constituted a tight core of political activists who shared many of the same beliefs, values, and concerns. They were movement coworkers, cohorts and comrades. As such, their lives often intersected. The biographies included herein reflect this and situate Communists within a small but impactful subsection of our nation's political history, a history that should be studied and appreciated.

Though *Let Them Tremble* does consult an array of primary and archival sources (speeches, personal letters, memos, pamphlets, articles, interviews), it also relies on secondary sources (published autobiographies, biographies, party histories, academic articles). By weaving together disparate sources largely available to general readers with archival material requiring ongoing research, this project aspires to be an easily accessible collection of narratives. Fortunately for the historian, the subjects of this study live(d) very public lives. They projected a vision – a vision worth exploring. As a result, they left an abundance of public statements (articles, press releases, interviews). While this study does utilize personal correspondences, letters and unpublished works, it also relies on public and previously published sources, many from scholars to whom I am very grateful.

Of course, the party wasn't perfect. While this study is a decidedly celebratory and positive appraisal of the work of individual Communists, the CPUSA also deserves criticism. Internal sexism and homophobia are two of the major shortcomings those interested in CPUSA history must grapple with. Dogmatism and a less than critical view of Soviet society are another set of challenges. Factionalism and party splits, including the 1991 split[107] that occurred amidst the collapse of the Soviet Union, are also worthy of more analysis. However, these shortcomings – among others – cannot and should not discredit the tremendous contributions Communists made to the struggle for democracy, workers' rights, African American equality, national liberation, peace and socialism. Hundreds of volumes have been written about the shortcomings of the CPUSA; this is not such a volume. Readers interested in a negative appraisal of the CPUSA and its leaders will not want for material elsewhere. Those stories have been told. The stories contained in this book, however, are still in the process of being explored, expanded upon and understood in their rich complexities.

* * *

In late 1988 reporters asked Gus Hall what he would show Soviet Premier Mikhail Gorbachev as he visited New York City. "I wouldn't show him Trump Tower," Hall responded. "I would show him the homeless, the slums. I think it would do him good not to get a one-sided view. Trump Tower is not New York."[108] Hall was astute enough to see the opulent symbolism of Trump Tower, its appeal, and he deliberately chose to highlight the billionaire's abode, to draw attention to income inequality, obscene wealth on the one hand and devastating poverty on the other. To the aging revolutionary, the contradictions of capitalism were as evident as ever. Trump Tower embodied one side of this contradiction. The rise of right-wing demagoguery embodied another.

During World War II, Hall volunteered to fight fascism abroad. Hitler's rise to power had turned Europe to ashes. It was in large part due to the monumental sacrifices of the Soviet people that the Nazi war machine was turned back and eventually defeated. In 1972, Hall's comrade and fellow veteran, Claude Lightfoot, soberly reflected on Hitler's rise to power, and asked himself: "If an American Hitler took power...would the democratic, freedom-loving forces be able to overthrow him as the allied powers had overthrown Hitler?" "On his way to the grave," Lightfoot continued, "Hitler was prepared to carry the whole German nation down to destruction. An American Hitler, on his way to his grave, would not hesitate to use nuclear power and attempt to destroy the entire human race."[109] Lightfoot's prediction is now a harrowing prospect.

Of course, Hall and Lightfoot could not have envisioned the rise of Donald Trump to the Presidency of the United States. But they feared that such a person *could* come to power, hence their decades-long defense of the Bill of Rights, democracy and peace. They also saw how racism, sexism, xenophobia, and war mongering would be emboldened by such a figure – the ongoing assault on Black lives, notwithstanding. That white nationalist militia groups have seen a marked increase in membership and activism in recent years should not come as a surprise.[110] They have found an enabler in the White House, which should give every democratic minded person cause for alarm. That Communist and left forces no longer have an international and internationalist counterbalance that can bring external pressure to bear against the most egregious aspects of 21st century capitalism is sobering. Communists lost a world power, a benefactor and a nation committed to at least the projection of a more egalitarian vision. The collapse of the Soviet Union has resulted in the dramatic shifting of the political terrain, domestically and internationally, to the right.

It wasn't hard for Communists to see the correlation between the decline of the Soviet Union and the ascendancy of the far right in the United States, a movement that has propelled one of the most incompetent, narcistic, and unqualified men to the highest office in the land. It is obvious to Communists – and to progressives of all stripes – that Trump has "revealed himself as a Nazi sympathizer and white supremacist," facts that are equally apparent to the so-called "alt-right," Trump's "core base of support." Trump appealed to "racism, religious fundamentalism, hate and fear" during his presidential campaign.[111] Now he is governing as "The First White President," as *The Atlantic* put it.[112] Regardless, Trump's rise should not be seen in isolation. Rather, it is the byproduct of several interconnected events, not least of which is the parallel development of the demise of Soviet socialism and the ascendancy of the far right.

Throughout the 20th century, Communists fought the right wing domestically and fascism internationally – a fight that took many forms. For example, the Communist seaman Bill Bailey in 1936 quietly climbed aboard the *Bremen*, then Germany's largest passenger ship,[113] as it sat in New York Harbor; 10,000 anti-fascist activists protested on the docks. After tussling with some crew members, Bailey found his way to the main flagpole, "tore down the huge Nazi swastika flag, and flung it into the water." Onlookers "cheered wildly."[114] According to Bailey, the sacking of the *Bremen* helped to initiate a "more aggressive drive against war and fascism" in New York City. A Madison Square Garden rally just days later had 20,000 people in attendance. Bailey spent the next several weeks speaking at "two meetings a day, gathering funds and support for the coming trial." A year later, he was in Spain with the Abraham Lincoln Brigade fighting Franco's fascists. During World War II, the Jersey born radical served as a Liberty Ship engineer in the Pacific, Okinawa, the Solomon Islands and the Philippines,[115] where William Pomeroy also served.[116] At war's end Bailey's comrade, Lightfoot, sailed home aboard the *Bremen*, now recommissioned as a transport ship.[117]

In the early 1960s, Communists would fight another type of battle. This time, however, their staunchest allies were students – another lesson not lost on astute

Communists. Hall, who would speak to tens of thousands of students during the early to mid-1960s, often connected the fight for free speech generally to the fight to hear Communists specifically. "There is a very deep feeling," he told students in New York City, "that if you can preserve the right of Communists to speak, then you can preserve the right of all to speak. That's true. But it's more than just a fight for the right of Communists to speak. The fact is that they [youth and students] want to hear a Communist speak...They are sick and tired of hearing the so-called Communist viewpoint from anti-Communists,"[118] he concluded.

* * *

In the biographies that follow you will hear directly from Communists, how they saw themselves contributing to the struggles of the day. They will tell their story, a story that has over the course of 100 years redefined our collective understanding of democracy, workers' rights, African American equality, peace and socialism. In the pages that follow, perhaps a little light can be cast during these dark times!

Chapter **1**

Arnold Johnson: A "consistent and vigorous" defender of the Bill of Rights and the Peace Offensive

It was spring 1944. Arnold Johnson, the Ohio secretary of the Communist Party, USA, proudly boasted of 1,233 new party members since the New Year. Nearly 700 new members had joined in Cleveland alone, making it the largest party membership in that city's history. Johnson excitedly reported to his comrades, "We have brought into our ranks a far larger number of trade union leaders, especially local officers, shop stewards and others." That Johnson was optimistic was evident. He and Earl Browder, the party's then general secretary, proudly shared a platform with Cleveland city council members – a jubilant event where "a number of leading Negro Democrats and some Negro Republicans" joined the party on the spot[1] – aiding his positive appraisal of the political moment.

This was a far cry from just a few years earlier when the Ohio Secretary of State had barred Johnson from being on the ballot.[2] Not only were well known Communists like Johnson and Browder now publicly sharing the stage with mainstream political operatives, they were also garnering impressive election results. In his 1943 and 1945 bids for the Cleveland Board of Education, Johnson received roughly 43,000 and 56,300 votes, respectively[3] – an impressive turnout for the son of

Scandinavian immigrants who started working in the lumber mills at age 12.

* * *

Born in Seattle, Washington on September 23, 1904, Johnson briefly attended UCLA after high school before moving to Washington, DC in 1924 to study law. He attended the National University Law School but returned to Los Angeles one year later. As a young man, Johnson had been attracted to Christian socialism, so it is no surprise that he began his studies at California Christian College. He received a Bachelors of Arts degree in 1929 and then moved to New York where he continued his religious education at Union Theological Seminary.[4] While at seminary, he began to mature as a workers' rights advocate and was arrested for distributing leaflets for the International Ladies' Garment Workers Union.[5] In 1931, Johnson received his Masters' Degree in Christian Education, and in 1932 his Bachelors of Divinity. He was well on his way to becoming a preacher.

Johnson was deeply religious, but he was also practical and wanted to engage in workers' rights struggles directly; as a result, he began to balance his spiritual work with practical work "as a means of effective social reform." In 1931, on assignment from the American Civil Liberties Union, Johnson went to Harlan County, Kentucky, where he was arrested for "criminal syndicalism."[6] The Harlan County coal miners – represented by the CPUSA-led Trade Union Unity League affiliated National Miners Union[7] – had been locked in a bitter, often violent struggle with "coal operators, representing some of the largest financial interests in the country."[8] According to Johnson's comrade Jim West, in Harlan the "coal bosses...hired killers and bought up [the] police and judges."[9] Jesse Wakefield, a Communist with the International Labor Defense, a legal aid organization initiated by the party, found his home destroyed by dynamite. A half-dozen miners and their supporters were killed. Union sympathizers were arrested, beaten or deported; some supporters were even flogged publicly.[10] Later in life, Johnson would look back on the Harlan County miners' struggle and remark that he "should have studied the role of the Communist Party and joined it at that time." He spent six weeks in jail for supporting the coal miners.

In 1932, Johnson joined the Conference for Progressive Labor Action,[11] founded by A.J. Muste; the CPLA would later be reorganized into the American Workers' Party and then merge with a Trotskyist group.[12] TUUL founder and CPUSA leader William Z. Foster called the CPLA part of the "pseudo-left," those "fake left groups" that act as "auxiliaries of the right-wing [labor] bureaucracy" and "create illusions among the masses." During what would be called the Third Period, party leaders labeled the CPLA a "left social-fascist" organization,[13] and directed their verbal and physical broadsides at other Marxist groupings. By 1936 Johnson had become disillusioned with the Trotskyist "lack of unity" and joined the Communist Party. He participated in the merger of the Communist-led Unemployed Councils with the smaller Trotskyist-led Unemployed Leagues, among other independent groups, to form the Workers' Alliance. At its peak the Workers' Alliance claimed 800,000 members in 1,400 local chapters. Johnson served as national secretary of the Workers' Alliance.

In 1939, he became the Ohio Communist Party state secretary and served as state chairman from 1940 to 1947. He was a respected organizer and leader. In 1947, Johnson moved to New York and became the CPUSA's national legislative director. Gus Hall, the party's future general secretary, replaced him as chair of the Ohio CP.[14]

* * *

The celebratory mood of 1944 quickly dissipated after the conclusion of World War II. Shortly after arriving in New York, Johnson was embroiled in controversy as City

College New York banned him and other Communist speakers, including Howard Fast, from its campuses. In a press release dated December 10, 1947, Johnson articulated a theme that became the cornerstone of his political thought for decades to come. "The action of the City College administration is in itself not only a violation of the Bill of Rights," but "also a subversion of the educational process." Mirthlessly, he joked that the reactionary Mississippi Congressman John Rankin had gained the "position of honorary chancellor of the college with absolute right to tell students what to think." However, Johnson wasn't laughing when he added, "No self-respecting student or citizen with a free mind can accept the dogmatic decree" of the college administration. He then challenged the Dean to a "full debate on the meaning of the First Amendment," a challenge that went unmet.[15] Oscar Berland, a student council member from the Marxist Cultural Society, which had invited Johnson, called the ban a "flagrant violation of the right of students," adding that he refused "to accept an intellectual strait-jacket."[16] Ira A. Hirschmann, a member of the Board of Higher Education, chastised the CCNY Dean, saying his actions "reflects deplorably on his high position." He called his red-baiting colleagues "pitiful," "frightened little men," who were attempting to "tear the First Amendment to tatters because of their fear." A few days later Johnson spoke with 100 students at Columbia University. There he castigated the emerging ban on Communist speakers on college and university campuses. He said college administrators were violating the "right of the student to think." Though "Columbia University has permitted me to speak and you to listen to me... [it] violates the rights of the students, however, when it bans Howard Fast and others who have defended the Bill of Rights against the Un-American Committee." According to Johnson, central to this right were controversial topics like Marxism-Leninism. He told the assembled students that the Communist Party struggles for democracy "the world over," a sentiment supported by the considerable sacrifice Communists had made during the recently concluded war. He also called on the university to give Fast a "honorary Doctor of Laws degree...for [his] defense of the Bill of Rights." That 300 students met just days earlier and "adopted a resolution protesting the college's [CCNY] actions," put Columbia University on notice, forcing it to acquiesce lest more dramatic resistance erupt. Within days, other Communists were invited to speak at Queens and Brooklyn College.[17]

Fortunately, this would not be the last time students came to the aid of Communists. Alongside his friend Gus Hall, Johnson participated in the 1960s wave of reds invited to speak on college and university campuses across the country. Perhaps protecting the Bill of Rights while directly challenging censorship was the goal when in April 1963 Johnson spoke at both the University of Connecticut and the University of Massachusetts, around 450 students listened at each event. Organizers said, "It is [our] purpose...to give the students the opportunity to listen and hear first-hand exactly what Communists believe" in defiance of faculty recalcitrance.[18] Johnson took this perspective one step further in December 1966. Roughly 20 years after CCNY initially refused to allow him to speak, he made a statement there that probably irked campus administrators. He urged the audience of 250 students "to seek a greater role in administrative decision-making at the college." "It is high time students start to challenge one point after the other in the administration of universities,"[19] he added. Johnson's advice to campus activists challenged those attempting to quash the then ascendant student movement and its welcoming of Communists. On other occasions though, right-wing campus administrators were successful in baring CPUSA speakers. For example, in February 1963, Johnson was scheduled to debate David Wright, an economist at the University of Georgia. The Faculty Committee on Student Affairs, however, cancelled the debate, dubiously claiming Johnson's appearance would cause a riot.[20]

Johnson didn't confine his defense of the Bill of Rights to college campuses. He also challenged academic anticommunism in the high schools. At a June 1960 hearing of the New York Board of Education, he articulated an unwavering faith in the Bill of Rights and blasted the "signing of a loyalty oath as a requirement for a diploma." The oath was a by-product of a state law passed in 1917 "during a period of chauvinist hysteria." It originated during the tumult of World War I with fears of rising Bolshevism. Johnson told Board members, "When hysteria replaces reason in the minds of those who administer our schools, the damage to the students and the community is far reaching and immeasurable." College students by the thousands apparently agreed with Johnson and would soon show their support by inviting Communists to speak on their campuses. "Patriotism is subverted," he continued, "and becomes not only the refuge of a scoundrel," but also "a tool to make scoundrels. Loyalty is cheapened and educational standards are handicapped," he added. Johnson likened loyalty oaths to the "gangsterism" and intimidation tactics of Al Capone, who also used "the smoke screen of fighting Bolshevism" for his own nefarious and illegal ends. Conversely, Johnson said, "Communists hold a high loyalty to the interest and welfare of the American people. We hold with many others, that that which is good for labor is good for the country" and "we oppose those who hold that profits and the interests of big business, the accumulation of the mighty dollar is the test of patriotism." To Johnson, the "first test" of loyalty was to embrace the growing demand to "abolish racist discrimination in our schools and in our schooling." By the mid-1960s this demand would enter mainstream political discourse. Johnson also called for an end to segregated schools and classes and the "elimination of every form of racist poisoning through our text books [sic], activities and practices." He demanded the "restoring to the teachers and the classroom the rights which are guaranteed by our Bill of Rights and the Constitution," an "essential element of academic freedom." Johnson also recalled that 300 teachers had been "driven from the [public] schools by political witchhunting [sic]" and that "hundreds of others...have been intimidated" into silence. In his conclusion, he urged the Board to "set an example of loyalty"[21] by defending the Bill of Rights and civil liberties.

Fortunately, not everyone was blinded by the anticommunist hysteria. As early as January 1947, some within academia were already beginning to see the assault on reds as not only an attack on democracy, but also as a harbinger of things to come, possibly fascism. Benjamin Mays, the then president of Morehouse College, noted in a letter to John Pittman, foreign correspondent for the *Daily Worker* and Morehouse alum, "I think there is no doubting the fact that the United States is much closer to fascism than it is to communism, and I fear, closer to fascism than it is to any form of genuine democracy."[22] Mays wasn't wrong. To Communists, fascism was a frightening prospect as the Red Scare intensified. Nearly a decade later, the American Association of University Professors would finally condemn "the practice of forcing teachers and other citizens to swear they have never been Communists as a job requirement,"[23] a belated, but still important contribution to the defense of the Bill of Rights. By the early 1960s, college and university professors from across the country called for dismantling the House Un-American Activities Committee, noting that it has "repeatedly undermined the freedoms essential for national well-being" by abridging "citizens' rights of free speech and association."[24] Loyalty oaths would eventually be declared unconstitutional. University presidents would also be recognized and rewarded by the AAUP for defending free speech and the Bill of Rights.[25] Communists and students challenged censorship in multiple ways. They protested and conducted polls designed to demonstrate a lack of support for the McCarran Act.[26] By December 1962, the ACLU got into the mix, praising O. Meredith Wilson, president of the board of the University of Minnesota, who "upheld the right of Benjamin Davis, Jr., the former Communist councilman from Harlem, to speak." In a statement Wilson said, "We do not fear Ben Davis, nor can we afford to allow the fears that others may have of him destroy our hard won right to free expression."[27] It was odd, however, that Communists – the main targets of the repression – were too toxic to acknowledge and reward.

Though Johnson was not permitted to deliver his remarks at CCNY in 1947 and at the University of Georgia in 1963, he repeatedly defended the right to peacefully assemble and hear controversial views. The CPUSA was consistently in the forefront of the war effort against fascism abroad, Jim Crow at home and the attacks on workers' and democratic rights generally,[28] which lends credence to Johnson's 1949 characterization of the party as a "consistent and vigorous" defender of the Bill of Rights.[29]

* * *

On July 20, 1948 twelve top leaders of the party were indicted and arrested,[30] signaling the beginning of the McCarthy era. Basic, fundamental democratic rights were trampled. A wide net of repression was cast, resulting in the imprisonment of party leaders across the country. Communists were hounded. Those associated with the left were investigated. The assault on the Bill of Rights forced a decade-long civil liberties retreat. Judge Harold Medina, who presided over the Foley Square indictment and trial of the CPUSA leadership, simultaneously became somewhat of a celebrity. He graced the cover of *Time Magazine* and by November 1949 proudly told reporters that he had received 50,000 letters of support. Medina likened the persecution of Communists and the accolades he received therefrom to "falling in love, over and over and over again."[31] Johnson remained both defiant and optimistic, despite the deepening climate of repression. The lunacy then enveloping the nation could be stopped, he argued.

In a July 1949 *Political Affairs* article titled "The Bill of Rights and the Twelve," Johnson called the jailing of party leader John Gates "a mockery." When Gus Hall and Henry Winston were jailed, he said, "the Court revealed the naked brutality of its justice." When Gil Green was also jailed, Johnson added, it is an attack on "the elementary democratic rights of the entire American people [who] were assaulted by the judicial arm of the fast-developing police state."[32] Eventually, more than 100 leaders of the party were indicted and convicted under the Smith Act. Thousands of Communists were harassed, intimidated, black-listed and hounded, while more than five million federal workers were subjected to "loyalty screenings."[33] Johnson remained steadfast in his belief that the party's "exercise of these rights [the Bill of Rights] is for the strengthening of democracy, for the improvement of the livelihood of the people, for the advancement of society." Furthermore, the "courtroom scene," the defendants who proudly refused to cower, embodied the "high quality and purposefulness which is in keeping with the best of American democratic tradition."[34]

Like Johnson, veteran Communist journalist Joseph North, highlighted the assault on civil liberties as the first step towards fascism. In his pamphlet *Verdict Against Freedom: Your Stake in the Communist Trial,* North ominously warned: "Dead men cannot speak their minds and live men who cannot may as well be dead. A nation gagged is a nation dead and we have recently emerged from the greatest of all wars [World War II] because a man named Hitler...sought to silence a world." To Communists, the domestic Red Scare was an act of fear and desperation. The civil liberties assault had to be stopped, they argued, lest it evolve into fascism. North appealed to friends and allies, and said, "bar them [Communists] the right to present their views in the public places and you end up by having your own views barred. That is the law of modern history," he continued. "You end in the quiet of the grave. Hitler, too, began by burning books and ended by burning men."[35]

"Our fight," the defense of the Bill of Rights, Johnson continued in his *Political Affairs* article, "affects the entire course of American history," especially African American civil rights. "It is, therefore, no accident that the Negro people are most alert as a people to the need of fighting for the rights of Communists" and "see the meaning of this struggle in terms of bitter experience of brutality and oppression...They [African Americans] see the common enemy. Ever greater numbers among them also see in the Communist Party the champion of their struggle,"[36] hence his optimism. He also articulated the centrality of African American equality to the struggle for democracy. Johnson's analysis was part of a long tradition within the party. It was part of a continuum of ideas that placed the struggle for African American equality and Black liberation at the center of the party's work. At a Welcome Home rally held on June 19, 1949 – nearly one year after the initial indictment and arrest of the CPUSA's top leaders – the legendary African American athlete, actor, artist, and secret party member, Paul Robeson,[37] echoed Johnson's optimistic sentiment. He told a crowd of 5,000 in Harlem, "I'm not afraid of Communists; no, far from that. I will defend them as they defended us, the Negro people. And I stand firm and immovable by the side" of the arrested CPUSA leaders. "Their struggle is our struggle,"[38] he said. Robeson's comments reflected the thoughts of many African Americans. That October, Alphaeus Hunton, Robeson's partner at the Council on African Affairs, voiced a similar sentiment while speaking in Philadelphia. "The people who are afraid to raise their voices and take a forthright stand for civil rights are only creating a quicker opportunity to have their own heads chopped off."[39] As Hunton indicated, the dragnet soon ensnared more than Communists. "The record will show that the fight for the freedom of the Communists is a fight for their right to fight for the rights of Negroes,"[40] he added in an August 1949 *Daily Worker* letter to the editor.

Johnson's faith in the Black community deepened as the U.S. government's assault on reds intensified. By 1951, Johnson would help lead the Civil Rights Congress, one of the most important civil rights organizations in U.S. history and lend his name to the CRC petition to the United Nations, *We Charge Genocide*.[41] The petition was simultaneously released at UN headquarters in New York and Paris by Paul Robeson and William L. Patterson, respectively. It not only embarrassed the United States internationally, as Gerald Horne notes, but also bolstered African American civil rights domestically, "virtually invit[ing] the international community to intervene forcefully in what had been seen traditionally as an internal U.S. affair." The petition "was a devastating indictment of...complicity and dereliction in lynching, murder, deprivation of voting rights, and all manner of crimes,"[42] which brought unwanted attention to the Truman Administration's mixed commitment to civil rights and equality.[43]

Johnson was arrested that spring along with dozens of other party leaders. Recall that the Korean War was then raging. Millions would soon be dead. School desegregation – with the aid of Communists like Lee Lorch[44] – was right around the corner. Protests erupted across the country after the brutal killing of Emmitt Till. Bus boycotts emerged and elevated debates around civil rights. Paul Robeson, William L. Patterson, Benjamin Davis, Jr., Alphaeus Hunton, Shirley Graham DuBois, James and Esther Cooper Jackson, Louis and Dorothy Burnham, Lloyd L. Brown and Lorraine Hansberry, among other Black Communists, were respected and influential. Black militancy comfortable with red allies looking East to an expanding socialist community of nations ready and eager to aid in the struggle for African American equality and Black liberation terrified the U.S. ruling class. Their fears intensified as lunch counter sit-ins and massive voter registration drives were initiated.

As the Chicago-area African American party leader, Claude Lightfoot, noted in his article "Black Liberation Impossible Without Communists," "If purges of communists are harmful to the nation in general, they are even more harmful to the struggle for Negro freedom – because their [the purge's] purpose is to deprive the black revolution of the services of some of the most dedicated and self-sacrificing forces our people have ever produced."[45] The centrality of African American equality to Communists in the struggle for democracy proved a formidable challenge to ruling elites. Additionally, the coalition of forces then coalescing around the party included cultural and artistic figures like Ossie Davis and Ruby Dee, which created a unique conundrum. Historian Gerald Horne argued, the government needed to "open democratic space for blacks while closing it down for their traditional allies [reds] – in other words *black liberation/red scare*...Creating an opening for Black Liberation while launching the Red Scare was akin to riding two horses going in different directions at the same time. Yet apparently," the St. Louis native concludes, "this maneuver was 'successful.'"[46]

In his *History of the Communist Party of the United States*, William Z. Foster asserts that the outlawing of the Communist Party served two purposes. First, "to illegalize the Communist Party and to destroy it," and, second, "to destroy democracy in general." The FBI's roundup of the party's leadership was "only the beginning," according to Foster. It also "had 43,000 Communists under surveillance for early arrests," as well as "half a million Party supporters [who] would be thrown into concentration camps" in the advent of war with the Soviet Union.[47] While Foster's fears may have been exaggerated, it is easy to understand his concern; most of his core cohort were now in jail or underground, and the Justice Department did – in fact – have *at least* six camps built "ready to confine American Communists" and the FBI had been "ready to seize some 12,000 'dangerous Communists'" in the event of a "general emergency,"[48] though what was meant by emergency was never defined. Government plots designed to put Communists in internment camps were not the party's or Johnson's only concern. Self-appointed, so-called patriots ratcheted up tensions and inflamed the hysteria, too. One such group of 100 veterans attacked Johnson and his comrades in Rochester, New York in mid-April 1948. A local reporter likened the scene to a "Nazi-style raid...culminating in a public book burning." Henry Farash, of the Rochester CP, pledged that the party would soon hold another public meet to "test whether the Bill of Rights and Constitution applies in Rochester." That the police stood around and did nothing to stop the assault,[49] likely served to dispel any lingering doubts Johnson may have had about the legitimacy of bourgeois legality.

Reds and Blacks fought a "common enemy,"[50] which made them both a threat to the ruling class. That the Communist Party had "unquestionably been a powerful factor"[51] in the advancement of African American equality, made Blacks less susceptible to anticommunism generally, and served to highlight "the obscenity of this trial of ideas," as the Trinidad born, Black Communist, Claudia Jones – a co-defendant of Johnson's – described the witch hunts. Just as it is a crime to be a Marxist-Leninist, a Communist, Jones added, it is also a "crime" to be Black, for both are "daily convicted by a Government which denies us [our] elementary democratic rights."[52] That the government denied Johnson, the party and the CRC – and its overlapping leadership – their democratic rights served not only to deprive African Americans of dedicated and self-sacrificing leaders, like William L. Patterson and Benjamin Davis, Jr., it also aimed to dismantle the budding organizational infrastructure – through the CRC and the CAA, for example – that bolstered collaboration between two key democratic forces, namely reds and Blacks, a collaboration Johnson had considerable pride in.

Arrested in June, 1951, Johnson – now the Pittsburgh areas' "new Commie Boss"[53] – expressed this sentiment during his court hearing: "This trial has been destructive of the welfare of the American people while pretending to protect the people...[it is] part of a war preparations program, with the Government making all kinds of slanders against Communist ideas in an effort to stop us from advocating [for] peace, democracy [and] security." "These trials are a smoke screen...[a] trickery against the American people. That is the price of destroying the rights of Communists." Like the other defendants, Johnson tied his fate to the fate of democracy, civil rights, workers' rights and peace. He boldly, defiantly told the court, "Your decision to jail us does not make us guilty," for the American people "will know that we are innocent and that they are also victims of this frame-up."[54] The courts offer to allow Johnson and the other defendants "to go to Russia rather than to prison" was met with indignation. Elizabeth Gurley Flynn told the judge, "We feel we belong here and have a political responsibility here. We feel we would be traitors to the American people if we turned our backs on them just to escape jail." Claudia Jones, who would soon be deported, told the judge, "The only act which I proudly am guilty of is membership in the Communist party which is not illegal."[55]

That Johnson, and 14 other party leaders, had their bail revoked – $175,000 secured by the CRC – added injury to insult. The court not only refused to accept the "legality of the [CRC] trust agreement," it also "disqualified" four CRC trustees "from writing bail" for any of the defendants. Additionally, the court sentenced three of the trustees – including African American party leader, Alphaeus Hunton – to jail for "criminal contempt of court," as they refused to disclose the source of CRC funding.[56] A "loyalty test" for bail was effectively created.[57] Another defendant, Manuel Tarazona, was refused bail when his wife "refused to answer questions pertaining to her organizational membership."[58] In total, bail was increased to $875,000 for Johnson and the other defendants,[59] while bail fund contributors were harassed and intimidated.[60]

The five million members of the All-China Federation of Labor protested the jailing of the CRC trustees and noted that the "prosecution of the democratic forces" was in "violation of the American Bill of Rights." Johnson and his comrades were "not fighting alone, but have the support of millions of democratic and peace-loving people throughout the world."[61] The New York Furriers Joint Council also protested the jailing and noted that the "refusal to accept bonds offered by the bail fund was a violation of constitutional rights."[62] In short, the assault on civil liberties necessitated domestic and international solidarity. By early August the CRC had issued a call to "all defenders of the Bill of Rights," which said, "The terroristic manner in which this Grand Jury has pursued the trustees...exceeds in violence any act of a similar character" in U.S. history. It was "a drive of terror"[63] directed against Hunton and the other trustees, a drive born of fear designed to isolate Communists and their allies.

Johnson remained defiant and optimistic. In a series of letters to his wife, the Seattle born radical continued to display confidence in the American people, especially African Americans. "Last night I had the most enjoyable time passing out leaflets on a street corner and then speaking...under the auspices of the CRC and its part in the fight to save Willie McGee." McGee was a Mississippi African American man falsely accused of raping a white woman; an all-white jury deliberated on the case for only three minutes before convicting McGee and sentencing him to death. "We had a picnic – and everything went well," he added, possibly reflecting on the attack and book burning in Rochester a few years earlier. The meeting was in the "heart of the Negro community." Just a few weeks later, Johnson was in Washington County, Pennsylvania meeting with "a few good coal miners. They are the salt of the earth," he wrote. "These are good days of activity," he reminded his "Dearest Love," who was still in New York facing political and financial burdens of her own as she searched for work. Perhaps a bit dismissively, Johnson told his wife, "a job is a job not a matter of enlightenment. The only really joyful work is work such as I'm doing," a reflection of his continued optimism. "It is good to see people grow," he added, reflecting on the changing political winds. "This fight for democracy is one which must always go forward even at such times that it appears as tho [sic] the forces in power would like to destroy democracy," first and foremost by attacking Communists. "Of course," he continued, "the final determination of the great majority of the people for their democratic rights must still be made." With clarity and thoughtfulness decades ahead of the times, Johnson also noted, "This period in history will probably go down in books as the one period most devoid of – not justice – no[,] but reason and logic – and injustice flows out of that I guess."[64] Johnson's faith in the American people and the Bill of Rights could not be broken.

To him, the jailing of party leaders served a multiplicity of goals – to destroy the party and to destroy the organizational infrastructure that facilitated collaboration between reds and Blacks, as a precursor to destroying democracy. Other Communists agreed. Howard 'Stretch' Johnson wrote in his memoir, the attacks on the CPUSA "were more damaging to democracy...than anything in [U.S.] history."[65] He could have rightly added that this assault was a product born of fear. In 1944, Arnold Johnson asserted that the CPUSA was quite likely "the greatest educational institution in the country."[66] During the early 1950s witch-hunt, he added to this critique, saying he "learned more in one year in the Communist Party about American history than in all those years of formal education. I learned more about the necessity of smashing jimcrow [sic] and of fighting for bread, and civil rights, and peace." Those who would destroy the Bill of Rights in their attempt to break the Communist Party "only further expose their cynical contempt for the American people and for democratic traditions," he added.[67] The party fought to survive and to defend basic democratic rights for all Americans through its defense of the Bill of Rights.

At times Johnson's defiance could turn to anger, and his more reasoned responses could turn vitriolic. The government's witch-hunt rested on "moral lepers, degenerates and stool-pigeons [which] indicates the rottenness of their plot," a plot aimed at destroying the Bill of Rights. "It is an insult to all decent Americans... [a] monstrous fraud foisted on the people," he added. Quickly, though, Johnson's optimism returned. "Such shameful perversion can never be the cornerstone of a sound [democratic] structure," only "its destruction." The assault on the Bill of Rights "demonstrates not only its [the government's] desperation and its degeneracy but also its disregard for the desires and decency of the people,"[68] whom Johnson had confidence would continue to aid Communists. If Millie Hamilton's letter from Youngstown, Ohio is any indication, his optimism was well founded. Hamilton told Johnson, "Hundreds of steelworkers and their wives" supported him and asked that she send regards. During the "mad days of jail threats and prison terms," she added, "through me they send best wishes." Commenting on the political climate, she wrote, "It is becoming ever plainer that the U.S. Constitution has been buried and the real 'foreign agents' have imported the German Nazi set-up." As "you and your co-workers walk into prisons, the hard-won liberties of America go with you,"[69] she concluded.

Johnson's optimistic view was buoyed by the steady stream of letters of support he received from the religious community. For example, the Rev. Kenneth Ripley Forbes called the indictment "an absurdity" and wondered "how much more of this abominable Fascist business the American people are going to stand for."[70] The Minister James K. Moore told Johnson, "You are on the frontier and battlelines [sic] of social change."[71] The Minister Lee H. Ball confidently told Johnson, "Those who are persecuted today will be respected tomorrow...

we are vastly indebted to those who speak their convictions and paid the price."[72] Congregations frequently stood with their pastors who dared to challenge the prevailing winds of the Red Scare. Rev. Marion Frenyear, of the South Hartford Congregational Church and a former student of the Union Theological Seminary with Johnson, sent $500 to help ensure a "fair trial." Even after the American Legion visited the church's deacons the congregation voted against censoring Frenyear.[73] Frank Heelen of Roman Catholic Maryknoll Seminary suggested bringing some theological students "to the *Worker* on an...informal basis (i.e. just dropping in on you)" and offered to have Johnson speak with his students, though he noted "we will have to maintain an absolute (on our side) secrecy about our talks," lest the "wrong people" hear about the discussions.[74]

By late 1954, the McCarthy Era was nearing its nadir. The U.S. Senate voted 67 to 22 to condemn the reactionary Wisconsin Senator,[75] who quickly became "persona non grata."[76] However, it would not be until 1957 and then 1967 that provisions of the Smith Act (which made it a criminal offense to advocate the violent overthrow of the government or to organize or be a member of any group or society devoted to such advocacy) and the McCarran Act (which required Communists to register as such), would both be declared unconstitutional, vindicating Johnson and his comrades. The 1955 confession by "professional perjurer" Harvey Matusow that he "deliberately testified falsely" put another nail in McCarthyism's coffin.[77] In a spring 1956 *Daily Worker* article titled "Is America Returning To The Bill Of Rights," party leader Si Gerson, rearticulated Johnson's ongoing faith that the tide was turning. "Whatever the ups-and-downs of the immediate struggles for constitutional rights in the days ahead – and there will be ups-and-downs and zigzags – the main direction is defined," the defense of the Bill of Rights will ultimately prevail. "While the tempo of the return," he continued, "towards the Bill of Rights is intolerably slow, it is already clear that some powerful currents are at work in the direction of a restoration of political rights for all,"[78] not least of which were the rights of Communists.

Johnson didn't limit his activism solely to the defense of indicted Communists, though. He also began to recognize the role of youth in the fight for peace – something that would become a cornerstone of his work by the mid-1960s. "Visit any active peace center and observe the participation of youth," he noted in the November 1958 *Party Voice*. Youth "give life to a movement," he told his comrades, which is why the party "must play a more responsible role answering their questions and strengthening their participation in the peace movement." His analysis soon became reality. "We must support, encourage and help develop the broad community peace movements" and "help unite people and organizations of diverse views" around "common fundamental peace activities in which they are *prepared to participate together*" [*italic* in original], he added. Johnson also encouraged party members to "independently, under our own name, issue statements, leaflets, documents, hold meetings, etc. expressing our own position." But he also implored his comrades to "learn from others" and "demonstrate our ability to function within the bounds of an organization program."[79] Johnson and the party had weathered the storm. They had checked the worst abuses of the far-right attack on democracy. The 1,300 comrades who gathered in New York's Carnegie Hall with Johnson to celebrate the Party's 39th anniversary that September [80] were cautiously optimistic.

After the 1958 elections Johnson excitedly asserted, "Any careful analysis of the character of the election... must lead one to the conclusion that this is the time to abolish [HUAC]...this committee is itself unconstitutional [which] has been repeatedly demonstrated by its usurpation of power in violation of the constitution." The president "abdicated responsibility," he said. But according to Johnson, "the American people voted for a change in [both] foreign and domestic policies – a

Leftward, liberal change." Additionally, he wrote, while "Widespread terror against Negro students, violence against Negro ministers, arrests and official murder of Negroes who stood for elementary rights" continued, the election was itself "a mandate for a 'radical' solution – an immediate halt to all Jim Crow, an end to segregation in schools, buses, parks, [and] housing."[81] Lunch counter sit-ins soon galvanized the civil rights movement, resulting in the founding of the Student Nonviolent Coordinating Committee. The young African American Communist Debbie Bell attended SNCC's founding conference in 1960. By summer 1963, she was working for SNCC in Atlanta, where she regularly dined with the Reverend Ralph D. Abernathy,[82] who roughly a decade later noted that it was an honor to work with Communists, such as Angela Davis.[83]

Though temporarily curtailed, the government's assault on reds wasn't over. By September 1959, Johnson was once again facing the inquisitors. He defiantly told HUAC, "the whole role of this committee violates the fundamentals of the Constitution and of the Bill of Rights" and "I have no intention at any time of cooperating or aiding any committee" that "is actually destroying the Bill of Rights."[84] Johnson had now spent more than 10 years of his life fighting to preserve and protect the ideals of this document. In all, he would be jailed from January 1955 until May 1957.[85] By summer 1960, Johnson was back in the spotlight as the People's Rights Party candidate for Congress; he called on the state legislature to extend voter registration dates and stop the "run-around in civil rights legislation."[86]

In 1961, just as Communists Gus Hall and Herbert Aptheker, among others, were preparing to crisscross the country and speak with tens of thousands of students, Johnson took direct aim at the McCarran Act, which required Communists to register with the U.S. Attorney General. In a series of articles in the *Worker* he wrote, "The court knows that nobody can register under the McCarran Act even if the court should order such registration. To register is to subscribe to a big lie as to the nature of our Party and to make oneself subject to all kinds of criminal prosecutions." He added, that the law was "directed against the Constitution itself" and is designed to "not only outlaw a political party," but also "mass organizations and unions." Optimistically, he noted that as Communists "intensify the fight for the Bill of Rights, we will not only gain strength among the people but also organizationally."[87] Reds would soon be overwhelmed with invitations to speak at colleges and universities, which bolstered Johnson's optimistic view. He declared, "The monstrous character" of the McCarran and Smith Acts "involves much more than a specific civil liberties violation. These laws smash at the whole foundation and structure of democratic rights. The issues involved are not limited to Communists," rather this is "a fight for the Bill of Rights and democratic liberties" for all Americans.[88] In a fall 1961 *Worker* article, Johnson added, "The Communist Party cannot register without committing perjury and submitting its officers, members and supporters to a whole series of criminal charges...[thereby effectively] scrapping the Bill of Rights."[89] In April 1962, Johnson spoke with a capacity crowd at Hamilton College. He told the audience of 700 students on a campus of 800 that the McCarran Act damages "the mental capacity...[It] not only [creates] political stupidity, which endangers the peace of the world but also personal lunacy. Everybody has a stake in ridding this country of the McCarran Act," he concluded, "which gives a legal sanction to lunacy."[90] A few weeks later, at a Washington University debate attended by 800 people, Johnson likened the McCarran Act as "basically an enabling act for Fascism in America."[91] "It violates the American way of life and destroys the American process,"[92] he added. Just a few days later, Johnson and nine other Party members, were ordered to register.[93] Despite the repression thousands protested. Just weeks earlier, 1,500 Communists and their supporters gathered at Carnegie

Hall; they "pledged...to defy"[94] the Act and refused to register.

James E. Jackson, editor of *The Worker*, echoed Johnson in a pamphlet that took specific aim at the attack on freedom of press within the Act's labeling provision. This provision "provides that 'Communist-action' and 'Communist-front' organizations," which *The Worker* had been labeled, "shall label any material which they send through the mail as deriving from such 'Communist-action' or 'Communist-front' organization." The intent was clear, "to restrict or destroy freedom of information by exposing those who receive such labeled mail to harassment and persecution," as the requirement would "not inform the readers," but would "incite his neighbors and confront him with the choice of canceling his subscription or suffering the social and economic reprisals and vigilanteeism [sic]," a tactic of the "ultra-right."[95] In March 1962, Jackson told the inquisitors, "I will never be an informer or a stoolpigeon...To inform or to become in any way an informer is repugnant to my conscience."[96] Jackson wasn't alone in his condemnation of the Act's labeling provision. That May, 31 college newspaper editors called on President Kennedy to "stop the harassment and jailings [sic]." They urged him "not to enforce the labeling provisions...and to preserve the constitutional liberties of all Americans."[97] Less than a year later, Jackson told students at the University of Connecticut, the McCarran Act "is incompatible with the democratic structure of our government; one or the other [fascism or the Bill of Rights] will prevail. I will never register under this law,"[98] he concluded. That March, 1,800 people celebrated the 39th anniversary of the *Worker* with Jackson.[99] He and other Communists defiantly fought to preserve the Bill of Rights. Johnson's comrade, Benjamin Davis, Jr., perhaps with a bit more dramatic flair, told 500 students at Upsala College that the "poison of the ultra-Right is not only politically dangerous," as evidenced by the McCarran Act, "but it also obviously creates a mental insanity," he added, echoing Johnson. "Neither the McCarran Act, nor all of the FBI cars that have followed me the last several days, can stop the American Communist Party,"[100] Davis told reporters in spring 1963, articulating the futility of the reactionary assault on both the Communist Party and the Bill of Rights. A year earlier Davis noted defiantly, "When the time comes for Socialism in the United States a thousand McCarran Acts won't stop it."[101]

When asked in 1961 if the party was again going underground as a result of the ongoing repression, Gus Hall replied in the negative. He added, echoing Johnson, that the Bill of Rights was instead being forced underground; it "is being buried," he said,[102] as evidenced by the continued harassment, which included dozens of uniformed and undercover police attempting to intimidate students while Communists spoke on college campuses.[103] In March 1962, after he and Davis were indicted, Hall called for "the dismantling and scrapping of the cancerous bureaucratic and oppressive apparatus that has grown up around the policy of political harassment," a policy that effectively put the Bill of Rights in the crosshairs. If civil liberties for all Americans were to be preserved, the government policy "of snooping, tailing, tapping, bugging, and the invasions of the home and private lives of citizens by J. Edgar Hoover's political police" must come to an end,[104] Hall concluded. In September, the Hall-Davis Defense Committee issued a press release enumerating the way in which the McCarran Act "Destroys the Bill of Rights":

"...it [the McCarran Act] undermines rights of free speech, free press and assemblage, and by outlawing a political party; labeling dissenting press and by legalizing guilt by association [1st Amendment;] it undermines guarantee against self-incrimination in demanding registration and thereby admission of non-existent criminal acts and conspiracy [5th Amendment;] it undermines guarantee of a fair trial and due process, in enforcing arbitrary rulings of an administrative board [6th Amendment;] it undermines guarantee against cruel and unusual punishment [8th Amendment]."

Further, the Defense Committee ridiculed the SACB's budgetary needs, as the Board requested an additional $545,000 "to continue the attack on the Communist Party" and the Bill of Rights. The Defense Committee then appealed to "the defenders of the Bill of Rights to meet the Board's challenge dollar for dollar. In defending them [Hall and Davis], we are defending you," they argued.[105]

"Frankly speaking, I think we'll lick the McCarran Act on the Hall-Davis case...And in so doing we shall render a tremendous service to the American people," Johnson noted in an October 1962 *Worker* interview. In the article, titled "Struggle Is the Secret of Arnold Johnson's Optimism," Johnson added, "We've got to get respect for our rights by PRACTICING them."[106]

That Johnson and his comrades were able to continue their work on behalf of social and economic justice – peace, jobs and equality – at all, should be viewed as both a personal and organizational victory. The entire weight of the U.S. government's repressive apparatus – including thousands of spies and informants[107] – had been let loose. Newspaper reporters were also pressured to act as informers in the witch-hunt against Johnson.[108] "Our telephone wires are tapped, our letters are filched from the mail," Johnson said. "Our leaders and members are followed wherever they go; brought before grand jury inquisitions and imprisoned without bail for refusing to surrender their Constitutional rights." The FBI, and its "parade of stool-pigeon witnesses...boasts that it makes a practice of infiltrating our Party...with spies and agent provocateurs,"[109] a sign of desperation, he argued. That Johnson was barred from visiting Canada[110] indicated that the repression wasn't confined domestically, as U.S. authorities colluded across borders in an attempt to stem a rising red tide. Regardless, despite the on-going assaults – the jailing, harassment and infiltration – the defendants, their organization, and the Bill of Rights persevered, though the collaboration between reds and Blacks was weakened. African American Communists like Paul Robeson were sidelined and replaced by those like A. Philip Randolph who were more willing to acquiesce to liberal anticommunism. African American cultural leaders, artists and authors, like Alice Childress – whose membership in the party is contested – would publicly deny membership, while defiantly participating in "subversive and illegal activity" by secretly hosting party meetings with well-known Communists at her uptown Manhattan apartment.[111] Regardless, Johnson and other CPUSA leaders soon refocused their energies on the youth and student upsurge and peace movements.

* * *

By the early 1960s Johnson would feel confident about the repudiation of anticommunism from within the ranks of the peace movement. He called Women Strike for Peace – an organization founded in fall 1961 by Bella Abzug, Dogmar Wilson and Amy Swerdlow (a Red Diaper Baby[112]) – "the most vital mass force in the peace movement."[113] According to CPUSA leader Roberta Wood, "lots of Communists were active and helped organize WSP, like me!"[114] To Johnson, WSP's willingness to dramatically challenge HUAC signaled a change in the political winds. More and more peace organizations – like Veterans for Peace in Vietnam, founded by suspected party member, Leroy Wolins[115] – began to also openly challenge anticommunism. Further, Margaret Russell, a leader in WSP, would in 1963 attend the World Congress of Women in Moscow and tell the 6,000 participants, "Our goals are inseparable. The movement for civil rights is part of the movement for a world of peace, freedom and justice to which we have dedicated ourselves," and which, undoubtedly, reinforced Johnson's faith in WSP. Billie Ashby, from the National

Association of Colored Women's Clubs, also attended the Russian confab.[116]

Johnson wanted his comrades to "support, encourage, and help the developing movement for peace. Peace is the central issue of our era," he said. "Peace must therefore be the central issue of our politics and our organization."[117] In the summer of 1960, Johnson began to connect the struggles for civil liberties and peace. In a prepared statement to the U.S. Senate internal security subcommittee, he said the witch-hunt "seeks to smash all struggle[s] for peace…[which] is the major demand of the American people." He added, "Communists are justly proud and vigorous advocates for peace" and support a program "vast numbers of other Americans also advocate."[118] That August the National Committee to Abolish the Un-American Activities Committee was formed.[119] In an April 1961 *Worker* article, Johnson noted that "the fight for Abolition [sic] of the House Un-American Activities Committee is an important part of the fight against racism, anti-Semitism bigotry and slander in our country. It is part of the fight for the Bill of Rights for all Americans." Further, he argued that "the defense of the rights of Communists, or of labor and progressive forces, results in strengthening the civil liberties of all Americans,"[120] including peace activists.

At a 1964 May Day rally at New York's Union Square, Johnson said, "We are a people of peace…As a people, we Americans want peace, and that demand will prevail." "The shift to peace is growing like a tidal wave," he added, partly due to the work of Communists who were increasingly being accepted as legitimate partners after years of Red Scare repression. Johnson called for the "outlawry of war and an end to the threat of nuclear suicide." "People today," he continued, "are not satisfied with just a little more democracy, or with just a little less poverty, or with only a bit more peace." To him, socialism's advances broadened the political terrain. "People want a full life – in a full democracy, without poverty and with peace." Despite the invasion in Cuba and the escalation in Vietnam, Johnson was optimistic. He said, "To evaluate the past years of struggle in this country," not least of which was the growing acceptance of Communists in the peace movement, "is to gain confidence for the future. That the future belongs to the people who will make it. That future is not an idle dream."[121] he concluded. Like Johnson, other Communists reached outward, sought allies and began to share leadership responsibilities in the emerging peace movement.

During the mid-1960s, Johnson became chair of the party's peace commission. In that capacity, he joined the steering committee of the National Coordinating Committee to End the War in Vietnam, the first nationally coordinated body to build opposition to the war.[122] In a report to party leaders after the November 1965 March on Washington for Peace in Vietnam, Johnson again highlighted the role of Women Strike for Peace. He also praised the party-led W.E.B. DuBois Clubs, which had been founded in June 1964. Both organizations, "played decisive roles" in the march of 30,000 people and "have taken the lead in varying degrees in the struggle against anti-Communism" by directing "attention to the key issues which Americans face in the struggle for peace." Their stance, as well as that of others, "is proving helpful...to the movement as a whole." He noted, CPUSA members "participated fully" in the NCC National Anti-War Convention in Washington, D.C. prior to the march. "We made our position known," he told his comrades, through *The Worker*, leaflet and literature distributions. The times, he argued, placed "a greater responsibility on us Communists." Self-critically, he concluded, "we cannot be satisfied that we did all that we should or could... We cannot afford to underestimate our responsibility."[123] As Johnson and other comrades began to take a more active role in the budding peace movement it was noted in a November 1965 party memorandum, "We are now an integral part of the peace movement...Excellent work was done and we have won a greater respect and recognition for our efforts," particularly in the New York

October Parade Committee. According to some, the party had "broken out of our isolation...as [the] fight for peace and the right to dissent, the essence of civil liberties, are merging,"[124] a characteristic Johnson embodied.

The DBC wasn't as generous in its report on the Convention of the National Coordinating Committee To End The War In Vietnam held later that month. DBC leaders noted that the convention was unfortunately mired in a "struggle over structure which dominate[d] the entire conference," and "reflected the attempt that was made by a minority faction" associated with YSA "to withdraw the more than one hundred independent Vietnam Committees out of a broad National Coordinating Committee...and to reorganize the independent committees into a narrow, self-isolating organization." The DBC's original approach to the convention, the report continued, "was to subordinate the question of structure to that of program. It was the feeling of our National Executive that if the convention was to be productive that it would have to develop a nationally coordinated program which could involve the broadest type of participation, and that to do this the structure should remain essentially unchanged, while the national center of the [National Coordinating Committee] should be strengthened to better service its constituents." It was said that the "DBC played a decisive role" and "the minority faction was thoroughly exposed and discredited. The caucus they called after the convention was a dismal failure."[125]

Worker reporter Tim Wheeler reflected on the party's role during this period. He said, "The Party played a huge role in changing the dynamics of the peace movement."[126] Johnson and the DBC were respected leaders. And the insistence on the open participation of Communists in the peace movement reframed the political debate as a defense of the Bill of Rights.

By the fall of 1966, the NCC began to fracture. In its place the Spring Mobilization to End the War in Vietnam (later, New Mobe) would emerge. Johnson was quickly added to its steering committee, which "adhere[ed] to the policy of 'non-exclusion' [of Communists], first and most of all, because it is right in principle, [and] necessary to the political health of the nation." "People of the Left (Communists with or without quotation marks)," it was noted in *Mobilizer*, the organization's bulletin, "should be permitted and expected to function normally in the political life of the country." Secondly, Spring Mobe recognized that "in practice a non-Communist coalition is in danger of becoming an anti-Communist one" and "its program will in the long run tend to be moderate and its resistance to the war restrained in policy." By excluding Communists, "It will tend to seek allies to its right,"[127] the bulletin concluded. Johnson had been articulating this sentiment for two decades now. Spring Mobe organized the April 15, 1967 national demonstration for peace.

Even as his focus shifted to war and peace, Johnson sought to develop ties with religious leaders and worked to sustain ties between the party and religious communities. He insisted upon on the party's participation in the February 1965 *Pacem in Terris* (Peace on Earth) Conference – The International Convocation on the Requirements for Peace. The conference, attended by 2,500 people, was designed to draw more Catholics into the peace movement. In a letter to Leslie Paffrath, the Convocation's secretary general, Johnson noted that when Pope John XXIII issued the encyclical *Pacem in Terris*, Gus Hall led a series of discussions on the subject and "made public his notes," which were sent to "leading Catholics throughout the country." The notes were "generally greatly appreciated in a wide circle of Catholic scholars." This was "an important development and represents part of an informal dialogue" between Communists and Catholics, Johnson added. He also informed Paffrath that "major Catholic publications" commented on "the substance" of Hall's comments, as well as a French Catholic scholar, whose comments were carried in *The Catholic Worker*. Additionally, *The Catholic World* published an article "devoted entirely to a discussion" of Hall's contribution which "indicates the continuing interest"[128] in what Communists have to say regarding peace. It is unclear whether Paffrath replied to Johnson's inquiries. Johnson did, however, attend all sessions of the convocation and reported on its importance to the budding peace movement.[129] Interestingly, *Continuum*, edited by Justus George Lawler, included brief articles by Hall, Johnson and another party leader, Hyman Lumer, on the impact of the convocation in its autumn 1965 issue. Hall was direct and to the point in his article. Since the convocation, he wrote, "the full sinister nature of U.S. intentions has come to the light of day." The goal, "to subjugate the people of Vietnam" and turn the region into "a vast U.S. military base of aggression, a time-bomb on the Asia mainland." Central to Hall's critique was the struggle for national liberation. "No amount of fakery can hide the fact that the people of Vietnam are fighting for their right to determine for themselves their own destiny. The people of Vietnam are fighting against an invasion...the only real invasion, that of U.S. imperialism." He did give praise where praise was due, though. "The speeches of Pope Paul place the authority and prestige of the Vatican on the right side of the struggle for world peace. This is a very important fact. But realities do not change without a struggle." Johnson's article noted that "obviously, the struggle for peace is not limited to pacifists, Catholics and Communists." To him, ascending socialism and "the new relation of forces makes war obsolete," especially nuclear war. "As a matter of survival," he continued, "modern weapons require that war be outlawed."[130]

That people of faith, Catholics and others, were engaging Communists wasn't new. For example, Johnson spoke at the Boston Community Church, and Herbert Aptheker spoke at the Jewish People's Forum in early April 1963.[131] Further, Benjamin Davis, Jr., addressed roughly 1,700 Los Angeles congregants that March at separate events sponsored by the Unitarian Church. Unity was the theme. "There are many paths to freedom," he said. "We say let history decide the best course while we unite on what we agree upon instead of letting our differences keep us apart." Johnson agreed. That Davis also raised the "possibility of convening every Negro organization in the country for the purpose of adopting a common program,"[132] lent credence to the ongoing desire among reds to focus their enegies on the struggle for African American equality as central to the struggle for democracy and peace.

In a November 1968 *Daily World* post-election article, Johnson noted "the 'law and order' police state threats, against the black liberation and all militant popular movements, call for further unity of the people." To him, "the continued upsurge of the people and the need of new political formations to express the will of the people" was essential. "The need for new alliances is a key lesson," he concluded.[133]

A 1968 statement issued by the party noted, "The peace movement has grown significantly. It has weathered a number of storms, gone through certain transformations, and achieved a fuller sense of unity." The growing acceptance of Communists was affirmed. "Two years ago the movement was sharply split over whether Communists and radicals should be excluded" from the peace movement. Today, however, "there is wide recognition that a policy of exclusion would infect the movement with the very virus of anti-communism that must be fought if peace is to be won." "The war will come to an end," the statement continued, "when it becomes untenable for the ruling class. This will occur when inability to win the war on the battlefield is coupled with such mass opposition and resistance at home that the only alternative is a reversal of course." To that end, the party argued that making "the war course untenable" should be the objective of every peace activist. Communists "urge[d] an intensification of the struggle on all levels, including the fight against the war within the old parties themselves." Reds also continued to articulate a special affinity for African American equality and Black liberation. They argued, "It is now necessary that increasing sections of the peace movement enlarge their concept to include the fight for Negro rights and freedom,"[134] a fight the party had been championing since at least the early 1930's with their defense of the Scottsboro Nine.

In a late 1969 report by the party's Peace Commission, which was likely written by Johnson, it was noted that the "potential of the peace movement is greater than ever before – the peace forces are on the offensive and they must be kept that way." Internally, Communists emphasized the "big job" of "advanc[ing] the peace movement, to find the means to involve thousands of workers" and "to deepen the anti-imperialist consciousness of the millions who are moving for complete withdrawal of our troops." Connecting the peace movement with the labor movement and the struggles for African American equality was a strategic goal for Johnson and his comrades, a task that could only be accomplished by growing the party, they argued. That fall, 30,000 copies of a special issue of the *Daily World* were printed for distribution at the November 15 Moratorium to End the War in Vietnam, where "a contingent of about 100 [party members] marched under the [CP] banner." "The party organization was better than on previous occasions," the commission added, "and many comrades were active in mobilizing the huge numbers which came out."[135] Johnson led the Party delegation and organized a meeting at George Washington University, where he, Charlene Mitchell and Daniel Rubin, and others, discussed the fight against racism and war.[136] According to Roberta Wood, "plant gate distributions" of the party's newspaper also helped mobilize workers for peace.[137] "The peace movement has reached millions of Americans and the Party has contributed to its growth," the Peace Commission report concluded. However, "the Party itself has not grown as a result." Apparently, "there isn't the conviction in our ranks that it is possible and necessary to build the Party at this time." While the Commission argued that Communists should play a "dual role of advancing and radicalizing the mass movement" and "build the Party and its press" the "latter role of a Communist has been forgotten, if it has ever been completely understood,"[138] an ongoing challenge.

In a March 1970 *World Magazine* article Johnson highlighted the anti-draft movement. He stressed that it is the "most important sector of the massive upsurge against the U.S. criminal aggression in Vietnam. It involves millions of Americans of diverse beliefs and many affiliations." It includes African Americans, "who are victims of racist discrimination by the draft process and in the army, and the Puerto Rican and Chicano who are also forced into the army of their oppressor." Johnson noted the contrast between the "sons of workers" and the "sons of the rich." To him, the "draft lottery is a fraud...The whole system of the draft is corrupt and unjust because the purpose of the army in this war is criminal aggression." He added that the anti-draft movement "must be appreciated if we are to understand the many forms and tactics used in the resistance, and the full potential of the movement." He called for "diverse tactics to create a meaningful massive unity" through New Mobe. Johnson argued for "greater inclusion" among a broad array of forces. "This is a key task for Communists and is an imperative for a majority expression" of peace. To him, "criminal atrocities committed by U.S. armed forces...[were] brutal, deliberate, murderous acts [that] represent the decadence of capitalism, and the barbarity of U.S. imperialism." However, he also praised "those who defied the military...and those who refused to be a party to atrocities," such as the Fort Hood Three. Their actions were "heroic," he wrote. He called the March 16-22 anti-draft week "part of a Spring offensive to end the war" and bring the troops home.[139] A month later, Johnson greeted the Young Workers Liberation League at the *Daily World*'s spring festival in New York City. He said, youth activists would "help reverse U.S. policy from war, racism and repression," while helping to build majority peace movement. He urged youth to "aid in the achievement of democratic rights for all the people," a necessary prerequisite in the "struggle for socialism in our time."[140] Just days later, Johnson's continued optimism shined through again. "The strength of the peace forces reaches far beyond the demonstrations and mass actions, far beyond the editorials, the pulpits and public forums, the debates in Congress, the Senate and the electoral arena." To him, the ruling class was now on the defensive. He said, it "can be forced to call a halt to present policy – and to reverse the course from war to peace." Johnson called for a "mighty movement – in action and in ideas – organizationally and politically – and that movement is in the making."[141]

The New York Times, however, dismissively called the Communist Party's work in New Mobe "relatively sedate." Johnson, the "C.P. warhorse," was considered "as ineffectual as he is sweet," while youth activists "simply don't care" about the presence of Communists, as many of "their elders belong, or once belonged, to some Marxist denomination."[142] Meanwhile, the newly renamed HUAC successor, the House Internal Security Committee, went a different direction and subpoenaed Johnson regarding his peace work. Johnson, unsurprisingly, refused to participate, seeing the subpoena as yet another assault on the Bill of Rights. As a result, he was cited for contempt of Congress and indicted in October 1970.[143] That June, Johnson sent a memo to the New Mobe steering committee informing them that he intended to not testify and thereby unwittingly add legitimacy to the Committee as it assaulted the Bill of Rights. He wrote:

"I have been active in the peace movement in this country for 44 years and hold that my membership in the Communist Party since 1936 has only served to strengthen my devotion and dedication to the struggle for peace and democracy, freedom and social progress. I hold that these objectives will be better guaranteed when this country changes from capitalism to socialism. Yes, I am proud of my Communist Party membership. [And] I am confident that the peace movement and the interests of the American people will be best served by my refusal to testify..."

With humility and a keen eye for the larger civil liberties implications, Johnson concluded, "If this move can halt the fishing and witch-hunting expedition" then "of course, the risk of contempt citation, trial and sentencing is worth it."[144] His decision to challenge HISC was reflective of a decades long commitment to protect and defend the Bill of Rights. In a legal memo, it was noted that "Johnson's defiance of the committee's attempt to investigate the peace movement has precipitated the first test of HISC's authority to subpoena witnesses and compel them to testify."[145] The committee dramatically failed this test. According to John Abt, Johnson's lawyer, this "was the first and only case of citation of contempt of a peace leader" by the HISC. "They picked me because they still think Communists are more vulnerable, and after they get me they'll be able to silence the other hundreds named in the HISC report and the thousands who think like them,"[146] Johnson added. Norma Spector, a founder of Women for Racial and Economic Equality, noted in a letter to other peace activists, "this renamed HUAC is preparing to launch a McCarthyite attack against all dissent" and if they "are permitted to again whip up anti-Communist hysteria in an effort to stifle dissent, we shall have lost the first, and perhaps most decisive battle to protect our freedom of speech and association."[147]

At the hearing, Johnson said, "These hearings are obviously calculated to intimidate and subvert the peace movement." If they succeed "the repression will grow to encompass every form of dissent – from civil rights demonstrations to peace pickets, from labor strikes to political actions."[148] After his indictment, the party's National Committee issued a statement calling the hearings "a calculated step of intensified repression and intimidation of the peace movement" and a "continuation of the government attack against the Communist Party and the liberties of all progressive Americans."

Their opinion that HISC should be "thrown into the Inquisition trash can,"[149] was shared by New Mobe, its leadership and most of the peace movement.

Further, it wasn't lost on Johnson, his comrades or the broader peace movement, that he was issued the subpoena just two weeks after the "nation's largest peace demonstration."[150] The FBI had wiretapped Johnson's phone without a warrant. Apparently, there was a truck load of recorded conversations, too.[151] Fortunately, Johnson could still rely on support from progressive clergy. Monsignor Charles Owen Rice, of the Holy Rosary Church in Pittsburgh, noted, "Our government's attempt to jail Arnold Johnson is part of its effort to discredit the peace movement." The "government's fear of opposition has become pathological. The repression grows," he added. Echoing what Communists had been saying for decades, the Monsignor concluded, "If they succeed in jailing Arnold Johnson, they can jail you and me."[152] The repression didn't deter Johnson. He was fighting on multiple civil liberties fronts. In fall 1970, he ran for U.S. Senate [153] and in early 1971, he was part of a lawsuit calling for "prohibiting and destroying a secret surveillance file" maintained by the State Department Passport Office.[154]

Ultimately, New Mobe, which had its phone service cut by the FBI,[155] split into two separate groups, the National Peace Action Coalition and the Peoples Coalition for Peace and Justice,[156] which the party helped to lead. Milwaukee area Communist, John Gilman, was considered one of the PCPJ's "most influential leaders" and served as its Midwest regional coordinator (which included five states) and Milwaukee chairman [157]; Jarvis Tyner, DBC leader and later national chair of the Young Workers' Liberation League, would serve on the coordinating committee.[158] In a report titled, *For A Majority Peace Movement*, Johnson updated his comrades on the split. He said, "representatives of thirty major national organizations and 17 area coalitions have developed a working relationship" through the PCPJ, "which is the all inclusive, multi-issue and multi-tactic section of the peace movement." To Johnson, the PCPJ "gains its strength by its diversity," something some sectors of the peace movement struggled with. "It is a coalition that does not claim to be the total of the movement," he added, "but is always in the process of growth, politically and in organized relations with other forces." The NPAC was dominated by the Socialists Workers Party, he told his comrades, which meant that the "struggle for unity must be made by involving the broader forces – many of them completely new to the organized peace movement." Rightly, Johnson added, "The approach is to the majority of the American people and not to an inner power struggle or counter-productive debates."

Despite the setback, Johnson once again saw the peace movement as being on the offensive. Its objective, to organize "such massive and varied actions by the majority of [the] American people that the ruling class and its Nixon Administration would be forced with only one alternative – end the aggressive war." To him, "U.S. imperialism is weaker today. Its criminal brutality, its greed, arrogance and avarice, its utter disregard of human and social values are signs of decadence and desperation – not of strength." Like other Communists, he saw parallel political trends developing on the global stage. The decline of capitalism and imperialism correlated directly with socialism's ascendance. As one system increased in power, the others' ability to unilaterally impose its will on the rest of the world diminished. Anti-imperialist forces "on the world scale," lead by the Soviet Union, "are a great source of strength to the peace movement" domestically, Johnson concluded.[159]

* * *

Johnson's involvement in New Mobe and the PCPJ weren't the only ways in which Communists helped to build the peace movement. The first call for "an international student [peace] strike"[160] was initiated by Bettina

Aptheker, a CPUSA, W.E.B. DuBois Clubs and Berkeley Free Speech Movement leader. As Aptheker, who was also a leader of the Student Mobilization Committee to End the War in Vietnam, or Student Mobe, recalled, "I proposed that we call a student strike...I called for it. I helped to organize it, but it was done through Student Mobe."[161] The strike, which took place on April 26, 1968, drew attention to the "horror that our government is perpetuating both in Vietnam and at home." The organization made a special appeal to high school students. One strike brochure urged student to "oppose the war that kills your fathers, brothers, and may kill you. Oppose the school administration that teaches that the killing or maiming of over a million Vietnamese in a racist war is legal and moral. Oppose racism," which "distorts everyone." "Oppose drafting our friends, brothers and ourselves to die in a war that we didn't start and don't want." Student Mobe called on students to think of the strike as a "political strike," as an "expression of opposition" and noted that "every student that engages in antiwar activities" during the strike "will be part of a huge international total, that may well encompass a majority of the world's students."[162] It is estimated one million students participated in the day-long strike.[163]

Considered a broad-based Marxist youth organization – with chapters across the country founded and often led by Communists – the DBC was named after the African American scholar-activist W.E.B. DuBois, who joined the party in 1961.[164] Like their namesake, the DBC faced unprecedented repression, including the March 1966 bombing of their national headquarters in San Francisco.[165] That same month, Richard Nixon attacked the DBC because of its name. He claimed it apparently "misled" people due to the similarity in pronunciation to the Boys Clubs of America, a "classic example of Communist deception and duplicity."[166] Students, however, mocked the Republican trickster and his outlandish claim.[167] Young Communists, like Jarvis Tyner, were also called before the Subversive Activities

Control Board due to their peace activism.[168] In 2013, Jay Schaffer, a member of the DBC Reunion Organizing Committee, said "the DuBois Clubs and the Young Workers Liberation League showed that it was possible to have a socialist-oriented, multiracial, multinational youth organization that was partisan to the working class and the labor movement,"[169] despite the repression. Robert Greenblatt, the national coordinator of the National Mobilization Committee, noted in early February 1968, that the attack on the DBC was a "new witch hunt...designed to destroy [the] movement and pick off its leadership," of which Communists were a part of. He urged solidarity with the DBC and encouraged protest rallies to be organized for the morning of February 27 at "as many" Federal buildings as possible.[170] Even anti-CPUSA Marxists, like Milt Rosen, chairman of the Maoist Progressive Labor Party, would declare the party-led DBC one of the most important groups in the peace movement, just after SDS and the May 2nd Movement.[171] Other PLP members were more generous; they praised the CPUSA's diversity, saying that it was "the best-integrated organization, by race, sex and age, that I've ever seen."[172] Just two months after the bombing of the DBC offices, the party's national office in New York was also damaged by a bomb.[173]

The party and DBC also helped lead the defense of the Fort Hood Three – three young soldiers who refused to deploy to Vietnam and were court martialed in 1966, marking "the genesis of the organized GI [anti-war] movement."[174] That two of the three – PFC James Johnson, who would later become city editor of the party's newspaper, the *Daily World*, and PVT Dennis Mora, a DBC leader – were party members [175] is illustrative of the multifaceted role young Communists would play in the emerging anti-war movement. Though Johnson and Mora's party membership was publicly denied, their example became "a cause celebre' spurring draft resistance and opposition to the war within the military."[176] At the 1967 DBC convention, Ronald Lockman, announced that he would also refuse to deploy. He told the 400 convention attendees, "I would like to see follow-the-leader in the army. I followed the lead of the Fort Hood Three in refusing to go. Who is going to follow me?" Grace Mora Newman, Dennis's sister, added, "Exactly one year ago the U.S. Army started court-martial proceedings against the Fort Hood Three. No doubt they are getting ready now to court-martial Ronald Lockman. One thing is sure," she concluded with no small amount of sarcasm, "the Du Bois Club will be well represented at Fort Leavenworth,"[177] which just happened to be a stone's throw from the Leavenworth Penitentiary where Gus Hall was imprisoned from 1951 to 1957. Grace Mora Newman would later run for office on the CP ticket as a peace candidate.[178] In mid-November 1968, after two and a half years in a military prison, the Fort Hood Three were released. Their patriotism was embraced by a 500 person DBC organized celebration that included folksinger Pete Seeger, actor Ossie Davis and others, including Cleveland Robinson, from District 65 of the Retail, Wholesale, Department Store Union.[179] During this period, party leaders Mike Zagarell and Paul Friedman also served in the leadership of the Stop the Draft Week protests.[180] The party-led DBC was very much a part of the G.I. anti-war resistance and the student peace upsurge.

Party members also helped initiate the aptly titled Vietnam Summer, which was "an attempt to expand and diversify the anti-war movement, [by] building a base outside of the existing constituency." The program hoped to recruit "1,200 full-time staff" and "as many as 10,000 volunteers" by summer 1967 to organize "broad, electorally-oriented educational projects aimed at middle-class adults to draft resistance unions and organizations for civil disobedience." The common theme, according to the organizers, was to "deepen and broaden" the anti-war movement, to "train organizers, develop educational materials, and provide funds for many types of activities." The program was supported by SDS, the

SNCC, the Baptist Student Movement, and the DBC, with party member, Franklin Alexander, signing the call.[181]

In December 1965, party leader and historian, Herbert Aptheker, led a delegation – that included Tom Hayden, founding president of SDS, and Staughton Lynd, professor of history at Yale University – to North Vietnam where they met with leaders of the Democratic Republic of Vietnam, Prime Minister Pham Van Dong and the National Liberation Front of South Vietnam. That Aptheker's companions were "people whose views and politics were different from my own" added legitimacy to the endeavor and broadened its appeal to a much more diverse section of the peace movement. To Aptheker, "Vietnam is the story of stories and I am going to examine it, first-hand, and then I am going to tell that story to as many of my fellow-Americans as I can." Aptheker, and his delegation, returned to campuses, rallies, protests, teach-ins, and newspapers eager to hear their "first-hand" accounts.[182] According to *Worker* reporter Tim Wheeler, the right-wing was "enraged." To them, Aptheker was "consorting with the enemy," though he and his travel partners ultimately became "heroes to the anti-war movement."[183] Earlier that year, James E. Jackson was in Moscow at a Consultative Meeting on the events then unfolding in Vietnam. He said U.S. imperialism would by its actions bring "progressive and peace loving forces, the popular masses," together in condemnation of the "open aggression against the Democratic Republic of Vietnam,"[184] which proved to be the case.

* * *

In 1972, party leaders Gus Hall, Jarvis Tyner, Rasheed Story, and Joseph North witnessed first-hand the barbarity of the U.S. war on Vietnam. "We saw with our own eyes that the main targets of the U.S. bombers were the heavily populated working class centers of Hanoi and Haiphong," they reported from Southeast Asia. "We saw the hospital and spoke with the women and children whose blood was smeared on the steps as we entered." "Civilian targets are the main objective," they said indignantly. "We saw market places bombed, restaurants bombed, factories bombed, waterfront warehouses bombed, vital watermains for the people's needs bombed," a war crime among many. "We have now seen crushed bodies of little girls who only moments before played peacefully with their dolls, and the bodies of small boys whose friendly game of marbles were disrupted forever by the massive tonnage of U.S. bombs." Hall and his comrades met with rice farmers in country villages; one man's family of seven had been killed earlier in the day. "In the name of our own children," the delegation continued, "we appeal to all Americans to save the children of Vietnam" and stop "the genocidal policies of the Nixon Administration." They implored fellow Americans to act with moral decisiveness. "Now that we know this, we must act now or accept the verdict of humanity, of complicity by complacency, in mass murder, in genocide...a national shame." Like other Communists, Hall and his comrades saw the attempt to destroy the National Liberation Movement of the Vietnamese people as an act of desperation, born of fear and weakness. "The bombings are the work of desperate men gone insane," they said. "Nixon's irresponsible acts of desperation are those of a mad butcher and can lead to a world confrontation," a harrowing prospect given the rise of Soviet socialism. Communists also saw materialist dialectics at work, too. For, "the very acts of desperation have opened up momentous possibilities of putting an end to the aggression now." This was an observation that would soon prove prophetic. "This moment in history," they concluded, "cries out for unity in action! This is a moment when we must unite and concentrate our total efforts to end this criminal war, to end this mass murder, to end this imperialist aggression." "We make this appeal from the air-raid shelters of Hanoi."[185] The YWLL also sent a delegation to Vietnam as guests of the Ho Chi Minh Working Youth Union.[186] The CPUSA's fraternal contact with Vietnamese Communists made a unique contribution to the domestic peace movement, especially as the crisis enveloping U.S. capitalism and imperialism intensified, eventuating in defeat in Vietnam.

* * *

Some within the party claimed that "peace activists seek Communist Party cadre to share a major part of the leadership and often even become dependent on our special contributions." At the party's February 1972 convention, national organizational secretary, Daniel Rubin, enumerated what was meant by "special contributions." First and foremost was the party's "approach to labor and the working class." This approach had helped birth the modern industrial union movement in the 1930s. Second, Rubin highlighted the party's "approach to Black and other specially oppressed national and racial communities." This is a role that has now been well documented. Third, "we have a mass, united front, coalition approach and are neither sectarians nor just out to feather our own nest," a polite jab at some other organizations less familiar with collective decision making and underground work. And finally, Rubin added, the party is "an organized, stable force that can impart organizational stability and dedication to the peace movement." However, Rubin also chastised some comrades for focusing too much energy on "intermediate forms," which have become "very dependent on staffing by Communists to carry out all their activities and to guarantee their finances." This was a peculiar conundrum for a small party attempting to have broad influence. Regardless, Rubin and other party members were optimistic and set new organizational goals of recruiting 1,000 new party members by the fall elections, increasing *Daily World* subscriptions by 7,000, and collecting 400,000 to 500,000 signatures to place Communists on ballots throughout the country, which would enable them to "talk directly to 2 to 3 million people."[187] Rubin's goals were likely born out of the electricity then surrounding the CPUSA and the successful campaign to free fellow Communist, Angela Davis.

* * *

In summer 1975 – during the 30th anniversary celebration of the birth of the Democratic Republic of Vietnam and shortly after the North Vietnamese People's Army liberated Saigon – Johnson traveled to Vietnam with his comrade Henry Winston. At a reception with Vietnamese Communist leaders, Johnson said, "Thirty years ago, a new Vietnam, the first Socialist state in South East Asia, the Democratic Republic of Vietnam was born... Today we celebrate and share that world historic event." The victory was proof of a shift in the world balance of forces, a shift toward ascending socialism. "The days, years, and decades of struggle for Vietnamese national liberation and independence should have been completed with the victory over French colonialism," were it not for U.S. imperialism, which "moved in with a madness, brutality and genocidal onslaught" reminiscent of "Hitler's ovens." "We could speak at length about the anti-imperialist activity in the United States," Johnson added, but "what was done by the heroic Vietnamese is so tremendous – and the role of the Socialist sector of the world was so decisive...that we prefer to express our appreciation" for what your struggle has meant to us, to the domestic movement to weaken international imperialism.[188] Johnson was pragmatic, too. His personal notes included exploring the possibility of initiating an American-Vietnamese Friendship Society upon his returned. "Such an organization is very much needed," he wrote, and should be organized "by people in the United States – and could involve many from the movement forces who opposed U.S. aggression,"[189] perhaps some of the same people Johnson had spent the past decade working with in New Mobe and PCPJ.

Winston told reporters, his visit to Hanoi "were six of the most inspiring days of my life." Le Duan, first secretary of the Vietnamese Workers Party, said the CPUSA played an "indispensable role" in the "Creation of a peace collation" that helped bring the war to an end. Johnson added, "Everybody greeted us without any reference to the fact that we had come from the country whose armed forces had inflicted such cruel blows against their people. They knew we were representatives of that America which opposed the war from the outset." The Vietnamese knew that "the majority wanted peace, and they singled out the CPUSA as being in the van[guard] of all friends of peace." It was noted that new schools and hospitals were being built. Johnson and Winston also laid a wreath at the door of the Ho Chi Minh mausoleum.[190]

* * *

In winter 1976, Johnson along with his comrade Roscoe Proctor, chair of the CPUSA's Black Liberation Commission, attended the First Congress of the Cuban Communist Party. According to Johnson, the Congress "was tremendous international event...the biggest international gathering of Communists and progressive forces in this hemisphere ever, I guess. And they [the Cubans] really made a big point of it." Johnson also highlighted the "emphasis on Marxism-Leninism and the interrelationship of the struggle for freedom in Cuba – the national liberation struggle – and the international support, each of which," he added, "contributed to making the revolution successful." Johnson and Proctor both reflected on the "socialist community, particularly the Soviet Union" in the consolidation of Cuba's revolution. The Cubans in turn expressed "their solidarity with the national liberation struggles throughout the world," noting that "what they can provide they will provide. Their support is not a matter of words," Johnson continued, "their support is a matter of deeds," which proved to be the case throughout Latin America and Africa, particularly Angola[191] ; the YWLL and the Communist-led National Anti-Imperialist Movement in Solidarity with African Liberation intensified their efforts to build solidarity for the People's Movement for the Liberation of Angola.[192] Over 400 Communists and their allies heard Johnson's report-back from the Congress at a February 2, 1977 *Daily World* forum. Reflecting on the "mass rally" in Havana's Revolution Square after the conclusion of the Congress, Johnson said, "It was not just massive...but colorful, alive, full of excitement. And it made you think: here is an example of a truly living relationship between the Party and the Cuban people." "It was a demonstration of confidence by the people in themselves, in their future, in their Party,"[193] he added.

Johnson also traveled twice to Europe and the Soviet Union (1961 and 1966). He retired from "active involvement" in the party in 1979 after a stroke and heart attack. He died on September 26, 1989 – a few days after his 85th birthday. He married Aurelia Ricci in 1933, while living in Ohio.[194]

* * *

In a February 1977 *Party Affairs* article, Johnson raised the question of "How to reach millions"? He wrote, "Let's get into the habit of mass work in the sense of the Party itself as well as the mass organizations," something the party-led National Alliance Against Racist and Political Repression was then exemplifying. We have a "great deal to learn about style of work. Reaching millions is different from talking to thousands," he added.[195] As a consistent and vigorous defender of the Bill of Rights, Johnson spent his entire adult life trying to build a mass organization capable of reaching millions. That he had an unwavering confidence in the Bill of Rights and democracy was unquestioned. That the ruling class did everything in its power to drive a wedge between

Communists and African Americans – as well as peace activists – is also unquestioned. The "long and arduous struggle to reestablish full citizenship rights of the Communist Party"[196] undoubtedly took its toll on both Johnson and the party. Fortunately for us, they had no other choice but to resist. As the party leader Elizabeth Gurley Flynn put it, "the Communist Party has been compelled to fight for its own existence. In so doing it has spearheaded the fight for the rights of others."[197] Additionally, the "refusal of the leadership and membership [of the party] to register" under the provisions of the McCarran Act, despite "severe penalties," Johnson wrote in 1967, "dramatically exposed the reactionary essence of the act and its threat to the democratic liberties of all Americans. For the Constitution and the Bill of Rights cannot be abrogated for one section of the people and preserved for all others."[198] His analysis easily applies to the Smith Act and McCarthyism generally. Johnson's friend and comrade, the lawyer John Abt, wrote in his memoirs, "After more than three decades as general counsel of the Communist party, I know as well as anyone the extent and extremes of repression to which this mightiest of all governments in history has gone to destroy a small Party of modest means because it sought to fundamentally alter the existing relations of economic and political power...Its leaders have repeatedly been imprisoned, often for years, without having committed a criminal act."[199] In February 1962, Abt told TV and radio interviewers, "It is one of the ironies of history that an organization accused of trying to overthrow the government is courageously defending the rights of each of us."[200] As Gerald Horne noted regarding the demise of the party-led CRC and its "vigorous advocacy" on behalf of democratic rights, "benefits were reaped by all freedom-loving people" due to the party's work, thereby "plow[ing] the ground that allowed for a revivified Civil Rights Movement to emerge,"[201] a movement partly birthed by Communists. In a September 1973 *Washington Post* interview, Johnson told reporters, "There is joy in the Communist Life,"[202] a life spent fighting for the Bill of Rights, peace, African American equality and socialism. Like other CPUSA members, Johnson paid a heavy price in defense of the Bill of Rights. Our nation is better, and our democratic safeguards are more secure because of him.

Chapter 2

Charlene Mitchell: Presidential politics, the National Alliance, and the fight against Reaganism

It was July 1968. Martin Luther King, Jr., and Robert F. Kennedy had both recently been assassinated. Earlier that year, the North Vietnamese People's Army launched the Tet Offensive, one of the largest and bloodiest battles of the Vietnam War – a strategic victory that marked a turning point in the war delivering a body blow that decisively put U.S. imperialism back on its heels.[1] African American Communist leader, James E. Jackson, after a visit to that war-torn country wrote of the "irreparable defeat" of a "sinister design to crush with military might the social emancipation and national liberation movement," a design, he added, which had failed completely.[2] The United States was in turmoil. Students, peace activists and civil rights leaders protested across the country. *Freedomways* editorialized that summer that "turbulence, and hard-to-predict cataclysms" marked the "political and social landscape," whereby "millions across the country are finding ways to express their dissatisfaction with things as they are." This expression of discontent, the editors argued, was a "*majority* opinion" capable of "opening a new period in the political life of the American people" [*italic* in original].[3]

It is in this context that the 38-year-old Charlene Mitchell – already a veteran of the class struggle and said to be the "country's leading lady Communist" – announced her candidacy as the first African American woman to run for president of the United States. She did not expect a huge vote, though. The CPUSA was, after all, still recovering from decades of repression. She did, however, hope the campaign would expose people to the party's ideas and policies. The campaign's success, she said, did not depend on actual votes cast. "I don't expect to win, except by some wild, miraculous stretch of the imagination,"[4] she told curious reporters. The "point of the campaign is not solely to amass votes," she added, while speaking with students at Fisk University. Nor is it "obviously, an attempt to actually get into office but rather to organize and bring the Communist Party before the people."[5] The campaign's success rested on the party's ability "to present to the American people their views and their platform in a way that the American people can begin to understand what communists [do] here," to present "some of the [party's] solutions to the problems of our country." She argued that racism was the "number one issue in the United States,"[6] second to the war in Vietnam.

In a 1968 CPUSA election brochure titled *Communist Candidate Speaks On Black Liberation*, Mitchell elaborated. "The economic system of capitalism and the political institutions which serve it have failed the people because it is incapable of destroying once and for all the racism that infects this nation." She said a fundamental, systemic change was needed, a change that would "put an end to the additional profits gathered by maintaining job discrimination and an unequal wage standard," while simultaneously removing the "ideological underpinning...that allows the waging of a racist genocidal war in Vietnam."[7] This was a theme the party had been articulating for years by 1968.

The party's leadership in the growing anti-war movement – not to mention, its well-documented vanguard role in the struggle for African American equality[8] – was multi-faceted. Mitchell was campaigning on the election trail – giving interviews, meeting with students, union members and community activists, publicly and persistently rearticulating the party's anti-racist and anti-war position. As early as 1966, others, such as the Fort Hood Three, were challenging imperialism and its racist manifestations directly within the U.S. military. PFC James Johnson and PVT Dennis Mora, both party members,[9] and PVT David Samas, then became the first G.I.s to publicly refuse to deploy to Vietnam and participate in what they termed an "unjust, immoral, and illegal war," a war demanding people of color make yet another blood sacrifice for a nation that still treated them as second-class citizens. That the Fort Hood Three were confined to prison, sentenced to years of hard labor, while simultaneously becoming "a cause celebre' spurring draft resistance and opposition to the war within the military,"[10] likely bolstered Mitchell's and W.E.B. DuBois Club's anti-war credentials, especially on the campuses, where party youth activists, like Bettina Aptheker – a leader in the Berkeley Free Speech Movement – helped to initiate student peace strikes.[11] Mike Zagarell, Mitchell's vice-presidential running mate and national youth secretary of the CPUSA, told reporters that young Communists helped to initiate anti-draft unions and served in the leadership of Stop the Draft Week protests; they also challenged racism within the predominantly white student movement. Zagarell told *The New York Times*, "the student unrest on college campuses and the antidraft demonstrations have been helped along by the Communist Party." He added, "there were 60 Communist party members who were marshals out of a total of 300" during the New York City Stop the Draft demonstrations.[12] The role of reds in helping to organize and mobilize the hundreds of thousands who protested has, unfortunately, often been ignored.

Communists spent much of the early 1960s speaking to tens of thousands of university and college students, helping to spur a rising tide of student unrest and activism – a fact that wasn't lost on ruling elites, and considerable effort were made to bar reds from campuses. That 250 students at Bloomfield College, a small New Jersey college, turned out to hear Zagarell in mid-October 1968 meant youth and students were still curious about what Communists had to say years after the initial upsurge in speaking engagements. That Zagarell also spoke at Northeastern College, Brandeis University, the University of Maine, Colby College, Amherst College, Brown University and the University of Rhode Island, among others that month[13] meant the 1950s Red Scare was not entirely successful. Mitchell was simultaneously on a speaking tour in St. Paul-Minneapolis, Minnesota where she was greeted with multiple radio, TV and newspaper interviews in between campus speaking engagements. This was an indication of the interest a young, African American woman Communist could spark in the heartland. Campus organizers told reporters, "dissident Democrats should consider voting for the Communist Party as one of the possible ways of expressing dissatisfaction with the nomination of Hubert Humphrey,"[14] which was likely music to Mitchell's ears.

The contradictions within U.S. capitalism were on full display, as Mitchell and her comrades were acutely aware. The punishment exacted on the Fort Hood Three – who after two and a half years in prison were released shortly after the November 1968 elections [15] – and others who dared to challenge imperialism and the presumed right of the U.S. to act as a global anticommunist police force, clashed with the reality of millions of students, peace activists and civil rights leaders protesting across the nation. This dialectic served to not only put the ruling class on notice as they scrambled to maintain the status quo. It also provided a spurious justification for intensified repression. New amendments to the unconstitutional McCarran Act – designating any organization as a Communist "front" in-which "*one* or more" [*italic* in original] members of the CPUSA participate in managing – was a case in point. President Johnson signed the new amendments into law. Not surprisingly, the newly resuscitated Subversive Activities Control Board immediately "scheduled the commencement of hearings against the DuBois Clubs under the amended act," along with thirteen other organizations. All but three were forced "to dissolve because of their inability to bear the burdens, financial and otherwise, of the SACB proceedings." Perhaps, as attorney John Abt suggested, the five SACB members were eager to continue receiving the "not inconsiderable rate of $26,000 per year" for a part-time job, while doing "virtually nothing,"[16] except harassing Communists and leftists, all on the taxpayers' dime. Such was the tumultuous political reality Mitchell confronted when she announced her candidacy.

Though the 38-year-old was keenly aware of the challenges, she continued to campaign vigorously – repeating the same themes that had turned her comrades into SACB targets. "Everybody says that the two problems facing our society are racism and the war. [Eldridge] Cleaver says it. [Dick] Gregory says it. The New Left says it," Mitchell told *The Harvard Crimson.* "More and more, however, their protest is turning inward, turning from racism and the war to the society which has brought them on and sanctions them." "The system itself is at stake – and the issue is the immense gap between the way people could live and the way people do live," especially African Americans. "What we need is a revolutionary transformation of this society to make it fit for men to live in, nothing else." We need a "counter-vision with counter-values," she argued. As an African American woman Communist, Mitchell pointedly challenged racism, imperialism and capitalism. She refused to allow her activism or Black radicalism in general to be confined safely within the acceptable boundaries of liberal anticommunism. Her advocacy for a third party angered and insulted political operatives wedded to and benefiting from a two-party political system; operatives who hoped to win African American votes despite centuries of slavery and Jim Crow. Mitchell argued, "It is time that workers run for public office and begin to build a political party of their own,"[17] an independent party, a party friendly to socialism and quite possibly aligned with the Communist Party, which the entire weight of the U.S. government was still trying to destroy, albeit unsuccessfully.

While a "revolutionary transformation" of society was her main objective, Mitchell also highlighted the role of education under capitalism in perpetuating an oppressive and exploitive ideology. In late October 1968, she spoke with students at Stanford University. She said students must "challenge the role of the university in a capitalist society. The student movement must move beyond the bounds and limits of a capitalist university" and, thereby, make it "dysfunctional" to capitalism. Universities function as a tool of the "corporate elite," she added, "and they all must be challenged by a movement with a different conception of the role of the university in society, a conception based on a different set of principles, priorities, and premises than those which flow from the private ownership of productive property."[18] Mitchell's message was generally in line with the mainstream of the Black left. The fall 1968 issue of *Freedomways* was entirely devoted to the crisis in education. While the language used by most of the contributors was considerably more tactful than Mitchell's, the conclusions they drew were remarkably similar: protests against "established authority" – in the public schools and in the private universities – were becoming a "proper and normal part" of everyday life, especially for Black youth who were "undergoing a process of inner re-examination and of incipient group self-awareness of such dimensions as to force a total restructuring of the Afro-American self-image."[19] That the *Freedomways* editorial board as well as its regular contributors included a considerable number of current and former party members – Esther Cooper Jackson, W. Alphaeus Hunton, Augusta Strong, Claudia Jones, Doxey A. Wilkerson, and Shirley Graham Du Bois,[20] for example – served to amplify the party's influence among African Americans during the Civil Rights era and to continue the decades long Red-Black alliance. On the one hand, some argued that party leaders benignly "discussed the content of the magazine" with some of the editors "and how to make it a better vehicle to influence the civil rights movement." Others, however, claimed that party leader James E. Jackson "determines the content" of the magazine,[21] thereby dismissing Esther Cooper Jackson's independent agency as editor. Still others argue that *Freedomways* was published by "Black Communists and funded by white Communists,"[22] or at least partially funded by the Soviet Union and Communist China.[23] Regardless, the quarterly journal remained a valuable tool by which Communists continued to gauge and influence African American political discourse. Additionally, *Freedomways* had a proud, radical lineage, too; it was born out of the ashes of Paul Robeson's *Freedom* newspaper, which also employed Communists, including Robeson's partner at the Council on African Affairs, Alphaeus Hunton,[24] an ideological mentor of Mitchell.

Mitchell applied Marxism to the university. She argued that the university "should be a self-governing community," just as workers should be empowered to govern themselves. The presidential candidate was expanding upon Karl Marx's well-known analysis, articulating the irreconcilable differences between workers and capitalists inevitably leading to class conflict. She argued that students and universities under capitalism have divergent interests. "The interest of the students is to learn how to think: the interest of a capitalist university is to teach them how to behave...The goal of [capitalist] education is the creation of docile people, the essence of general society is the subordination of people to things: commodities and the production of commodities," she concluded.[25] "[A]s a communist," she continued in the election brochure, "I have decided that in time we will have to face that ultimate business" of ushering in "a system where the people own and control the wealth together." We must "bring on socialism." Her election was between campaign intended to educate voters about socialism and to announce the party's return to the electoral arena. The party hadn't put forward a presidential candidate in 28 years. Mitchell appealed to Civil Rights and Black Power activists, boldly declaring capitalism "represses us. The men who hold power in the country fear black people and the potential power that lies in black communities. Now black people have moved to assert that power and the repression follows." Police clubs, water hoses and rabid dogs were "sent to meet the protest of black people."

In her campaign, Mitchell specifically appealed to "my black brothers and sisters to consider the alternative my party offers. If you agree with all or most of our program, vote with us. If you want to get in this thing, join up."[26] According to Mitchell, some African Americans did join the party demonstrating the continuing resiliency of a Red-Black alliance less susceptible to anti-communism. "We're going everywhere, even the South," she told reporters, "as symbols of the problems and the people in this country that the two major parties ignore – a black woman representing the struggle against racism and for peace, and a draft-age man [Zagarell] representing the struggles of students and draft resisters."[27]

In early October, Mitchell spoke at the "first political forum" of the San Fernando Valley State College Students for a Democratic Society chapter. More than 200 students heard her blast the "dog eat dog" nature of U.S. capitalism. She added, the "racist war in Vietnam should be ended right now. It was started by presidential decree and can be ended by presidential decree." It is time "to turn this country around, and we Communists are ready to do this," she concluded. Mitchell also did numerous TV and newspaper interviews, including a "national CBS-TV show on minority party candidates."[28] A few weeks later, she was at City University-New York, telling 100 students there that the "[George] Wallace movement contained the seeds of fascism." She urged the creation of a "Left Alternative against the Center and the Right" and "warned against supporting Humphrey" as a "lesser evil" candidate. "We need an effective Left instead," she argued. "The only real alternative is the Left," she added, in alliance with the Communist Party, which "stood for community control of the schools and police,"[29] a call eerily relevant today. A few days later, she was in Austin, Texas, where she was greeted by local Student Nonviolent Coordinating Committee leaders and spoke with 120 students at the University of Texas.[30] At Fisk just days later, she told students, "Organize and mobilize the people in the black communities on the basis of what **they themselves** describe as their needs and demands" [**bold** in original],[31] not predetermined ideological ideas.

Just days before the presidential election, Mitchell spoke at Lowell State College, Harvard, Boston State College, Massachusetts Institute of Technology and the University of Massachusetts.[32] She told about 150 Harvard students, "the old grey goose of liberalism is dying and after Tuesday, it may be dead." While she exaggerated the impact her candidacy would have on the outcome of the presidential elections, her criticism of liberalism was incisive and withering. "American liberalism has perverted itself," she added. "The liberal coalition brought on the war in Vietnam. Liberals say that violence has brought about the crisis in our country. It is, instead, the failure of liberalism that has driven demonstrators and rebels into the streets." She implored the assembled students to get involved, and asked: "What are you going to do with your lives? Are you going to be on the side of Che Guevara or of [Secretary of State, Robert] McNamara? Are you going to join the movement, or will your life be one of quiet desperation?"[33] In all, Mitchell spoke at 16 colleges in 9 days leading up to the election.[34]

Mitchell appeared on the ballot in just two states and received only 1,075 votes,[35] a predictably dismal result; most Americans did not know she was on the ballot. Additionally, her electoral results should not lead to the erroneous conclusion that support for Communist candidates – even at this juncture of the Cold War – was infinitesimal. Just two years earlier the well-known Southern California Communist, Dorothy Healey, received over 85,000 votes in her bid to become the L.A. county tax assessor, a non-partisan position.[36] Several factors coalesced to hinder the success of Mitchell's electoral campaign – the party itself being one of them.

* * *

As early as June 1967, the party had begun internal discussions on whether to run a presidential candidate in the 1968 election. That spring, party general secretary, Gus Hall, broached the topic. He said, "In one form or another the central issues, movements and trends in our country will be shaped and influenced by the 1968 election." At the spring National Committee meeting, it was said, "we need to hammer out the political guidelines for the 1968 elections." Additionally, he continued, we must reject "classical tailism – tailing events and movements, tagging along after them. It is reacting but never acting. It is supporting but never initiating or leading. It is political 'milk-toasting.'" Clearly, Hall was ready for a shift in the party's approach to the elections. He was ready to go on the electoral offensive. "We are going to decide *now*," he added, "whether in 1968 we and the independent forces are going to be an electoral tumbleweed blown about by political breezes and currents, or whether we are going to be a force that influences the decisions of others who are hesitantly moving" [*italic* in original]. To Hall, the answer was clear. "It is in this same spirit that we have to take up *now* the question of Communist candidates – again, not as a substitute for other independent forms, but in addition to them" [*italic* in original], he added. And he urged his comrades to "give serious consideration" to running Communist candidates. "Our Party is fortunate," he concluded. "We have many able men and women to pick from," who should run for House and Senate seats, as well as local elected offices. "And we must now make a fight against state laws banning Communists from the ballot by challenging them with Communist candidates."[37] Gaining ballot status, though, proved very difficult, as evidenced by Mitchell's campaign. "The bosses and boss politicians know the meaning of a vote for Communists candidates, no matter what the number. That is why they continue to try to keep the Communist party off the ballot," read one campaign flier.[38] Regardless, the party's general political outline or direction was decided. However, it would ultimately be another year before Mitchell would be chosen as the organization's standard bearer.

At the CPUSA's July 1968 Special National Convention, national chair Henry Winston outlined the party's electoral tactics. He told the assembled delegates and guests, "it is necessary to understand that the policies which we advance in regard to the electoral struggle of 1968, policies which are three-pronged in nature, are not things in themselves." Rather, he continued, "The three prongs – work within the two parties, building of independent political formations, and the participation of the Communist Party through its own candidates – are not isolated from a general policy, a general strategy, but involve tactics in relations to a general objective, that of moving people from many levels in one direction – the direction of an anti-monopoly coalition." Mitchell's electoral results are much more difficult to gauge when viewed through this Marxist prism. For, as Winston put it, the party was articulating a "class concept" capable of challenging "monopoly power and wealth," a concept that "alter[ed] power relationships" and ultimately "entails a breakaway from the two-party system and the formation of a new mass-based popular party." Unfortunately, this was something most Americans were leery of. According to him, the creation of an anti-monopoly coalition, "a qualitatively new formation – one that is pitted against monopoly rather than one that is...subordinated to a sector of monopoly," was a "intermediary strategic aim" on the long road toward winning socialism.[39] He and his comrades, saw in Mitchell a reflection of the modern civil rights movement, a symbol with the potential to harness and direct mass energy. As the candidates' sister-in-law and comrade Kendra Alexander later recalled, Mitchell's "nomination was symbolic of the Party's firm and principled position on the Black liberation struggle,"[40] a position born out of a decades-long commitment to democracy, equality and socialism. Further, in many ways, Mitchell simply had "the credentials" and was "poised to take advantage of the 'Black Power' movement," as David Cullen and Kyle G. Wilkison have written,[41] though she only had four months to campaign. "We are proud to be the only political party in the United States to have nominated a woman, Charlene Mitchell, as candidate for president of the nation," Clara Colon, wrote in *Political Affairs*, the party's monthly theoretical journal. However, she critically added, as inspiring as Mitchell's campaign is, it – along with other examples – "will remain little more than tokens" unless "the whole mass of women [move] forward, freeing them to become human beings, to exercise their full rights and talents, and to help solve the crisis facing us."[42] A young African American woman could signal, after years of repression, a new, vibrant Communist Party, a party reflective of the emerging movements – including feminism – and a party poised to go on the offensive, which was a reasonable conclusion given that tens of thousands of students across the country had recently flocked to hear party leaders like Gus Hall and Herbert Aptheker speak on college and university campuses.[43] Mitchell agreed with this assessment, telling students at Fisk University that she saw herself as "a symbol in that the major question of the day is how to end racism and oppression of black people in this country, and who is better able to handle these questions than a black person. It naturally followed that the candidate would have to be black," she concluded.[44]

By running Mitchell as a presidential candidate, Winston argued, the party also hoped to fight for its "full citizenship" as a political organization. To him, "the struggle for democracy is incomplete so long as discrimination exists against Communists." Additionally, "our Party, fighting for its equal rights and equal citizenship in all movements, must necessarily be connected with this massive movement in order to deepen its consciousness. This is the contribution which Communists can make in present-day struggles." As a result, Winston concluded, "our Party will grow and become a more powerful force for progress in our country." Perhaps unintentionally, Winston – and the party, generally – was acknowledging a weakened status after decades of repression. They were now attempting to connect with mass movements, rather than found and lead them as they had done in the 1930s. They were hoping to engage present-day struggles as equal partners. While Winston implored his comrades to "approach this task [the 1968 elections] seriously," he also admitted the organization's limited capacity as a "small party." Long-time party leader, Arnold Johnson, went so far as to criticize some sections of the party for underestimating "the significance of this campaign in reestablishing the full legality of our Party." "Regardless of the many other tasks in which Communists are involved, it is essential," Johnson continued, "to get our candidates," especially Mitchell, "before the people," though the "campaign will in the main be a 'write in,'" which proved to be the case. Johnson called Mitchell's campaign a "meaningful protest, one that could strengthen the forces of peace and progress." Ever the optimist, Winston added, in "short time" the CPUSA could be "transformed into a mass party leading tens of thousands and hundreds of thousands of workers" in an "anti-monopoly coalition that must come and for a socialist America which must follow."[45] In her acceptance speech at the convention, Mitchell said, "in 1968 the people *must* have a chance to *consider the left*" [*italic* in original],[46] her four month campaign window notwithstanding.

"We are not out to compete with anybody for votes. The aim of our campaign is to compliment and strengthen the work being done by other independent forces," Matthew Hallinan wrote in the September 1968 issue of *Political Affairs*. Hallinan, son of the wealthy West Coast lawyer Vincent Hallinan – known for his defense of the ILWU President Harry Bridges – and W.E.B. DuBois Clubs leader, continued, "Our campaign, however, is no public relations stunt. We will not be satisfied with just television appearances, news conferences, and campus rallies. Our candidates...were chosen for a purpose; they were born of black and white, working-class America, and that is where they intend to focus the campaign." He wrote, "The political tasks of our campaign are clear. We must spell out in clear and concise terms the class interest that lie behind the imperialist adventure in Vietnam. We must put forth a program for black liberation that deals with the underlying economic forces that act daily to push the masses of black people more deeply into super-exploitation and poverty."[47]

Bettina Aptheker reflected on Mitchell's campaign and suggested that some within the party were "very ambivalent about Party candidates" at that time. "They wanted to support the most progressive major party candidate, Eugene McCarthy," she added. "It was a complicated decision. I felt like it was a mistake for her to run, which had nothing to do with her. She started so late and had no hope of getting on the ballot [in most states]. Party energy should have been put elsewhere," Aptheker concluded. Divisions were also growing within the party in the wake of the Paris and Prague Springs, which complicated the overall political calculus.[48] That the *Daily World* gave considerable positive attention to Dick Gregory and his Freedom and Peace Party presidential ticket, often featuring him above the fold while Mitchell was noted afterwards, is illustrative of the point. A *DW* editorial just days before the election highlighted the "three outstanding black spokesmen – Dick Gregory, Eldridge Cleaver and Mrs. Charlene Mitchell," all presidential candidates, which likely served to reinforce the ambivalence Aptheker spoke of. As the election neared, party leaders would also discuss "the limited expression for a new party and independence from the established political system." They noted that this sentiment would impact the coming presidential elections.[49] Despite his support for Mitchell's campaign, even Johnson hedged his bets. "Whatever differences may exist on one or another programmatic demand or personality, these formations [the Gregory and Cleaver campaigns] do offer an alternative to independent voters and to many who are disillusioned with Humphrey and Nixon."[50]

Later in life Michael Myerson would paint a much more cynical picture. According to him, "Party leadership came into the [1968] convention with the determination and decision to nominate Gus Hall for President," to the displeasure of a "new generation of comrade delegates," who had joined during the recent youth and student upsurge. After a "wide-ranging debate," they nominated Mitchell. Rebuffed by the younger generation of activists and new members, according to Myerson, Hall engaged in "the virtual sabotage" of the campaign and refused to prioritize "Party resources...funds or personnel,"[51] thereby adding one more obstacle to an already perilous endeavor. In 1972, Hall would in passing reflect on Mitchell's 1968 presidential campaign and acknowledge, "though we didn't put everything into it, it was a good opening."[52] The party began to once again test the electoral waters. Betty Gannett argued in the December 1968 issue of *Political Affairs*, "People in the millions, under the leadership of a conscious vanguard, make revolutions. Only *their* actions can guarantee success in any effort to replace the monstrous system of capitalism with a new society" [italic in original]. That Mitchell's presidential campaign attracted but a handful of votes did not mean that lessons were not learned, that the party shouldn't continue to articulate its vision – in a multiplicity of forms, including running candidates. "How to win the people – first of all the majority of the working class, black and white – to the path of revolution,"[53] Gannet wrote, was the real question, not how to win votes, especially in a system rigged against third parties. That Communists did *not* analyze in detail Mitchell's campaign in the late 1968 or early 1969 issues of *Political Affairs* lends credence to the ambivalence Aptheker spoke of. In an 11 page January 1969 post-election *Political Affairs* article, a paltry three paragraphs were devoted the Mitchell's presidential campaign.[54]

* * *

Considered one of the "most important" in a wave of new Black women to join the CPUSA, Mitchell as a child "never imagined becoming a revolutionary." Born in 1930 in Cincinnati, Ohio, she grew up in what would later be called Chicago's Cabrini-Green Housing Projects, was educated at Waller High School on the near north side, and then at the Moody Bible Institute. She had planned on becoming a missionary. "I joined so many churches and got baptized so many times," she later recalled. However, her experience with racism and the struggle against it, often led by local Communists, as well as her father's activism, prompted Mitchell at the age of 13 to join American Youth for Democracy,[55] a party-led youth organization, "which has had tragic success in spreading communism," as the *Chicago Daily Tribune* reported; the youth groups was also termed "a training school in lawlessness," while being called "a mere Charlie McCarthy to the Communist party" by others,[56] a reference to the Edgar John Bergen's ventriloquist character.

Mitchell's "very first political activity" was with the AYD, which organized white and Black youth to desegregate Chicago's Windsor Theater, at North Avenue and Clark. As she recalled, "they [management] made African American youngsters sit up in the balcony, and the white kids sit down below. And one day we just decided we weren't going to do that, and we just exchanged places. And so white kids went upstairs, we went downstairs. And then the management didn't know quite what to do because they couldn't tell the white kids they couldn't sit in the balcony, so what to do?" Soon other youth from the neighborhood joined the AYD and young Communists in their protests, pickets, demonstrations and sit-ins. The theater was de-facto desegregated. "That was the very first thing I did." At age 14, while protesting at a local segregated bowling alley, Mitchell was arrested for the first time.[57]

The spark was lit. Mitchell soon became a leader in the Labor Youth League, another party-led group, and the NAACP Youth Council, among other organizations. She started taking classes at the party-led Abraham Lincoln School for Social Sciences, founded by well-known Communist William L. Patterson.[58] In 1946, Mitchell officially joined the Communist Party. "I fell in love with the Communist Manifesto," she said later. Reading and studying Marx "opened my eyes...the way that he understood the development of the Western world in-terms of the role that slavery played" in capitalisms genesis[59] provided an ideological foundation for her activism to come. In 1948, like other Communists, she was active in Henry Wallace's Progressive Party bid for president.[60]

During the early 1950s Mitchell began to focus her energies on African Liberation, especially in Apartheid South Africa. "I was taught that the struggle in Africa was part of the struggle for socialism all over the world. And that it would never be complete unless the colonialists were forced out of Africa."[61] She became friends with W. Alphaeus Hunton, veteran of the National Negro Congress, and mainstay of the Council on African Affairs, "the leading U.S. organization" committed to promoting "the independence of all African colonies and to support the full freedom of colored peoples throughout the world."[62] During this time there was "a tremendous bringing together of the struggles in Africa and those for liberation in the United States...I really began to see the importance of it," Mitchell added. As one commentator noted, "veteran activists with links to Communist Party networks in the labor movement and other local struggles were almost always valued participants if not leaders of local anti-apartheid coalitions. Their ideological grounding in class analysis, their mass organizing skills, and their strong links within the black community were a significant part of ongoing African solidarity activity." Unfortunately, they were rarely, if ever given credit for their contributions; many CPUSA activists did not announce their membership, both as a protective measure for themselves and the movements they helped to build. Mitchell traveled to Algeria, Morocco, Sierra Leone, and Guinea, among other decolonizing nations, and met with leaders of national liberation movements on behalf of the CPUSA.

During the McCarthy era – as her friends and comrades, like Henry Winston, were either underground or in jail – Mitchell emerged as a CPUSA leader. "They [the CPUSA's national leadership] were all in jail, and it was clear that the intent was to jail anybody who was openly a communist," she later recalled. By early 1952, Mitchell – along with other party cadre – went underground; she lived under an assumed identity for nearly two years in St. Louis and New York City. This was a very trying time for both Mitchell and her party. People were frightened, but we had to "try to keep up the work of the Party in some way, to keep the Party functioning." It was "very difficult to be part of a mass movement," as Communists were hounded, harassed, spied on and attacked. However, despite the repression, people of color still joined the party, "not out of love for the Soviet Union but because they believed socialism to be the necessary response to capitalism and oppression," which undoubtedly provided Mitchell and her beleaguered comrades with hope.

By 1955, Mitchell had moved to Los Angeles; in 1957, at the age of 27, she was elected to the party's National Committee.[63] A little over 10 years later she was thrust into the spotlight as the first African American women to run for president of the United States, a watershed moment for civil rights, feminism and the party.

* * *

Within two years of Mitchell's Presidential bid, her life and work took another dramatic turn when her friend and comrade, Angela Davis, was charged with conspiracy to kidnap and commit murder. She allegedly supplied a 17-year-old Jonathan Jackson with the weapons he used in a California courtroom shoot out, resulting in four deaths. Fearing for her life, Davis went into hiding and was placed on the FBI's ten most wanted list. Her comrades felt she was framed for her leadership role in the struggle against racism in general and her fight to free victims of racist and political repression in particular. Two months later – after an extensive nationwide manhunt – Davis was arrested in New York City.[64] Shortly thereafter, Communists led a historic domestic and international campaign for Davis' freedom – ultimately, achieving her exoneration and the birth of the National Alliance Against Racist and Political Repression, headed by Mitchell.

In early December 1972, roughly six months after Davis' acquittal, Mitchell outlined her experience as executive director of the National United Committee to Free Angela Davis and All Political Prisoners to a meeting of the party's Central Committee. She told the assembled party leaders, "The major lesson we learned was that the legal and mass defense of political prisoners is an inseparable entity; that you cannot free a political prisoner in the courtroom alone, and you cannot, without a good, political legal defense in the courtroom, make a mass defense," or create a mass movement. Connecting the campaign to free Davis to the earlier campaigns to free the national leadership of the Communist Party, Mitchell urged her comrades to not only address the political reality of the day, to not only address "the freedom of political prisoners who are presently on trial, but of those that are probably going to be on trial. And more importantly," she added, "we must discuss the role our Party can play" in forming a national defense organization – the genesis of which would come from the roughly 200 local Free Angela Davis Committees.[65] Mitchell was articulating a long-held understanding within the beleaguered party, which had been given tangible form nearly 25 years earlier with the emergence of the Civil Rights Congress. The CRC was formed by the merger of the International Labor Defense and other party-led defense organizations. At that time, Communists agreed that the party should not itself become a defense organization. Defense work was needed, they argued, but a "separate permanent nonpartisan organization devoted exclusively to this purpose is required," as Elizabeth Gurley Flynn said.[66] That party stalwarts led this broad formation augured well for its working class orientation as well as the centrality of African American equality. Mitchell, in many ways, was walking in Patterson's footsteps, building on the proud traditions of the CRC. Ruling elites were simultaneously reeling from the defeat of the Davis frame up.

Mitchell's report to the Central Committee also highlighted weaknesses in the party's defense work, mainly "organizational weaknesses." The party "did not somehow train sufficient cadre to be able to continue the movement now that Angela is free...[As] broad as we were finally able to make the campaign to free Angela, within that breadth there still remained a certain degree of sectarianism. First of all, within our Party." After highlighting the party's short comings, Mitchell added, "there are people literally all over this country who are interested in what Angela Davis, Black woman Communist, has to say," a clear rebuttal to the decades long attempt to dismantle and isolate the Marxist organization. Further, the Davis case also illustrated the centrality of the struggle for African American equality. The central question for Mitchell and her comrades, revolved around how to harness the energy then given form by the Free Angela Davis Committees. Moving forward, the party had to provide leadership and "single out...priority cases," while acknowledging "that it is impossible at this moment" to find "a single political prisoner that is going to be symbolic in the same way that Angela Davis was." Mitchell continued, "when we started to think of how to single out cases, we thought it was absolutely necessary to single out *representative* cases throughout the country" [*italic* in original], cases that embodied the systemic, racist nature of what is now called the prison-industrial complex.

Mitchell outlined a proposal for building a national defense organization, arguing "that it is very possible for us to be the leadership" of such an organization "and for that leadership to be completely accepted." She urged initiative and creativity if the party was going to "live up to our leadership potential," a potential severely hampered by decades of Red Scare repression. "People will not accept our leadership just on the basis that *we* are the Party that spearheaded and led the movement to free Angela Davis" [*italic* in original], she added, urging her comrades to not rest on their laurels. "So, the need for organizers, both locally and nationally...is most important," she concluded.

Mitchell stressed that focusing on building a national defense organization wasn't naive or altruistic. She saw its formation – and projected mass character – as a matter of collective self-interest. She feared a return of the 1950s witch hunts; party memories of that repressive period remained fresh. "We're going to have to have a movement that is so unified and so organized that we will be able to defend, not only our own comrades, but the mass movement. After all, that is exactly what is under attack."[67] Like Patterson, Mitchell had no illusions about bourgeois legality. The "first line of defense for civil liberties in the United States was defending the rights of Communists," a comment "repeated so often... that it bordered on the trite – but it remained no less true," as Gerald Horne indicated regarding the CRC.[68] Urgency was the order of the day – to protect the party and the movement. Mitchell hoped to call a national conference by March 1973, a conference to "represent [defense] organizations from all over the country." Optimistically, she said "it will be possible for us to have a mass defense organization no later than the Spring of 1973,"[69] a lofty goal, indeed.

Of course, Mitchell was no stranger to defense organizing. Even before the Angela Davis campaign, she had organized against police brutality; she built the Community Alert Patrol in Southern California to monitor police activity; convened the Emergency Conference to End Repression Against the Black Panther Party; and coordinated the Committee to End Genocide, which like the CRC before it, presented to the United Nations a petition signed by tens of thousands highlighting systemic racism. She also served as executive secretary of the "largest political prisoner campaign in the United States," the National United Committee to Free Angela Davis and All Political Prisoners.[70] And in May 1973 – roughly two months later than her initial optimistic projections – Mitchell became the founding executive director of the National Alliance Against Racist and Political Repression.

The call for the founding conference of what would become the National Alliance boldly proclaimed, "forces of racism and repression can be defeated. We know that victory can be won." The campaign to free Angela Davis was evidence. "We can free political prisoners. We can free victims of racist and political repression. We can stop the increase of police aggression and the unbridled terrorism which pervades the prisons." Like the Davis campaign, the newly formed defense organization argued, "we can only succeed in turning the tide of repression through a united, nationally coordinated effort," an effort not unlike those led by the CRC. "The repression of this period is calculated, organized and systematic," the call continued. "In its center is the seed of fascism, which, if allowed to sprout, would strangle us all. To successfully confront and bring a halt to this systematic, nationally organized repression, we need a national apparatus to organize our resistance."[71] This was a sentiment the entire party – as well as the broad array of progressive forces then coalescing around Mitchell and Davis – were keen to agree with. Over 800 civil rights leaders and organizers attended the founding Conference.

It wasn't long before the National Alliance was in the thick of struggle. For example, at a July 4, 1974 rally in Raleigh, North Carolina, the NAARPR led 10,000 protesters "past [the] notorious 134-year-old Central Prison" to the State Capital, where they railed against the so called "administration of justice"; 45 people were then on death row, more than in any other state, and 14,000 were housed in that state's prisons, which was "one of the highest prisoner ratios in the nation." The main speaker, Angela Davis, called North Carolina "the No. 1 disaster area in terms of racial justice," which was a partial explanation for the NAARPR's decision to rally there. Davis' goal, to lay "to rest the myth that the oppressed people of this land – Black, Brown, Red, Yellow, and white, and people of varied political and religious beliefs – cannot work together," to lay "to rest the myth that people will no longer take to the streets for freedom and justice." Speaking alongside Davis was the Rev. Ralph D. Abernathy, head of the Southern Christian Leadership Conference. He called North Carolina "the most repressive state in America." Perhaps more damning to the right wing though, was his willingness to publicly work with Communists, like Davis, something Dr. Martin Luther King, Jr., was becoming more comfortable with prior to his assassination. "They must be trembling in Washington to see us holding hands today," Davis said as she put her arm around Abernethy. "Because...here is a minister, and here," tapping her chest, "is a Communist." Abernathy addressed the crowd, saying, "my Communist brothers and sisters...

[if] that trickster in Washington [President Nixon] can go to Russia and sit down with the head of the Communist party, it is with pride and honor that I march with Angela Davis." The Red-Black alliance Communists had spent decades building still posed a formidable challenge, a challenge that brought the SCLC and the NAARPR together in North Carolina to draw attention to death and prison sentences disproportionately handed out to people of color. "Now we must consolidate our unity, make it firm as a rock," Davis concluded.[72]

At a January 1975 New York conference called by the NAARPR, the questions of immigrant rights and police crimes were discussed. The NAARPR called for "an end to harassment and repression of foreignborn [sic] workers." With the ongoing civil liberties violations directed at immigrants, this call is just as relevant today. "The racist and unconstitutional mass arrests and deportation of foreignborn [sic] workers" by the Immigration and Naturalization Service was racial profiling. According to the NAARPR, police and INS officers targeted anybody "who looks Latin or dark-skinned." The NAARPR emphasized that the terms "alien" and "illegal" were themselves "derogatory," preferring the term "economic refugees," as workers "were forced to leave their country" due to "economic oppression...created by U.S. multi-national corporations which exploit their natural resources."[73] The conference, which took place at the Church of the Resurrection in Harlem, hoped to "bring together both experts and victims of police violence to testify." Mitchell, who gave the conference's opening address, said the NAARPR and its allies needed to "compel the lawmakers to start making laws against police violence and crimes, and compel enforcement of the laws." She added, "We have got to develop ways to mount such an organized offensive that it compels the police and their political superiors to accept responsibility for their criminal acts." Though Mitchell was running a national organization, she didn't hesitate to emphasize the fact that organizing starts at the grassroots. "We must start knocking on doors, speaking before church congregations and local unions. We must start taking depositions, building community support. We must begin to build a movement that compels certain officials to come along with us." She urged the Conference attendees to "involve as many people...as possible, as long as they are organizations of the people."[74]

On May 10-12, 1975, the National Alliance held its 2nd Annual Conference. Celebrating their early accomplishments, it was noted, "we can already say that our timing answered a real need," a need made even more urgent by the corruption then being exposed in Washington, D.C. with the impeachment of President Nixon. "The Watergate crimes have shown our people what movement activists have been saying for years; the real criminals in our society are those that victimize us with war, corruption and oppression." Inversely, though, "revelations of those crimes have presented us with new opportunities to build our democratic movement in defense of our rights and to extend our liberties. Those who rule us have to retreat – at least in their rhetoric," it was added. The NAARPR claimed a partial victory. At the conference it was also noted that "Our first year of existence was largely devoted to laying our organizational base for sustained struggle,"[75] an organizational base that gained the attention of some in Washington determined to stunt the growing thrust towards Communist leadership in the struggles against racist and political repression. Apparently, Black militants were still comfortable with red allies, despite the on-going assaults on civil liberties.

In fact, the specter of repression remained. Right-wing Ohio Senator John Ashbrook spoke for many of his ilk when he castigated the NAARPR: "[It was] a direct outgrowth of the Communist Party-directed Angela Davis defense movement...[that] conduct[ed] extensive agitation around the phony [sic] issue of alleged repression of minorities."[76] Ashbrook was half right, the NAARPR was indeed founded and led by Communists; however, the repression exacted upon national minorities, especially African Americans, was anything but "phony." JoAnn Little, a working class Black woman from North Carolina was a case in point. Little, only 20, was facing the death penalty in 1975 for killing a white male prison guard in self-defense; he attacked her with an ice pick with the intent of sexual assault. Mitchell and the NAARPR put Little's assault into political context. She became "a symbol of the economic exploitation, sexual violation, political persecution, and denigration of black womanhood," as Erik S. McDuffie noted. She was truly a "*representative* case" [*italic* in original], something Mitchell had earlier thought impossible. Ultimately, with the help of the NAARPR, Little became the first woman in U.S. history to be acquitted by arguing that she "used lethal force in self-defense against rape," thereby again illustrating the power of legal defense and mass defense as "an inseparable entity."[77] "If justice is to prevail, there must be a struggle. And the only force powerful enough to reverse the normal, repressive course of events is the organized might of great numbers of people," Angela Davis, wrote regarding the Little case. Davis, who developed a relationship with Little and helped her prepare for her trial, added, "JoAnne Little may not only have been the victim of a rape attempt by a white racist jailer, she has truly been raped and wronged many times over by the exploitation and discriminatory institutions of this society,"[78] a society that all too often denigrates and exploits womanhood, especially Black womanhood.

Prior to the Little victory, Mitchell began laying the groundwork for a legal offensive amongst Communist lawyers. She wanted all Communist lawyers and law students involved in legal defense in one way or the other. At a party-sponsored conference of lawyers in January 1975, she put the issue thusly: The party's "fight against repression has been from the outset part and parcel of our approach to struggle...we have always been guided by the principle of the preservation and extension of basic civil liberties and rights." Fortunately, she added, "At this moment...there does exist an organization [the NAARPR] that has the potential to defeat this massive onslaught of repression and to mount an offensive," an organization "based on the principle of unity [and] the acceptance of the leadership role of the Party," an organization "whose integrity cannot be successfully challenged." However, she also cautioned against viewing the NAARPR "as a Party organization," which would "deny its defined united front character." While she encouraged party lawyers and law students to give "time and talent" to the defense organization, she also urged her comrades to "influence other legal organizations," like the National Conference of Black Lawyers. "With a bourgeois superstructure of courts, police and prisons, who better than a Communist lawyer has the necessary tools to wage successful legal struggles," she asked the assembled Communists. She also called on them to "give vanguard leadership"[79] on the legal front in the fight against racist and political repression. Just a few months later, Mitchell welcomed 3,000 protesters as they rallied at Lafayette Park just across the street from the White House. They chanted, "We did it for Angela, We can do it for JoAnn!."[80]

That November, Mitchell told the *Daily World*, "From its inception those of us who helped shape the Alliance believed that we could unite representatives of every racial and ethnic group on a non-partisan political basis into a nationwide, united organization. The defeat of racist and political frameups over the last few years shows what a united movement can accomplish." Mitchell also noted the representative nature of the three NAARPR co-chairs: Clyde Bellecourt, of the American Indian Movement; Bert Corona, of the Centers for Autonomous [Independent] Social Actions; and Angela Davis, of the CPUSA. They "reflect" a "unity of purpose," she added, which was more important than ever, as "we faced a nationally-coordinated pattern of repression from the federal government and that only a nationally functioning organization could combat such a threat. All the revelations of Watergate, domestic dirty tricks, etc., have demonstrated that our analysis was correct. But more important, we have proved that you can conduct a nationwide fightback campaign, involving the broadest range of groups and people,"[81] which the CRC had done decades before.

At the Third Annual Conference of the National Alliance police violence continued as a focal point. Not unlike the attention brought about by the #BlackLivesMatter movement today, it was noted that "nearly 1,000 citizens [are] killed and 10,000 wounded each year by police bullets. Underlying this drive...is the ideology of racism, used to divide our people." According to Mitchell, "The repression we have witnessed and fought – wholesale wire-tapping, infiltration of government agents into democratic organizations and institutions, arming of police into municipal armed forces...massive imprisonment of the poor, repressive legislation and the use of grand juries to prosecute and jail militant leaders and organizers of mass movements – all have been preparatory steps toward the ultimate destruction of the rights of all working people and their organizations." For too many, especially for people of color, it was added, "The peace that they [the police] seek is the peace of the cemetery." It was concluded, that the "tasks ahead are enormous, the stakes great. In balance are the lives of our people and the future of our country. Our ranks must grow and our unity must deepen." That Communists, and those associated with Communists, continued to articulate a unifying theme, a theme embraced by tens of thousands – though the party's ranks remained small – could not have been lost on the ruling class. They continued to grapple with a decades-long failure of isolating the CPUSA and its leaders. Mitchell, and the NAARPR, boldly proclaimed: "Our method is mass struggle – informing and mobilizing millions of people to unite in word and action," to build an organization "that can't be ignored by those in power."[82] As Davis indicted in her

Raleigh speech, this was a goal quite possibly causing ruling elites to tremble.

In an August 1977 *World Magazine* article, Mitchell boasted of the NAARPR's successes. She wrote, the National Alliance is "an attempt to bring into coalition the maximum participation of all who recognize that repression – in all its facets – is a direct threat to all who would engage in progressive struggle." The NAARPR "has emerged as one of the most significant united front organizations in our country. Its significance stems from its program, based on the principle of unity." It has become a "unifying force whose integrity cannot be challenged," Mitchell added.[83] True to its mission, the NAARPR sought ways to reach out, to broaden its connections and build a modern-day united front organization. For example, when North Carolina textile workers at J.P. Stevens in their long struggle to unionize urged supporters to purchase stock shares and confront shareholders at their 1977 annual meeting the NAARPR stepped up. Mitchell, Abe Feinglass, the NAARPR's co-chair, and Michael Myerson, then an executive board member and CPUSA leader, attended the confab and registered their protest to the company's anti-union tactics. During the mid-to-late 1970s, Angela Davis spoke at over 100 college and university campuses on behalf of the National Alliance,[84] recalling the college tours of CPUSA leaders during the previous decade when Communists collectively spoke with tens of thousands of students.

Throughout the 1970s and 1980s, the CPUSA continued to embody what Chicago area African American party leader Claude Lightfoot called a pioneering aspect of Black liberation. It was the party in the 1930s and 1940s that built "the foundations of struggle against race and class oppression" and "brought the nature of Negro oppression to the attention of the entire world and thereby made the fight against it worldwide," Lightfoot wrote in his collection of essays, *Ghetto Rebellion To Black Liberation*.[85] The NAARPR's campaign for Little's freedom, among other examples, not only brought domestic pressure to bear, it brought world-wide attention – and continued condemnation – to the ongoing reality of U.S. racism. Further, the NAARPR continued to exemplify the necessity for external, international pressure – a hallmark of the Communist-led fight against Jim Crow a few decades earlier and a unique contribution largely lost with the demise of Patterson's CRC and the Hunton's CAA. As Horne noted, the 1960s civil rights organizations, even those connected to Dr. Martin Luther King Jr., "did not have the international ties of the CRC, nor the global reach of the CAA, which amounted to a net loss for African-Americans and their allies,"[86] a qualitative loss the repercussions of which are still being felt to this day.

"There is no question that there is a re-emergence of the ultra-right in our country today," Mitchell told party members at a spring 1980 seminar. This re-emergence, she added, "is simultaneous with the increasing crisis that exist in the country – the economic crisis, the political crisis, and the moral crisis – all justified by the concept of placing the blame on the victim," primarily African Americans. She said the "fanatic right," the Ku Klux Klan and domestic Nazi groups, were "to the right [of the] interests of monopoly and the rightest elements within the government" and make them "appear legitimate." While she praised the spontaneous fight back directed against the "fanatic right," she also saw troubling signs ahead as the lack of "consistent development" opened the way "for the pseudo-left." Groups like the Communist Workers Party were then attempting to organize direct confrontations with Klan members in Greensboro, North Carolina. Mitchell warned against this tactic. To "confront any enemy at his front door is stupidity," she said. For Mitchell, "To arrive at a correct strategy it is important to have a correct assessment of the forces at play and the balance of those forces." While Mitchell and the party regretted the loss of life, they also saw the CWP's actions as left adventurism. "Fundamental to organizing against the ultra-right," she continued, "is the winning of the broadest unity," something ultra-left forces were loath to do. Additionally, "While cementing left unity is imperative, it is not sufficient to halt the advances and victories of the ultra-right," which then – with echoes of today – had an enabler in the White House. Mitchell also tackled anti-communism. She argued, "if the monopoly ruling class views the Communist Party, USA, as its main domestic enemy," doesn't it logically stand that "any sincere left organization or party will view the CPUSA as its friend and ally." To Mitchell, the old maxim 'the enemy of my enemy is my friend' took concrete, tangible form. Regardless, she said, "We must always be mindful of time, place and circumstance. The movement that must be built to stop the ultra-right has to be won but it has really only begun. The mass sentiment is growing but mainly unorganized...Communists must be in the forefront of this very important struggle," she concluded.[87]

On March 4, 1980 Mitchell testified before the House Subcommittee on Crime in Washington, D.C. Like William L. Patterson before her, she called the Federal government's response to "the current crisis of racist violence and terror" in the U.S. "alarmingly inadequate." She said the KKK "and other white supremacist, para-military hate groups are today engaged in open avowed race warfare against the Black people of our country." Mitchell highlighted "terroristic tactics, [including] killing, shooting, kidnapping, arson, assault, and other forms of harassment and intimidation," which was "No longer limited to the South." "Klan terrorism has occurred in every state in the union," she told the lawmakers. She described "widespread cross-burnings, bombings, shootings, beatings, and harassment" uncovered by the NAARPR in Birmingham, Alabama. Mitchell had also recently been the victim of an attack "by Klan thugs" after urging the San Diego Democratic Party to withdraw "its nomination of Klan Dragon Tom Metzger," then running for

Congress. She also told the subcommittee about *The Turner Diaries*, which was "published, ironically, by a group calling itself the National Alliance." The novel is seen by many as a "blueprint and manual for the Klan's race warfare." Mitchell also chastised the House members for the ongoing terror being directed at Africa and Latin America, "as evidenced" by the killing of "[Patrice] Lumumba, [and Salvador] Allende," and the attempted killing of "[Fidel] Castro and others." She asked: "If we are to have a crusade against terrorism, should it not begin at home with the Ku Klux Klan?" She attacked the Reagan Administration for its "indifference...in the face of a growing mass people's movement." She added, "Klan terrorism is a nationwide phenomenon that demands a national response by the federal government. To date, that response has been limited and totally inadequate," which "legitimizes the organization" providing a "climate conducive to the growth of radical violence and terror." In contrast to the FBI's endless attempts to discredit and otherwise delegitimize the CPUSA and other radical groups, continued Mitchell, "no more than 50 – 100" acts of "Klan-inspired terrorism" have been investigated by the FBI, and "pitifully few – scarcely a handful – have resulted in prosecution." Nor has the federal government taken "preventive action in advance of racist acts of terror," she added. Of course, the NAARPR "has frequently criticized abuses in the use of federal grand juries by the Criminal Division in its attempts to manufacture cases against those who struggle for Black equality and national independence, peace advocates, draft resisters, opponents of nuclear arms, and other left and progressive individuals and groups." Why, she queried, "such timidity in asserting jurisdiction" when it comes to domestic hate crimes perpetrated by white nationalists? "Is it not strange," she continued, that the "Civil Rights Division remains hobbled." Mitchell then proposed "that an interdepartmental task force be set up" including the DOJ, FBI, ATF, "naval and army intelligence, as well as non-governmental agencies and individuals to investigate and prosecute all violations of federal law by the Ku Klux Klan and other white supremacist para-military groups." "Congress has an historic obligation to see that laws protecting people from racist terror are enforced and implemented at every stage," she concluded.[88]

On February 1, 1982, Mitchell, herself became a victim of police brutality and terror when she and her husband, NAARPR organizer Mike Welch, "were brutally dragged off a New York bound Amtrak train by local police and a railroad security agent." As the assault transpired, "No rights were read; no warrant was shown; no reason was given." Mitchell and Welch were "injured, arrested, and later charged with traditional charges of racist harassment – public drunkenness and obstructing an officer." For Mitchell and the NAARPR a number of interconnected issues were raised by her treatment: "the right to interstate travel free from racist harassment and violence; the right to be active in movements for social change without facing government inspired attacks; and the right to judicial due process and trial by a jury of one's peers,"[89] which was denied to Mitchell and countless other African Americans throughout U.S. history. To the *Daily World,* "the extremely suspicious unfolding of events resulting in their arrests raise the question of whether the whole scenario was police motivated and instigated." Ben Chavis, a Wilmington Ten defendant and NAARPR leader, told reporters, "I am outraged that the physical brutality against progressive forces in the U.S. continues to escalate...the vicious attack" against Mitchell and Welch were part of "a combined government, federal, state and local conspiracy to stop what I believe to be one of the most effective anti-racist, and anti-repression organizations in the country." The Wilmington Ten were nine young men and one woman wrongfully convicted in 1971 in Wilmington, North Carolina of arson and conspiracy; they were sentenced to between 15 and 34 years in prison; all 10 served nearly a decade in jail before an appeal won their release; they were pardoned in 2012. It was also revealed to the press after a Freedom of Information Act request that COINTELPRO (the CIA's Counter-Intelligence Program), "a federal spy network," was keeping track of Mitchell's "movements, activity and associates."[90]

Henry Winston, called the assault on Mitchell and Welch "a new and renewed attack against our democratic liberties," "policies and practices,"[91] an attack the Reagan administration approved of. Angela Davis noted the irony of the situation while at Wheat Street Baptist Church in Atlanta, the same church nearly 10 years earlier she addressed after her release from prison. She said, "It is ironic because we are here to defend Charlene's freedom when she was the genius behind the struggle to gain my freedom,"[92] which partly explains the attacks levied against her.

In order to publicize the case and create a "Fact Sheet" on similar cases of police brutality, the NAARPR requested $5,000 dollars from the William L. Patterson Foundation. In the request letter, it was noted, "Continuing the tradition of Patterson and [Paul] Robeson at the United Nations, the National Alliance is launching a mass educational campaign to 'expose the nature and depth of racism in the United States; and to arouse the moral conscience of progressive mankind.'" It was added, that the "lives and rights of these movement leaders [Mitchell and Welch] must be protected, and only a mass movement based on an understanding of the issues can do that." It was proposed that 25,000 copies of both a "Fact Sheet" and a pamphlet dealing with the "Southern Attacks on Movement Leaders"[93] be printed and distributed in Georgia, where Mitchell and Welch were attacked. In *The Organizer*, the NAARPR newsletter, Mitchell likened the assault to "a throwback to the days of collusion between the government and the railroad in defense of segregated facilities."

She stressed that the assault was "aggravated by the fact that my husband is white and I am Black." Frank Chapman, elected executive secretary of the National Alliance in 1983, put the assault in larger political context. He said, "This is a classic racist frame-up, under the guise of criminal charges, [whereby] the state in fact persecutes our leadership and our organization...fabricating a case against civil rights leaders."[94] Chapman himself had been a victim of police frame up; he was wrongly convicted in Missouri of murder and armed robbery in 1961 and spent 14 years in jail before the NAARPR secured his release.[95] Mitchell would later file a $2 million lawsuit against Amtrak.[96] In a memo signed by Angela Davis, Pete Seeger and Haywood Burns, the founder of the National Conference of Black Lawyers, it was noted that the assault "was a signal to the leadership of all organizations and concerned people, that the Reagan Administration was heightening its attack against the movement for change in this country." The assault was a warning to progressives and radicals of all stripes. "We knew that the history of the National Alliance and its impressive list of victories against racist and political repression have made it a target of government inspired 'terrorism,'" the memo concluded. It was also announced that the NAARPR planned to print and distribute 100,000 brochures to "heighten awareness of the case." Davis, Seeger and Haywood then asked for financial contributions to help fund the campaign.[97]

By spring 1984 Amtrak, Mitchell and Welch reached a settlement agreement; Amtrak paid an undisclosed amount to the victims. "We consider it to be a significant amount of money," Welch told reporters. "We feel that our position has been vindicated and that we have been exonerated from the charges on which we were arrested." To Welch, the assault and frameup "was an attack on the movement and this settlement therefore represents a victory for the movement."[98] Mitchell and Welch's victory illustrated the impact internal and external pressure can have on the outcome of political frame ups, a hallmark of party-led legal campaigns starting with the defense of the Scottsboro Nine in the 1930s.

* * *

By the late 1970s, Mitchell had begun to refine her analysis of political repression to include the death penalty under capitalism, an analysis at odds with "the bigotry of the cop on the beat or the judge on the bench." As an advocate for an end to the use of capital punishment, Mitchell argued, Marxists "believe that the best and most convincing argument from a moral, political and legal point of view is that, in a class and racist society, the entire arsenal of weapons at the hands of the criminal justice system – the death penalty in the first place – will be meted out disproportionately and unequally against the poor and powerless, the working class and people of color in the first place." Her contact and personal relationships with prisoners through the NAARPR, like Joanna Little and Frank Chapman, added urgency to her sentiments.

According to Mitchell, "Of 35 death-row inmates charged with rape (as of March 29, 1976), 26 were Black and one was a Native American Indian, for a non-white total of 77.1 percent." While she undoubtedly agreed that "rape is among the most horrible of crimes," she also highlighted "the use of rape charges as a means of victimizing Black men," thereby allowing racist police, prosecutors and judges to legally lynch men of color, a tactic used innumerable times throughout U.S. history. Additionally, Mitchell continued referring back to the Little case; during "exhaustive research" the NAARPR found that "not a single instance was discovered throughout the entire history of the United States of a white man being executed for raping a Black woman. In fact, rarely are white men executed for rape at all." She also speculated, wondering if Little's rapist had survived would he had even been charged? The likely answer would only serve to reinforce Mitchell's jaundiced view of the criminal justice system. "The democratic and progressive movement, including Communists, can not [sic] fail to understand that the drive for the death penalty is a response of the bourgeoisie attempting to tighten its 'dictatorship.' We can not [sic] fail to act, in concert with others, to abolish the death penalty," Mitchell concluded.[99] She also began to highlight the threat to democracy posed by the Reagan Administration, the ascendancy of the right wing and the retreat of socialism globally.

In April 1981, Mitchell presented a paper on *Afro-American Equality vs. Reaganite Racism* at the party's Second Extraordinary Conference held in Milwaukee. She urged her comrades to "make a change in pace – an all-around immediate change – in giving leadership in the fight for Afro-American equality," a struggle that "cuts across every aspect of the Reagan/monopoly offensive." She called for an "All-People's Front against Reagan," where party members could "fight for clarity and project solutions," like strengthening the Voting Rights Act and the fight for affirmative action. She called "Reaganite attacks" a "treacherous design." "No Communist, no one who fights for peace jobs and justice – no democratic-minded person can dare be complacent," she added, while highlighting the role of the National Alliance, "the only organization that is doing mass grassroots work around the Voting Rights Act." The defense organization had already turned in thousands of signatures to the Senate subcommittee demanding "extension and enforcement" of the Act. "In the struggle for Afro-American equality, the Voting Rights Act is a major vehicle,"[100] Mitchell, now the executive secretary of the CPUSA Afro-American Liberation Commission, added. To illustrate the seriousness with-which the party took the struggle for African American equality the *Black Liberation Journal*, which was first published in winter 1976 and then "suspended" in early 1981, was restarted. "We're back now primarily because these are no ordinary times," the editors wrote in the reconstituted journal. "[T]he Black Liberation

Movement needs direction. It needs a forum to discuss and debate from a Marxist-Leninist point of view the path out of the crisis." Articles focused on *Black People and the Economic Crisis – The Impact, Reagan's Nuclear War Policies and the Struggle for Equality, The Case for Sanctions Against Fascist South Africa*, among others.[101]

Nine weeks before the CPUSA's 23rd National Convention the commission held a special conference to assess the status of Black-white unity against Reaganism. Optimistically, as the title of her remarks – *New Levels of Struggle – New Levels of Unity* – illustrate, Mitchell said, "the all-peoples' front against Reagan continues to grow and the number of coalitions, either temporary or longer-lasting, is increasing," as evidenced by the September 19, 1981, Solidarity Day, the June 12, 1982, March for Peace and Justice, as well as the 400,000 people who marched to the Lincoln Memorial commemorating the 20th anniversary of the historic 1963 March On Washington. Mitchell said, "All these major mass actions had a common theme – Reagan Must Go." She added, "The multi-racial and multi-national working class composition has been qualitatively strengthened and the leadership [initiatives] of the Black liberation movement have reached new levels of struggle and unity."

However, while focused on mass organizations like the NAACP, PUSH, the Urban League and the National Council of Negro Women, she also highlighted and encouraged her comrades to "reaffirm our determination to be a part of these mass movements." She added that Communists should "learn from masses in action and [work] to influence their direction."[102] Mitchell expanded on these thoughts at a June 16, 1984 meeting of the party's Central Committee and National Council. She called the "new movement," led by the Rainbow Coalition and the Rev. Jesse Jackson, "one of the most positive historical developments within recent times." "This movement is not however an organization," she cautioned. "It is not the formation of a new political party. It is a movement that takes place within the Democratic party," a movement struggling for "independent politics within that party,"[103] a delicate balance.

This analysis was a reaffirmation of Henry Winston's "three-pronged" tactical approach formulated in 1968, which encouraged Communists to work within the two-party system, to help build independent formations and to run Communist candidates – with some successes. For example, the successful campaign of Communist Kenny Jones to the St. Louis City Board of Aldermen (Ward 22).[104]

However, Mitchell also expressed criticisms. The "class stratification" within the emerging Rainbow Coalition left it blind to "the need to win labor. More precisely it does not see the imperative of winning white workers who are in the organized labor movement." Communists, she added, should work to build a "strategic alliance" able to challenge Reagan, "his racism" and his "penchant for lying." "Black workers can not [sic] win this battle alone, nor should they be asked to wage it alone," Mitchell added. Echoing earlier sentiments, she concluded, "Our Party, the Communist Party, must be seen as the party that gives ideological and practical leadership in the struggle for equality,"[105] in the first place by recruiting white workers to the cause of African American equality. In June 1985, Mitchell continued to hammer away at a recurring theme, highlighting the importance of the Rainbow Coalition and the role of Communists. In 1985, she told participants at the Conference on the Present Stage of Struggle for Afro-American Equality, that the Rainbow Coalition "remains the underpinning of many independent forms...It is an important arena of struggle and the Communists must be involved. We must bring the Communist essence – the class content – to the struggle," she emphasized, thereby "showing the labor movement as an ally that is also under attack."[106] For Mitchell, this broad coalition of forces was a bulwark against Reagan era reaction and the ascending right-wing – a coalition that included Communists.

* * *

The NAARPR held its 10th national conference in Chicago in May 1990. Mitchell told the conference attendees, "While the task seems overwhelming, we have the experience of the past 17 years. We know how to fight and to stop these attacks." By any objective assessment, the NAARPR won significant victories in the fightback against racist and political repression as evidenced by the Little and Chapman cases, and many others. Speakers at the conference included Dennis Rivera, president of Local 1199 Hospital Workers in New York and Representative Charles Hayes (D-IL). Chicago Alderman Jesus Garcia summed up the conference sentiment when he sent greetings from the Windy City to the gathering "for each and every minute, every hour and every year that you have held up the banner of freedom for everyone." At a pre-conference kick-off rally attended by 400 people Lindiwe Mabuza, of the African National Congress, recalled that she "had attended the NAARPR's founding convention in Chicago in 1973, and that one of the slogans at that meeting was, 'Free Nelson Mandela and All Political Prisoners.'"[107] Communists, going back to Robeson and Hunton's CAA, helped initiate the call to free political prisoners in South Africa. Nelson Mandela, a member of the South African Communist Party,[108] celebrated the assistance given by Communists in the struggle against apartheid even as the 20th century entered its last decade and as socialism retreated. Black liberation in Africa sought and received substantial financial, technical and military aid from the Soviet Union and Cuba, which exacerbated the crisis then enveloping capitalism. This may be part of the reason why Nelson and Winnie Mandela held a dinner and reception at their Soweto home for Mitchell and Angela Davis in September of 1991 as the two U.S. Communists visited their South African comrades. At that dinner and reception Mandela noted that the ANC-SACP alliance "has proven to be effective" in the struggle for Black liberation. "We will never permit our enemies to tell us who our friends should be," the future Nobel Peace Prize recipient, told Mitchell and Davis. He was acknowledging the importance of an enduring Red-Black alliance. Shortly after returning home, Mitchell and Davis embarked on a nation-wide speaking tour,[109] a bitter-sweet celebration. The ANC and SACP had emerged victorious in South Africa, though socialism was in retreat and would soon collapse. Mitchell editorialized that the Soviet Union's "assistance to the national liberation movement is an honorable page in the history of humanity," of which "none of its mistakes can blot." Additionally, she continued, "We can never let the imperfections of socialism blind us to the cruelties of capitalism,"[110] especially the African slave trade, the genocide of indigenous peoples, fascism and war.

During a speech at the Voices of the Left Forum in December 1990, Mitchell, who had now been a member of the CPUSA for nearly 45 years, said, "To denigrate in anyway the role of the Communist Party, simply does not square with history. We stand upon a firm foundation on which to build." Despite the "problems of existing socialism," Communists remained "convinced that it [socialism] is a higher state of social development...[a] more democratic, more humane system; a system without racism, discrimination and exploitation."[111] While Mitchell still believed "that socialism is, ultimately, the only guarantee of democracy," her confidence was beginning to waver. The events in Eastern Europe took the world by storm and made the Communist stalwart add the qualifier, "That does not mean that democracy will automatically come with socialism," a courageous acknowledgment, especially as socialism retreated. Socialism, Mitchell added, "on which we have placed all of our hopes and dreams, is seemingly falling apart," which "demands of us, the opportunity to reassess our beliefs and policies,"[112] something Mitchell was keen to do.

Nevertheless, only one year later Mitchell, along with other party leaders, including Angela Davis and Herbert Aptheker, left the CPUSA and helped form the Committees of Correspondence. [113] Mitchell said this departure was due to a lack of internal democracy within the CPUSA.

* * *

Roughly 17 years earlier, at a spring 1974 reception honoring Mitchell at the W.E.B. DuBois Community Center in Harlem, Davis said, "I owe my life to Comrade Charlene. When I was under attack, she came to my aid, risking her own life to save mine. She helped many attain clarity in the political movement, including myself," Davis added. She then thanked Mitchell "for your courage, commitment and revolutionary leadership."[114].

In mid-May 2014 on the 41st anniversary of the birth of the NAARPR, a two-day National Forum on Police Crimes was held at the University of Chicago, the birthplace of both the National Alliance and the CPUSA. Over 250 people attended the forum, including the NAARPR's founding executive director, Charlene Mitchell. At a fundraising banquet during the conference, Mitchell was honored with the establishment of the Charlene Mitchell Human Rights Award. Her friend and comrade, Angel Davis, was the first awardee.[115]

Chapter 3

Gus Hall: The "Right to Speak," young Communists and strategic relationships

It was early February 1963. Gus Hall, general secretary of the Communist Party, USA, sat patiently as more than 1,000 students from the University of Virginia packed Cabell Auditorium. Students came "in droves," the *Worker* reported, which forced a smile from the steel-worker turned union organizer turned CPUSA leader. The auditorium was already at capacity when an additional 1,000 students were turned away. The overflow crowd was proof, according to Hall, "that the probing minds of youth" know no political boundaries – that they would not acquiesce to anticommunism. Hall viewed their eagerness to learn about Marxism-Leninism "as a reassertion," a commitment "to defend your right to hear whomsoever you choose,"[1] thereby challenging the McCarran Act and the House Un-American Activities Committee and helping to spur what would become known as the student free speech movement – a movement partly led by Communists.[2]

Later that month Hall spoke at Yale's Strathcone Hall. I'm the "real article," he told the assembled 500 students, not a "caricature," not a Cold War boogeyman – a theme he would articulate repeatedly. Playfully, Hall brought Yale's "political skeleton" out of the "socialist closet," informing the assembled students and faculty that another longtime CPUSA leader, Alexander Trachtenberg – the director of International Publishers – was in his youth the chairman of the Yale Society for the

Study of Socialism, which then had about 200 members. Hall challenged the assertion that there was no freedom of expression in the Soviet Union. He added, "I won't slander the Soviet Union to win my place and my right to fight for socialism here." Hall's perspective on the same basic freedom in the United States had been soured. After all, he had spent most of the 1950s in hiding or in jail due to his political beliefs. "Maybe the fact that I served six years in jail for thinking makes me a little prejudiced. Or perhaps I am prejudiced because I face a possible 30 years in prison under the McCarran Act." Adding insult to injury, Hall noted that he "had to get permission to [travel and personally] appear" before his HUAC inquisitors. Just days before the engagement, Senator Thomas Dodd unsuccessfully attempted to force Yale to cancel the event, and thereby deny Hall his First Amendment rights. The irony was certainly not lost on the assembled Handsome Dans. They responded with "appreciative laughter" when Hall joked that Senator Dodd will sleep well knowing his appearance did not constitute a "clear and present danger"[3] to national security. The irony thickened when just four years later Dodd was "censured by his [Senate] colleagues for improprieties in his financial affairs." Apparently, the New England lawyer had diverted "to his own use over $116,000" in campaign contributions.[4] One can imagine Hall being tickled by the news.

By mid-March, Hall had completed two Boston speaking engagements – at the Jewish People's Forum and at Brandeis University. In what was "the biggest meeting of the year on a campus of 1,200," more than one-third of the student body filled Schwartz Hall on the Brandeis campus. The visit, sponsored by the Student Political Education and Action Committee, was a huge success. Every seat was taken, and the doors were closed a half hour before Hall's appearance. Arnold Johnson, the general secretary's friend and comrade, reported, "more [people] were turned away than were able to get in." At Brandeis, Hall urged peace in a polarized world.

"Peaceful co-existence is a necessity...A course must be chartered to world peace with honor to all countries,"[5] Hall concluded.

The success of Hall's early 1963 East Coast speaking tour wasn't an aberration. Communists were speaking on college and university campuses in front of large and enthusiastic audiences all across the country. Marxist historian Herbert Aptheker addressed 250 students at Michigan State University in January. That March, he spoke with 400 students at the University of Michigan, 1,200 students at Howard University, and about 125 students at Roosevelt University.[6] In June, Aptheker spoke to a packed hall at Bard College; that December he also spoke at Harvard University.[7] Ben Davis, Jr., one-time Harlem councilman, addressed 500 students at Brown University in February. He told curious students there, "I joined the Communist Party as a result of my experience as a Negro...looking for freedom and first-class citizenship," emphasizing that his Communist beliefs were "made in the U.S.A." This particular discussion lasted until after 1:30 a.m., as curious students talked with Davis well after his presentation had ended.[8] That fall, Davis spoke to about 100 students at City College of New York. He proclaimed, "We live in an epoch of transition of capitalism to socialism." This transition included the "struggles of Negro Americans to pass from a status of indignity and second-class citizenship to first class citizenship and dignity." He called this movement towards dignity, "a social revolution, although not a socialist revolution." "It is a revolution designed to overthrow the jimcrow [sic] system," not necessarily capitalism, "a revolution to enforce our democracy against the Dixiecrats and the ultra-right."[9] In an interview with the *Detroit Free Press* Davis expanded upon his CPUSA membership. "I am discriminated against by virtue of being a black man and I am a Communist by virtue of the fact that I want to fight against that discrimination."[10] That the Communist Party had "unquestionably been a powerful factor" in the advancement of African American equality, as CPUSA leader William Z. Foster wrote,[11] led thousands of Blacks, like Davis, to align with reds, and thereby dismantle Jim Crow, spark the civil rights movement and dramatically reshape U.S. politics. Further, Communists were now embarking on successful college and university speaking engagements, helping to spur a student-led revolt against the political straitjacket of McCarthyism.

In April 1963, 1,500 students heard party leader Hyman Lumer at Rhode Island College[12] and 2,500 heard Daniel Rubin, the party's youth coordinator, at Colorado State College. Rubin defiantly said, "the world [is] heading toward socialism and eventually communism." According to him, this "is both desirable for mankind and inevitable."[13] In June, Carl Winter told 150 students at the University of Michigan, "Peaceful co-existence cannot mean merely the absence of war." This theme seemed to resonate with students "since the cold war – so long as it continues – prepares the conditions for the outbreak of an atomic holocaust." To Communists, Winter added, "peaceful co-existence cannot mean the preservation of the status quo but, rather, a new system of international relations."[14] With socialism then ascending, this was a reasonable conclusion. In November of 1963, more than 2,000 students filled "every inch of space" in the Student Union Grand Ballroom "and adjoining lounges" at UCLA to hear southern California party leader, Dorothy Healey. Earlier that year Healy spoke at Riverside, Cal-Tech and Occidental College, among others. She told students, "I became a Communist because I despised a system in which human beings could be degraded and oppressed while property rights were exalted. I remain a Communist, despite harassment and persecution, because I believe in man's capacity to build a society where all mem are free and where, therefore, each individual can freely develop."[15] In July, Albert Lima, another California party leader, helped break "the 12-year ban against Communist speakers" on the Berkeley campus.[16] Less than a year later, he spoke in front of

2,500 students at San Mateo College, though a so-called Taxpayers Committee to Oppose Communist Speakers on Campus tried to bar his appearance.[17]

In short, Communists were speaking with large crowds of enthusiastic students across the country. Apparently, the party's emphasis on peace, civil rights, democracy and socialism resonated and helped spark a student based assault on censorship, a free speech movement.

On February 12, 1962, one year prior to his University of Virginia engagement, Hall addressed 12,000 students at the University of Oregon. Police on horseback nervously observed in the backfield and cheerleaders ushered students to their seats as he gave his presentation and then took questions well into the evening. "[T]his was a serious discussion," Hall later wrote. "The questions on a whole were on a rather high political plane." Veteran Communist journalist Joseph North wrote, students "listened intently, respectfully, and gave him a warm round of applause...So it was wherever he went." Later that evening Hall spoke at Oregon College in Monmouth to 3,000 students. On February 13, he spoke with 1,000 students at Lewis and Clark College and then on the 14th to "only 800" at Reed College, as Portland officials refused to let Hall speak at the city auditorium, which could have accommodated the additional 1,000 students who "stood around trying to get in." According to Philip Bart, one-time chair of the party's history commission, Hall spoke in front of a cumulative 19,000 students on five campuses between February 10 and 15, 1962,[18] including the University of California, where "a spontaneously organized gathering of hundreds" met with Hall after he concluded his remarks. Hall told students, "Anti-communism is just a smoke-screen, the real aim is to destroy the Bill of Rights." During this trip, Hall also held a press conference at the International Longshore and Warehousemen's Union.[19] ILWU international president Harry Bridges was known for his close ties to Communists. Hall also spoke at Stanford University in front of 1,500 students,[20] while his comrade Arnold

Johnson jammed the 700 person capacity auditorium at Hamilton College. According to the *Utica Daily Press*, "There were people sitting in the organ loft and on stairs, the floor and window ledges" to hear the party stalwart.[21] Also in February, 350 students heard Bart at Bowdoin College in Maine and hundreds more heard Aptheker in St. Paul, Minnesota.[22] Aptheker also addressed 250 students at the University of Pennsylvania in early April,[23] while Benjamin Davis, Jr., addressed 600 at Harvard.[24] African American party leader, James E. Jackson, told 1,400 students at Colby College in May, "The problem of problems of our nation and of our times is that of prevention of the outbreak of thermonuclear war." Jackson, who helped found the Southern Negro Youth Congress, added, "To secure the peace of the world is the primary task of all mankind, the indispensable enabling measure for the solution of all other questions on the agenda of history."[25]

It was reported in early March 1962 that Hall gave 37 separate speeches in just 12 days.[26] In April, he told 400 students at CCNY that if the McCarran Act prosecutors succeed in jailing him and Benjamin Davis, Jr., "no American...will be free." "You can't make Socialism in a hot-house." "The soil must be ready. But thoughts, like seeds, unless the soil is ready for them, they will not grow." The ravages of capitalism were preparing the soil, he concluded.[27] The political winds were shifting. Nearly 1,000 students at Swarthmore College agreed, as they "turned out" for Hall on April 29.[28] Earlier that month, the American Association of University Professors presented its annual Alexander Meiklejohn Award to Arthur S. Flemming, president of the University of Oregon for defending the Bill of Rights and supporting Hall's right to speak there.[29] On May 1, Hall addressed 7,000 people at the Union Square May Day rally.[30] Days later, he spoke with 400 students at Hunter College,[31] 700 students at the University of Chicago[32] and 1,800 more at the University of Wisconsin, where another 1,500 were turned away due to a lack of seating.[33] By mid-June Hall could declare, "During the past six months I have spoken to some 50,000 students and youth directly...The tide has turned."[34] Communist speaking engagements continued into the fall. For example, in late November, Michigan party leader Carl Winter spoke with 900 students at Kalamazoo College,[35] traditionally thought of as a conservative stronghold. Communists had reason to believe it was time to go on the offensive.

That spring Hall noted, "In the mass movements, the most important and most active contingent are the youth." Jubilantly, he added, the "student demand" to hear Communists was "completely without precedent." "It is of such magnitude that no force is able to ignore it," including the FBI. "It has become a point of discussion on all levels of political life," he continued. "We are so close to it that we do not fully appreciate it." Hall called the growing demand for Communist speakers "a mass break-out from the conformist strait-jacket of McCarthyism" and a "rejection of anti-Communism," a bewildering defeat for the ruling class. Though many of the emerging student groups were "loose and even temporary in nature," Hall was still optimistic. He saw the potential for a "spark that can fundamentally change" and challenge the contours of U.S. anti-communism, a spark spearheaded by youth. Additionally, he noted the array of self-published journals students were then printing. "Isn't it fantastic that in a number of colleges, there are two, three or four monthly magazines and newspapers," Hall continued, many with a Marxist outlook. That Communists "must be a factor in finding forms through which this tremendous energy can best express itself," was a given to Hall. That "We must not be mere observers," was also a given. Hall's perspective, that Communists "must be a force in helping to initiate forms of united action in this upsurge and help give it cohesion and direction,"[36] wasn't just rhetorical. Soon party-led formations like the Advance Youth Organization, the Progressive Youth Organizing Committee and the W.E.B. Du Bois Clubs would emerge. Hall regarded the string of Communist speaking engagements in the early 1960s as "victories for free speech and democratic rights, won in the face of a powerful campaign organized by the Ultra-Right,"[37] a campaign youth and students defiantly challenged.

The substance of Hall's campus presentations often focused on free speech, democracy, the defeat of the ultra-right and peace. Speaking to students in New York, Hall hailed freedom of speech as vital. "It's a weapon," he added. It must be preserved if we hope to collectively "thrash out the very complicated problems [youth] face." He connected the fight for free speech generally to the fight to hear Communists specifically. "There is a very deep feeling that if you can preserve the right of Communists to speak, then you can preserve the right of all to speak. That's true. But it's more than just a fight for the right of Communists to speak. The fact is that they [youth and students] want to hear a Communist speak...They are sick and tired of hearing the so-called Communist viewpoint from anti-Communists." As a result, elites attempted to again curtail civil liberties and free speech in an effort to stunt the party's then growing appeal among youth and students. Hall was undeterred, though. To him, a shift in consciousness was taking place. The "fascist-like assault" designed to "transform the American people into a hysterical anti-Communist mob" had failed. Senator Joseph McCarthy had been silenced. The Smith and McCarran Acts would both be declared unconstitutional. Communists were now on the offensive, regularly speaking to thousands of students across the country and playing an important role in the emerging civil rights and peace movements. The "squirming of politicians," the "fanatical fascist-like fringe of the ultra-Right" was being "pushed back into its lair,"[38] Hall concluded. This was partly due to the courage of student activists who spearheaded the right of Communists to speak on college and university campuses across the country, a strategic relationship Hall would not soon forget and one that would become a prominent feature of the general secretary's work for many years to come.

According to long-time Communist journalist Tim Wheeler, "The country had been pulled into an atmosphere of fear and intimidation by McCarthyism" and was just now coming out of the darkness. "The Party estimated that youth weren't going to buy into the scare tactics. They were responding to lunch counter sit-ins and freedom rides. They could see the evil right in front of them and the Party knew they would be responsive." Indeed, tens of thousands of students gathering to hear CPUSA speakers was quite the response. "Campuses and universities were a logical center for anti-war, civil rights activity,"[39] Wheeler added, a sentiment the party was keen to acknowledge and embrace.

Foreshadowing years of successful college speaking tours, in a June 1961 television interview Hall blasted HUAC thought police. He advocated for a democratic free flow of ideas. He told reporters, "The attempt to jail ideas cannot succeed...Thought cannot be outlawed." The party, he continued, will "struggle for every breath of legality."[40] That fall, Hall was speaking at Cornell University in front of nearly 2,000 students as an additional 2,000 were "turned away."[41]

This years-long struggle for legality partly explains Hall's willingness to traverse the country, to speak at college and university campuses and to act as a conduit by which student radicalism could express itself. Students challenged campus faculty, administration and right-wing community leaders by defiantly inviting Communists to speak. Hall, and other CPUSA leaders, discussed Marxism-Leninism, peace, workers' rights and the struggle for African American equality with students. Young Communists who joined the party as a result, aided campus organizing. This was a free speech movement, a broad-based, multi-class assault on censorship.[42] While protest tactics received more attention, student resistance took many forms, and Communists often urged students to take a more active role in campus administration[43] – which, obviously, did not curry favor among administrators. They also encouraged students to conduct polls to challenge McCarran Act thought control,[44] which many were inclined to do.

Hall soberly asserted in fall 1965, that the left, including the CPUSA, can best "exert its influence" if it is "united around issues and methods" broadly, and not bogged down in sectarianism. "On this basis we are working with and are a part of most of the movements and struggles of the people – including the student upsurge."[45] This was an understatement of sorts. As historian, Gerald Horne pointed out, "the party had a major role in igniting these [student] protests, insofar as an initial grievance of students was the effort to bar them from hearing Reds on campuses."[46] That many of these same students became young Communists served to bolster a strategic relationship that ultimately proved fertile ground from which the party would attempt to rebuild its hounded and depleted ranks.

Even non-communists acknowledged the CPUSA's growth among youth. James H. Forest, national secretary of the Catholic Peace Fellowship, in 1966 told reporters, students see the CPUSA as "a moderate, well-established, well-known left-wing organization," not an ultra-left group "aligned...with violence."[47] In short, the party's appeal to youth and students was not surprising. This sentiment was shared by others, including J. Edgar Hoover. The FBI director tacitly acknowledged the impact reds were having on college and university campuses [48] and ordered his underlings to keep tabs on Communists and their student allies.

* * *

Gus Hall was born Arvo Kusta (Gustav) Halberg on October 8, 1910 in Iron, Minnesota. His parents were charter members of the CPUSA. He would reflect later in life that he "drank in socialism with his mother's milk." Raised in a family of ten brothers and sisters, Hall, "from infancy was moulded [sic] by the class-struggle into which he was born." By 14, he had left school and "took whatever job was available...whatever came along that would mean food on the table." By 15, he had joined a lumber union, by 16, he had joined the Young Communist League, and by 17, the Communist Party. "My life seemed to have prepared me for the books of Marx and Lenin," he would later write. Soon Hall was organizing workers across the upper Midwest.

By 1932, Hall had already felt the sting of the policeman's baton, as he marched alongside 35,000 unemployed workers in Minneapolis. Singled out as a march leader, he spent months in jail, along with fellow CPUSA leader, Sam 'Red' Davis. "Repeated marches, repeated demonstrations, repeated arrests...It became a way of life" for the young Communist. In 1934, Hall moved to Ohio and began working at Republic Steel and then Youngstown Sheet and Tube. He helped organize the Rank and File Steel Workers' Committee. In 1936 Hall, now 26 years old, became a fulltime organizer for the Steel Workers' Organizing Committee, where he helped recruit 10,000 workers into the fledgling union.[49]

Communists were not strangers to industrial unionism and were instrumental in building the Congress of Industrial Organizations. Of the roughly 200 fulltime SWOC organizers – in the late 1930s – about 60 were party members.[50] Communists quickly became "a major force" within the CIO and "play[ed] a foremost role in the great [organizing] triumphs" to come[51] due to their years of organizing experience in the party-led Trade Union Unity League, which had dissolved in the spring of 1935, just months before the CIO left the American Federation of Labor. As Michael Dennis points out, CIO President John L. Lewis recruited "Communist Party activists – who had proven to be tough, skillful, and implacable organizers – to conduct field work...[They] provided vital leadership, fostering a sense of class awareness and political coherence among workers."[52] By 1939, Communists had earned positions of influence in a number of CIO unions; by 1948 they led about one-fourth of the CIO's then membership.[53]

Hall was one of those "tough, skillful, and implacable organizers." However, in a 1949 *Political Affairs* article, he modestly deemphasized his own role in the SWOC organizing drives. Instead, he highlighted the role of the party. "It is a matter of record that the only working class organization which had continued to provide genuine leadership to the steelworkers since 1920 [was] the Communist Party." "Our Party was already engaged in mobilizing capable forces for the campaign long before S.W.O.C. had established its offices or staff. It was inevitable therefore," he concluded, "that the various district directors of the S.W.O.C. established close working relations with the local leaders of the Communist Party. Many leading Communist went on [to join] the staff."[54]

In 1937, as the Little Steel Strike unfolded, Hall courageously led the strike in the Warren-Youngstown-Niles, Ohio area, the heart of Republic Steel and Youngstown Sheet and Tube. Battles there were bitter. "[B]loody confrontations with the National Guard, the armed gangsters and the police"[55] were a daily occurrence. Hall was implicated as the "brains" in a bomb plot to "dynamite bridges, railroad tracks, steel mills and the light and power company, and to blow up the homes of non-strikers with high explosives." Hall would eventually plead guilty to "a charge of malicious destruction" and was fined $500. That one of his accusers "spent six years as an undercover [FBI] spy"[56] called into question the evidence and motives fingering Hall.

In Chicago – the strikes' storm center, where party leaders, Joe Weber, the SWOC sub-district organizer, and Hank Johnson, an activist in the party-led National Negro Congress, among others, organized – police and Republic Steel thugs busily prepared for "imminent confrontation." Republic stockpiled weapons, including four submachine guns, 525 revolvers, 64 rifles, 245 shotguns and employed 370 police guards. In what became known as the Chicago Memorial Day Massacre, police and Republic thugs opened fire on peaceful protesters. Ten strikers and supporters, including party member Joseph Rothmund, were killed and hundreds were wounded.[57] Shortly thereafter, another Communist, John Abt, helped lead a 10-day investigation into the massacre through the LaFollette Committee, a special committee of the U.S. Senate established by the National Labor Relations Board.[58]

The Little Steel Strike bolstered the entire CIO union drive. Workers in other industries, especially auto, surged into action. There were an estimated 5,000 strikes involving around two million workers in 1937 alone.[59] Communists, like Hall – and Wyndham Mortimer, the leader of the General Motors sit-down strike in Flint, Michigan[60] – led many of these battles.

In Ohio, Hall's leadership of SWOC was indispensable. According to some, when he informed SWOC of his plans to resign and work fulltime for the CPUSA, the "leaders of the Steel Union were startled." Philip Murray, the new head of the CIO, personally sent Hall a letter urging him to reconsider. Hall's comrade, James E. Jackson, later remarked, "Gus Hall had no peer as a strike strategist and inspiring organizer of masses."[61] Others, however, claimed Hall was unceremoniously ousted from SWOC due to charges labeling him as head of a "dynamite ring."[62] Whatever the details of Hall's departure, later in life he would be recognized by the union he helped to found. In June 1995, he was invited to Steelworkers' Union Local 1375 in Warren, Ohio to be recognized; the then president of Local 1375, Mike Rubicz, was also a party member. Hall was introduced by Rick Nagin, the then CPUSA national steel coordinator and future executive assistant to Cleveland councilman Nelson Cintron.[63] Hall was also part of a panel presentation sponsored by the Ohio Historical Society titled *The SWOC Years, 1937-42.* He talked about his early organizing experiences.[64] Additionally, the Steelworkers' Organization of Active Retirees – which continues to welcome Communists into its leadership – issued a resolution recognizing Hall as a "pioneer" founder of the United Steelworkers' Union of America.[65] Two years later, the AFL-CIO repealed its anti-communist clause.[66] A new generation of party members[67] began to openly serve as union officers, leaders and organizers.

By 1939, Hall became the Youngstown party organizer. Two years later he was elected head of the Cleveland party organization and began working closely with Arnold Johnson, whom he replaced as Ohio state chairman in 1947. In 1949, he was elected national secretary, and in 1950, after Eugene Dennis – the party's then general secretary – was sentenced to jail under the Smith Act, Hall became acting general secretary, a position made official in 1959.

Hall's leadership in the Ohio Communist Party was interrupted, though. He volunteered to serve in the U.S. Navy in 1942 as a machinists' mate in the Pacific.[68] Hall, along with an estimated 15,000 other Communists,[69] joined the war effort against fascism. Hall was still serving overseas when he was elected to the party's National Committee in 1944. Upon his return to Ohio, Hall was elected state chairman and then to the national executive board. By his mid-30s, Hall had already "play[ed] his part in helping the hungry defeat starvation, [and] in building the trade union movement." He had served in prison and in the Armed Forces,[70] acts of radical patriotism by a son of the American working class. In late July 1948, Hall and 11 other party leaders would be indicted and thrown in jail for supposedly advocating the overthrow of the U.S. government by force and violence.[71]

Even during this tumultuous time, Hall still devoted considerable attention to youth and their capacity to organize for progressive social change. At a September 8, 1950, Youth Rally for Peace and Freedom sponsored by the Labor Youth League, Hall said, "I don't know how many atom bombs the government of the United States has stockpiled. But I do know that they are too few to impose Wall Street's so-called peace terms on humanity." He urged the assembled youth and students to act else the possible destruction of humanity weigh on their shoulders, a terrifying prospect with war in Korea then taking thousands of lives. "I know that your generation will have to share the collective guilt of our nation, and suffer the collective wrath of all mankind, if we permit our government to bring upon the world the horror of an atomic war." He said the country was led by "atomic-maniacs." He called atomic weapons "fascist weapons." He added, "To accept in silence the prospect of using them is itself brutalizing. It is a step toward accustoming oneself to the idea of gas ovens and the other refinements of fascist torture and murder." But, Hall continued, it "is not too late to save our country." The "frightened men of Wall Street and Washington" can be stopped, lest their trembling hands accidently initiate nuclear war. However, if they "succeed in outlawing the Communist Party...then I cannot give you any guarantee that the point of no return will not soon be reached." Thankfully, he concluded, "Our youth love America. They love it not only because it is their own, their native land – but because of what it has been, what they want it to be and believe it to be," though "evil forces have betrayed and are remaking this America we all love."[72] At least one youth, Roosevelt Ward, Jr., the 21 year old executive secretary of the LYL, followed Hall's suggestion and was sentenced to three years in jail for violating the draft,[73] a tactic young Communists would emulate during the Vietnam War.

William L. Patterson blasted U.S. militarism in Korea at a Madison Square Garden rally. He said, that "Aggressive war abroad – and that's what we're in – means fascism at home." Further, "jails are being glutted with peace defenders." Communists, like the LYL leader Ward Jr., were among them. Hall added, U.S. involvement in Korea was a "naked armed struggle for the imperialist domination of the Far East,"[74] a struggle that would cost millions of lives.

As the Red Scare and Cold War intensified, Hall – along with other party leaders – were compelled to go underground. After being captured in Mexico, he spent six years in Leavenworth prison and another two years on conditional release, sequestered away from party work.[75] During that time, Hall ran a gas station in Ohio; comrades would visit, seek political advice and attempt to win him over to various factional positions.[76]

* * *

In fall 1958, Communists held an East Coast conference to assess their status among youth and to discuss recommendations for growth. It was noted confidently at the conference that the party "has emerged from its internal crisis."[77] The cause of the crisis was multifaceted; domestic political repression, the Khrushchev revelations, the suppression of the Hungarian Revolution, sectarianism and damaging internal security measures. The party was bruised and battered, but not broken. It was ready to refocus energies on youth and student recruitment.

Robert 'Bob' Thompson, a distinguished World War II veteran – later denied his pension and burial rights at Arlington Nation Cemetery[78] – was direct and to the point in his report on the conference. "Loss of ties with youth" was highlighted as a major concern. The "small number of youth comrades and their relative isolation" was acknowledged. However, optimistically it was added, the party "has the capacity to re-establish these ties and to re-acquire an intimate knowledge of youth activities and problems and needs," which proved to be the case. Though the party had "not developed a definitive approach towards a youth organization yet," Thompson continued, "there has been much thinking and discussion" on the subject. It was urged that a "Party thesis" be adopted "within the next few months."

Numerous proposals came out of the conference. Some attendees envisioned "a Marxist-Leninist youth organization, to serve as a guiding force among youth to consolidate and give direction in the various aspects of youth activity towards socialism." Other comrades favored "some sort of Marxist youth organization," perhaps something "similar to the L.Y.L.," which had been disbanded in 1957. Still others argued for "Party youth clubs" and saw the creation of a youth organization with a "broad progressive pro-labor, pro-peace character" as an initial first step in the right direction.

It was suggested that a "National Party Youth Conference" be held in early 1959.[79] In short, 1958 marked an important turning point for the CPUSA. Communists were preparing to go on the offensive after a decade of playing defense. They were ready to put considerable time, energy and resources into reconnecting with youth, an effort that would soon pay considerable dividends.

* * *

Hall returned as a fulltime revolutionary in 1959 and at the party's 17th National Convention was elected general secretary. He quickly initiated "an intense period of intellectual and organizational activity."[80] He appointed Daniel Rubin the party's youth secretary.[81] College and university speaking tours, which put Communists in front of tens of thousands of students across the country, were right around the corner. Former Communist councilman from Harlem, Benjamin Davis, Jr., echoed Hall's sentiments at a spring 1960 National Committee meeting. He said, "our Party [must] give special attention to youth, particularly Negro and student youth with a view to solidarity actions on all campuses."[82] It wouldn't be long before Hall and Davis' projections took concrete organizational form. That fall, party leader, William L. Patterson, talked with students about emerging national liberation struggles in Africa. He asked 500 students at Simmons College, "whether human values would be measured by color and creed as in the West or through universal recognition of the inherent dignity of mankind regardless of nationality, color, religious beliefs or political philosophy"? With socialism then in ascendancy,

Patterson also predicted that "the nations of Africa would turn toward the East,"[83] toward the Soviet Union and China. Black Americans also increasingly looked to the East[84] due in part to the work of Patterson and other Communists. Patterson had spent the past 30 years cultivating a domestic and international Red-Black alliance. The following spring Davis pulled on a similar thread in an address to 100 CCNY students. "The growing strength of the socialist world has weakened the hold of the imperialist powers on Africa and Asia,"[85] he said. Black liberation aided by Soviet socialism fueled world historic changes and forced an agonizing retreat away from colonial subjugation and imperialism.

Hall prioritized the building of a broad based Marxist-oriented youth organization. The diversity of forms created by young Communists reflected the discussions held at the fall 1958 Conference. Hall saw college and university speaking tours as one way to introduce Marxism to students, while identifying potential new recruits. The party-led Advance Youth Organization (which included future Communist leaders like Bettina Aptheker, Angela Davis and Margaret Burnham),[86] as well as the publication, *New Horizons for Youth*, were successful organizing tools[87] despite government harassment. Youth Publications, Inc., publisher of *New Horizons*, was subpoenaed to appear before the McCarran Act Grand Jury. According to Lionel Libson, the publication's editor, *New Horizon's* was "born out of the growing need for young people to have a periodical which reflects their interests and answers the burning questions" such as "peace, employment and desegregation." That the youth publication "answers these questions" with an eye towards "our own democratic traditions, and scientific socialism" meant it had to be silenced through the Act's labeling provision. However, it was noted that "If this attack succeeds, all other youth publications of social concern"[88] would soon face the inquisitors too. Advance pledged "to work for the repeal of the McCarran Act" and urged Attorney General Robert

Kennedy "to uphold democracy by rescinding this order," requiring that the youth group register as a Communist front. The party-led Progressive Youth Organizing Committee founded New Year's weekend 1961, blasted Kennedy, too. Alva Buxenbaum, the African American chair of the PYOC, said the fight against the McCarran Act "will be the focus of the youth movement nationally and will draw international support."[89]

The assault against Advance gained the attention of the Citizen's Committee for Constitutional Liberties and the National Student Association, which collaborated on a McCarran Act information kit distributed to student leaders across the country. Included in the kit was a letter from Miriam Friedlander, Advance's executive secretary, and future New York City Council member. "It is clear that the action against Advance is calculated to suppress the voice of democratic youth which has broken through the pail of the McCarthy era." The McCarran Act was a "dangerous invasion" on civil liberties, she wrote. Also included in the kit was an NSA resolution against the Act.[90] NSA would also help organize a CCNY debate on the McCarran Act, featuring former Assemblyman Mark Lane who said, "The defense in this country of Advance...[is] the front line of defense of the rights of America's people and youth." According to the *Worker*, Lane's comments received "Thundering applause" from the assembled students.[91] That September, Mike Stein, Advance's president, sent a letter to "several hundred national and international youth and student organizations," indicating that the McCarran Act "endangers the rights and freedoms of all youth and student organizations." Advance, which had been scheduled to appear before the Subversive Activities Control Board on September 9, called for pickets to protest the hearing.[92] Students for a Democratic Society and Campus Americans for Democracy sponsored actions in support of Advance for early October, while the Student Nonviolent Coordinating Committee encouraged individual members to show support.[93] The support was on-going and growing. In late October, over 300 people rallied in support of Advance outside of the SACB hearings. SNCC leader Jim Monsonis, said, "Advance is being interrogated under the McCarran Act not because of the possible political associations of some of its members but because of positions which it has taken and argued for." Stein "noted it was Halloween night, and declared [that Attorney General] Robert Kennedy was witch-hunting in the wrong places."[94]

Despite the witch-hunt, the party was optimistic. Advance and the PYOC brought young Communists and their allies together to fight against political repression. In a press statement, the PYOC said it was "dedicated to the examination and advancement of the democratic labor and Socialist traditions and aspirations of the American people." Greetings were sent by Harry Bridges, international president of the ILWU and W.E.B. DuBois, among others. Buxenbaum, the future chair of the party's women's commission, told reporters, "American youth ar [sic] apart [sic] of the worldwide movement (for progress)" and they "demand" a "life that measures up to today's possibilities." Reflecting on the lunch counter sit-ins in North Carolina, she added, "A year ago there were only occasional rumblings among youth. But since the first sit-ins...an ever growing number of youth, Negro and white, have been raising their voices, [and] demanding a brighter future." Emboldened by the upsurge, the youth group also adopted a Youth Bill of Rights. It said in part: Youth have the "right to plan our own lives free from the threat of nuclear annihilation and the burden of military service," the right to "organize freely; to examine all ideas," the right "to an education based on ability to learn, but not on ability to pay," and the right to "job training and full employment."[95]

Praising student leaders, like Buxenbaum, Hall remarked that the PYOC "constitute[s] an important step in filling the organizational vacuum that has existed. This vacuum has always been a weakness, but in the light of the rise in the movements [among] the youth, it has become a serious political question. The Party," Hall concluded, "must give higher priority for the work among youth."[96] Concomitantly, Hall also "confronted the urgent job of rebuilding and unifying the Communist Party."[97] The two were connected, as thousands of youth and student activists would soon join Advance, the PYOC, the W.E.B. DuBois Clubs, and later the Young Workers' Liberation League, and the Communist Party – thereby, replenishing the ranks.

As noted above, the "objective situation was becoming more advantageous" for the party. After ten years of playing defense, "no longer were they virtually isolated in protest."[98] While speaking to 450 students at Columbia University in November 1961, Davis personified a larger trend then propelling the party once again into the spotlight, to the dismay of ruling elites. Mockingly, he said, "All the publicity I have received couldn't be bought by all the gold in Moscow," though his Soviet comrades were likely pleased by the reception Communists were then receiving. "Telephones are constantly ringing at Communist party headquarters," he added triumphantly. That 1,000 CCNY students rallied the next day and called for a strike in support of Communists served to highlight the failure of the speakers ban. At CCNY Samuel Hendel, chairman of the political science department, told assembled students, the ban on Communists was "a gross violation of academic freedom unsupported by law." CCNY students did get to hear Davis' voice though, as a tape-recorded speech was played at a rally highlighting the ridiculous nature of the ban. Apparently, students could hear, but not see a Communist speak. On the recording Davis said, "if this ban is allowed to stand, academic freedom will go out the window."[99] By mid-November 3,000 students were on strike and boycotting classes at Queens College; 1,500 protested the ban on Communist speakers; they held signs that said, "Ban the Ban!"[100] Just weeks later, PYOC chair Alva Buxenbaum wrote to President Kennedy demanding the creation of a National Youth Act, which included "apprenticeship and skilled job training for 200,000 additional youth providing jobs with union conditions."[101] On and off the campuses, young Communists were ambitiously making demands. By mid-December the ban was lifted; two days later Davis was again invited to speak at CCNY, an engagement which he regarded as a "fitting tribute to the 170th anniversary of the Bill of Rights."[102]

Unsurprisingly, the FBI took note. Cartha D. De Loach, assistant director of the FBI, speaking at an American Bar Association conference in January 1962, told reporters, "the Communists have grown increasingly ambitious in their designs upon youth." He noted that the PYOC was created "to pave the way for greater Communist influence" among "broad segments of our college students." He also credited Hall with the party's "renewed emphasis on youth."[103] By May 1962, *Time* would report that "some 100 campuses" had extended invitations to Communist speakers.[104] It did not, however, report on the number of colleges and universities that had denied Hall, and other Communists, their First Amendment right – which was likely a considerable number. That same month, Arnold Johnson spoke to an audience of 800 at Washington University in St. Louis.[105] In April he spoke with 700 at Hamilton College,[106] and in December he spoke with 450 students at Trinity College.[107] Hall told 1,000 students at Swarthmore College also in April, that "anti-Communism has become a big business, a profession which is a racket...a smoke screen behind which all kinds of crimes are committed against the American people." He likened anticommunism to "a weapon, a studded club...a political poison," the horrific "basis of Hitler's brutality...the cornerstone of his gas chambers and concentration camps."[108]

That September, the party's Lecture and Information Bureau sent a series of letters to various professors, college papers, student councils and organizations requesting that "you invite representatives of the Communist Party to speak." This was a deliberate, systematic approach to reach students. In "the past year Communist spokesmen addressed more than thirty colleges and universities" where "approximately 75,000 students and townspeople" attended. "It is clear from this," the letter concluded, "that students wish to hear the Communist viewpoint from bona fide spokesmen. Students in their search for knowledge apparently are not satisfied to learn about communism from anti-Communists."[109] Those hoping to stunt the then ascendant youth and student movement and its welcoming of Communists were reeling in defeat.

By spring 1962, Hall increasingly framed the Cold War as a struggle between life and death. He attacked Cold War policies "at home and abroad" as undemocratic and even suicidal. He acknowledged that the domestic and international aspects of the Cold War differed tactically. However, he stressed that they were both geared towards the same strategic goal – the destruction of the domestic Communist left and the dismantling of international socialism. He called the "policies that sacrifice the interests of the people and [the] nation to those of a few monopolies," a foundational concept of Cold War politics. That the Cold War is "self-defeating" was obvious, he told students. To Hall, these policies were of a "bankrupt and dead-end character." They were "suicidal policies of the ultra-right," designed to propel our nation down "a totally reckless" path towards nuclear war. He said, "Anti-Communism has truly become a big business," as weapons manufactures were living high off the government hog due to the increased military spending. Ominously, Hall added, the Cold War was "Political lunacy combined with nuclear power," an "unthinkable danger to all of mankind,"[110] especially youth and students who would bear the brunt of a new war. Fortunately, this same demographic was flocking to campus auditoriums and stadiums by the thousands to hear what Communists had to say. Al Richmond, editor of the West Coast *People's World* echoed Hall. He wrote, "The cold war is the malignant core of the social status quo." It was a cancerous growth then being excised by youth and student activists, Communists among them. "HUAC is among the monsters guarding it," he added. "'Anti-communism' is its weapon,"[111] a weapon then losing its effectiveness as youth and students by the thousands continued to welcome Communists to their campuses.

Daniel Rubin, who spoke on about 40 campuses in the early 1960s, boasted in fall 1962 that the PYOC had grown. Its growth suggested that "many students consider the CP a legitimate and necessary participant in the great debate on communism and our country's objectives." To Rubin, Communists were "taking a number of steps to increase their influence among youth." The party's support of the PYOC, the numerous college speaking engagements and the considerable mobilization for the 8th World Festival of Youth and Students in Helsinki, in which 450 young people from the U.S. had attended, a large and representative delegation,[112] was his proof. In August 1962, Rubin and other young Communists also attended the annual congress of the National Student Association, which had earlier partnered with Advance in the fight against the McCarran Act. Over 1,000 students, leaders from the PYOC, *New Horizons for Youth,* Students for a Democratic Society, the Committee on Racial Equality, and various campus groups attended the 12-day conference.[113] Young Communists found common ground with moderate NSA members like future Congressman Barney Frank who argued during the plenary that the "McCarran Act is an abomination and I'm against abominations. It should be repealed." It was noted that "thousands" of fliers and other party literature were distributed, including Hall's *End the Cold War,* which was "especially well received."[114]

Rubin, Hall and their comrades were far from satisfied. They saw "that improving drastically the size and quality of the Communist youth is essential for influencing the mass democratic youth movement in a progressive direction." The party needed to do more, they argued. Hall and Rubin emphasized the creation of "an extraordinary organizational form, a Communist Youth Division" designed to "give proper emphasis, push and scope to youth activity." Coupled with their successful university and college speaking engagements, Communists also experimented with new and even "spontaneous forms" of youth organization.[115]

Hall was once again indicted in March 1962 – this time, under the McCarran Act – which, added to his and the party's sense of unease. To Hall, the ruling class was once again acting out of desperation, which wasn't lost on youth and students. Yes, Hall was a victim of "a police-state law…a fascist enabling act," a "monstrous law" and "cowardly capitulation" to right-wing extremism.[116] Uniformed and undercover police watched his every move; *The New York Times* reported that 22 uniformed police and 15 detectives attended an early May Hunter College speaking engagement.[117] Hall and the beleaguered party were still defiant, though, as the continuing "lunacy" was in the process of birthing its antithesis, an upsurge led by youth and students powerful enough to win "the decisive case for democracy in our land." That Communists had "confidence in the American people," especially youth, was undeniable. That "victory can be won" took convincing. The CPUSA believed that "The Bill of Rights can and must be the effective law of our democracy."[118] This belief, along with the tens of thousands of students then clamoring to hear CPUSA speakers, gave Hall and his comrades the strength to muster on.

Hall was relentless and would not let the renewed assault slow him down. He even reached out to the Socialist Party. He asked SP leaders, "What issue is supposedly of such all-consuming magnitude that it can blot out these great issues of the day? What issue has thus far divided the socialist forces and thereby weakened their contribution to a united struggle of our people." The answer: "It is in fact NOT an issue. It is a POISON. It is ANTI-COMMUNISM. The price our people have paid and are still paying for anticommunism, particularly in the last decade, is beyond calculation. The price the Left, and especially the Socialist forces, have paid for either falling prey to its insidious influence or retreating before it, has been a catastrophic weakening in their historic role in the political life of our nation." Hall wasn't arguing for a merger of the two organizations. He was far from naïve. His proposal did "not mean an end to, or the submerging of, differences. But," he continued, "it would mean an end to...'socialist' campaigning on the 'anti-communist' issue," a capitalist wedge tactic used to divide left forces. He echoed his friend and comrade Arnold Johnson, "The Communist Party, not by its choice, has become the battleground in defense of the Bill of Rights and the Constitution," a reality being recognized by "all thinking, democratic Americans." How did the so-called socialists respond to this overture? They said in part, "The Communist Party today has asked the Socialist Party to join it in common action, saying that this would unite 'some of the best fighters for peace and democracy.' We reject this appeal,"[119] a rejection that not only harmed the CPUSA, but also democracy and socialism.

While Hall made unrequited overtures to the Socialist Party, the CPUSA continued scheduling university and college speaking engagements. In fall 1963, Herbert Aptheker, considered by some 'The Most Dangerous Communist in the United States,' spoke at Los Angeles State College, the University of California, San Jose State College, Oakland City College, San Francisco State College, the University of California (Berkley), University of the Pacific, and the University of Oregon. As Aptheker put it, "Audiences were not only large – that is not new; they were genuinely interested...*Anti-Communism, as an intellectual weapon, is losing its effectiveness*" [*italic* in original].[120] Hall couldn't agree more. He urged his comrades to see this upsurge as an opportunity to "put our house in order" with an "emphasis on party building" among youth. Self-critically, he told his comrades that the party needed to "correct the damage done [in the 1950s] through excesses in the name of security" and "take a fresh look at the problems and the tasks of party building." "We must find the way, in spite of, and in defiance of, harassment to build the party and the press, to increase our public activity." Though the party's "public activity" was at a high level, recruitment lagged. "The political needs of today make a breakthrough a real possibility. We must guarantee it," Hall added. "We had to fight to break the isolation of our party," after years of concerted political repression, "and we still need to do so," he continued. Hall was not willing to let the party rest on recent successes. "The task ahead is a big one. We need simultaneously to mobilize the party and to strengthen ourselves – organizationally, politically and ideologically. And we must do this while doing ever more in the field of mass work." Hall had called for "a 3- or 4-month intensive period of Party renewal, a period of rejuvenation, refreshment and revitalization." We "must get with these historic times" and "make history," he added, which required "more alertness, more boldness, more determination."[121] Communists seemed ready to take on this task.

* * *

James E. Jackson, in a letter to Henry Winston, was exuberant. He shared Hall and Aptheker's optimistic outlook. Like his comrades, he saw the party's work among youth as essential and noted, by "early in '64 there will be born a real union of youth for socialism [the W.E.B. DuBois Clubs]," an organization "with an explicit program, banner and leadership." Jackson added, that it "will carry forward in present times and circumstance" the work of comrades like Winston, Gil Green and Claude Lightfoot, Communists who "gave leadership" to the youth and student movement in the pre-war years. It "is gratifying to witness how people are emerging from the long night of McCarthyism,"[122] Jackson continued. The recent wave of successful speaking engagements as well as the historic 1963 March on

Washington was fresh on his mind. Dawn brought tens of thousands of youth activists now packed into university stadiums fighting for the right to hear Communists speak. Rubin would note, in retrospect, that the forming of the DBC was designed to attract young people to the party, "and it did to some extent."[123] DBC national chair, Philip Davis, articulated the youth organization's main goal: To become "a potent force on the American political scene,"[124] a goal young Communists strove towards.

Spur, the DBC's newsletter, echoed Jackson's sentiments. The "new organization was born to fill a gap felt to exist by many young people who have been involved with the movements for peace, civil rights, and economic security for the American people." Youth across the country "agreed that an organization was needed which would stand for the goals of all these democratic movements, and at the same time go beyond them to point the way towards a socialist society." The newsletter's editors urged youth and students to "break out of the overstuffed [arm-]chair socialism which has become so comfortable for us." They criticized the "fireside discussion groups which analyze and reanalyze the movement – [a] searching of the line with which to 'guide' the movement, and of the proper book with which to establish our authority," as if "worship[ing] the printed word [was] an end in itself." The newsletter then briefly highlighted the work of DBC chapters across the country, including the organizing of vigils in honor of James Chaney, Andrew Goodman and Michael Schwerner, civil rights activists murdered in Mississippi that spring.[125] That Schwerner was a Red Diaper Baby (his parents were New York party members) brought the horrific murder too close to home for many Communists; Larry Rubin, Daniel Rubin's cousin and SNCC Mississippi field secretary, like other youth activists, noted in retrospect that he came to terms with the prospect of death while in the South.[126] That Phil Davis urged DBC members to "put our bodies on the line" for civil rights,[127] wasn't empty rhetoric. It was a terrifying reality. Black and white Communists saw the struggle for African American equality as central to the fight for democracy and did everything in their power to bolster unity.

In a September 1964 *New York Times* article, party leaders estimated that they spoke with "more than 100,000 students on 100 college campuses" between the fall of 1961 and summer of 1964.[128] Just a few months later the Berkeley Free Speech Movement emerged and propelled Communist Bettina Aptheker into the spotlight as a national leader of the youth and student upsurge. To Arnold Johnson, Communist speaking engagements influenced students "far beyond the campus[,] through the radio, television and the press."[129] Johnson also noted in fall 1964 that 50,000 copies of Hall's pamphlet *The Eleventh Hour* had been printed and distributed, with an additional 50,000 on order; 100,000 copies of the party's *Economic Program*; 50,000 copies of a pamphlet titled *End the Ghetto*; and 30,000 copies of the *Appeal to Youth* had also been printed. "Thus, some 250,000 copies of our literature have been distributed within the past several months,"[130] he added excitedly. Speaking to 300 students at Columbia University in December 1965, Hall called anti-communism a "demagogic appeal to utter falsehoods," an "**ideological narcotic**" [**bold** in original], designed to put students "under its spell."[131] Fortunately, however, youth and students seemed immune to this particular opiate. That October young Communists on the Harvard campus said, reds "work in a large number of organizations other than their own. We seek to expand the membership, and to democratize the structure of these organizations." Work within other organizations created both obstacles and opportunities for growth, and young Communists bolstered youth and student activism. "We will be found in almost any organization for peace, jobs, or for freedom," it was added.[132]

At the party's 18th National Convention in spring 1966, it was said, "a Communist speaker on campus can outdraw all other speakers," and that "large numbers of youth" have recently joined.[133] Hall told reporters that the party was "again the largest and most decisive influence on the left," a boastful and exaggerated claim. He added, new members were "75 per cent [sic] youth." Actual party membership remained relatively small, though, at about 12,000. As part of the party's outreach, observers from Students for a Democratic Society, the Student Nonviolent Coordinating Committee, and other youth groups were invited to the confab. Hall also criticized media outlets for "playing up every small left sect that makes bombastic outlandish statements."[134] Two years later, *Daily World* reporter Carl Bloice asserted, "There's no generation gap in the Communist Party... youth are proud of the principled position the Party has consistently taken on public issues."[135] Its leadership in the struggle for African American equality, workers' rights, and peace were highlighted. And in spring 1969, Henry Winston reported on educational and ideological work to the party's 19th National Convention. He said, "It is with pride that I note that there is one institution [International Publishers, the party's book publishing arm] which is the recipient of orders by the hundreds of thousands." Winston then added glowingly, "In the past six years this institution has issued" more than 105,000 copies of the *Communist Manifesto*, 24,500 copies of *The German Ideology* by Marx and Engels, 33,500 copies of Lenin's *Imperialism*, 40,500 copies of his *State and Revolution*, and 29,000 of his *What Is To Be Done?* This was a considerable accomplishment from both a political and business perspective. Winston continued, "Universities and colleges order Marxist works. Hundreds of thousands of them. There is a mass hunger for our literature,"[136] which was likely bought and read by the tens of thousands of students then gravitating around CPUSA speaking engagements. That 1,500 students called for a general strike throughout the University of California system in 1969 in support of the recently dismissed Communist professor, Angela Davis,[137] was reflected of the strategic importance party leaders had placed on youth and students at the 1958 conference and the 1959 convention.

In short, reds had a lot to boast about. Even former members of the Maoist Progressive Labor Party noted in retrospect, "the CP was the best-integrated organization, by race, sex and age, that I've ever seen,"[138] though not necessarily the largest. Regardless, tens of thousands of youth and students were eager to hear Communists on university and college campuses, while thousands of young Communists simultaneously made their mark on the civil rights, peace, and student movements through the DBC. Young Communists and DBC members worked for SNCC,[139] helped organized peace marches[140] and helped lead the FSM,[141] among other activities. That nearly 120,000 cumulative votes were cast for L.A. Communists William C. Taylor in 1964 and Dorothy Healy in 1966[142] was reflective of the shifting political winds buoyed by youth and student activists – of which young Communists constituted a healthy contingent.

While the March 1966 bombing of the DBC headquarters in San Francisco had a devastating impact on the youth group's physical offices, it actually bolstered the organization's recruitment. In the weeks following more than 1,500 young people joined. At that time, more than 60 clubs were active "in cities and on campuses across the country,"[143] despite ongoing harassment, intimidation and violence directed at youth activists.[144]

That fall and into early 1967, the Northern California District of the party reviewed its work among youth; similar conversations were taking place across the country. The conclusion was mixed. It was noted, "The key policy since 1964 for the youth in the Party has been to build a socialist youth organization," i.e., the W.E.B. DuBois Clubs. Why? Communists argued that there was a "need for an explicitly socialist youth organization not hostile to the CP and not hostile to socialism." Such an organization had the potential to "influence directly and demonstratively the course of the movement by putting words and theories into action," while also helping "to build the Party among youth." It was argued that the DBC "would afford young people who were active on a variety of political issues and on a variety of political levels to have discussions on Socialism and Marxism," and "at least for some people" it would provide political space to "transition toward being able to come to the Party."

DBC members helped to lead many of the most important movements of the period, but the party also grew. The Northern California District "doubled or tripled our youth membership," which it was added "was a good thing." The review, however, also highlighted a problem unique to the CPUSA – "probably the single most important problem" Communists then faced. How would they continue to put considerable time, energy and resources, and "a great many Party youth," into the "sustaining of the non-Party [youth] organization," the DBC, while simultaneously building the party?

Complicating matters, it was added that there "is a desire of young people not to be constrained in only building the DuBois Clubs." Youth, "young comrades" in particular, wanted "to be in the mainstream of youth developments." It was suggested that youth cadre be "active wherever the people are on all levels of their development,"[145] a suggestion that also created additional hurdles to sustained growth as some youth found fulfilling avenues for activism without the added burden of Communist affiliation and eventually moved on.

Communists remained optimistic. Another report from the Northern California district noted, "the youth policy as developed nationally and as implemented locally, has been the most effective and successful of all policies in the past period." "Large numbers of youth have been recruited into the Party, and youth activity in general," the report continued. As noted above, Communists not only built the DBC but also helped build the broader civil rights, peace and student movements. "Our problems today are largely problems of growth, not problems of decline,"[146] the report concluded. Many DBC members were integrated into the party's still considerable organizational apparatus.

At a 1967 CPUSA National Youth Conference Mike Zagarell reported, that "in the past three years it [the DBC] has rapidly grown into one of the most important [organizations] on the Left, with a membership of some 4 thousand and a following that far surpasses that." He said, the DBC "served as both a leading and mass organization," which "has placed added organizational tasks [before] the Party." The "increasing public role and influence [of the DBC] is not a guarantee for building the Party," he continued, and urged comrades to be patient with youth and student activists. "Naturally they will not be developed theoreticians. They will bring with them some of the misconceptions current within the movement." However, "if the Left moods among the youth are to [be] won for the Party, the Party must be more visible." Youth "will be searching" for an organizational home. "They must have the opportunity to find, examine and judge our Party," Zagarell concluded.[147]

While some questioned the CPUSA's influence and impact on the 1960s wave of youth and student uprisings, Charlene Mitchell wasn't one of them. In a 1968 newspaper interview, the CPUSA presidential candidate said, "There are some young people, some black militants, who think we're irrelevant." But, Mitchell continued, "each new generation comes along and thinks it invented progress, invented radicalism – until it learns better...they'll learn, like I did, that we've been there before."[148] In fact, Communists had been leading the struggle for workers' rights, African American equality, Black liberation, peace and socialism since at least the 1930s. Others, however, were less charitable. According to Michael Myerson, for the party "this was a real opportunity for renewal, for a replenishing of forces and of leadership. A number, a modest but nonetheless significant number [of youth], joined the Party" during this time, which constituted "real growth." This was the first real upswing since the dark days of McCarthyism. "The

Party leadership of course welcomed these new faces but," Myerson added ominously, "never knew what to do with them." They were largely unaccustomed to the party's decision making structure and embraced "real debate." "Frankly speaking, the center in New York never really trusted the DuBois Clubs," Myerson added. They "managed" to move its national office from San Francisco to New York, where "more 'mature' and 'responsible' leadership" could "embrace it like a fist and smother all the life out of it."[149] While Myerson's comments are indeed worth noting, they also likely reflect the times in which he wrote them – June 1990. Socialism was collapsing around the world and the CPUSA was embroiled in an internal conflict culminating in a split at the December 1991 Convention.[150] Regardless, as Myerson indicated, a "significant number...[of] new faces" joined the party for several reasons – the cross country speaking tours Communists were then initiating coupled with the work of the DBC are just two.

Bettina Aptheker argued, "Not infrequently" students "challenged the basic structure of power in the universities and in society." Asking Communists to speak on their campuses was one way they "challenged the basic structure of power." She added that this movement began in spring 1960 and "reached its first plateau in the fall of 1964 with the Berkeley Free Speech movement."[151] Aptheker articulated a cumulative, quantitative swell of activity. While the FSM "raised questions and challenged educational assumptions. It [also] offered a minimal program for and succeeded in gaining certain political rights for students" on and off the University of Berkeley campus. Additionally, and perhaps more importantly, it "lent direction and gave impetus to a student movement seeking redress of grievances on campuses throughout the nation." Though Aptheker saw the FSM as "the beginning of a long process of change," students had actually begun their revolt much earlier – in the late 1950s and early 1960s. Students had been leading a fight against censorship, a free speech movement, since at least the early 1960s, which wasn't lost on Aptheker. She credited her own activism in the FSM as a direct result of the 1959 party convention and its decision to focus on youth recruitment. Aptheker had initially hid her CPUSA membership, which led some to see her attendance at the University of Berkeley "as part of an insidious Communist plot." To Aptheker, this was a ridiculous proposition. Instead, she argued, public knowledge of party membership "would have meant cooperation with a red-baiting attack on the FSM by helping to focus attention away from the issues raised by the FSM and onto the question of Communism." The Berkeley activist saw herself as a student, as an American and as a Communist, as someone participating "in common struggles for democratic liberties, for civil rights and for peace...I believed [these struggles] to be virtuous struggles commensurate with socialist aspirations. I am a member of the Communist Party because, as I see it, that Party upholds principles which combine a particularly enlightened view of society, with a sense of humanity and peace not to be found elsewhere. As a Communist I believe in the fullest expansion of the democratic liberties of the American people," she concluded. That at least 100,000 students had heard Communist speakers prior to the political quake that rocked the Berkeley campus lent credence to Aptheker's report to the party's Youth Commission in 1966. "It is clear that when thousands demonstrate over a prolonged period dramatic change can be made. People have wrought changes in the past, and they will continue to do so,"[152] she concluded. Hall agreed.

Communists were making some gains among students, though they could only claim a modest increase in actual membership. By spring 1966, membership hovered around 12,000,[153] not the upsurge in dues payments they had hoped for. Communist speakers still addressed huge crowds. And DBC members made positive contributions to various movements. But Hall was concerned. U.S. combat troops had been deployed to Vietnam in early 1965. As early as 1964, Hall warned audiences of a "New Fascist Danger!" He said, "The Republican Party is now transformed. It is now an instrument of extreme reaction. It can become the instrument of fascism." The Republican Party was now controlled by "fanatical fascist groups" and "virulent McCarthy[ists]," he added. Building on his earlier sentiments, Hall continued, the Republican party hoped "to provoke and to increase world tensions," though a Democrat, Lyndon B. Johnson, sat in the White House. They wanted to "put into practice a plan for a world-wide network of nuclear bombs to use as nuclear extortion. It is a policy of nuclear war – a policy of nuclear suicide,"[154] he concluded. To say Hall was worried would be an understatement. Nuclear annihilation was a very real possibility. At Columbia University in 1965, he told students that escalation in Vietnam could result in nuclear war. "It could be the war to end all wars," he said, "because it could end all human existence." Hall called American policy in Vietnam a "war of depopulation" and said the U.S. military was "putting the nation to the torch" with its indiscriminate use of napalm. With an eye towards the economic aspects of the war, Hall also noted that Chase Manhattan Bank and Bank of America had recently "announced the openings of their Vietnamese branches." He concluded, "This is what the war is about."[155] By 1967, Hall was blasting the Johnson Administration and its "dangerous illusion, futile and costly effort" in Vietnam.[156]

In June 1969, Hall delivered a speech in Moscow at a World Conference of Communist and Workers' Parties. He said, "U.S. imperialism remains the most aggressive, war-like force in the world...It is *the* main force of military, political and economic aggression...It is the greatest danger to world peace" [*italic* in original]. President Nixon's pledge to withdrawal 25,000 troops from Vietnam, while the U.S. military "resumed its bombing," was nothing more than the "illusion of disengagement," Hall told his comrades. The Nixon Administration, he said, "is placing a higher priority on the use of open terror" in Vietnam.[157] Hall could have highlighted any number of human rights abuses to make his point; for example, the "wrist slap" Platoon Sgt. Roy E. Bumgarner received after he murdered three unarmed villagers as part of a "body-count contest." Bumgarner, who "fostered a reputation as a prolific killer," was found guilty "of unpremeditated murder," and received "a reduction in rank and a $582 fine."[158] This was an illustration of Nixon's tacit support of the "open terror" policy Hall warned of. According to Hall, "Nixon will continue the tactic of the carrot and the club – but with less carrots."[159] Bumgarner's actions were simply part of an international Cold War policy personified. The 1968 My Lai Massacre, where over 300 Vietnamese civilians – men, women, and children – "were tortured, mutilated, then killed" by U.S. soldiers is another example. Nixon had Lieutenant William L. Calley – the only officer convicted in the massacre, though 14 were charged – released from an Army prison and put under house arrest pending review. Calley was freed three months after Nixon left office,[160] possibly a reward for carrying out the "open terror" policy endorsed by the ruling class.

While 58,000 U.S. soldiers died in Vietnam, a staggering one to three million North Vietnamese were killed. The "plan was to kill as many enemy soldiers (and their civilian supporters) as possible,"[161] it was said, which confirmed the depopulation campaign Hall warned of while at Columbia University. The "bloated innards"[162] of US imperialism were exacting a heavy price on the Vietnamese people who dared to develop their own economic and political model. However, Hall continued to be optimistic as youth and students revolted across the country, in part by welcoming Communists to their campuses.

Herbert Aptheker – who led a delegation to Vietnam in December 1965[163] – noted in *Political Affairs*, the war on Vietnam "is illegal; it is immoral; it is militarily untenable; it is diplomatically disastrous; and – perhaps decisive – *it cannot work*...With world opinion horrified, with U.S. opinion at least suspicious, with the vast strength of the Socialist world, with the fierce determination of the people of Vietnam, with the realities of U.S. politics...there is every reason to believe that a cease-fire in Vietnam can be compelled." A peace policy, Aptheker added, "can be forced upon Washington; it must be *forced* since the natural proclivities of monopoly capitalism are towards greater and greater monopolization, exploitation and domination. That is, the natural proclivities of monopoly capitalism are towards war" [*italic* in original].[164]

Hall agreed with Aptheker but emphasized the role of domestic political action against state monopoly capitalism as the movement's main strategic goal for achieving peace. To him, the ongoing Cold War – and the concomitant buildup of U.S. military capacity – was a byproduct of "monopoly's fusion with the state and its increased domination of the state apparatus." Ultimately, he added, "All [anti-monopoly forces] are compelled to take up seriously the task of electoral work." For nearly 40 years now Hall had been fighting for legality within right-wing bourgeois democracy. His emphasis on electoral work was simply an extension of that long-term policy, though rebranded to hopefully appeal to student activists. Further, "The anti-monopoly struggle of today takes place within the context of a new balance of forces," as "the existence of a world system of socialist states – of a world in which monopolies have been not merely controlled but eliminated," he added. Optimistically, Hall argued that the anti-monopoly struggle could quickly transition into an anti-capitalist struggle, "especially within the working class contingent."[165]

In spring 1970, Hall reported to the party's National Committee that imperialism was "headed for a crisis because its mainstay is a miscalculation...on the balance sheet the position of U.S. imperialism in Vietnam has become weaker and more vulnerable. And as a result the forces of world imperialism are also weaker."[166] That fall, Hall told 350 people at the Cleveland City Club, "The United States cannot win in Vietnam because our own people will not support criminal policies of brutal aggression." The millions of protesters who had poured into the streets over the past few years was Hall's evidence. As an internationalist, though, Hall also highlighted the resilience of the Vietnamese people themselves. "The United States cannot win because of the determination and unbelievable tenacity of the heroic Vietnamese people... their struggle against foreign oppression is a way of life," he added. "It has been a way of life for generations. In their very being, there is no separation between life and independence or death and oppression. To conquer them is to destroy them as a people. Any attempt to subjugate them is an act of genocide."[167] By summer 1971, Hall would add to his critique of U.S. imperialism. The Cold War was showing signs of "disintegrating," he said. "For U.S. imperialism this is a moment when the headwinds are threatening to take over. This is a period when the counter forces [of world socialism] have become an effective counterbalance to U.S. imperialist policies. Increasingly they are canceling out the U.S. influence. This is a moment when the [c]limb has become slippery and precarious" for imperialism.[168] In short, ascendant socialism compelled retreat at home and abroad.

Hall's comments proved prophetic. The U.S. withdrew unconditionally from Vietnam on March 29, 1973. That Communists continued to receive an "unbelievable response" on college and university campuses – coupled with the recent success of the campaign to free Angela Davis – served to give the ruling class another black eye. That "students have not yet accepted Communism" mattered little to Hall, though, as "their questioning shows they are beginning to regard it as a thinkable alternative"[169] despite a decades-long attempt to destroy the CPUSA and discredit socialism.

By late June 1975, the CPUSA convened its 21st National Convention, culminating with a Bicentennial Festival to Advance the Struggle for Jobs and Democracy, Against Racism and War. "Political history will be made when 5,000 Communists, friends and political activists from the working class and people's progressive movement" meet at Chicago's International Amphitheatre Convention Arena, wrote Arnold Johnson in *Party Affairs* one month prior to the Convention. Johnson predicted the Bicentennial Festival will be a "political breakthrough."[170] It was, as attendance surpassed 6,000.[171] Kathy Kelly, president of the National Student Association – the nations' oldest and largest student group which would become the United States Student Association – was scheduled to speak.[172] Her planned appearance was illustrative of the party's broad strategic approach to youth and student organizing. That she was unable to speak, due to a last-minute trip to the Soviet Union to meet with youth and student leaders there,[173] served to confirm the party's positive assessment of Communist influence in the youth and student movement. The former steelworker had spent the better part of 15 years helping to build a Communist contingent among youth and students – a strategic relationship – and he seems to have succeeded.

That 3,000 youth "cheered and applauded" Hall when he spoke at the Young Workers' Liberation League Youth Rights Bicentennial Festival in New York City in February 1976, likely jettisoned any lingering doubts he may have had. "All the hoopla and hullabaloo, the empty bombast and rhetoric, are not honoring our revolutionary past," Hall said at the Festival. "It is clear the big business bandmasters are trying to use the past to drown out the cries of protest over the problems of the present." They were attempting to cynically reshape the past to fit the political needs of the present. However, Hall added, the heirs of our legacy, "The millions of young people who have never signed paychecks, unemployment checks or dividend checks...who have no credit cards, union cards or calling cards...who are in those trying, 'teen-and-in-between' years, too young to be hired and not old enough for old age pensions...find themselves asking: 'What have we to celebrate?'" To Hall, "Our youth have a right to ask, and society has a responsibility to provide an answer," as the "cold, harsh, ugly reality" of youth unemployment was becoming a growing reality for millions. "The economic crisis may be over for some, but it is far from over, and in fact will never be over, for millions of young people who are on the **outside**, on the side-streets [sic], **looking in**!" [**bold** in original]. "[Y]outh DO have the right to earn, learn and live,"[174] James Steele, the national chair of the YWLL, said, echoing Hall.

As part of a Bicentennial discussion on democracy, Steele added to Hall's critique while speaking at Tuskegee Institute in late October 1976. He told students, "we Communists and YWLLers [sic] proceed in our assessment of things from a working class perspective," which forced them to view politics a bit differently. He argued that "Alabama in particular, the South in general, is as much the cradle of liberty as Boston was two hundred years ago. Yes, I say the cradle of liberty." When people celebrate July 4th "they are compelled to also celebrate the Montgomery [Bus] Boycott." He added, "when black people, inspired by the heroism of Rosa Parks, declared their independence from gradualism and tokenism, declared their independence from the status of being in the back of the bus of the country's social, political and economic life." Steele asked, "Where would democracy in this country be if the million-fold movement of the Black masses and their white allies had not played a signal role in helping shatter the floodgates of cold war and McCarthyite reaction which had damned [sic] up the people's movement with rabid anti-communism and racism."[175]

* * *

According to Bettina Aptheker, the youth and student upsurge of the 1960s was met with a mix of "controversy and ambivalence by some within the Party."[176] Indeed, some older Communists questioned the staying power of emerging youth organizations, their predominantly white, middle class composition and a lack of working class background. Regardless, by the mid-1970s, Hall could look back with pride at the role of young Communists in the anti-war movement within the military and on college campuses. It had been less than 10 years since the Fort Hood Three – three young soldiers who refused to deploy to Vietnam and were court martialed – sparked "the genesis of the organized GI [anti-war] movement." Their example became "a cause celebre' spurring draft resistance and opposition to the war within the military."[177] Their courage helped spur the ongoing crisis within imperialism. That two of the Three were party members[178] – PFC James Johnson, who would later become city editor of the party's newspaper, the *Daily World*, and PVT Dennis Mora, a leader of the DBC[179] – is illustrative of the multifaceted role young Communists played in the emerging anti-Vietnam war movement, thereby challenging Nixon's "open terror" policy within the military.

The first call for an "an international student [peace] strike" against the war in Vietnam, was initiated by Bettina Aptheker.[180] Aptheker, also a leader in the Student Mobilization Committee to End the War in Vietnam, recalled, "I proposed that we call for a student strike. The strike could take various forms." However, the goal was for students in campuses across the country "to hold some kind of action to protest the war." An estimated million students participated. "I called for it. I helped organize it," though it was done through the Student Mobe.[181] Clearly, the party had a broad tactical approach to ending the war. It hoped to weaken imperialism internally, while simultaneously developing new cadre within the youth and student movement. Charlene Mitchell, the first African American women to run for president of the United States, said the party also gained a considerable number of new members: "the times that we have recruited the most people and had the most impact was when we were most active in the mass movement... around the work in the anti-Vietnam [War] movement, you know, within the Peace Movement itself, this was the time that we had recruited more people than ever before."[182] Though the party did not regain its 1930s Popular Front or World War II era peak membership, it did grow in the 1960s and 1970s and played an important role in many of the struggles of the time. As noted above, in the 1960s Communists and DBC members worked for SNCC, helped lead the FSM and the peace movement, while speaking with tens of thousands of youth and students. Additionally, in the 1970s, Communists led the efforts to free Angela Davis, initiated the National Alliance Against Racist and Political Repression, which Mitchell served as the founding executive director,[183] the National Anti-Imperialist Movement in Solidarity with African Liberation,[184] led by fellow Communist Tony Monteiro, and Trade Unionists for Action and Democracy,[185] among other examples.

Further, it had only been five years since the founding of the party-led Young Workers' Liberation League. The YWLL recruited "the best of the working class – black and white,"[186] it was said. At its founding convention in February 1970, Hall urged youth to think broadly and challenged sectarianism within the youth and student movements, a recurring theme for the aging revolutionary. He said, "We, like many others, are fighters for reforms – higher wages, against all practices of discrimination and segregation, electoral reforms, voting rights, housing, day care centers, etc. But we are the most effective fighters for reforms because we are revolutionaries – not reformists. Reformists tend to ask... Revolutionaries demand." Hall emphasized tactics within a Marxist-Leninist lens to YWLL delegates. He said, "In Marxist-Leninist terms, tactics is a word meaning how to move people into struggle based on their understanding of their own self-interests. How to move the struggles to the next stage. That must be the test of all tactics – how do they move people into struggle." According to Hall, "Social progress is being propelled by a worldwide revolutionary process. It is sweeping capitalism before it – root and branch. The question before mankind is not whether socialism. In a basic sense it is not even how socialism. The only unanswered question is how soon. The founding convention has helped with the answer to this question...it is sooner than you think,"[187] he concluded.

"The significant thing about it [the YWLL] was that up till then it was assumed that the 'socialist left' was white students," Jarvis Tyner recalled. "There was this idea of parallel development: Black youth were supposed to go into the Black Panther Party and student radicals into SDS." The DBC was considered part of the socialist left. Though it was never as large as SDS or as provocative as the Black Panther Party, its diversity challenged the "idea of parallel development" Tyner spoke of. James Steele, who served as YWLL national chair from 1974 to 1983, added in retrospect, "The League attracted some of the best radicalized youth of the period" and "broadened their outlook. It helped equip them with tactics based on unity. It made a rather remarkable contribution." According to Judith LeBlanc, "The League hit the nail on the head for me...it exemplified equality and brotherhood." To LeBlanc, the YWLL emphasized "uniting young people from different walks of life and different nationalities."[188]

Like the DBC, the YWLL was tactically flexible. It viewed domestic struggles for peace through the lens of a worldwide revolutionary process, thereby connecting youth and student movements internationally and historically to the movement for socialism. In a 1972 *Party Affairs* article Philip Bart wrote, the party and the YWLL's participation in and leadership of the anti-war movement "helped elevate the consciousness of many sections, especially youth." This "enhanced anti-imperialist consciousness"[189] weakened domestic support for the war, while engendering youth and students to Marxism and the party. Illustrative of the point is Jarvis Tyner's comment in 1972 to the Subversive Activities Control Board: "There are Communists and non-Communists within our [the YWLL's] membership and leadership. We are a legitimate organization and have every right to exist and carry out our program within the framework of the Constitution and the Bill of Rights."[190]

That 8,000 Communists, trade union and student leaders came to hear Hall at a "kickoff rally for a new people's political movement – a mass movement that will bring about people's power, working people's power," in August 1979[191] at the party's 22nd National Convention in Detroit served to confirm his optimism. Hall and his comrades prepared for a new decade of struggle. Youth and student activists – from Advance, the PYOC, the DBC and the YWLL, like Alva Buxenbaum, Jarvis Tyner, James Steele and Judith LeBlanc – were fully integrated into the CPUSA, leaving their own mark on the then 60 year old organization.

That youth leaders, like LeBlanc, who lived on the Pine Ridge Indian Reservation in 1973 during the historic stand-off at Wounded Knee, found a political home in the CPUSA wasn't surprising. The American Indian Movement activist recalled, "That experience [Wounded Knee] more than anything else, convinced me to join the Communist Party."[192] In fall 1978, LeBlanc, along with other YWLL leaders, organized 300 people to attend the opening program of the party's new People's School for Marxist Studies in New York.[193] Similar in content and theme to the party's flag ship adult education institution, the Jefferson School for Social Sciences[194] – though considerably less ambitious – the People's School main goal was to "serve the needs and interests of working people, of Black, Hispanic and other minority peoples, to serve the struggles of women for full equality and youth," as Hall put it. The goal of "directors and deans of corporate funded schools," he continued, "is to deceive, to make it easier for the monopolies to exploit the working people and govern society." The aim of the People's School, however, was to "attract a wide-range of people, from unemployed youth to trade union and community activists." Students "will consist mainly of those whose education has been deliberately restricted and limited by the ruling class." This is a cry gaining considerable resonance today as the student debt crisis reaches staggering proportions. While the school's curriculum included classes on the history of the Communist Party, women's equality, Black liberation, the freedom struggles in Africa and Latin America, political economy, and philosophy, it also offered "practical courses" on "writing and speaking skills and housing and community organizing."[195] As a new decade neared, Hall continued to search for ways to reach youth and students.

Roughly one year later, young Communists convened a symposium that included Frank Jackalone, chairperson of USSA; Kujaateli Kweli, director of youth development for the National Urban League; and James Steele, national chairman of the YWLL. Their focus: The "prospects for youth in the presidential year [1980] and into the new decade." Steele and Jackalone weren't strangers; they had co-chaired the U.S. delegation to Cuba during the 10th World Festival of Youth and Students a decade earlier. Young Communists under Hall's leadership continued to play a unifying role as the right wing began its ascension with the election of Ronald Reagan.[196]

The relationship between the Party, the YWLL and the youth movement wasn't always clear, though. According to CPUSA national co-chair Joe Sims, "folks didn't quite understand what they were in, [or] what they were doing, and it created a lot of problems." Questions were raised regarding the "nature of the organization. What were we trying to build?" Hall and Winston "came to the conclusion that we were going in opposite directions at the same time [and] out of that [discussion] came the idea to build a Communist-led youth movement," what would become the Young Communist League. YWLL leader James Steele "was surprised" by the shift in emphasis, he recalled. Sims who had been assigned to Budapest to represent the U.S. youth movement at the World Federation of Democratic Youth, noted that he "didn't realize the state of the organization was dire. We really didn't have much on the ground then," he added. "The question was to figure out what we actually had and then to rebuild." Sims, LeBlanc and John Bachtell subsequently met with Winston to discuss "the character of the organization that we were trying to build. We had a back and forth about it." Ultimately, the YWLL was disbanded and in its place the YCL was re-founded. According to Sims, "there was a special approach to USSA," an approach that had proven very valuable in the defense of Advance, the PYOC and well into the 1970s. Sims said, comrades in Baltimore were in touch with a young Tupac Shakur, who had joined the YCL; that there was a "substantial club" on the University of Massachusetts Amherst campus, where YCL leader, Jason Rabinowitz, had been elected student council president. YCL members were also active at Rutgers University, Brown, Wesleyan, "and throughout the New York system, City College, Hunter, Brooklyn College, Medgar Evers College." During his years as a YCL leader, Sims found Hall "to be a reservoir of advice, knowledge and information. His council was invaluable. He could be biting and supportive at the same moment." Sims harbored no doubts regarding Hall's support of the youth and student movement. "He supported student concentration immediately. College students are working class youth." Additionally, Sims said Hall's Marxism was neither "rigid nor dogmatic."[197]

Hall, however, was always self-critical; despite myriad accomplishments, youth recruitment and retention remained a challenge for the CPUSA into the 1980s. In 1984, shortly after the re-founding of the YCL, Hall criticized his comrades for failing to make youth recruitment a centerpiece of their work. He said, "we have said all the right things. We have made important decisions. We have passed very basic resolutions. We make very fine speeches...We have said many times youth work is critical for the Party, especially for the Party's growth...And then we don't follow through – in the center, in the districts... nothing happens." Hall still saw youth as "a reservoir of political strength...a tremendous reservoir," while also acknowledging that "each generation is different" and comes to socialism in different ways. Hall wasn't just worried about the long term health of the CPUSA, his concern was much broader. "We have to convince trade unions that for their own good they have to take special steps to attract youth, to take up youth issues, to fight for the needs and future of the young generation," he added. The mainstream labor movement today is articulating a similar theme as it fights back a decades-long shrinking membership. Hall even argued that party centers across the country should be turned into youth centers, perhaps "unemployed youth centers" organized in tandem with the party-led National Congress of the Unemployed. Hall called for "immediate action" coupled with "a basic long-range change in attitude. We have to realize that when we do not do youth work we are leaving a big gap on the class struggle front."[198] This component of the class struggle had proven indispensable to the party in the 1960s and 1970s.

That Communists were able to mobilize nearly 300 U.S. youth from 70 different cities, 42 states and 40 campuses to attend the 12th World Festival of Youth and Students in Moscow in July-August 1985 is a testament to the endearing strategic relationship between youth and the CPUSA. In all, 60 grassroots groups were a part of the U.S. National Preparatory Committee, while nearly 500 "prominent organizations and individuals, from the grassroots to the national level, endorsed the Call to Action" issued by the NPC; nine members of Congress also endorsed the call. Further, the festival movement received proclamations of support from the mayors and/or city councils of New York, Chicago, Cleveland, San Francisco, Atlanta, Philadelphia, Baltimore, Toledo, New Haven, and Madison, Wisconsin. Delegates were acknowledged by the governors of New York, Massachusetts, and Minnesota. A number of unions, including the Steelworkers, the Auto Workers, AFSCME, UFCW, SEIU, National Union of Hospital and Health Employees, Teamsters and IBEW, sent delegates to the Russian confab. According to James Steele, co-chair of the U.S.

Delegation, the festival "represented hundreds of millions of young people throughout the world. It was likely the broadest and most representative gathering of youth in history." It was also largely subsidized by the Soviet Union, another example of socialism's commitment to international solidarity. The festival "symbolized the beginning of a new phase, a new level of self-assertion on the part of hundreds of millions of young people whose representatives were there in Moscow." Steele concluded, the "unity of the youth and the truth...blossomed" in the land of socialism. Additionally, the festival movement "brought into being a veritable network of unity, initiative, cooperation, exchange of experience, progressive political education and internationalism." "Properly developed, such an ongoing" youth and student "structure can make a weighty contribution in the days ahead," a contribution that was needed more than ever with the rise of far-right demagoguery. "Such a united front movement of the young generation," Steele said, "has unlimited potential."[199] Hall agreed.

In 1989, during a speech in front of 1,500 students at Harvard University, Hall returned to a familiar theme, one he had discussed 25 years earlier at Yale. He challenged the popular caricature of Communism, as a subject that has "left skeletons in millions of closets." However, CPUSA members, remarked Hall, "deal with anti-communism somewhat differently than most. For us, it is a more direct challenge...many of us served rather long prison terms for thinking." Others were "hounded, harassed, fired from their jobs and blacklisted from their professions." Still others, "to this very day," are being imprisoned, tortured and murdered. Anti-communism's foundation, continued Hall, is based on "a false, caricature concept of the Communist Party...Anti-communism is based on and deals only with a false caricature. In a real sense it is a confession that it must create a big lie myth because it is not able to deal with the real thing."[200] The real thing was much more nuanced and complex. The real thing had fought hard and sacrificed dearly to protect the Bill of Rights and expand democracy. That the real thing had been able to survive at all is a testament to the resiliency, commitment, and dedication of Communists like Hall.

Throughout his long life Gus Hall weathered many political storms. However, he never wavered in his commitment to socialism and his confidence in youth. While still a young man, he battled steel barons, police batons and fascists. As he grew older, he fought state sanctioned, domestic terrorism, political repression and petty thieves – like Senator Dodd. Yet, he held firm and soldiered on. He was a catalyst for the student free speech movement. He presided over the birth of the PYOC, the DBC, the YWLL and the re-birth of the YCL. He mentored thousands of youth and student activists. That he is – often and unfortunately – remembered only as "a powerful, deceitful, dangerous foe of Americanism,"[201] belies the awesome contributions he and his party made to the social and economic justice movements of the 20th century, even in the post-1956 period. CPUSA involvement in the 1960s and 1970s era student, peace and civil rights movements have been largely neglected. The historic record, however, tells a different story. The CPUSA was far from marginal. It brought "back [the] Old Left ideology,"[202] built alliances and grew. Though it's membership gains were modest, the CPUSA nonetheless continued to play an outsized role. A thorough reexamination of 1960s and 1970s era student, peace and civil rights organizing is long overdue. Contemporary observers agreed with *The Cornell Daily Sun*, when in February 1962 it editorialized: "On U.S. Campuses... Gus Hall Provokes 'Right to Speak' Battles."[203] Student newspapers honestly reflected the realities of the time. As Hall said shortly after his 12,000 person University of Oregon visit, "this need to probe the problems of the day which fortifies our democratic traditions" helps explain "the mass character" of the struggle for "my right to speak, and their [student's] right to question and listen."[204] Unfortunately, though, a Red Taboo[205] in

American historiography still exists, obfuscating Gus Hall and the party's many contributions.

* * *

Gus Hall died on October 13, 2000, five days after his 90th birthday. He spent over 60 years of his life as a fulltime revolutionary, 40 years as head of the CPUSA. He ran for president of the United States four times,[206] shook hands with world leaders and rank and file workers. Hall was a prolific writer, authoring a number of books – including, *The Energy Rip-Off: Cause and Cure*, *Basics for Peace, Democracy and Social Progress*, *Karl Marx: Beacon of Our Times*, *Fighting Racism*, and *Working Class USA: The Power and the Movement* – dozens of pamphlets and hundreds of articles. He and his party endured. At a New York City memorial at the Great Hall of The Cooper Union, 500 people celebrated Hall's life. New CPUSA national chair, Sam Webb, called Hall "a working class intellectual." He said, Hall "had a life-long love affair with the American people and its working class. He loved our country and its rich democratic traditions." Reflecting on Hall's contributions to the anti-Vietnam war peace offensive, Nguyen Dhanh Chau, Ambassador to the UN from the Socialist Republic of Vietnam, called Hall a "great friend of the Vietnamese people."[207] Greetings were sent from around the world.

* * *

At a spring 1989 CPUSA national board meeting John Bachtell, then chair of the YCL, told his comrades, "The youth and student movement today is extremely volatile. It is marked by the biggest upswing in activity, primarily on the campuses, in perhaps twenty years." He highlighted "important struggles" led by YCL chapters at the University of Massachusetts Amherst, Arizona State and Brown University, among others, "where multi-racial coalitions [often led by YCL members] have been formed and huge demonstrations were organized."[208] The YCL continued to work with and within broad based youth organizations, like USSA. Hall undoubtedly felt confidence in the emerging young Communists who would lead the CPUSA into the 21st century.

One of those young Communists was Anita Wheeler, an African American Baltimore high school student, City School Board member, and future editor of *Dynamic*, the magazine of the YCL. At a May 1999 Congressional hearing on violence in city schools, Wheeler, granddaughter of longtime Communist journalist, Tim Wheeler, connected violence in schools to poverty, lack of opportunity, and parents working multiple jobs. She told the assembled politicians about the "economic strains of the household," as parents are forced to spend more and more time "away from the home," resulting in children raising themselves and their siblings.

She advocated for the "social needs of students," cultural diversity and stress management, school forums that emphasized parental involvement, and "federally funded programs" that address systemic issues working class youth face. No parent should have to choose between their child's safety and education, she added, emphasizing the role of student leaders as a "vital resource" capable of solving larger social-economic problems, like gun violence,[209] foreshadowing the vital role youth and students would play in the not too distant future as gun violence reached crisis proportions. In a winter/spring 2000 issue of *Dynamic*, Wheeler wrote, "YCL members, including myself, are faced with many challenges within our schools concerning anti-capitalist and anti-imperialist views, especially with school administration." She added, the shootings in Columbine have provided a pretext to stifle YCL organizing. Violence has "created a situation within our schools in which freedom of speech, assembly, and expression are under attack. The right-wing is using this as an excuse to suppress the rights of all students and create a more repressive atmosphere," she concluded.[210] The National Rifle Association is today employing this tactic in its attempt to stifle youth activists. That YCL members, along with hundreds of other youth activists, were arrested by "rampaging police" in November 1999 during the Battle in Seattle against the World Trade Organization[211] reinforced Wheeler's concerns about the stifling of civil liberties.

The YCL continued to organize, though. Campus and community clubs across the country mobilized into the National Youth and Student Peace Coalition – led by Jessica Marshall, YCL national coordinator – and United for Peace and Justice, in which Marshall served on the national steering committee; Judith Le Blanc, long-time CPUSA national board member, served as national organizing coordinator and national co-chair.[212] That Marshall led the NYSPC as an estimated "30,000 to 50,000 students at 400 to 500 colleges walked out" on Wednesday March 5, 2003 as part of a national Books Not Bombs student peace strike[213] served to illustrate the ongoing strategic role of young Communists in the student and peace movements. Young Communists also waged campus sit-ins in places like St. Louis, Missouri where Student Worker Alliance members Ojiugo Uzoma, Danielle Christmas and Katie Castellano helped win higher wages and better benefits for low wage janitorial and other service employees on the Washington University campus.[214] Simultaneously, other young Communists, like Treston Faulkner and Erica Smiley, helped lead the Student Labor Action Project and Jobs with Justice,[215] which emerged as one of the most influential and powerful grassroots labor-community coalitions of the new century.

Perhaps, it was just this type of leadership Gus Hall envisioned when he said, the party "must give higher priority for the work among youth." It was at the YWLL's 10th Anniversary where Hall talked about yet another misadventure of US imperialism. He told youth and student leaders there:

"The problem for youth is not the Persian Gulf, but the political and economic gulf between corporate interests and the people's interests...There is nothing more criminal, more insane, unpatriotic and Un-American than spending billions for the military, than permitting rich families to plunder and pillage our economy out of hundreds of billions of dollars while tens of millions of Americans live below the official poverty level. The policy of austerity and scarcity creates a crisis for the whole working class, but for working class youth it is an absolute catastrophe, a dead-end. Because of this policy, you are not to be allowed to enlist in the future of the United States, except as cannon fodder to kill and be killed for Exxon and Shell."[216]

Hall's remarks could easily have been written in 2003 when Communists – like Marshall and Le Blanc – helped lead the peace movement.

At this same YWLL anniversary celebration, Jarvis Tyner, the YWLL's first national chairman, connected the growth of the league and the party to the growth of an anti-monopoly movement. He wrote, "It is not possible to build a mass anti-monopoly movement and mass Communist Party without the full and active participation of the youth. That is a fact."[217] Gus Hall agreed.

Joseph North, editor of *World Magazine*, in fall 1970 reflected on the party's work among youth and students in the 1960s. He noted, "Few people in the Party today will ever forget the example Gus afforded at that time. He roamed the country, speaking at every type of meeting. He made an especial [sic] impact on the youth; they saw him on TV, on radio, they read the questions and answers published after the press conferences...He spoke on campuses from coast to coast...He made himself available to speak on college campus and in [the] ghetto, before television and to student reporters for youth periodicals...The party began to speak to millions. It began to teach them the new truth. Its literature, the works of Marxism-Leninism began to catch hold on the campus. No longer was it possible to ignore the ideas of socialism, of Communism...A new day was dawning,"[218] North concluded.

Thousands of students fought to hear Communists speak at their university and college campuses. Tens of thousands attended, listened, and learned. DBC members helped shape the youth and student upsurge, civil rights and peace movements. Communists helped redefine 1960s and 1970s student radicalism, peace and civil rights. In short, the Communist Party, and its leaders, like Hall, were far from marginal. In a January 1961 TV interview, Hall commented on the enduring impact he hoped Communists would have on future generations. He said, "In a sense" the CPUSA is an "advanced detachment of American society and projects advanced ideas," ideas which "only years later are accepted more or less by other sections of the population."[219] His comments have proved remarkably resilient today, 100 years after the birth of the CPUSA. According to recent polls, youth view Socialism more favorably than capitalism.[220]

Chapter 4

Henry Winston: Sight, Vision and Black Liberation

It was March 5, 1956. African American Communist Party leader Henry Winston, in hiding since spring 1951, walked up to the Foley Square Courthouse steps in Manhattan to turn himself in. Over 500 friends, family members and fellow Communists solemnly protested as the beleaguered revolutionary willingly surrendered.[1]

Less than four years later, Winston, now "gravely ill" and "stagger[ing] about in anguishing pain" due to "long years of neglect and abuse in the dungeons of a Federal prison," was on the operating table, his life hanging by a thread. According to *The Worker*, "pure sadists, capable of the most barbarian cruelties" had neglected Winston's cries of pain for months as a tumor grew in his head. Guards, "armed and swaggering," waited patiently outside his hospital room. They were "ready to wrap him in chains and leg irons and haul him back to the steel and concrete tomb...should the surgeons succeed in saving his life."[2] To his comrades, the horror was bizarre, surreal even.

Why was Winston treated so cruelly? He had "never committed a crime against anyone and never hurt anyone." In fact, his entire adult life was spent in "devotion and service to the people of our land, to the workers of our nation and the defense of our country against Hitler." Winston served with distinction during World War II. Maybe this was his reward now that our wartime ally, the Soviet Union, had become a feared enemy.

Winston, "a political prisoner, in whose situation is merged the abominable credulity of American racism against the Negro people and [its] viciousness towards Communists,"[3] embodied a Red-Black alliance, an informal collaboration spanning decades, a collaboration many in Washington were determined to destroy. Like his friends and fellow Communists Paul Robeson,[4] Benjamin Davis, Jr., and William L. Patterson, Winston brought the struggles for African American equality, Black liberation and ascending socialism together domestically and internationally.[5] For this, he had to punished.

It wasn't lost on McCarthyite witch hunters that 500 protesters called for Winston's freedom on July 3, 1960, while he recovered.[6] Interestingly, however, history seemed to play a cruel joke on the red-baiters. Just 24 hours later – on Monday, July 4 – the new U.S. flag with 50 stars representing the addition of Hawaii as a state was debuted for the first time in Baltimore. That in Hawaii "the power of the Communists...is a thousand times stronger" than on the mainland, as the Mississippi Senator James Eastland would earlier quip, made the joke mirthless. Some politicians even argued that the addition of Hawaii would be akin to giving the Kremlin two votes in the U.S. Senate.[7] Fortunately, for those in Baltimore, 40,000 strong cheering the new flag and joyously singing the *Star-Spangled Banner*[8] – that ode to and glorification of the slaveholding republic, not inconsequentially written by a slave master[9] – racism was still the law of the mainland. That Winston was both Black and red legitimized his tortures.

By the fall of 1960, Winston had been transferred from the Staten Island Hospital, "whisked away" to the federal prison in Danbury, Connecticut.[10] Though blind, his morale was high as his comrades intensified efforts to gain his freedom. Winston's comrade Benjamin Davis, Jr., at a spring 1960 party National Committee meeting, put Winston's treatment in political context. He said, "special attention [must] be given to the fight for the freedom of Henry Winston." To Davis and other comrades, "racist cruelty" wasn't just directed at Winston. It was part of a larger assault against an entire people, which made Winston's struggle symbolic.[11] Shortly thereafter, William L. Patterson toured the Soviet Union, Czechoslovakia, Hungry, France and Great Britain to build international support for the ailing revolutionary.[12] By September, the Chicago-based Communist-led Afro-American Heritage Association issued a World Appeal for his freedom. It said in part, "pimps, panderers, dope-peddlers, and ex-public officials who steal from the public are treated with greater humanity"[13] than Winston. In late October, Winston's case was scheduled to be brought before the United Nation's Human Rights Commission, where it was said, he was being persecuted "in the dark of his blindness and in cruel isolation from his loved ones." Apparently, the witch hunters wanted him to "repent." His subversive "ideas of peace, of justice and equality for his people, and ideas of a better life for all humanity,"[14] had no place in American political discourse. This seemed to be a recurring theme. Prison and blindness weren't enough. The forces of reaction wanted contrition. Mike Newberry, in the pamphlet *The Cruel And Unusual Punishment Of Henry Winston*, framed this logic as thought control. Winston, "a Negro leader and a Communist, who was convicted not of a crime, but of teaching and advocating his political philosophy," was still in jail because he would not denounce his party, nor debase himself as a turncoat.[15] The now blind revolutionary sought legal redress as well; by November, Winston had filed a one million-dollar law suit against the U.S. government, claiming his blindness was caused by "delay...negligent and willful conduct."[16] William Z. Foster, by then retired and soon to leave for the Soviet Union, said he was filled with "revulsion and anger." He called Winston's treatment "barbaric," and added, that his comrade was "in jail for no crime at all."[17] *The Worker* summed up the situation in fall 1960: "Winston walked into prison a strong and healthy man. But because he is a Negro and a Communist the government authorities deliberately brought on his blindness" by refusing to treat him. This was an "obvious effort to crush him."[18]

The Rev. Dr. Martin Luther King, Jr., also supported Winston's freedom, which was a testament to the Red-Black alliance Communists had spent decades building and solidifying. In correspondence with his friend, the former Communist councilman from Harlem, Benjamin Davis, Jr., King wrote, "I think it is both immoral and tragic for a nation to allow any human being to face such an inhuman situation." Characteristically, King backed his words up with action. The pastor also spoke at a testimonial dinner for Winston at Harlem's Hotel Theresa in September 1961.[19] Seven years later at a *Freedomways* banquet honoring W.E.B. DuBois, the African American scholar-activist, King – not six weeks before his assassination – conversed with Winston and told him it was an "honor" to finally meet him.[20] That night, King directly challenged anticommunism, noting that DuBois "was a genius and chose to be a Communist...Our irrational, obsessive anticommunism has led us into too many quagmires to be retained as if it were a mode of scientific thinking."[21] Winston, was undoubtedly smiling from ear-to-ear, as the political implications of King's comments were enormous. King wasn't the only person of note supporting Winston, though. DuBois, who also spoke at the 1961 Hotel Theresa dinner, noted – less than a month prior to officially joining the CPUSA – that "Henry Winston had suffered for his determination to think and act in accord with what he believed was right. It is a great honor to stand in the presence of this man, beholding his wounded body and undaunted soul."[22] Eleanor Roosevelt and A. Philip Randolph, among others, advocated for his freedom, too. Perhaps inflicting another black eye on U.S. backed international anticommunism was the goal when Fidel Castro, though still consolidating his new revolutionary government in Cuba, offered to swap Winston for terrorists captured during the CIA-backed and botched Bay of

Pigs invasion.[23] Castro wasn't alone among world leaders now advocating for Winston's release. In late April 1961, shortly after Winston's 50th birthday, long-time party stalwart, Arnold Johnson, articulated the passion of millions around the world when he said, "Everything about Winston calls for his freedom."[24] Though blind, Winston – and his comrades – were optimistic and could see a shifting of the political winds.

Their confidence proved prophetic. On June 21, 1961, President Kennedy granted Winston executive clemency.[25] Less than a month later, Winston held a press conference alongside his comrades Gus Hall and Benjamin Davis, Jr. He said: "Despite my handicap, I intend to resume my part in the fight for an America and a world of peace and security, free of poverty, disease, and race discrimination...I return from prison with the unshaken conviction that the people of our great land, Negro and white, need a Communist Party fighting for the unity of the people, for peace, democracy, security and socialism. I take my place in it again with deep pride. My sight is gone but my vision remains."[26]

When asked how he weathered such a tumultuous storm, Winston expressed confidence in his comrades and his party. He said, "My confidence in the Communist Party helped me a great deal in prison. In life it is necessary to have an anchor. That is primary...I have great confidence in Socialism. I have great confidence in the Communist Party. That was my anchor."[27]

Increasingly, Winston and his comrades were being seen as defenders of the Bill of Rights. In March 1961, 350 professors from 79 universities and colleges railed against the House Un-American Activities Committee, arguing that it has "repeatedly undermined the freedoms essential for national well-being" and "continues to abridge citizens' rights of free speech and association."[28] The treatment of Winston was a case in point. In August, Charles Allen, Jr., national education director of the United Electrical Workers' – a union less susceptible to anticommunism, with prominent reds like William

Sentner playing a public, leadership role[29] – told a rally of 1,200 in New York City, "History has seemingly anointed the Communists with the oils of struggle. They are the first to bear the brunt of repression. They are always on the front line in the everlasting struggle for the Rights of Man."[30] That September the Oil, Chemical and Atomic Workers' Union, representing 200,000 people in a strategic sector, called for the "abolition" of HUAC, stating that the infamous committee "consistently attacked only liberals and nonconformists...[not] truly dangerous conspirators."[31] Cultural and civil rights leaders, such as folk singer Pete Seeger and novelist Gore Vidal, as well as the Rev. Fred L. Shuttleworth, vice president of Dr. King's Southern Christian Leadership Council, got into the mix, too. They held a massive New York City rally at the Manhattan Center that December demanding the abolition of HUAC.[32] Despite decades of repression, the CPUSA still managed to wield considerable domestic and international support; still advocated for an internationalist idea, a worldview, Marxism-Leninism; and still managed to draw tens of thousands into its orbit. Gus Hall – who was now regularly speaking in front of thousands of students on campuses across the country[33] – wasn't wrong when he told reporters just days before Winston's release, "The attempt to jail ideas cannot succeed...thought cannot be outlawed."[34] Was this the real danger posed by Communists like Winston? The treatment exacted upon him was a manifestation born of fear and weakness, Communists argued; fear of another generation of Black luminaries, like Paul Robeson and W. E. B. Du DuBois, comfortably situated within the red orbit; fear of an emerging youth and student movement defiantly challenging McCarthy era thought control by inviting Communists to their campuses.

After spending over 10 years in hiding or in jail, a prisoner in his own country, Winston, in September 1961 – just as construction of the Berlin Wall was beginning – left for the Soviet Union, where he would remain until February 1964.[35]

* * *

Henry Winston was born April 2, 1911, in Hattiesburg, Mississippi, a mere generation removed from slavery. He faced the hardships of poverty early in life; by eight or nine, young Winston was already working, helping to put food on his family's table. In 1925, his family moved to Kansas City, Missouri, where his father had gone three years earlier to work at a steel mill. By 18, Winston was washing dishes 12 hours a day and trying to finish school. During this period, as the Great Depression struck the nation, Winston's love of reading blossomed. He read Frederick Douglass, W.E.B. DuBois, Upton Sinclair and Theodore Dreiser. They "echoed" what he "saw and knew" from experience. After happening across a Communist Party rally in defense of the Scottsboro Nine and meeting party leader Abner Berry, Winston became curious about Soviet socialism. He read John Reed's classic *Ten Days That Shook The World*, which left a lasting impression. The writings of Marx, Engels and Lenin became cornerstones of Winston's political beliefs, an ideological foundation that would remain throughout his life – and see him through the darkness of prison and blindness. Shortly thereafter, Winston was working with the party-led Unemployed Councils and later the National Negro Congress. In 1931, now 20 years old, he joined the Young Communist League, quickly becoming a YCL leader. Later in life, Winston recalled: "Lenin's teachings showed the way. It was these ideas which influenced and molded my life and led me to understand questions of the leadership of the working class. I also learned that victory for the class, and my people, could come about only if there was a Communist Party guided by a Marxist-Leninist theory."

It was in the thick of struggle against racism that Winston emerged as a CPUSA organizer. The campaign to free Barney Lee Ross, a Texas Black youth falsely accused of rape and sentenced to death, became Winston's focus.

He helped lead the campaign to free Ross in Kansas City, as a wave of protests swept through the South. Outrage was so intense that the governor of Texas delayed the execution. The reprieve was short-lived. As preparations for execution moved forward, the governor said in part, "The boy [sic] may be innocent but sometimes it is better to burn a house to save a village." Though innocent, Ross was sent to the electric chair. Such experiences with racism "steeled [Winston] in the struggle against the racial oppression of his people."

In 1932, Winston was invited to the YCL's national school in New York City. It was there, while attending party meetings, that he would meet Fern Pierce. Soon they were married; in 1934 they had a son. By 1936, Winston had joined the YCL's National and Executive Committees; he had officially joined the party in 1933 and that fall was sent to the Soviet Union. In spring 1935, Winston returned to the United States and became the YCL's organizational secretary in Cleveland, Ohio. However, his time in the Buckeye state was short lived. In January 1936 Winston was elected YCL national organizational secretary; he returned to New York shortly thereafter.[36]

Back in New York, Winston made building the National Negro Congress, one of the party's most successful Popular Front organizations, a priority. At the NNC's second National Convention, Winston told the 1,100 delegates and guests, "Today it is glorious to be alive. The people throughout the world are no longer patiently submitting to tyranny and oppression...A new hope pervades the world. We are uniting for the freedom and progress of our own people...[the] entire South is dominated by **Wall Street**" and so long as they "are able to play white and black, so long will the poverty of the South continue," an observation still relevant today. He called for "**united action**. Only unity of the white and black can save the South" [**bold** in original], he concluded. He also highlighted the growing role of organized labor, especially the newly formed CIO, which "is moving our whole society."

"Realignments are taking place in politics," not least of which were the political shifts initiated or led by Communists. "Our people have begun to realize that it is only with labor that we can achieve our aims." Like other Communists, Winston was engaging in mainstream political discourse. He even paraphrased President Roosevelt's 1936 acceptance speech and called on African Americans to abandon "economic royalists...[while joining] with labor politically,"[37] something many were keen to do with the passing of the Wagner Act in 1935 and the upsurge in organizing efforts.

Meanwhile, fascism was on the rise across Europe. It was a mortal threat to *both* democracy and socialism. The CPUSA mobilized over 3,000 volunteers – mostly fellow Communists – to fight against Franco in Spain.[38] They were attempting to stop fascism in its tracks. Simultaneously, the *United Front Against Fascism And War*, a historic speech defining the worldwide strategic perspective of Communists for generations to come, was given life by Georgi Dimitrov, a Bulgarian party leader who courageously defeated the Nazis during the frame-up Leipzig Trial; he later became head of the Comintern. Appropriately, Winston who spent the entirety of his life following in Dimitrov's footsteps was in Moscow in 1934 when the Bulgarian, now "freed from the fascist beasts," arrived.[39] Winston was again in Moscow in spring 1937 as a representative of the YCL at a meeting of the executive committee of the Communist Youth International, where he and other youth discussed how to stop the spread of fascism.

By age 27, Winston was elected to the party's National Committee; World War II was on the horizon. After the German attack on the Soviet Union Winston told radio listeners, the Red Army has "shown the people of the whole world how a free people, thoroughly organized and brilliantly led, can beat back the nazi [sic] hordes."[40] Eventually, 26 million Soviet citizens and soldiers would lose their lives defeating the Nazis, and defending socialism; Stalin was unprepared for the attack (many of his most experienced generals had been executed),[41] which Winston had no way of knowing. Regardless, Winston, along with an estimated 15,000 other Communists,[42] joined the U.S. armed forces and served in World War II, despite a segregated military. In a 1941 pamphlet, *Old Jim Crow Has Got To Go!,* Winston challenged the "ruling circles of this country" on the question of military segregation. He said, they "fear the prospect of intermingling 'colored and white [military] personnel in the same regimental organization.'" They dubiously claimed desegregation would "be 'destructive to morale' or 'detrimental to preparations for national defense.'" To Winston, their real fear "is that such intermingling may spill the beans," and build comradery, as a "fusion of the common problems, a recount of the of common experiences in civilian life, a growing collaboration and understanding between Negro and white" may foretell broader unity – something that had to be avoided. The "possibility of such intimate contact may well result in recognition of their common destiny, directed...against imperialist oppression in general." According to Winston, at this time "only two Negro units completely officered by colored personnel: the 184th Field Artillery and the 369th Coast Artillery" existed,[43] which hamstrung the effort to defeat fascism abroad.

Despite segregation, as party leader James West recalled, "Over 30 per cent [sic] of the leadership from [the] club level upward had taken up arms within nine months after the Pearl Harbor attack. Many never returned."[44] Fortunately, Winston would, but he wouldn't see Fern, his comrades or his party again until the summer of 1945.

* * *

By spring 1946, Winston was elected to the party's central committee and named its organizational secretary. Two years later, the Mississippi born revolutionary – along with most of the party's national leadership – would be indicted and arrested under the provisions of the Smith Act and thrown in jail. A lengthy and costly trial followed.[45] The Red Scare was now in full swing, fueled in large part by the uncorroborated claims of paid FBI informants. Hyman Lumer, educational director for the United Electrical Workers' Union District 7 and party leader, noted that professional informing could be a lucrative business. "[A] common feature of these high-minded 'patriots' is that they are paid – and often very well paid – for their 'patriotism,'" he wrote. In a 1955 pamphlet, titled *The Professional Informer*, Lumer gave several examples: Mary Stalcup Markward, received $24,026 over a ten-year period and Berenice Baldwin received $16,717, while William G. Cummings only received $11,023 over eight years, *not* inconsiderable sums in the late 1940s and early 1950s. Lumer emphasized, "these are only the amounts the FBI *admits* giving them" [*italics* in original]. Additionally, the professional informers also received sizable paydays for "performing on the witness stand," an additional fee, of course. Lumer pointed out, "there is money to be made from lectures, writing, radio and television, movie rights, etc...Such is the 'self-sacrifice' of these stool-pigeons."[46] Unfortunately, real patriots, many of whom happened to be red and Black, like Winston, ended up in jail cells due to the stool pigeon racket.

At Foley Square, Winston defended his party: "I am a Negro...I have experienced jim crow [sic]. I have seen lynchings. I have experienced segregation, brutality of every possible kind, insults and abuses, and I have always searched for a program for my people that would liberate them...This is my life...[and] I shall never forget the fact that the Communists Party was the first organization in this country which offered a program for my people as well as my class."[47] Unlike the paid informants, Winston could not be bought. Instead, he fired back at his accusers: "We shall prove by a wealth of incontrovertible facts that Wall Street and Park Avenue control the jury system and have converted it into a conviction machine." His political insight fell on deaf ears. By fall 1949, Winston and his comrades had been sentenced to five-year prison terms and hefty fines.[48]

In a March 1950 report to the party's National Committee, Winston remained defiant. "This is a supreme test for our Party...We can win that test, we can rout the enemy." Specifically, Winston was referencing the Mundt-Ferguson Registration Bill, which would have required every member of the CPUSA to register with the attorney general's office. Not only were leading Communists being rounded up on charges of conspiring to overthrow the U.S. government by force and violence, now all Communists – if Mundt-Ferguson became law – would have to register based on this falsehood.[49] According to party stalwart Arnold Johnson, Mundt-Ferguson "would nullify the Bill of Rights, cripple the trade unions, and advance the establishment of a full-fledged fascist dictatorship."[50] The message was clear, civil liberties for Communists would not be recognized. The August 1950 cancellation of a Council on African Affairs sponsored rally at New York's Madison Square Garden "pending action on the Mundt-Ferguson Communist-Control Bill"[51] was evidence. Winston, Johnson and the entire party had reason to fear the worst but were not deterred. "[T]hings seem very placid at [Party] headquarters," *The New York Times* noted in September. "The [CP] is conducting a membership registration of its own, and it does not seem to worry anyone that the F.B.I. might swoop down on the offices...and cart off an up-to-date roster." Winston defiantly told reporters, the CPUSA could not be destroyed.[52] That December, over 2,000 New York Communists held three separate (Manhattan, Bronx and Brooklyn) pre-convention meetings to challenge the growing repression. Carl Winter, Michigan Party leader spoke in Manhattan; he said, "the Communist party will not register as felons."[53]

"The working class in American does not want fascism. It wants democracy," Winston's report continued. He called on all party members to put forward their "maximum effort" and "go to the working class" and "draw upon the most democratic and best organized forces in the nation – the industrial workers."[54] This wasn't empty rhetoric. As organizational secretary, Winston well knew the party could count on considerable support from within several industrial unions, at least at the onset of the Red Scare. Outside observers agreed: "The Communists were [then] the best-organized political group within the CIO." As Judith Stepan-Norris and Maurice Zeitlin note in *Left Out: Reds and America's Industrial Unions*, Communists still led a combined union membership of about one million, roughly one-quarter of the CIO's 1949 total membership.[55] Communists "must show the way," emphasized Winston, especially among industrial workers. "Never was the responsibility of the Party as leader, guide and organizer of the people as great as today." The party's existence hung in the balance – as did the democratic liberties of all Americans.

In Winston's report, *Building the Party – Key to Building the United Front of Struggle*, he told his comrades, "We [have] registered to date 83 percent of our 1949 membership." Though the domestic Red Scare was ascending, Winston was still confident that "registration will no doubt be increased to 85 percent, meaning a 15 percent fluctuation for the year 1950." Additionally, many districts were above or at the national average: Montana, 94; Florida, 90; Indiana, 86; Georgia, 85; Iowa, 85; California, 85; Minnesota, 85.5; New Jersey, 85; Connecticut, 84; New England, 84; Wisconsin, 84; Illinois, 83.5; New York, 83; Northwest, 83.

To Winston, "These figures indicate the high level of organizational political struggle conducted for maintaining the Party membership." After detailing the percentages in districts below the national average, Winston highlighted two factors that continued to fuel his optimism. First, he was confident "that the raising of the national average from 83 to 85 percent will be solved primarily here" at the National Committee meeting, as comrades would – in a spurt of activity – likely "guarantee completion of registration in the next two or three weeks." Secondly, he urged his comrades to pay special attention to "registering our industrial membership in general, and our Negro membership in particular," a section of the working class historically less susceptible to anticommunism. He then highlighted the status of the party's industrial concentration policy and recruitment of African Americans in the key districts of Ohio, Western Pennsylvania, Illinois, Michigan, California and New York.

In Ohio, membership increased among coal miners, with a "slight dip" among auto and railroad workers, which put "in sharp focus" completing registration among electrical, steel and rubber workers, all hovering around 85 to 87 percent of 1949 membership. In Western Pennsylvania, comrades registered 93 percent among coal workers, and 80 and 71 percent among electrical and steel workers, respectively. The high registration among coal workers was partly due to the "outstanding role" of party members in the recent coal miners' strike, where they "were active in raising relief for the strikers...distributing many thousands of leaflets, as well as the *Daily Worker*, and...obtaining scores of subscriptions to the *Worker*." However, as Winston noted, "these activities were undertaken at the expense of completing the registration" in other areas. Additionally, Communists in Pittsburgh faced "concerted attacks...against foreign-born comrades in particular, by the press, the use of stoolpigeons, and the printing of lists of names, also tended to divert our comrades... from completing the registration," he added, understating the gravity of the accomplishment given the repression. In Illinois, the party grew among steel, farm equipment and railroad workers, with a slight decline in meat packing. The "biggest drop" in membership was among auto and electrical workers, roughly 71 and 76 percent of 1949 membership. In Michigan, the party grew by 5 percent in auto; Winston did not report on other industries. In California, the party increased membership among carpenters and teamsters, and among auto, electrical and radio workers, with a "slight decrease" among steel workers. Winston told his comrades that he did not have the percentages for the International Longshoreman and Warehousemen's Union, considered a party stronghold; he did note, however, "some loses have taken place,"[56] though the ILWU did decisively reject anticommunism in a resolution adopted unanimously at its 1949 convention.[57] In New York, membership was increased in electrical, longshore, railroad and auto, while steel was down 1.5 percent. Winston also noted the sharpening confrontation with Joseph Curran, president of the National Maritime Union, one-time ally of the Jamaican-born Communist, Ferdinand Smith – the NMU's former secretary-treasurer and perhaps the most influential Black labor leader in the country. Curran had hoped red-baiting would shield his union from the ravages of the witch hunt.[58]

Winston also examined party membership among African Americans in these key districts. In Ohio, membership was up from 11 to 13 percent; in Illinois, from 25 to 28 percent; in Michigan membership fell from 19 to 17 percent; in California, from 14 to 13.5 percent; in New York membership stayed constant, at 9.5 percent. According to Winston, "These figures show the fundamental health of our Party, its stability." In the face of repression and "sharpened class struggle" – and to the surprise of many – Communists did *not* abandon the organization in droves. Winston even went so far as to suggest, "our Party will continue to grow," and criticized some comrades for their pessimism. As he saw it, repression was the inevitable "logic of the class struggle." Therefore, he continued, "Ours is the job of learning and mastering our science in such a way as to steel the Party, ideologically, politically and organizationally," to find ways to grow even under harsh conditions. Winston said, we need to make "our policies the policies of the masses in struggle." He was defiant and optimistic.

Winston had much to boast about. The "full weight of the reactionary, imperialist bourgeois state apparatus" was attempting "to isolate our Party from the working class, and to outlaw it," but the assault failed. Party membership not only remained healthy, but comrades also fulfilled their financial goals. The 1949 fund-drive goal was met, bringing in an accumulative $2.5 million, while a special "bail fund" raised more than $1 million "in less than 10 days," not an insignificant amount; roughly $36 million in 2018 dollars. The "Party has become hardened in struggle, better consolidated, ideologically and organizationally. Our membership has shown increased activity, self-sacrifice and devotion,"[59] Winston added, a conclusion hard to dispute given the details of his report.

While it is difficult to know the party's actual membership for the years 1948, 1949, and 1950, and into the early 1950s, by mid-1956 Communists would still claim 20-25,000 members, though membership lists had not been kept for "a great many years."[60] As a security measure the party had "abolished the use of membership books some years ago," Arnold Johnson noted, though they knew it would create "organizational difficulties."[61] One FBI report written in spring 1949 estimated the New York State Communist Party alone had a membership of about 28,000 divided into approximately 1,200 clubs,[62] indicating a dramatic fall by mid-decade. In September 1950, roughly two years after the initial indictment of the party's top leadership, it is worth noting that Communists could – with only 10 days' notice – mobilize 14,000 members to fill Madison Square Garden to denounce "American intervention in Korea,"[63] not an insignificant accomplishment, especially since the party-led CAA had been barred from the venue just the month before.[64] Based on Winston's analysis, the immediate impact of the early Red Scare was only a partial success. Not only did the CPUSA retain the bulk of its membership, at least into the early 1950s, but it also still enjoyed residual support well into the decade – that is, until the Khrushchev report in 1956 documenting Stalin's crimes against humanity and socialism. As party leader and World War II veteran, Robert Thompson – a recipient of the Distinguished Service Cross who would later be denied his VA benefits – noted in retrospect, "The historic significance of the 17th National Convention [held in December, 1960] of our Party lies in the fact that it symbolized, after more than ten years of ramified and vigorous efforts, the defeat of the ruling class objective of destroying the CPUSA."[65] Historian Maurice Isserman would note, "the fact that so many [party members] persevered through the worst of the anti-communist hysteria of the late 1940's and early 1950's stands as eloquent testimony to their courage and commitment."[66] As a percentage of membership, it is fair to suggest that the party saw a sharper membership decline due to security measures (the decentralizing of membership lists, for example), infighting, factionalism, sectarianism, the Khrushchev revelations and the suppression of the 1956 Hungarian Revolution, than due to direct government repression. From their own internal estimates, the party saw a more significant drop in membership after the bombing of Pearl Harbor (about 30 percent) – as Communists volunteered to serve overseas in the armed forces and let their membership lapse – than during the early Red Scare (about 15 percent). Though weakened, the CPUSA persevered throughout the Red Scare. Over 3,200 "friends" of the *Daily Worker* would fill New York's Old Carnegie Hall in late January 1956 to celebrate that publications 32nd anniversary despite the repression.[67] One observer at the party's 1957 convention noted, "the American Communist Party has been greatly weakened by the events of recent years, but not destroyed. Its organization is intact and functioning, and it still has resources of men, money and ideas. The very fact that under present conditions 300 people from all over the country could gather for this convention is a demonstration of strength."[68] Additionally, 1,300 New York Communists would gather in

September 1958 to celebrate the Party's 39th anniversary.[69] The CPUSA would end the decade with about 10,000 members,[70] but it would enjoy a resurgence in the early 1960s, especially on university and college campuses.

The McCarran Internal Security Act, which passed Congress in September 1950, further complicated matters for Winston and his comrades. McCarran Act differed from the Smith Act in that it attempted to force so-called communist front organizations to register with Federal authorities. Any organization with Communists in leadership was considered a communist front. As Winston and the party warned, the anticommunist web had now ensnared the entire progressive movement, causing organizations like the Civil Rights Congress and the Council on African Affairs, led by William L. Patterson and Alphaeus Hunton, respectively, to dissolve by mid-decade.[71]

In this context, with the fear of emerging domestic fascism – in the form of the Smith and McCarran Acts – the party decided in spring 1951 to send some of its core leaders, including Gus Hall, Gil Green, Robert Thompson and Henry Winston, underground. It would be five years before anyone – except Winston's most trusted comrades – would see or hear from him. Winston reemerged in spring 1956 at the Foley Square Courthouse steps. As he surrendered, "police rushed in from all directions," handcuffed him and shoved him into a police car.[72] Years of prison, torture and finally a presidential clemency – after a worldwide campaign – awaited Winston.

* * *

Elizabeth Gurley Flynn, the 'Rebel Girl,' wrote to Winston in early 1962 while he was recovering in the Soviet Union. "I hope you are in good health and are enjoying your experiences in the land of Socialism. Soak up all you can, it will be of great help when you finally return."

Flynn's playfulness masked caution, as the assault on domestic reds was far from over. "But don't be in any hurry. Let us see what develops here first,"[73] she added, eluding to the renewed assault on civil liberties and the recent indictments against Winston's friends Gus Hall and Benjamin Davis, Jr.

Flynn's frequent letters kept Winston abreast of the party's successful college and university speaking tours. "Lots of news," she wrote in one letter, "Ben [Davis, Jr.] and Gus are busy speaking at colleges."[74] Another relayed that Hall's speech at the "football stadium in Eugene, Oregon," where 12,000 students attended, would soon be printed as a pamphlet. "Gus spoke at City College and Hunter. Ben is going this weekend to Minneapolis and Chicago. They are really going places,"[75] she added. Reds continued to fill university and college stadiums with thousands of youth and students eager to hear what Communists had to say. "Gus had several fine college dates...Virginia, Brandeis and Yale. [Herbert] Aptheker went to Howard. Ben had a splendid trip to the Coast. Hy [Lumer] is leaving shortly for the mid-west and coast."[76] Jessica Smith, editor of *New World Review,* also shared with Winston the excitement surrounding the college speaking engagements. "The reports are that Gus had a most remarkable experience on the coast. After his meetings first being banned, students, faculty and city officials insisted that they be held, and there were big crowds everywhere."[77] Communists found receptive student audiences around the country willing to buck campus faculty, administration and conservative community leaders in defense of the Bill of Rights. Ever the realist, though, Flynn also reflected on the continuing anti-Soviet sentiment among many liberals. They are "so anxious" to distance themselves from Soviet socialism, she wrote, "that they espouse the unrealistic and dogmatic views of Soviet critics [and] feel super revolutionary that way...and quite safe too from the McCarran Act,"[78] she concluded, while her friends Hall and Davis faced the inquisitors.

Writing to Winston of the historic 1963 March on Washington for Jobs and Freedom, Flynn could hardly contain her excitement. She noted, it "was a day to go down in history."[79] Other comrades shared their elation with Winston, too. Clara Colon, secretary of the Defense Committee, said, the March was the "height of inspiration."[80] Phil Bart, then the party's organizational secretary, echoed Flynn and Colon. "[T]his development [the Freedom March] is revolutionary in character and the movement reflects it," he wrote, as the "movement – now national in character – is no longer Southern alone. It has reached into every area of our country." For Bart, "this development requires a thorough revitalization of our organization," something Winston also called for in the coming decades. "We must again move in fully into the struggles of the Negro peoples [sic] movement. It requires some fundamental changes," Bart continued. The "hangovers of the recent past," which have admittedly "taken their toll," have handicapped the party's ability to change and adapt to the "new conditions," he added. However, "If any single group in American life is playing the part to advance our country to a higher stage of democratic development – it is precisely this movement,"[81] a movement led by African Americans and their white allies. "Events are moving rapidly," Bart continued. "This is, of course, true on an international scale as well."[82] Winston was acutely aware of this fact as socialism continued its ascent and as national liberation movements broke free of colonial subjugation.

"Gus made a remarkable report," James E. Jackson wrote to Winston regarding a recently concluded leadership meet. It "evokes expressions of determination... [to] really tackling the problem of outfitting our vehicle with well formed and controlled organizational wheels, in order that the power in the good motor of our policies will roll our vehicle forward to the front ranks." Jackson said the party meeting concluded "on a high note of unity and a new sense of dedication." He added, that "neglected aspects of the system of [party] organization" would soon get renewed attention "so that we can get more milage [sic] out of our sound mass politics."[83] Considering the party's then growing acceptance on university and college campuses, this wasn't an unrealistic goal. Some Communists shared a less optimistic assessment of the political climate in their correspondence with Winston. Claude Lightfoot wrote, "The black muslims [sic] continue to make headway and [it] is becoming very dangerous. They seem to have money to burn." Lightfoot mirthlessly added, "I sometimes wonder if they aren't financed by the Texas oil Billionaires."[84] Flynn echoed Lightfoot's concern writing, "The only divisive elements are the muslims [sic]." They "oppose desegregation, are for a complete separation of the races and" they apparently "'hate the whites,'" she concluded. Fortunately, "they are pretty well repudiated by all the responsible Negro forces."[85] Victor Grossman, a U.S. Army soldier who defected to the Soviet Union in 1952, also wrote Winston. Grossman, now in East Germany, asked Winston to vouch for him as the Berlin correspondent for *The Worker*.[86]

The immediate issue of concern for Winston was his desire to visit Africa and get a first-hand account of the national liberation movements there, though such a trip could risk placing his U.S. passport in jeopardy. Writing to Winston in April 1963, his attorney John Abt asked if he had "given full consideration to the possible legal consequences of such a trip." Abt noted that travel outside of the Soviet Union or Eastern Europe, would, "of course, require you to use your passport and will therefore violate the provision of the McCarran Act which makes it a criminal offense for a Communist to use a passport." Abt continued, "As you know, about a year ago, the State Department revoked the passport of Elizabeth Flynn, Jim Jackson, Arnold Johnson, Bill Albertson and Herb Aptheker." According to Abt, Winston wasn't included in this list due to "fear of the public reaction since it was known that you had gone to the Soviet Union for medical treatment" and since the "revocation would have been ineffective...since none of them [the socialist countries] would have recognized it or deported you for lack of a passport. Once you travel elsewhere, an entirely different situation will arise," as it would no longer be for medical purposes, "and you will no longer have the good offices of a socialist government to rely on." Sanctuary was just one of the multiplicity of ways the Soviet Union and other socialist states aided revolutionary movements the world over. Abt was particularly concerned about "travel to Africa," as the State Department "for obvious reasons" would "want to stop you." Also "obvious" was the State Department's acknowledgement of the still potent international Red-Black alliance Communists had spent decades building. Abt warned, "If the State Department acts to revoke your passport on your arrival in Africa (or perhaps en [sic] route)," what African country would "receive you or allow you to remain there without a passport." This was an intriguing question. Black liberation in Africa backed by ascendant world socialism helped propel some, like Kwame Nkrumah, to power; the socialist first president of an independent Ghana had recently welcomed U.S. Communist W.E.B. Du Bois (and later Alphaeus Hunton). Abt continued, "if your passport is revoked...you might not be allowed by that country to return to the Soviet Union." Likely Winston would be returned to New York "at a time and in a manner that is not of your choosing." Complicating matters for Winston was the ongoing Flynn-Aptheker passport case. "Your appearance in Africa" coupled with the "publicity that is sure to attend it" would undoubtedly be "used in Congress and in the court room"[87] and potentially create an excuse to prejudice the outcome.

Winston was understandably reluctant to return to the U.S. while Red Scare prevailed. He called the McCarran Act "a very savage attack by reaction...a Hitlerite dictum in every way...a barbaric law" designed to stifle the "will of [the] American people for peace and democratic rights."[88] Abt warned Winston in October 1963, "once you [come] back here, your return to Moscow would not be possible so long as the passport provision of the McCarran Act remains in effect." Winston had to remain in the Soviet Union or Eastern Europe, or risk having his passport confiscated. "If your passport has not expired, it will be picked up upon your arrival. And the State Department has no discretion under the law but to deny you a renewal." Aside from its other harmful effects upon democracy, the McCarran Act also made "it a crime for any government official to issue a passport to any person he has reason to believe is a member of the Communist Party," which clearly included Winston. While Abt was optimistic that the Aptheker-Flynn case would eventually be ruled in their favor, he didn't expect a decision before the spring of 1964.[89] Meanwhile, Winston's comrade James E. Jackson was depressed because he could not then travel to the Soviet Union to visit his friend and mentor. "I hope against hope that we will win the right to travel again soon," he wrote his comrade, "so that I could spend a few days basking in the Black Sea sunny beaches with you before your return." Like Winston, and thousands of other revolutionaries, Jackson concluded, "Boy, I could really use a couple of weeks of socialist hospitality right now."[90]

Writing from the Soviet Union, Winston kept Abt informed of his travel plans and asked him to attempt to postpone his deposition until early 1964 after the Aptheker-Flynn decision. "I do hope the callous and cold-blooded policy which is responsible for my blindness will not manifest itself [again] at this stage of the treatment," Winston wrote. However, "It is clear that the humanism needed in such a case...does not rest with us. But life presents us with such challenges," he added whimsically and apparently in good spirits. "I look forward to doing my share in the very near future to make whatever contribution I can for the forward march of my people, my class and my nation,"[91] he added, a nation that had been complicit in taking his sight. Writing to Jackson, Winston continued to be optimistic. We "are on the threshold of a great democratic upsurge and the battle for social advancement along the entire front. What a joy it is to be an active participant in such a struggle,"[92] he concluded. Winston's optimism again shined through. He also emphasized that the "lesson from the struggles of the Negro people has real meaning in terms of helping to throw light on important international questions,"[93] questions he would soon reflect on in published form.

* * *

A few months later, Winston was back in the United States. However, even his return was racked with controversy. His new booklet, *New Colonialism: U.S. Style*, printed abroad as *The Challenge of U.S. Neo-Colonialism*, was barred by U.S. Customs. The pamphlet, a stinging critique of U.S. imperialism, situated Winston as a foremost working class intellectual of international Black liberation foreshadowing his future contributions. Winston continued to have considerable influence in the movements for Black liberation well into the 1970s and early 1980s.

New Colonialism outlined the emerging dynamics of U.S. imperialism alongside then ascendant socialism. Winston understood that capitalism and imperialism worked hand-in-glove, and though they could act with "open, direct coercion, domination and conquest," they could also employ "concealed and more cunning forms of exploitation." These new forms, wrote Winston, were "introduced because of the powerful sweep of the national liberation movements and the aid given them by the socialist countries," primarily the Soviet Union – another illustration of capitalism's retreat. Jim Crow and colonialism both had to contend with "New World Realities," namely the emergence of a Red-Black alliance and an ascendant international socialist challenge to capitalist hegemony. A "distinction must be drawn between the appetite of U.S. imperialism and the practical possibilities for satisfying it," Winston wrote. The modern empire was "doomed to remain a pipe-dream" due to "changes in the world balance of forces in favor of socialism, democracy and peace." Black liberation, backed by world socialism, had become a potent force.

Though socialism and Black liberation were both in ascendency, Winston wasn't naïve. He urged a realistic assessment. "The goal of world domination has not been renounced," he added, "for the striving towards this goal is inherent in imperialism. But it has been pushed somewhat into the background." Keeping Asia, Africa and Latin America safely within the orbit of world capitalism became the ruling class' immediate goal. Through "aid, trade, recommendations for agrarian reform...and the creation of conditions favoring" capitalism generally, the ruling class hoped to win over hearts and minds and thereby isolate socialism, national liberation and the democratic upsurge. While the former colonial empires sought "*direct* political rule...neocolonialism aims primarily to direct the development of these countries," thereby employing "an optimal strategy aimed at consolidating and possibly expanding the sphere of capitalism." Winston likened this form of imperialism to an "invisible colonial empire" [*italic* in original][94] albeit, an empire then in decline, as Blacks and reds held considerable influence domestically and internationally and were in the process of reshaping the political balance of power with the aid of ascendant socialism.[95]

Winston expanded on this issue in a letter to James Jackson. He wrote, U.S. imperialism had to take the upsurge in national liberation movements and the corresponding shift in the world balance of power "into account. It had to make concessions on the home front as a condition for the pursuance of its neo-colonialist policies." He argued, "it is a class necessity which compels U.S. imperialism to act this way." It is attempting to "cloak its aims," "to conceal its neo-colonialist role...just as it is attempting to cloak its real role within this country" by making overtures toward Black civil rights, while hounding African American's most consistent allies, Communists. Winston's solution to this conundrum was simple: Carry "the struggle for black and white solidarity to new heights."[96] In short, Communists should keep doing what they've been doing since the 1930s, grow the domestic movement for African American equality and civil rights, e.g. the long civil rights revolution.[97]

Winston's comrades were already working in this direction. Ishmael Flory and William L. Patterson, for example, collaborated with John Henry Clarke, a prominent historian, Pan-Africanist and *Freedomways* associate editor; Carlton Goodlett, a leader in the World Peace Council and prominent West Coast publisher; Dick Gregory, comedian and peace activist; Lincoln Lynch, the associate director of the Committee On Racial Equality; and C.T. Vivian, a leader in the Southern Christian Leadership Council and confidant of Dr. King. They collectively sponsored the call for a Conference For Solidarity With African Freedom. In the call it was noted, "This is the age of Africa's emergence from the yoke of imperialist bondage," as "liberation struggles have weakened colonialism" thereby enabling some "African peoples" to "secure national independence." According to the call, and by extension, large segments of the civil rights and Black liberation movements, the "imperialist powers, with their vast business and banking operations and their military basis [sic] located inside newly independent countries, have never reconciled themselves to their losses and continuously strive to turn the clock of history back." Though colonialism was "mortally wounded, [it] is not dead," they added. "Like a vampire, it feeds on the blood of millions of Africans," people striving for equality and independence often with the aid of Communists, domestically and internationally. Conference themes included: *Africa's New States and Statemen, African Roots of our Heritage of Culture and History, On Foreign Trade and Freedom, Lessons of African and Afro-American Freedom Struggles,* among other topics.[98]

Some within the party, however, were nonplussed. A group calling itself the Ad Hoc Committee For A Scientific Socialist Line based in Chicago, argued in November

1963, "If the leadership of our Party persists in its refusal to get the Party moving into the forefront of the struggle, history will leave us in its dust." The Committee condescendingly wrote in its *Bulletin*, "Negro masses are floundering in a sea of misleadership [sic]." Rhetorically they asked, when the "Negro has the militancy, the will, the courage – where do we find the Party?" To them, the party's "leadership remains aloof...They call for a policy of moderation, of gradualism, of tokenism – a policy of passive resistance."[99] Their sentiments had little bearing on reality.

The fight against colonialism and imperialism, and for Black liberation was a delicate issue both within the U.S. and internationally. Some white student and Black Power organizations – often inspired by Maoist guerrilla movements internationally – like the Ad Hoc Committee, leaned toward left-adventurism domestically. Winston took this tactic to task in a February 1968 *Political Affairs* article titled, "Unity and Militancy For Freedom and Equality."

Winston's article acknowledged that "we have much to learn from the new courageous leaders who widened and deepened the freedom path," but he also urged his readers to "reject the organizing of armed uprisings in the black communities today." Ironically, this was the pretext given for Winston and his comrades indictments and jail sentences roughly 20 years earlier, though neither he nor his comrades had ever advocated for the use of force and violence. Winston bluntly condemned "conspiratorial, terroristic actions." They "are adventurous, provocative and politically irresponsible, inviting reprisals against the black community. They should, therefore, be rejected." Directly challenging some of the more charismatic Black leaders of the era wasn't beyond Winston either. He knew from experience the depravity of capitalist barbarity and urged caution. Additionally, on a political level, he knew – again, from experience – how mass movements were built. He chided gently, telling young activists, "The door should be wide open to any new and effective forms of struggle forged in the fires of the freedom fight." He added, "tactical weapons of the freedom struggle" should be put to the test. Moreover, movement leaders should ask basic questions as plans are being discussed and decided upon: "[W]ill they advance or set back the struggle? Will they unite or divide the mass of the black people? Will they aid in winning allies or isolating us?" To Winston, militancy "has to meet the test...the militancy of individuals lies in the ability to inspire *mass* militancy. It can never be a substitute for it" [*italic* in original]. "Unity of the black communities can truly spell black power," he added, not the actions of isolated adventurists. He urged young activists to commemorate "our black heroes," like W.E.B. DuBois, Paul Robeson and Benjamin Davis, Jr. Ever the optimist, Winston concluded, "conditions exist for opening wider the door of democracy" through Black-white unity. "To achieve such unity in struggle, it is incumbent upon white progressives and revolutionaries to conduct a consistent and courageous battle against racism,"[100] partly by steering clear of adventurism and terrorist tactics.

Winston wasn't alone among Communists in this opinion. Claude Lightfoot, the party's Negro Commission chair, told reporters in spring 1966, Communists support "self-defense for Negroes," but "we are not advocates of violence." However, it should be added, Communists were not strangers to self-defense either; their leadership among sharecroppers in Alabama, for example, is worth noting. Lightfoot continued, "the argument that we [African Americans] could win the struggle [for equality] without communists had failed."[101] Others have documented this fact regarding the demise of the Communist-led Civil Rights Congress and Council on African Affairs.[102] Regarding the question of self-defense, Lightfoot elaborated. African Americans had a right to "use violence to achieve change" when "channels for democratic change are closed to them." It was even argued that African Americans should "police their own communities." Due to the continued assault on

Black lives today, this call has again gained resonance. To Lightfoot and other Communists, the main question confronting the nation, African American equality and Black liberation, wasn't "violence in the Negro community but the increasing violence being directed at it." A party statement issued in fall 1967 added nuance. "We believe that conspiratorial, terrorist actions which are not based upon a program aimed at improving the conditions of life for the masses and which do not receive the support of the masses are reckless, adventurous, provocative and politically irresponsible." But, "armed self-defense, if necessary," was a legitimate tactic. For, "black people not only have the right but the responsibility to defend their persons, their homes and their community."[103] Lightfoot concluded, the struggle for African American equality and Black liberation must go beyond "the norms of bourgeois legality."[104] As Communists saw it, the political superstructure, the police and the courts, continued to fail Black Americans despite some modest gains.

In spring 1970, with recent Weathermen bombings likely in mind, Gil Green echoed Winston and Lightfoot's remarks in pamphlet titled *Terrorism – Is It Revolutionary*. In that document, Green wrote, terrorism "is a dangerous manifestation...capable of great harm to the whole Movement. It disorients honest, self-sacrificing young fighters. It creates a disruptive nihilistic element inside the Movement. Above all, it feeds its opposite: it gives the liberals and reformers a freer hand within the mass movement and gives the ruling class the public legitimacy it seeks for a policy of increasing repression."[105] Winston, Green and the entire Communist Party fought for broad-based unity and shunned terrorist tactics.

* * *

While Winston made many ideological contributions, especially after his return from the Soviet Union, his organizational leadership was equally impressive. Much of this work centered on the confluence between African American equality, Black liberation in Africa, and socialism. At the founding conference of the National Anti-Imperialist Movement in Solidarity with African Liberation in October 1973, Winston – who was considered "the moving force"[106] behind the organization – demonstrated both his ideological and organizational prowess. He told the conference, "Black folk in the USA, together with the courageous and valiant fighters of liberation movements in Africa...symbolize to me the road ahead, the road to complete destruction of imperialism in general, and the defeat of U.S. imperialism in particular." Though "we fight on two different fronts," he emphasized, we also fight "against a common enemy...U.S. monopoly, U.S. imperialism," a system then in retreat. For Winston, "The African Liberation movement has given to us...the extended hand – will we accept that hand," he asked? Like Alphaeus Hunton and the CAA before him, Winston urged the conference attendees to focus their energies against apartheid South Africa. He argued that a "massive anti-imperialist movement to compel the unseating" of South Africa from the United Nations was particularly important. "These fascist, racist beasts have no place among civilized nations," he added. To him, this was the "test of internationalism...how we Black folk in the United States, together with our allies, white, Black, Yellow, Brown, Red, can unite our voices in such a way as to develop that kind of attack which will compel American imperialism to reverse its policy." "We cannot do less," he continued, "for in doing it we help not only the people of Africa, but we are [also] helping to advance the fight of Black folk here at home for full equality." Communists could justifiably be proud of their history, particularly the struggle against racism. This was a fight Communists had been leading since at least the 1930s with the defense of the Scottsboro Nine. Winston also attacked the remnants of anticommunism, saying, "if you are going to defeat the man, you cannot play the man's game and the man's game is Anti-Communism."[107]

Within six months, NAIMSAL was participating in mass rallies for Black liberation and assumed the mantel left by the CAA when it "launched a national campaign to collect signatures...demanding that the Republic of South Africa be expelled from the UN"; the campaign was initiated at the May 1974 African Liberation Day rally attended by 7,500 people in Washington, D.C.[108] NAIMSAL leaders also participated in international conferences, like those called by the Afro-Asian Peoples Solidarity Organization, which coincided with the 15th anniversary of the founding of the Popular Movement for the Liberation of Angola. Delegates from "more than 80 countries, including at least 20 African governments," attended the February 26, 1976 Angolan confab. The U.S. delegates included Tony Monteiro, acting executive secretary of NAIMSAL, who was "spearheading much of the Angola solidarity activity" in the U.S.; Carlton Goodlett, a leading endorser of NAIMSAL's petition campaign to expel South Africa from the UN; and Roscoe Proctor, chairman of the CPUSA's Black Liberation Commission. NAIMSAL "called on trade unions, churches and other U.S. groups, as well as students, workers and the unemployed, Black and white, to demand U.S. recognition of the PRA [People's Republic of Angola] and [to] condemn U.S. government support for the pro-imperialist factions," trying to undermine the new socialist government through the "financing, training and arming [of] mercenaries from several countries."[109] Monteiro would spend three weeks "on the Angolan battlefront" as a guest of the MPLA, which has "waged a tremendous struggle" for national liberation. "I personally saw that the MPLA has tremendous support all over the Angolan countryside," Monteiro told the *Daily World*. South African mercenaries "invaded Angola [with] a go-ahead from the Pentagon," he added, while the MPLA received Soviet and Cuban support, people who "worked as engineers to repair dynamited bridges, clear mined roads, etc." Monteiro said the Angolans were working to "consolidate, build up, and disentangle itself from the web of imperialist investments while developing its economy." By mid-March Monteiro was speaking to domestic audiences across the country about his trip and celebrating the delivery of 100,000 signatures to the UN calling for the expulsion of South Africa.[110] By late June, Monteiro, now considered the "youthful head of the movement that spearheaded the campaign to expel South Africa," was addressing the UN's Special Commission on Apartheid. He said, the "tide of liberation engulfs the entire apartheid regime," a tide given substantial support by ascendant socialism. Conversely, Henry Kissinger's hands were "soaked with the blood of the African people," Monteiro added, as "his actions implicated the U.S. government as direct participants in the crime of apartheid." Like Alphaeus Hunton and the CAA, Monteiro brought domestic attention to the fight for Black liberation in South Africa and U.S. imperialism's support for the apartheid regime.[111] NAIMSAL and Monteiro didn't just support Black liberation abroad, though. They protested the granting of visas to racists, like Ian Smith, "head of the illegal Rhodesian regime." "By inviting Ian Smith to be a guest of the White House," a NAIMSAL spokesperson said, "President Carter is saying that Blacks in southern Africa have no human rights that the white racist regime must respect." And that "transnational corporation profits come before the human rights of the African people." NAIMSAL called on Carter to "recognize that the struggle for liberation in Zimbabwe [Rhodesia] is essentially a fight by the majority of the people to decide their own future." NAIMSAL also charged Carter with "ignoring the plight of racially oppressed youth who are unemployed in his own country."[112] Further, U.S. hypocrisy was on full display when NAIMSAL invited Duma Nokwe, deputy secretary of the African National Congress, to New York in June 1976. NAIMSAL sought to enable "U.S. citizens [to] get the facts on the Soweto massacre and the continued wave of arrests and murder of Black South Africans." That the visa was initially denied meant that "the same government that allows mercenary recruitment to take place within our shores...[also] refuses to let the representatives of the struggling Black majority...tell [us] about the real situation in South Africa."[113] This was a tacit acknowledgement of the continuing potency of an international Red-Black alliance.

Local NAIMSAL chapters were just as dynamic in their demand for Black liberation. In Philadelphia, for example, NAIMSAL protested against South Africa's participation in the International Lawn Tennis Association's Federation Cup tournament. That the tournament was "backed by $130,000 from Colgate Palmolive Co.," which has "large investments in South Africa" served to illustrate the corporate interests in maintaining the status quo in the land of apartheid. Additionally, the inclusion of South Africa "is in clear violation of the international sports boycott," a boycott "backed by the UN." Adding insult to injury, the apartheid regime was participating in the tournament here while its "fascists are increasing their genocidal assault against freedom fighters there," with the aid of the U.S. Conversely, tennis players from the Soviet Union, Czechoslovakia, and Romania had withdrawn from the tournament in protest.[114] Additionally, the Rhode Island NAIMSAL chapter "initiated" and "is leading the struggle...against the sale of the South African Kruggerrand." A "monopoly of the sale of the gold piece symbolizing racism and apartheid" was then held by the Rhode Island Hospital Trust Bank, which "control[s] a large portion of the market for importing gold." NAIMSAL leaders "met with the bank's vice-president for international banking" and spoke at Brown University, which then held "$23 million in investments" related to South Africa. They demanded divestment from the racist regime.[115] That December, the Chicago NAIMSAL chapter organized for Dr. Callistus Ndlovu, a member of the Revolutionary Council of the Zimbabwe African Peoples Union (ZAPU-Patriotic Front) and chief UN representative, to speak at its fourth anniversary dinner, along with Congresswoman Cardiss Collins.[116] They were continuing to build a cross Atlantic Red-Black alliance. Three months later, the Rhode Island chapter invited ANC leader Themba Vilakazi to speak. He said, "mass pressure" has "slowed the buying of South African gold by U.S. banks, which was a victory against apartheid."[117] By late March 1979, the Philadelphia chapter hosted Ndlovu at a gathering of 150 people. They commemorated the 19th Anniversary of the Sharpeville Massacre in South Africa on March 21, 1960 where 69 people were killed, and hundreds were wounded; "police opened fire on unarmed people peacefully demonstrating against the hated racist pass system." "There can be no fair and democratic elections in an unfair and undemocratic system," Ndlovu emphasized. Earlier that week NAIMSAL sponsored a rally attended by 200 people at the First Pennsylvania Bank. They wanted "to expose the bank's policy of investing $50 million in South Africa while disinvesting its funds from housing, jobs, public schools and supermarkets in Philadelphia."[118] Four months later, NAIMSAL organized a speaking tour for Eric Mtshali, of the South African Congress of Trade Unions. Mtshali praised NAIMSAL for its work and told reporters, "a strong and powerful NAIMSAL is not only good for the struggle in the U.S. but will also be a blessing for the struggle in South Africa...we support NAIMSAL and NAIMSAL supports us."[119] The bonds of struggle shared by Africans fighting for Black liberation and African Americans fighting for equality were again highlighted. That fall the Chicago chapter hosted Mtshana Ncube, of the Zimbabwe Patriotic Front. She said, "the enemies of the Zimbabwe struggle for self-determination are the same enemies of Afro-Americans fighting for human rights." "We must remember that without freedom in Africa, there can be no freedom for Blacks in any country," she added. State

Senator and soon to be Chicago Mayor Harold Washington also addressed the banquet.[120] Washington's right-hand man among Latino voters in his mayoral bid was the Communist Rudy Lozano,[121] an indication of the political bonds Communists were building decades after their supposed demise. Like the CAA before it, NAIMSAL chapters also helped organize food, diaper and cloth drives.[122]

That Communists Angela Davis, Franklin Alexander, Tony Monteiro and others, led NAIMSAL served to illustrate Winston's role in mentoring young Communists for leadership in mass organizations. Additionally, with Winston's guidance NAIMSAL continued the internationalist traditions of the party-led CAA. In part, it was his relationships to fraternal Communist Parties and Black liberation movements in Africa that shaped the domestic anti-imperialist movement against apartheid in South Africa – a role played Paul Robeson, W.E.B. DuBois and Alphaeus Hunton two decades earlier. According to CPUSA national co-chair, Joe Sims, "the party took the initiative to find ways to do mass work. After McCarthyism, we were driven out of all sorts of groups. So, we had to find ways to carry on our activity. We had to create political space to do the work that was needed." NAIMSAL and the NAARPR were born out of this concept. "We knew that the SACP and ANC were calling for sanctions," Sims recalled. "NAIMSAL provided the opportunity to place that issue front and center. It laid the basis for the broader anti-apartheid movement to grow." To Sims, NAIMSAL and other party-led formations, "were left-center formations that gave us the ability to influence anticommunism, to question our defacto illegality, to do mass work, to build relationships."[123]

In spring 1978, NAIMSAL brought John Gaetsewe, the general secretary of the South African Congress of Trade Unions, to the U.S. He told a New York audience of 700, "The purpose of my coming to this country is to appeal to the American people, the American workers to support us in our struggle for the liberation of our mother land." Gaetsewe connected the struggle against apartheid to "other parts of the world." He told the audience, "your support is [part of] an international action of solidarity against oppression all over the world." It was an international struggle then backed by ascendant socialism. There can "be no compromise" with apartheid Gaetsewe added. "Workers struggling in South Africa face not only the brutality of the South African fascists, not only the genocide that is apartheid, but the combined power of international capitalism, of imperialism." Other speakers included, John Makatini, ANC representative to the UN; Leslie Harriman, Nigeria's UN ambassador; Zehdi Labib, chairman of the UN's special committee against apartheid; Jarvis Tyner, chair of the New York State Communist Party; Charlene Mitchell, executive secretary of the National Alliance Against Racist and Political Repression; and Monteiro. Harriman noted, "The gold in Fort Knox, the uranium in the atomic bombs, and the diamonds that help high society glitter all come from South Africa as the product of slave labor." Tyner "articulated the consensus" of the groups when he added, "No sports, no loans, no business transactions, no nothing with apartheid until it crumbles." NAIMSAL also organized a speaking tour for Gaetsewe, which attracted crowds at union halls, churches and community centers across the country.[124]

Roughly three months later, NAIMSAL hosted a conference at New York's Great Hall at Cooper Union with representatives from the Soviet Union, Vietnam, and Cuba who "spoke out on why they support the liberation movements" in South Africa. The presentation titled *Salute to the Freedom Fighters of Southern Africa* and also included speakers from Namibia, Zimbabwe, and South Africa (SWAPO, ZAPU and the ANC, respectively) and marked the first time a panel discussion of this type was held in the U.S.[125] Winston was proud of the Communists he had mentored and the movement he helped birth.

* * *

Winston's remarks at the party's 21st National Convention in spring 1975 focused on a theme he would emphasize for the remainder of his life. According to the aging revolutionary, the party still had "a unique role to play. It alone sees the need for a broad mass movement of the people and the possibilities for building such a movement. It alone understands the decisive role of the working class." Unfortunately, this class was now on the defensive. Union density was beginning a decades long decline into the single digits, a partial result of the purging of Communists in the late 1940s and early 1950s. For Winston, though, the immediate struggle was "not an end in itself." Rather, it was a "means by which to improve the lot of masses today and lead to the kind of popular movement that can curb monopoly power, nationalize the great industries, and move [us] towards a socialist reorganization of society." He said, "you can't get to socialism except on the road of immediate struggle...[the] compass which guides us make mandatory the active and creative leadership to the immediate and future interest of our class."[126] To the 6,000 trade union, community, and student leaders attending the convention's culminating event – a "gigantic Bicentennial Rally,"[127] highlighting the party's commitment to peace, jobs, democracy and socialism – Winston wasn't far from right. Communists had to confront immediate and long-term struggles on the road to socialism. That thousands of movement leaders still had confidence in the CPUSA and its strategic outlook – after decades of repression – was evident. That the CPUSA was considerably smaller than its late 1930s to mid-1940s peak mattered little to the beleaguered organization. The trajectory was one of growth. A resurgence similar to the early 1960s influx was a distinct possibility. Communists were still riding high from the successes of the campaign to free Angela Davis and the birth of NAIMSAL and the NAARPR. "For a short time – the period of Comrade Angela Davis' arrest, trial and aftermath – there was another growth spurt of young people," Michael Myerson later recalled, though he added, it "soon tapered off."[128] Party organizational secretary Arnold Brecchetti went so far as to title his post-convention report *Toward a Mass CP* and note that the 21st National Convention was "some 40 per cent [sic] larger" than the prior held in 1972, "reflecting the growth in the Party in the intervening years."[129] The internal conclusion was unanimous: Communists were poised to make a comeback.

Three years later, however, Winston would chastise himself and his comrades. The optimism on display at the 1975 convention failed to translate into sustained growth. Our Party's "structure...has become too top heavy." He told his comrades, "basic sections of the Party are crying out for cadre...Total reconstruction of our style of work brings before us the question of re-examining the entire process of decision making. Proper organization," he added, "means proper deployment of cadre" away from the center and into the Districts, primarily into industry. "It is imperative to move with speed," he urged, while clarifying what is meant by party building. To Winston, "Party Building is not simply recruiting into the Party. That is only one aspect of Party building – and a useless aspect unless one understands...[that] it is not Party building if it severs the Party center from the mass movements," a tendency to turn inward and focus on ideological questions alone. He argued, "A small Party with a correct line can overnight become numerically strong. Everything depends on how we organize, organize on the basis of an industrial concentration policy. If there isn't a struggle for such a policy, growth will be slow, the Party will remain small. This is sectarianism," he said pointedly, and perhaps surprisingly to some. "We must see to it that at the core of our daily activity there is the constant development of living ties with mass movements. This is the criterion of Communist work."[130] The blind revolutionary still had a radical vision.

This wasn't the only time Winston was critical of the party's direction. In a memo to Gus Hall and James E. Jackson from mid-December 1978, Winston "urge[d] that steps be taken, and especially with our leading cadre, to involve them in [party] schools 'of a special kind,'" schools geared toward achieving "major objectives by the time of the Convention," i.e., schools geared towards tangible, demonstrative goals; results reflective of the types of reports Winston used to give as organizational secretary roughly 30 years earlier. Somewhat sarcastically, Winston added, "I believe that the projected plan of the Education Dept. is a beautiful plan on paper," while the "implementation" would be "an achievement of great significance." However, to accomplish such tasks "means all hands must be on deck" with a "political mobilization different, in concept and practice, from the routine and the administrative only." To Winston, the "potential for growth" was "unprecedented." He said, "we must do everything to guarantee success." He stressed the "necessity of retooling all our work. This especially applies to style of work." The former organizational secretary then lamented the low level of party organization. "In the whole state of New York there is but one shop club...this is true of other districts as well," he added. To resolve the "fundamental question" of why required the "collective effort of everyone. *This is a school*" [*italic* in original], Winston told his comrades. What better way to train emerging leaders than to have them address the low level of party organization on the ground, asked Winston? In conclusion, to Winston, cadre problems need to be solved "and most of them quickly,"[131] a challenge reds would continue to grapple with.

Winston further argued for a different approach to party membership; to open up and welcome outsiders, to become a mass organization. He told comrades, "dues payments [should] become the barometer of a member's understanding of the Party. There must be an approach in which finances are not collected primarily from Party members, but based on mass struggle, mass participation, mass planning." This approach harkened back to the party's Popular Front organizing in the 1930s and 1940s, and which helped to build mass organizations like the Unemployed Councils, the NNC, and the CIO. Later popular front efforts included the CRC and the CAA, and most recently, the NAARPR and NAIMSAL. Winston believed that the thousands of activists attracted to these formations exemplified the soundness of this tactic. Winston wanted to bring people into the party who were well intentioned, hard-working activists and organizers, committed to struggle, though not necessarily concerned with the nuances of Marxism-Leninism. Winston would even advocate for a loose organizational model emphasizing outward projection similar to that employed by the National Council of Churches, which "speaks for some 40 million people." "This is the way,"[132] he said. Winston also argued for a robust electoral approach against the right-wing. "In 1968 our Party was on the ballot in two states; in 1976 we were on in nineteen states and the District of Columbia and in 1980 we're fighting to be on the ballot in thirty states,"[133] he said earlier that same year.

It was the wedding of Winston's tactics – a focus on industrial concentration, membership based on mass struggle, and a robust electoral policy often in the industrial heartland – that garnered the most impressive results for the party. For example, in 1980 Rick Nagin, the party's then steel coordinator based out of Cleveland, would receive 42,410 votes as a candidate for U.S. Senate,[134] while Barbara Browne, a Chicago candidate for trustee of the University of Illinois, received 46,956 votes. Throughout Illinois, 92,000 people cast ballots for Communist candidates that year.[135] 8,300 people cast their votes for a Communist in the District of Columbia,[136] not an inconsequential amount for a city council race. In the 1982 elections Communists received 36,000 votes for state treasurer in Minnesota and 28,000 votes for board of education in Michigan,[137] while Communist Kenny Jones was elected to the St. Louis City Board of Aldermen in 1983, representing the 22nd Ward.[138] Jones also helped lead the anti-apartheid divestment movement in the St. Louis Board of Aldermen, while his comrades in the St. Louis Coalition of Black Trade Unionists, known as a Red Chapter, did the same.[139] In fact, Communist candidates ran throughout the 1980s and into the 1990s. Exemplifying this trend was Evelina Alarcon, the party's Southern California chair, who received over 144,000 votes in her bid to become Secretary of State in 1990.[140] Judged by Democratic Party standards, the CPUSA could legitimately claim nearly 162,000 members in Ohio, Illinois, Minnesota and Michigan in the early 1980s – never mind Jones' victory in St. Louis or Alacron's impressive election results less than a decade later. Winston, however, wasn't satisfied.

Winston thought that Communists should be leading mass movements of the unemployed, and that new cadre would likely emerge out of these struggles; Winston himself had been steeled in the party-led Unemployed Councils and NNC. In spring 1983, Winston's prescription for the ailing party began to take organizational form. On the weekend of July 4, party leader Scott Marshall convened the National Congress of the Unemployed in Chicago attended by nearly 500 delegates from 81 cities, including 32 union unemployed committees and 60 independent community organizations, representing tens of thousands of unemployed workers. According to Marshall, "People came to Chicago because their local experiences convinced them that a national crisis requires a national movement." The Congress accomplished a number of overlapping goals. First, it "answered Reagan" and his anti-worker, anti-union policies, while affirming the collective power of the unemployed. Second, it gave participants "a sense of the depth and breadth of this movement – that we are a growing, developing movement of incredible diversity." Congress registration was 30 percent African American; 20 percent Latino; over 25 percent were women; and 60 percent were under forty. Additionally, participants "came from church groups, cooperative societies and food pantries. They came from union committees and coalitions of union and community committees. They came with discount programs, job banks and self-help programs – but they all came ready to build a movement."[141] Party member and chairman of the Wisconsin Steel Save Our Jobs Committee, Frank Lumpkin, keynoted the Congress; the Save Our Jobs Committee would later win multiple lawsuits against Wisconsin Steel totaling $14.5 million in back pay, pensions and benefits.[142] The Congress posthumously elected Rudy Lozano, the Midwest director of organizing for the International Ladies Garment Workers' Union and Communist who had been assassinated in his home in early June, as chairman emeritus; as noted above, Lozano had been Harold Washington's righthand man among Latino voters in his bid to become Chicago's first Black mayor.[143] Marshall, who also led the Chicago-based Jobs Or Income Now!, would be named the Congress' national organizing director. In summary, he told his comrades, the Congress "is the natural inheritor of the proud traditions of struggle left by the Unemployed Councils of the 1930s," and it has the potential to "develop a mighty unemployed component of the antimonopoly coalition."[144] It could challenge both the Reagan Administration and conservative labor leaders slow to address the unemployment crisis. To Winston and his comrades, the CPUSA was once again leading a movement of the unemployed.

Roughly one month before the Chicago congress, Winston reflected on the dangers of an ascending far-right and Reaganism. He told the party's National Committee, Reaganism "is a new effort of reaction at a different stage, to crush Communists and establish the preconditions for smashing the liberties of all." Winston, and his comrades, feared a return to the Red Scare and the concomitant outlawing of Communists, labor leaders and progressives, as well as the prospect of nuclear annihilation. The "central problem," he emphasized, "is to prevent the outbreak of nuclear war. The danger of nuclear war emanates from our shores...No greater task has ever been faced by any people in the capitalist world." Winston also addressed the administration's assault on labor unions, particularly the firing of 11,000 air traffic controllers in PATCO, the Professional Air Traffic Controllers Organization. "PATCO was merely the demonstrative aspect of the process of monopoly reaction's offensive against the labor movement as a whole," he added, foreshadowing the managerial offensive that would decimate the labor movement in the years that followed. "The most immediate problem for us is to deepen and widen the struggle for democracy," he concluded. "The practical struggle must at all times be realistically based."[145]

* * *

Winston kept a grueling organizing and speaking schedule into his twilight years. During an early 1985 trip to Ohio, Winston participated in an hour-long radio talk show, and two TV interviews in Youngstown; he spoke at the Arab Community Center and Youngstown State University; he did a radio show in Cleveland, spoke at a *Daily Worker* forum, and a Black studies class at Akron University.[146] Apparently, audiences were still receptive.

Unfortunately, less than two years later, on December 12, 1986, Winston, now 75 passed away in Moscow. His comrade Gus Hall lauded Winston as a "heroic U.S. figure of the world revolutionary movement." His "confidence in the future was unshakable and his revolutionary enthusiasm was a source of inspiration." Hall recognized Winston as "an internationalist who saw his duty as a U.S. patriot in [an] unsparing struggle to save humanity from the perils of nuclear holocaust."[147] Jarvis Tyner, Winston's longtime friend and comrade, remembered him fondly. "Winnie grew up to become one of the finest Marxist-Leninist thinkers and organizers that the U.S. working class has ever produced." Tyner continued, Winston and his comrades "should have been treated like heroes for their great work...Winston showed no bitterness. He was warm, kind and confident." He would often call sick or ailing comrades and host meals at his East Harlem apartment. He had a "wonderful smile and infectious sense of humor."[148] James E. Jackson, at the January 1987 memorial tribute to Winston, reflected on his relationship to the Mississippi born revolutionary. He noted, "The power of Henry Winston's example will ever be an impulse for action," for African American equality, Black liberation and socialism. "We had a rarely experienced friendship that spanned 51 years of intensely political activity," Jackson added. "He was my buddy as well as my comrade and leader."[149] He was a dignified and confident, humble and patient, mentor to thousands of young revolutionaries, who cut their political teeth guided by his experiences.

Among those young revolutionaries was Angela Davis, herself a political prisoner freed after a massive, global campaign. At a party-sponsored centennial celebration of Winston's birth, on Sunday, February 19, 2012, Davis, though no longer a CPUSA member, told the capacity crowd, "Henry Winston was indeed revered throughout the world. Communists and those who were not deterred by anti-communism had no problems openly declaring their admiration for him." He "was a constant inspiration to me," she added, reminiscing on his support during her imprisonment. Not only was his "love for the struggle...matched by his love for all of the individuals in his life," but he was also a foremost Black intellectual who "imbue[d] an important internationalism into the Black Liberation Movement" and "helped Communist and progressive activists to develop a conceptualization of solidarity...grounded in antiimperialist unity." The "spirit of Henry Winston will always be with us."[150]

Chapter **5**

Judith LeBlanc: Indigenous Marxism, **Changing America** *and United For Peace & Justice*

It was Saturday, January 21, 2017. More than 1.5 million women – and their allies – took to the streets of Washington, D.C. to protest the inauguration of Donald J. Trump, the 45th President of the United States, a man who as a celebrity had bragged about grabbing women "by the p*ssy."[1]

Before the march, prominent women's rights leaders spoke to the assembled "nasty" women, a reference to candidate Trump's comment during a presidential debate to Hillary Clinton,[2] a comment that had now been co-opted as a term of endearment for a growing women's rights movement. While a sizable majority of non-college educated white women (64 percent) voted for Trump on November 8, 2016, an astonishing 95 percent of Black women, 81 percent of non-white and 70 percent of Hispanic women voted for Clinton,[3] thereby associating themselves with a progressive majority sentiment that would cast roughly three million more popular votes for the former Secretary of State; Clinton would lose the presidency due to the outmoded and antidemocratic electoral college. According to the assembled protesters, a misogynist disdainful of women of color had become president on January 20.

It was in this context – the assault on women, especially women of color, and the concomitant threat to democracy – that a sea of activists cast a pink shadow over Trump's inauguration crowd, a fact the new president bitterly denied to the amusement of comedians and late night talk show hosts. The organizers had facilitated in the creation of an intersectional, multi-issue women's rights march – a march focused on democracy, choice, peace and indigenous rights, a march that signaled the beginning of the resistance to Trump's presidency. This partly explains the administration's early insistence on "alternative facts."[4]

As the speakers' list neared its end, Judith LeBlanc, director of the Native Organizers Alliance and a member of the Caddo Nation, calmly walked up to the microphone.

"President Trump, we have heard you are considering privatizing Indian land for oil. You will not steal our land," LeBlanc thundered. "And President Trump, let me break it down for you, this is a Standing Rock moment," which "means our power is rooted in love for humanity. Our strength is drawn from our ancestors. Our medicine is stronger than rubber bullets or water cannons"; both had been used on Native peoples as they peacefully protested the construction of the Dakota Access Pipeline on sacred lands.

"President Trump, the movement we are building is driven by faith, by hope, by love and prayers. We will stop the carnage of Mother Earth. Water is sacred. Water is life. Women are life,"[5] LeBlanc concluded. Her message effectively linked women's rights, environmental sustainability and respect for indigenous communities into one cohesive narrative, a unifying narrative.

Within a month, after Trump had reversed President Obama's earlier order and gave the Army Corps of Engineers permission to begin construction of the Dakota Access Pipeline, LeBlanc told an interviewer, "We knew as soon as President Trump entered office that he signed an executive memorandum on expediting the process... [and that] we have to stand even more with Standing Rock Sioux tribe...The fact remains that the [tribe] has a legal right and a moral responsibility to protect the land, water and air, not only for their tribe but for the 17 million people who live along the Missouri River."

"Standing Rock is everywhere. It is a beautiful thing," LeBlanc added, emphasizing the new level of unity and coordination among the various Native tribes, even those who rely on fossil fuels for revenue. "We have the right to decide for our land, our water and air, and how our people are affected by these greedy corporations who will stop at nothing to maximize their profits."[6] Central to LeBlanc's and the NOA's strategy was a divestment campaign that had succeeded in convincing the city of Seattle to withdraw three billion dollars from Wells Fargo[7] over the pipeline conflict; they hoped to compel more cities to do likewise.

According to LeBlanc, fossil fuel companies have left "generations of disease and death in their wake," which partly explained her desire "to get at the systemic nature of the role fossil fuels play in the economy and in creating the huge threat to the existence of our planet." However, LeBlanc – a movement veteran – had no illusions. She also saw corporate self-interest as a potential wedge tactic capable of stopping the pipeline. "At this point, the pipeline is losing money. It is not a good business investment,"[8] she said, highlighting the divide between different sectors of the energy industry and their deep-pocket investors.

* * *

Standing Rock wasn't the first-time LeBlanc or the Communist Party had advocated and organized for the rights of Native Americans, nor was it the first time the party would speak out against pollution and environmental degradation. At a party conference on Indian liberation in late 1969, it was noted, the "monstrous crimes against the Indian people committed by the capitalist ruling class in the course of nearly five centuries of genocidal onslaught" – a "brutal and barbaric onslaught," it was added – has "from the first 'discovery' of the western hemisphere to the present period of dying imperialism pursued the single aim of extermination, cultural and physical." Communists claimed the ruling class were responsible "for the death of more than seventy five million Native Americans." However, despite the slaughter, the "heroic resistance of the Indian people, with the proud record of never having surrendered to the conqueror and the invader," has now witnessed a "fresh upsurge." It is the "responsibility of the working class and democratic forces in our country and on a world scale to give maximum support to the Indian Liberation struggle," a conference press release noted.

Henry Winston, CPUSA chairman, participated in the conference and called upon his comrades "to help develop a movement such as has never been seen in this country in support of the struggles of the Indian people for liberation, and for partial compensation for the first great crime of the ruling class in this country, Indian genocide." Winston argued for collaboration. He said the fight for Indigenous rights was "part of the general class struggle, and a part of the struggle for liberation of all oppressed peoples." To Winston, "Indian Liberation...can come about only in the struggle to put an end to racism, by the struggle to win our class," especially white workers. "We must win our class to make this struggle," he concluded. Winston also noted the "distortion of Indian history," like that of African American history. He said, both histories are "consciously and deliberately" obscured so as to ensure that "neither white nor black – nor anyone – will get a correct interpretation of history." "No people... including the Indians, get the truth," Winston concluded.[9]

To LeBlanc and her comrades, Native American rights and the struggle to preserve and protect the environment were intrinsically connected. In his 1972 booklet *Ecology: Can we survive under capitalism*, Gus Hall wrote, "Our nation is being poisoned with the ultimate threat of extinction by pollution and destruction of our environment." He said, the "real source of the problem" is the "very nature of the social system under which we are forced to live," namely capitalism.[10]

LeBlanc, already an activist, was living in the Pine Ridge Indian Reservation during the 1973 historic stand-off at Wounded Knee. Part of the "AIM [American Indian Movement] generation,"[11] LeBlanc had gone to Wounded Knee as part of the Legal Defense/Offense Committee; she worked with indicted defendants collecting evidence and affidavits. It was at Wounded Knee where she "got to know folks connected to the party who helped me understand the nature of systemic racism." "That experience [Wounded Knee] more than anything else, convinced me to join the Communist Party," she recalled in 1998 during the 25th anniversary of the stand-off. To LeBlanc, Native Americans are a "part of a growing movement... [that is] taking aim at the problems of the system – at the problems of the capitalist system. It is a new day," she added, "and the struggle of my people is part of the larger struggle against the right-wing offensive."[12]

LeBlanc joined the Young Workers Liberation League in 1973 and that July she travelled to the German Democratic Republic as part of an American Indian contingent within the U.S. delegation to the 10th World Festival of Youth and Students. By 1974, she was officially a member of the Communist Party, USA.[13]

Like her comrade Lonnie Nelson – who participated in the 1972 takeover of the Bureau of Indian Affairs building in Washington, D.C., as well as the Wounded Knee stand-off[14] – LeBlanc became an outspoken advocate for Indian liberation. She reminisced: "the lives of Indian people are inextricably linked to the political direction of the country. Yes, separate problems reflect segregation and racist discrimination against Indian people and yet these problems are so connected with the political and economic conditions for the working class in every community, for every race or nationality." To LeBlanc, Pine Ridge "is a 'showcase' of what centuries of capitalism has done to a people; it contains the poorest county in the country. [It] has become, in some ways, a prison of poverty and racism."[15] A once thriving people and culture were nearly decimated. In LeBlanc's critique capitalism, colonialism and genocide were tightly intertwined. To her Marxism had the potential to unify divergent sectors of the working class, while emphasizing the unique role Native Americans could play in movements for environmental sustainability and economic justice.

LeBlanc sees "a lot of parallels between [the early 1970s] and today": "inaction of elected officials, denial of equal rights, and the destruction of Mother Earth." "Our historic ties to Mother Earth give Indians of all tribes on all continents a duty to lead and build strategic alliances before our planet is destroyed."[16] LeBlanc connected her 1970s era activism and organizing to the contemporary concept of intersectionality. The CPUSA's slogan would also eventually evolve from "People Before Profits" to "People and Nature Before Profits."

Like her comrades, LeBlanc was harassed for her political activism. For example, in 1975 while hosting a National Alliance Against Racist and Political Repression fundraiser in Springfield, Massachusetts, LeBlanc and David Cohen, a YWLL activist and union leader, were arrested for "disturbing the peace." Two officers entered the dinner party premises "without a warrant." They were told to leave and returned later with three additional officers. Upon their return they arrested LeBlanc and Cohen, who were acquitted of all charges.[17] According to LeBlanc, intimidation was the goal. That she helped establish and led a Citizens Police Review Board "to investigate the murder of Black and Puerto Rican youth by the Springfield Police Department" provided the spurious justification for the harassment. LeBlanc, a trained paralegal and an associate commissioner on the Massachusetts Governor's Commission on the Status of Women,[18] would not be silenced though.

Coupled with her Native rights activism and advocacy were electoral politics. In 1976, LeBlanc ran for the Massachusetts State Senate on the CPUSA ticket. During the campaign, she chastised both Republicans and Democrats who "have long viewed Native American Indian people's votes, and therefore their needs, as insignificant." LeBlanc also declared the 1976 Bicentennial of the United States a farce. The U.S. government refused to "acknowledge the centuries of crimes against Native Americans, nor has either of the [two] major parties pledged to make amends for the centuries of genocidal oppression – the land grabs, the racist deprivation of civil and legal rights, the attacks on culture and religion, the impoverishment, exploitation and police repression which capitalist development has forced upon the Native American Indian peoples."[19] In short, to LeBlanc U.S. history was a history of genocide and resistance.

While indigenous people's rights were her primary focus, LeBlanc also made youth rights a central theme of her state Senate bid. At a Youth Rights Rally attended by 100 people, she charged incumbent Senator William Bulger with "crimes against youth," adding that his "repeated statements against school desegregation... encouraged violence," especially against African American youth. That Bulger (brother of the infamous crime boss James 'Whitey' Bulger), other elected officials and anti-busing racists called Roxbury, a predominantly African American area in Boston, "unsafe" and hinted at "the necessity of vigilante action from white communities," was "part of a series of crimes against youth and crimes against our future," she added.[20] LeBlanc also pledged to "fight the corporations [which] perpetuate unemployment, crime, deteriorating housing and [create] obstacles to quality integrated education in Boston." They determine the outcome of local elections by "buying off elected officials," a familiar scenario. "What we desperately need," the Caddo youth activist added, "is responsible government...responsive to the needs of the masses of people." To LeBlanc, "Responsibility means fighting for legislation to provide meaningful jobs at union wages...It means fighting for legislation to control exorbitant rents and extend rent control to public housing...[and] It means taking the tax burden off the backs of the people least able to carry the load," a progressive taxation platform that would also "slash the military budget, and use our money to meet the needs of the people." LeBlanc argued that it should "be a crime to incite racism and use it as a weapon to confuse and abuse people." This was a demand Communists had been making since at least the 1930s. "We need to recognize that racism oppresses us all and we can never have a free democratic society until we create the condition of full equality for everyone." Additionally, LeBlanc saw school desegregation, curriculum reform and affirmative action as "but first steps in overcoming centuries of racist oppression against the Black, Chicano, Puerto Rican, Asian and Native American Indian peoples of the United States,"[21] a step in the right direction; demands that continue to resonate today.

LeBlanc called for the "Guarantee [of] the Reservation land base" and urged Federal authorities to "restore it to at least 110 million acres." She also called for "full Indian control of the land and resources, with Federal funds for full development." She wanted to "abolish the present BIA [Bureau of Indian Affairs] and establish a national agency under democratic Indian control that would end big business plunder of Indian resources and would have power to enforce Indian claims for restitution." LeBlanc believed that Native Americans were best suited to represent their interests in the halls of power. As such, she also urged "the fullest representation of Native American Indians at all appropriate levels of community and state government, trade unions and peoples organizations." She boldly called for "additional Federal funds for the specific educational and health needs of Native Americans to quickly overcome the legacy of special oppression and exploitation."[22] "We are giving people a chance to vote for themselves," LeBlanc argued. According to the *Daily World*, LeBlanc's campaign wasn't just an electoral campaign. It was "a crucial step in the struggle of nationally oppressed working class men and women to exercise their political right to serve in government," to represent themselves and advocate for their interests. "It is absolutely essential," LeBlanc added, "that young people" have "an opportunity to be represented by a member of a minority [group] and a youth." She also stressed the need for "a women's bill of rights, guaranteeing paid maternity leave, daycare, and job safety, as well as public housing and recreation." These demand were then gaining international attention by women's organizations in the Eastern European socialist nations and their Third World allies. Perhaps overly optimistic, LeBlanc concluded, "Communists should, must, and will be elected to local offices. We are a valid political force,"[23] a force the U.S. government had spent decades trying to destroy.

LeBlanc was actually part of a slate of Communist candidates that ran in the 1976 elections. Along with the Gus Hall-Jarvis Tyner presidential campaign, LeBlanc's comrades Ishmael Flory, Herbert Aptheker and Joelle Fishman, among others, challenged anticommunism by putting Communist candidates on the ballot across the country. Unfortunately, these campaigns met with limited success. LeBlanc received about 2,000 votes or 7.5 percent of the total in her state Senate bid, though "where I lived I got 33 percent of the vote."[24] Remarkably, she was "unable to vote for herself." Apparently, her polling location's voting machine was defective and "failed to respond when the 'Communist' lever was pulled." Voter complaints "brought only surly responses"[25] from poll workers and elections officials who had done their utmost to create additional obstacles for Communist candidates and the people willing to vote for them. This wasn't the first time Communists complained of being unable to cast votes for themselves.[26] It seemed to be a recurring theme. "We didn't have the capacity to know how wide the suppression was," LeBlanc noted. To her and the party, the campaign was a success regardless of the number of votes cast. "It was an amazing experience. I debated Bulger. Got lots of media. The campaign received a lot of attention. We raised a lot of issues. We were part of a national political dialogue that revolved around how and in what way Communists should participate in elections. We were fighting for the right of third parties to be on the ballot, to be a part of the electoral arena."[27]

Further, LeBlanc's campaign laid the groundwork for future gains, like that of Communist Polly Halfkenny, who would receive 4,363 votes for City Council during a runoff primary election in Boston roughly a year later. Like LeBlanc, Halfkenny "talked with thousands of people in the neighborhoods and across the city, stressing [her] commitment to equality, integrated education, continuation and strengthening of rent control, meaningful charter reform and jobs."[28] Communist candidates effectively forced others to respond to the issues they raised.

In December 1976, LeBlanc's advocacy for Native American rights took a uniquely Marxist turn. She led a "historic delegation of Native American youth to Soviet Tajikistan, a mountainous republic in central Asia." According to LeBlanc, "we went to study the implementation of the national question, to learn about the relationship between political systems and the development and deepening of national culture." After her return, LeBlanc told an audience of 100 people at the Community Church of Boston "the story of a peasant-landlord society jumping to socialism as a result of the socialist revolution in Russia in 1917," an event unmatched in world history. She said, "Tajik women with the help of women communists from Russia, Lithuania, and elsewhere fought to free themselves from the degradation imposed on them" by male supremacy and traditional customs. Now, "fifty years later" different nationalities live in "comraderie [sic] and commitment to a better way of life." Joining LeBlanc at the Community Church was Massachusetts State Representative Saundra Graham, who had recently returned from a peace conference in Moscow. Graham told the audience, "Peace can be a time of a booming economy. We must say to our government –

cut the military budget and put the money into the needs of the people." This was a theme LeBlanc would make a centerpiece of her political identity by the early 2000s. Graham also noted that trade with socialist countries could be "a source of economic stimulus and jobs" domestically and a way to ease Cold War tensions. As a mother of three children, she told the audience, "I am tired of living under the threat of war,"[29] a threat that would increase dramatically with the ascension of the far-right and the retreat of socialism.

* * *

LeBlanc returned to a familiar theme in a July-August 1983 *Political Affairs* article. "Indian reservations with rich resources are a prime target of the energy monopolies,"[30] which pipeline developers confirm by their continuing actions. LeBlanc proposed a strategic alliance between labor unions and Native tribes throughout the 1970s and 1980s; some unions, though, ignored the concerns of American Indians for the promise of jobs.[31] Leblanc wasn't deterred, urging fellow Communists and their allies to "encourage the trade union movement to fight for jobs with affirmative action for Native American Indians." "The protection of reservations and their natural resources from monopoly plunder needs to be a major point of struggle for the U.S. working class," she argued. Communists needed to highlight the "sharper antimonopoly character emerging" from within the struggle for sovereignty and natural resources – a precursor to the contemporary movement for environmental sustainability.

LeBlanc saw the struggle for Native rights as having a "fundamental interconnection" to the Party's strategic focus of "the developing antimonopoly struggle," and she criticized her comrades who viewed the plight of Indigenous people as a "side issue." In some Districts, the party "had very little relationship to native leaders on the ground," she recalled. LeBlanc wasn't deterred, though.

"This was part of the dialog and of being a Native American woman in the Communist Party," she added. To her, regardless of its shortcomings, the party "recognized the role of various liberation struggles. Native, Asian, Puerto Rican, Mexican and African American activists were brought into the leadership of the party. The party mentored and educated in special ways. This was one of the biggest contributions it made. It was fully wide-open."

Regardless, LeBlanc argued that demands for good jobs could unite Native tribes with unions. We need to "strengthen and expand" Native resistance in collaboration with unions, she emphasized. "The central issue in cities and [in] reservations is jobs. We can not [sic] talk about protection and further development of [Native] culture, language and religion without a major emphasis on the fight for jobs with affirmative action," including for Native Americans. "We must work for multiracial class unity in a way which *convinces* Native American Indian workers that their natural allies are to be found in the working class" [*italic* in original]. To LeBlanc, "The Communist Party had a healthy political strategy of building the unity of the working class, of the various people of color communities. It recognized the fact that there was special problems and needs and ways that the working class could move together in a more unified way despite racism," LeBlanc recalled.[32]

LeBlanc, and other women Communists – Evelina Alarcon, Carole Marks, and Mildred Williamson – appeared on the popular *Sally Jesse Raphael* syndicated TV show in spring 1986.[33] Communists were seen as a curiosity to some, not necessarily a force to be taken seriously. Regardless, Party members were energized when 700 reds attended a special conference on the midterm elections just a few months later. At the conference members were urged to "step up their involvement in electoral forms such as Political Action Committees (PACs) in the unions and elsewhere." It was emphasized that "local party clubs [should] work on voter registration and mobilization." Emergency "membership mobilization meetings to discuss the final stages of the congressional elections" were also encouraged and a "goal of building 50 [new] party shop clubs" was adopted. LeBlanc, now national cadre director, called for an "all out push to increase the circulation of the *PDW* [*People's Daily World*] to 100,000,"[34] which was an ambitious goal.

To LeBlanc, building the movement for Indigenous rights and working class power complimented building the Communist Party and the *PDW*. In a spring 1987 pre-convention report, LeBlanc said, "We are a minority party with majority ideas and the potential for great growth." "In every area [of struggle] there is tremendous flux, tremendous possibilities to influence the development and the thinking of masses, and tremendous opportunities to initiate Left forms, new coalitions and alliances...Objective developments dictate that we must grow rapidly. Life is making this a necessity,"[35] she added. This "necessity," however, was made considerably more difficult by Reagan-era anticommunism. LeBlanc had a response for the critics, though. "The bottom line on anti-communism," she told a conference at Harvard University in fall 1988, "is that it has always been used to derail unity in the people's movement, disarm their militancy, and undermine the struggle against capitalism," a sentiment then born out of nearly 70 years of struggle. "It is essential for Americans to hear straight from the horse's mouth, so to speak, about communism. Then they can make up their own minds about capitalism, socialism and communism," LeBlanc added. Anticommunism "attempts to camouflage the existence of the class struggle. It has taken its toll on the labor movement, on every progressive movement,"[36] she concluded.

At a spring *PDW* picnic in Los Angeles attended by 200 people, LeBlanc took aim at President Reagan and Reaganomics. She asked, "what the country would be like if Reaganism were defeated in November," if the country "turned around," turned away from the policies of the right-wing then exemplified by the coming George

H. W. Bush presidency. "What would life be like in our country if you could organize without government interference," she asked? What if "the government stopped funding contra wars...[and] all children were guaranteed daycare...All this is possible with mass struggle," she concluded, calling on Communists to "bring together Democrats, independents and first-time voters for mass action."[37]

Like other Communists, LeBlanc rooted her political activism in international solidarity. While in Managua, Nicaragua in fall 1988, she and party leader James Steele, along with representatives from 130 other political parties from Asia, Africa, Europe and the Americas, demanded that the U.S. government end its "aggressive and interventionist" policies through the CIA backed Contras and "pay for damages it [has] inflicted on the Central American nation." LeBlanc and the other delegates were attending the 25th anniversary of the founding of the Sandinista National Liberation Front, which had won state power in 1979 after overthrowing the dictatorship of Anastasio Somoza DeBayle.[38] Unfortunately, with the former CIA director and Reagan vice president on his way to the White House, Reagan era domestic and international politics were continued. LeBlanc told her comrades in Detroit in late November 1988, "Reagan's voodoo economic dreams are about to explode into our very worst nightmare." She predicted that "economic problems will become the key battleground for the people's movement in coming months." She also called capitalism an "economic time-bomb" and noted that the National Economic Commission, a bipartisan U.S. deficit reduction commission headed by corporate elites, had already drawn up "battle plans" for "austerity economics," which was akin to "asking bears to refrain from eating honey." The nightmare was beginning; 80,000 farmers were served foreclosure notices, 7,000 GTE middle management workers were laid off, cuts to Social Security were proposed, while 2,000 state workers in New Jersey were laid off shortly after the elections. More "layoffs are in store for autoworkers after the holiday break," she predicted. "Monopoly capitalism is in trouble," she added. "The only way out of the impending crash...is to tax the rich and cut the military budget." LeBlanc's call would not come to fruition even after the collapse of socialism; U.S. imperialism soon embarked on military adventures in the Middle East with horrific consequences.

LeBlanc said the formation of a "people's party" was not on the agenda, arguing instead that "the most effective way to end corporate rule on Capitol Hill is for the trade unions, the Afro-American community and peace, women's and environmental movements to run their own candidates," Further, she argued that "there is a newly developing understanding of the limitations of the Democratic Party and the role of the media in trying to influence and manipulate the fears of the people." LeBlanc would reflect more on the role of media in democracy in the coming decade. Despite the outcome of the presidential elections, LeBlanc urged Communists to organize "independently of the Democratic Party – politically, financially and organizationally."[39]

* * *

Though LeBlanc's focus was frequently on immediate demands, she viewed the world through a Marxist-Leninist lens and articulated a world-view that centered on broad-based unity. In a spring 1989 article titled "The Communist Party and Its Ideology," LeBlanc wrote, "We help build coalitions so that the people's movement can win reforms. This energizes the movement and sharpens the class struggle." She articulated a working class focus, a collaborative endeavor with the party seen as *a part* of a larger mass movement. "Communist participation adds working-class direction, solidifies and unites... We never attempt to take over coalitions. We never try to go it alone...We know that neither the Communist Party, nor the working class, nor the people's movements can, on their own, separate and apart, make fundamental, long-lasting changes." To LeBlanc, this was a time tested sentiment born out of years of experience. "Our work in coalitions is a critical and decisive element of our Party's contribution to raising the level of class consciousness in the democratic movements." For LeBlanc organizing and ideology were inseparable.

Unlike some other Marxist groups, the party has often shunned the public spotlight. Whether out of fear of repression and anticommunism, or as activists focused on specific issues within broad coalitions – something LeBlanc would exemplify throughout her career – the "Party [often] makes important contributions for which it cannot take credit." In LeBlanc's words, "There is no better way to fight anti-communist stereotypes than through our presence and our participation in struggle," even when membership was often relegated to one-on-one discussions. Fear of Communists, she added, "relies on a lack of knowledge," on a stereotyped caricature. Communists must engage, build trust and demonstrate their commitment to struggle because anticommunism doesn't just affect the party, "It affects how the left is organized." To LeBlanc, anticommunism weakened the entire movement for social and economic justice, while isolating movement leaders from their natural allies. The demise of the party-led CAA and CRC are just two examples.

To LeBlanc, the party's influence could not "be measured with a gauge or a computer" and remained larger than its formal membership. Demonstrable contributions, "in people's day-to-day struggles, armed with, and creatively applying our ideology," would not only shape and influence political discourse, but would also help build the party. For LeBlanc, this was the articulation of a class analysis situated within the context of world historical forces competing for power, a context that would be dramatically reshaped in the coming years with socialism's retreat. "Our future as a Party is tied to the fate of that most important class in the history of civilization," the working class; its ascendance or decline impacted the party's ability to influence, recruit, and grow. "We have projected the building of a mass Party with its ideological and numerical foundation in the working class because only such a party can lead political struggles."[40]

Largely absent from the party's analysis was an understanding of the ongoing and precipitous decline of those traditionally seen by Communists as constituting the key link in the chain of the working class, industrial workers. Only belatedly did they begin to see the larger shifts in the economy away from industrial production and towards service sector and tech jobs as necessitating a shift in concentration. The party's "industrial concentration" policy marred Communist organizing and tied its recruitment to an ever-smaller section of workers, a section that would become increasingly insecure about its future.

"Our Party is shaped by objective circumstances, by the dynamics of the class struggle," LeBlanc emphasized. "On the positive side, we are involved in many of the most important struggles of the day," including the fightback against factory closures. "On the negative side, we are not big enough and we are not growing fast enough." Focusing their still considerable energies on a declining sector of the economy with a shrinking workforce isolated some party leaders from the emerging movements then springing into action as the economy continued to change. Unsurprisingly, growth suffered. Reflecting on these conditions in 1992, LeBlanc noted, "We cannot be a working class party in the abstract; it is not an academic question. We cannot build a mass Party without concentrating on the majority class, the working class. We must be a Party of, by and for the working class."[41] "Our Party must inspire people to take matters into their own hands; to fight for what is needed, not simply what is possible," LeBlanc added. "We must work on three levels; we must work in our own name, in a public, visible way as a political Party; we must help to build coalitions to support this initiative [on the Rebuild America Act, for example] and we must organize the victims of the crisis at the grass roots," which they did. "We must spark a national movement that fights for jobs and equality."[42] Communists were still searching for a return to the Popular Front. However, unlike in the 1930s, industrial workers were now a sector of the working class increasingly in decline.

In spring 1992, LeBlanc would be appointed national field secretary. Her main responsibilities were to "represent the CPUSA in national coalitions," a role she would excel at over the coming decades, and to "assist the districts and clubs" by helping them develop "work on the economic crisis and other fields of mass activity." She also became the chairperson of the Secretariat, "a national collective of Communist mass activists."[43] The following year, LeBlanc became chair of the Party's Mass Action Department.[44] A year into the Bill Clinton presidency, LeBlanc had few positive things to say about the Arkansan. She denounced the administration, saying, the "social policy is reflected in their inaction on the economic crisis," a crisis initiated under Reagan. "The best thing the administration and Congress can do to combat racism is to make a job a human right," she added.[45]

LeBlanc would continue to focus on the struggle against racism. At a January 1994 New York party meeting, she said Dr. Martin Luther King Jr.'s "bold, militant, dramatic mass action" was coupled with "his vision of ending the racial injustices of hundreds of years," starting with the African slave trade. "His vision expanded as the struggle for civil rights expanded," she added, an expansion partly led by Communists. For reds, though, "the basic truth is that racism is...generated, promoted and organized by the ruling class in its efforts to make maximum profits, to cloud over the class nature of our society...Our Party's contribution to the fight against racism is unique," she continued. "We see what needs to be done in the current situation. We link it to the long-term necessity to get to the root causes of racism and to put an end to the system that gave birth to racism. This can only be done by bringing into existence a new system...that has as its constitutional, political, economic and social basis equality and an end to exploitation."[46] This goal, however, was made considerably more difficult with the collapse of the socialism in Eastern Europe. Just a few days later, LeBlanc would report on the party's Jobs and Equality Campaign, telling 125 Communists, "The Party is calling for an emergency, massive public works program with enforced affirmative action and the right of trade union protection." She called it, "an anti-scab bill and a new civil rights bill," which will "strengthen contract fights for the organized section of the working class."[47]

The CPUSA's emphasis on the use of emerging technologies also began to generate excitement within party circles. In spring 1994, Communists called for a People's March on the Information Superhighway, April 4-10, culminating with a "National Town Hall Meeting that links 50 cities by telephone." The main topic was, *For Real Change Today and Socialism Tomorrow.* LeBlanc led the discussion on *Jobs and Equality, the Crisis in the Cities and the Struggle Against Racism.* The Young Communist League took out an ad in the *Village Voice* and asked, "Are you a Communist? If you think the system doesn't work, you might be. Call 1-800-READ-PWW." And the *PWW* set a fund-drive goal of $400,000 by July 4.[48] On April 4, the anniversary of the assassination of Dr. King, Communists urged their readers and members to "Call, fax, E-mail," to "let the Congress and the White House know that we need immediate emergency action to address the crisis of joblessness and discrimination."[49] They also said, "Let's talk, modem to modem." "Computer buffs, unite!,"[50] it was added, as Communists began experimenting with non-traditional means of mass communication.

LeBlanc's activism and advocacy as a Native American has never taken a back seat, regardless of her other responsibilities. She argued, "Basic challenges face the movement for equality" for Native tribes, challenges that "flow from the corporate drive to keep the Clinton Administration and Congress 'on course' – [by] cutting the budget deficit and the national debt on the backs of the multi-racial working class." Since the "initial colonial land grab [the] result has been the continued destruction in living standards, segregation and unemployment, alongside attacks on culture, customs and persistent efforts to take away our land." "Indian people suffer under conditions of the long-term crisis of the capitalist system," a crisis exacerbated by the ascendance of the right-wing. The "struggle for jobs is therefore key to a successful fight for equality," as Native people suffer unemployment rates "from 60 to 80 percent on Indian reservations." She continued to criticize the administration for "proposing to cut Indian programs further," since "some tribes are 'non-historic,'" meaning they came "together as a result of special oppression of Indian peoples – tribes that came together after being driven off the land, or from loss of great numbers due to epidemic disease." To LeBlanc, "This policy is a new form of racism." It is an attempt to "pit tribes against one another to compete for federally funded programs... [to] keep us all fighting over smaller and smaller pieces" of the federally funded pie. The administration "has proposed $248 million in cuts" to the Health and Human Services budget covering Indian health services, she added, while increasing the overall Health and Human Services budget by $23 billion. "This strategy is as old as dirt," LeBlanc continued, "pit one group against the others." The "administration's demagogic call for tribal sovereignty is in effect a policy of asking Indian tribes to tighten the economic noose around their own necks." LeBlanc called instead for an "emergency increase in funding for Indian job training and health care until such time as a universal socialized medical system is enacted and a job guaranteed for all in our country." To her, the right of Native American "self-determination will continue to be discussed, but it can never be taken out of the political and economic context unfolding in our country."[51]

Le Blanc would next shift her considerable focus to an emerging political outlet, public access TV, through the party-sponsored weekly news-show *Changing America*, which continued the legacy of *People Before Profits*, a political talk show created by the party's video department in the mid-1980s and ran until 1990.[52]

* * *

At a January 1999 CPUSA National Committee meeting, LeBlanc reported on the coming launch of *Changing America*. She also previewed "a work-in-progress video of the program." The show, produced by LeBlanc and edited by YCL leader Noel Rabinowitz, was funded by the Chelsea Fund for Education, a 501(c)3 non-profit. "It was a big innovation," she recalled. "Gus [Hall] was very excited about it. Plus, it built off of the organizing relationships party members had across the country."[53]

Changing America's First Episode was released early that March and focused on the February police killing of Amadou Diallo, an unarmed 23-year-old Guinean immigrant; four plainclothes officers mistook Diallo as a rape suspect and shot him 19 times (41 shots were fired) while he stood outside his apartment.[54] Protests soon erupted. While the officers were charged with second-degree murder, all were acquitted. For *Changing America*'s inaugural episode, LeBlanc interviewed Ron Daniels, the executive director of the Center for Constitutional Rights, who noted that his organization was "overwhelmed by the issue of police brutality." Daniels said, police misconduct "is horrible" and likened the New York City Street Crimes Unit to "para-military warriors... hitting the streets harassing people on the basis of a profile." Daniels said, Diallo's profile to police "by definition...[was] threatening, dangerous [and] suspicious." He likened racist police to the Ku Klux Klan and the White Citizens Council; they are the "same animal," he added. Daniels called for the creation of civilian review boards, "independent bodies...[with] prosecutorial, investigative, subpoena power and the ability to recommend penalties." He said, police must be "compelled to change their behavior." This demand is just as relevant today as the assault on Black lives continues unabated. Daniels urged *Changing America* viewers to "march on the streets...[and] the ballot box."[55]

For the Second Episode, LeBlanc interviewed Congressman John Conyers, Jr., who not only called for civilian review boards "in every city," he also blasted private prisons, "corporations who are trying to make a profit...[which] makes doubly certain that no rehabilitation will occur." Conyers didn't mince words. The "racial violence of police...police misconduct, violence and abuse is worse than civilian violence," he said, as trained police are supposed to be held to a higher standard. Conyers also connected the diverting of tax dollars to private prisons with a constraining of funds for other social services. "That doesn't work when you talk about who's gonna provide health care, hospitals, doctors, clinics. Who's gonna provide educational opportunities...government functions that are very important," he concluded. Conyers also called for a hate crimes bill. Hate crimes should be "federal crimes," he said. "We're trying to stop people from being dragged along by a car... that's a lynching, a modern lynching," Conyers added,[56] a reference to the spring 1998 brutal torture and killing of Texas African American, James Byrd, Jr.[57]

As a public access TV show, *Changing America* provided in-depth interviews coupled with a "pulse on the streets" section and a recap of the week's news by *People's Weekly World* editor Tim Wheeler. It was a uniquely CPUSA approach to the emerging independent media movement.

Episode Four's focus was on the Newport News, Virginia shipyard strike. On April 5, the 9,200 members of the United Steelworkers of America Local 8888 began a four-month strike against the Newport News Shipbuilding

Company. Local 8888 was asking for a $3.95 per-hour raise. The shipbuilder designed and constructed nuclear powered aircraft carriers and submarines, and said its final offer included a $2.49 per-hour raise over the life of the contract.[58] LeBlanc discussed the cause of the strike with Local 8888's president, Arnold Outlaw. He told *Changing America*, "the company had no intention of actually bargaining with us." They are doing "any and everything they can to break the spirit of the union," Outlaw added. Emphasizing the power of collective action, he concluded, "A strike is what's needed today to bring them back to the table." That sentiment proved prophetic. According to Dewitt Walton, assistant to the USW international president, "The issues are clear... world class defense workers, second class wages. World class defense workers, third class pensions. [There are] people working this shipyard 30 to 35 years [who] can't look forward to quality retirement."[59] The party's newspaper, the *PWW*, covered the strike as well. Reporters interviewed Dan LeBlanc (no relation), president of the Virginia AFL-CIO, who said, "I don't have respect for a corporation that runs a plantation and takes advantage of the right-to-work (for less) laws in this state." He added, that Newport News workers "are worth no less than the workers at any other shipyard. We're tired of our workers...being treated like second-class citizens."

Central to the striking workers demands were increased pension contributions. Solidarity poured in from across state lines. William Postler, a retired boilermaker from Electric Boat in Connecticut, held up a "poster-sized blowup of his monthly pension check totaling $1,965." Rick James, a retiree from Newport News, then held up a poster of his monthly pension check totaling $204. Barry Credle told the *PWW*, "These are world-class ships and I'm a first-class shipfitter [sic] but I'm paid only $13.48 an hour."[60] According to Stephen Francisco, USW legislative representative, the shipbuilder "made a serious miscalculation." He said their contract proposal was nothing more than "greed...pure and simple greed."

It was noted that NNS "made $266 million dollars last year." Francisco added, that OSHA and the Navy had initiated an "extended safety investigation." USW members also planned to protest at the NNS shareholder meeting[61] where USW secretary-treasurer Leo Gerard, put the issue thusly: "I want to ask the management of this company...The majority of the workers in Connecticut [at Electric Boat] are white. The majority of the workers at the [NNS] Yard are southern and they're Black. Are you perpetuating poverty because the workers are southern or because they are Black or both? Neither one is acceptable to the Steelworkers Union and I think they have to answer for that."[62] Roughly a month later about 800 Local 8888 members went to Washington, D.C.; they gathered at the Navy Memorial and marched to the Capitol demanding that the Defense Department and Congress pressure NNS "to return to the bargaining table." It was noted that NNS shipbuilders were paid as little as $12.59 per-hour, "less than the wages at a nearby brewery."[63] Ultimately, Newport News came back to the bargaining table and proposed a 58-month contract that included a $3.10 per-hour raise over the life of the contract, and improved pension benefits,[64] a clear victory for the striking workers.

By late July, Communists were boasting about *Changing America*'s early successes. In a *PWW* article it was noted that the show was "on the air in 32 cities," potentially reaching millions of viewers, and that it is "one of a handful of independent cable TV news shows distributed to public access channels nationally and one of the few to cover working-class culture and struggles." The "crew has burned up the highway miles traveling to towns and cities to film strikes, mass demonstrations, and to conduct interviews," it was added. Communists hoped to establish a "pro-socialist and pro-working class" TV show capable of reaching a diverse audience. LeBlanc highlighted the show's emphasis on rank-and-file workers and union leaders. She said, "We want to tell the whole story in their words, in their views, about how they are struggling against big, greedy corporations like Newport News Shipbuilding." This focus partly explains why union leaders like Leo Gerard granted LeBlanc and other Communists special access and exclusive interviews. "When workers fighting for their lives call us to thank us for our support and coverage, we know that 'Changing America' is really a part of the fight against the corporations," LeBlanc added.[65]

International solidarity was also a regular *Changing America* theme. LeBlanc interviewed Rev. Lucius Walker, from Pastors for Peace, in Episode Seven. With the recent Baltimore Orioles vs. the Cuban National Team baseball game at Camden Yards fresh on everybody's mind, LeBlanc asked Walker about the campaign to challenge the U.S. blockade of Cuba. "Everything helps a little," Walker said. "I don't want to overplay the significance of the game," he continued, "but it at least provides an opportunity for people to think of Cuba in a more normal, natural light. They play baseball like people in the United States." At the very least, the game "forced a lot of U.S. citizens to ask questions." He urged *Changing America* viewers to "imagine what the relationship [between Cuba and the U.S.] ought to be." Walker and Pastors for Peace not only challenged the embargo, they also delivered aid. "We see the value of the aid we deliver. We see the lives affected by the aid we give...We know that ultimately, because right is on our side, the force of history is on our side, that the blockade will be ended. And we think that would be a tremendous contribution towards strengthening Cuba's determination to perfect its revolution. That revolution, the Cuban revolution, is such a precious gift and a fine example to especially Third World countries...They need that example," Walker concluded,[66] as Communists and their allies sought ways to build international solidarity with the small socialist island.

Popularizing working class culture was another regular theme. LeBlanc interviewed the Tony Award winning actor and activist John Randolph; he had been blacklisted in Hollywood during the McCarthy era witch hunts.[67] Jazz musician Sarah McLawler was also interviewed. For LeBlanc and *Changing America*, working class culture included art geared toward political ends. For example, LeBlanc interviewed Esther Cohen, the curator of Gallery 1199, a project of the Service Employees International Union Local 1199. Cohen said the union had the "foresight...to understand the relationship between culture and working people." She said the Bread and Roses project, initiated by Moe Foner, reached 1.5 million workers nationally. The Gallery's current exhibit brought teachers, union organizers and students together to discuss sweatshops in New York's garment district. The project was supported by SEIU, the Union of Needletrades, Industrial and Textile Employees and United Students Against Sweatshops.[68] *Changing America* also met with the students responsible for creating the anti-sweatshop artwork.

Interviewing workers and union leaders was at the heart of *Changing America*'s vision. In Episode Eleven, LeBlanc interviewed Randi Weingarten, president of New York's United Federation of Teachers and future international president of the American Federation of Teachers. Weingarten and LeBlanc discussed the New Century Coalition and a revived NYC labor movement. "Anything that is worthwhile takes an inordinate amount of time, energy and effort to accomplish," Weingarten said. May 12, when tens of thousands of unions and community activists rallied, "was a first step, the beginning of a revitalized labor movement in this city," Weingarten said.[69] The rally was meant to send a clear message to then Mayor Rudolph Giuliani regarding contract negotiations involving 250,000 city workers set to expire in 2000. LeBlanc also interviewed Lee Saunders, who had recently taken the helm at the 120,000 member American Federation of State, County and Municipal Employees District Council 37. Saunders told *Changing America*, "The issues that impact our members are community issues, also...better education, health care, quality of life." We consider ourselves as "not only a labor institution," he added, "we are also a social institution." Indicative of the changing mood within the halls of labor, Saunders concluded, "A sleeping giant is awake and we are going to make some very strong statements."[70]

Others agreed with Weingarten and Saunders. Leslie Frane, vice president New England Health Care Employees 1199 in Connecticut, told LeBlanc about her union's multipronged approach to winning victories for working families. "Yes, we are struggling against our employers. And, yes, the employers are corporate entities that make huge profits...[They] have big CEO salaries. And yes, they can afford to do better. But we were also saying that we have to target the state," as that is "where roughly 75 percent of the income...Medicaid money, which is direct state money [comes from]." So, Frane concluded, "we really began to view it as a triangle where there are three sides. The workers, the employers and the state." Frane's union represents nursing home workers, people who take care of the day-to-day needs of elderly residents. She added, the "members are incredibly united." They know they "share a common enemy – the employers."[71]

Jonathan Hiatt, special counsel to the AFL-CIO, agreed, but was a bit more reserved in his interview with LeBlanc. "The right to organize in this country is at the present time not a real right to organize. The law is very, very deficient," he said. "Many employers...have decided [they] should dictate whether or not their workers are going to have an independent voice in the workplace." As a result, they are spending hundreds of millions on anti-union consultants and are "thwarting workers' freedom to make their own decisions." He said, employers hire "union busters...[that] operate in the shadows." They surveil workers, interrogate workers, hold captive audience meetings, make employees watch anti-union videos, and fire union leaders. According to Hiatt, "They realize that it's unlawful, but they also realize that our labor laws are so weak that in the long run there is nothing to lose." They know "down the road all they will be ordered to do if the workers in the union...brings a case before the labor board... [that] the worst that will happen is that in maybe a year or two years they'll have to bring the worker back to work and pay back wages, but no punitive damages, to compensatory damages, no attorney's fees, but by that time the campaign is over," he concluded. He thanked *Changing America* for helping to put "employer interference under the spotlight."[72]

By September, the *PWW* was praising *Changing America* as the "most talked about national public access [TV] program," a program that "continues the proud tradition of distinguishing itself apart from corporate sponsored TV shows." It was noted, "You'll see the class struggle up close and personal," as Communists continued to experiment with independent media.[73] Another *PWW* article noted that the list of cities and towns across the country airing *Changing America* "continues to grow," while the show has become "an indispensable tool in analyzing the mood and direction of working-class people across the country." *Changing America* was contrasted to the "corporate sponsored TV news and magazine shows [that] rarely show working people," which was "an integral part" of the party-sponsored show. It was also noted that volunteer correspondents were needed to continue growing the shows viewership and coverage.[74]

September also marked the beginning of the second season of *Changing America*. Episode One featured an interview with Linda Chavez Thompson, executive vice president of the AFL-CIO. Chavez Thompson noted the excitement in the air, "especially with people of color and women. They see a change that the labor movement is listening." She took aim at the growing wealth gap, too; "the tragedy of America today" is that workers "are not sharing in that economy, not sharing in that wealth...they're not sharing in the fruit of their productivity." Chavez Thompson told LeBlanc, "Time and time again we see CEO's that are getting millions of dollars in stocks and bonuses and salaries and if we were to have kept up...workers today would be getting $100,000 a year and $20.18 minimum wage...but we have not... The worker is forgotten. And they are the ones living paycheck to paycheck, trying to make ends meet." Like LeBlanc, Chavez Thompson blamed the rich and powerful, and their political allies. "All they want is more and more and more and they want to keep it in their pockets." She also talked about the AFL-CIO Labor 2000 program, which aimed to elect 2,000 union members to public office in the year 2000 – candidates who understand the plight of ordinary, working people. "We kept looking for candidates that were pro-labor, candidates that were friendly to labor. And we decided why not from labor, why not people who have lived it. People who fight every day on the jobs," Chavez Thompson emphasized.[75] Party leaders across the country, within and outside of organized labor, supported the campaign.

In Episode Two, LeBlanc interviewed Amy Dean, of the South Bay Central Labor Council, one of the youngest AFL-CIO, CLC leaders in the country. Dean emphasized labor's "renewed emphasis on rebuilding the grassroots of the American labor movement." She urged labor and community activists to take "a page out of our history, out of our past" and to look "towards the future...[to]... build capacity in every community across the country to rebuild the labor movement." This was an ambitious goal reminiscent of the alliances that were built during the emergence of the CIO in the 1930s. The AFL-CIO should "reposition the labor movement to be the moral voice in our communities, aligned with community allies, aligned with women's groups, aligned with religious organizations, aligned with communities of color and aligned with the very groups we need to be aligned with if we are going to rebuild a progressive agenda," she added. Significant to Dean's outlook was a keen understanding of the increasingly dominant role of the service and tech sectors of our national economy, what she called "the new economy." By this time, party leaders began to better understand the emerging service and tech sectors. "We are rebuilding the role for the American labor movement in the heart of the new economy." Dean added that "a renaissance [is] taking place" in the labor movement, especially among women, people of color and youth. She also urged the creation of "on the ground fighting [political] machines"[76] led by labor and its allies.

In Episode Four LeBlanc spoke with Brian McWilliams, president of the International Longshore and Warehousemen's Union about the upcoming World Trade Organization meeting in Seattle. McWilliams said, globalization was "lowering the standard of living" for all workers. "Workers here will never get a fair shake until workers everywhere around the world get a fair shake," he added, telling LeBlanc that the ILWU and other unions hoped to mobilize 100,000 protesters into the streets during the trade negotiations set to take place that fall.[77]

Changing America was on the front lines during what became known as the Battle in Seattle. Trade union, community, youth, and environmental rights protesters clashed with police who repeatedly used tear gas, rubber bullets, and percussion grenades. Ron Judd, president of the Kings County (Seattle) Central Labor Council, was one of those protesters. He told LeBlanc, "We need to have rules that put people before profits, rules that put the planet before profits." This was a unifying theme, one Communists, Socialists, and progressives of all stripes shared. He said, the WTO protests were a "cornerstone for change." He urged all workers to "stand together united as a global trade union movement." Atlanta Labor Council president and party ally, Stewart Acuff, pointedly added, "The underlying issue is corporate greed." "We came with a message to represent our people, to say: 'Hell no!' And we're taking a message back more unified than ever and we will win," Mark Fromke, vice president of the North Dakota AFL-CIO and party leader, told LeBlanc. Despite the violence inflicted upon protesters by police, morale was high. "Today we made a statement not just for our workers, but for workers all over this country," Linda Chavez Thompson noted, as hundreds of thousands of protesters shut down the WTO negotiations. James Clawson, of the U.S. negotiating team, told reporters, "The protesters were successful in stopping the negotiations."[78] The WTO protests were a stinging rebuke against unregulated, anti-worker, anti-environmental global trade.

As the 2000 presidential elections neared, *Changing America* also directed its attention at Governor George W. Bush's administration in Texas; the Lone Star silver spoon was then running for president. In the special pre-election video *Texas Trail: First-Hand in Bush Land* LeBlanc met with labor and community leaders to assess Governor Bush's devastating tenure. "Governor Bush has been the most dangerous politician I've known in my lifetime," Joe Gunn president of the Texas AFL-CIO, told LeBlanc. "He's got a pleasant appearance. He's got a boy scout smile. But he's got a mean streak as broad as he is tall." In an attempt to interview Bush campaign staff, the *Changing America* crew also went to the Bush National Campaign Headquarters but were turned away as security guards escorted LeBlanc off the property. LeBlanc also spoke with Samantha Smoot, executive director of the Texas Freedom Network, Thomas Webb, of AFSCME Local 1550 and Dale Worthman, president of the Harris County AFL-CIO CLC,[79] all of whom said that Bush would be a disaster for the country.

In all, *Changing America* spanned three seasons. "Nationally, we were distributed in 60 cities and we won a number of awards," LeBlanc recalled. Its potential viewership was in the millions. "We covered stuff that wasn't getting covered. *Changing America* was used and bought by unions in the battle grounds states, too. It was also part of the founding of the Independent Media Movement. We went on to develop and support the Independent Media Center around the Democratic and Republican Party National Conventions. We were the first independent TV media team to be given media credentials during those conventions." *Changing America* was a unique attempt to provide regular news and analysis from a working class, CPUSA perspective without being overly ideological or politically heavy handed. LeBlanc interviewed a wide array of community, labor, religious and cultural figures. Additionally, *Changing America* sought to broaden and deepen the party's relationships to mainstream political leaders, especially in the labor movement, though "it wasn't a CP show." LeBlanc and the *Changing America* crew were a welcomed sight on picket lines and at rallies and protests. The USW even gave *Changing America* an award for its coverage of the NNS strike. "We got the NNS CEO to admit on camera that he hired replacement workers. It was the key link that compelled the company to come back to the bargaining table," LeBlanc concluded.[80]

* * *

In spring 2000, LeBlanc was elected as a vice chair of the CPUSA responsible for producing *Changing America* and coordinating party communications work,[81] which included organizing speaking engagements for party leaders returning from international trips to China, Cuba and elsewhere.[82]

A year later she was again in Texas visiting comrades in Corpus Christi, Houston, Austin, San Antonio, Denton and Dallas; she also spoke with students at the University of North Texas. Her trip was part of the "CPUSA leadership's plan to travel to every corner of the United States to hold discussions and share observations about the country today."[83] Those discussions were part of what the party called the "pre-Convention discussion period." One such pre-convention question LeBlanc addressed in a *PWW* letter to the editor. She wrote, the "discussion has been interesting." Communists from across the country were then evaluating Gus Hall's legacy. They continued to assess the impact of the collapse of socialism in Eastern Europe. And they began to address questions of what socialism in the 21st century might look like. It was asked, "What is a vanguard party?" and "Is the CP a vanguard revolutionary party?" To LeBlanc, though, this wasn't the "starting point for discussing the role of the CP in our country today." She acknowledged the limited resources of the party and its shrinking cadre. She said, we "are a small party in a rapidly growing left movement," though it was added, Communists "are very well connected to struggles," as indicated by the response LeBlanc and others received with the TV show *Changing America.* She praised the recent upsurge and activism within "labor and [the] people's movements," calling it "fantastic." She characterized the left as "those who are willing to get involved to fight for social justice and who realize that there is no hope unless they do." Communists worked to include as broad an array of community groups, labor unions, religious organization and students in their analysis of what constituted a broad-based people's front. According to her, the "CP's greatest contribution... [was] to unite the left and help to keep the focus on class struggle issues." To her, "the left must be measured by its attempts to unite with mainstream America in struggle against the many-sided rightwing political agenda." LeBlanc emphasized the "strength of the left, along with its continuing search for how to organize and mobilize majority movements against the daily crimes of this system, is in a basic sense the determining factor in making social change." To her, this analysis "begins to answer the question what is revolutionary, since revolution ain't going to happen until millions see it as the way!" She added, "the Party can be and is, in our modest way, helping to organize for dramatic and, yes, revolutionary change." In conclusion, she wrote that "the word [vanguard] is hollow...[It is] a word that doesn't really fit with today's left movement and the Party's incredible possibilities." Ultimately, the "bottom line is unity," she continued, "in the fight against corporate domination," which required a "stronger more united left and a bigger Communist Party!"[84] Sam Webb, who became CPUSA national chair after Hall's death, agreed with LeBlanc. He noted in a spring National Board report, "We adjusted our strategic and tactical policies in the early 1980s because of the growth of reaction and the extreme right. What impelled us was the fact that the most anti-labor, anti-women, anti-people, racist and militarist sections of monopoly capital and their political representatives in our nation's capital were in ascendancy," and would soon be firmly in control. "Similar dangers, though greater, exist today," he concluded. "Thus, there is absolutely no reason to change our policy now."[85] LeBlanc would soon exemplify this policy through her leading role in United for Peace & Justice, the nation's largest peace coalition which was formed in fall 2002.

* * *

The horrific events of September 11, 2001 would not escape LeBlanc's or the party's analysis. "In moments of natural disaster people come together to respond," LeBlanc wrote just days after terrorist attacks. "Yet the destruction of the [World Trade Towers] is not a natural disaster, like a tornado or earthquake. It is a political disaster, an international disaster, a human tragedy that moves people to respond." She noted the patriotism on display; "flags are flying from windows," the U.S. flag "side by side with the Puerto Rican, Mexican and Irish flags...On street corners and doorsteps in neighborhoods around Manhattan burning candles stand as small monuments to hope and peace. Tens of thousands have participated in candlelight vigils. It's a city coming to terms with one of the most horrific events in U.S. history," LeBlanc added. She highlighted unity. Her main theme was ordinary working class people coming together during times of crisis. She noted the "Latino, Black and white, Arab, Asian and American Indian, immigrants and citizens" gathering at "command central" to help in whatever way possible. "Many are skilled workers wearing T-shirts of the Electrical Workers,

Ironworkers or Laborers unions," she added, emphasizing organized labor's contribution to the removal of debris and the search for life. "I'm an electrician," Lee, a member of the International Brotherhood of Electrical Workers Local 3, told LeBlanc. "We're just here to help and do whatever we can. Move rubble and whatever else they need us to do." "It's ugly, it's like a war, just be prepared," he continued. "This is the most horrendous thing I've seen in my life, just unnecessary carnage and pain," Barry, a laborer from Manhattan, told LeBlanc. According to her, a "sense of urgency and frustration" lingered on the faces of the tradesmen and women "as they anxiously wait for their name to be called for assignments at Ground Zero." LeBlanc added, "search and rescue teams have come from 15 countries." She also noted with pride that teams "have also come from the Pine Ridge Indian Reservation," where LeBlanc had lived during the historic stand-off at Wounded Knee. She said, "one of them was Wendell, who had organized an American Indian team made up of police officers, EMT's and firefighters." Conversely, *The New York Times* "interviewed CEO's to capture what they termed 'their wisdom' on how to handle this catastrophic event." LeBlanc saw this as an insult to the thousands of ordinary people desperately offering their help.

A few themes emerged in LeBlanc's conversations: "Unity and solidarity can make us stronger. Mourning is not a cry for vengeance. Together we have to find a way out of the crisis. [And]...Ground Zero solidarity can be turned toward the problems we will face in the days to come." As the Bush Administration began to rattle the sabre of war, New Yorkers resisted. "The president said we're at war. We don't want to become the people that we're dealing with now," Nancy, an onlooker holding a sign appreciating the Ground Zero crew, told LeBlanc. A college student told LeBlanc, "Yes, we believe that justice should be served, but you can't shed innocent blood because if we do, we become just like them. And if we become like them, then they are the ones that win."

Hector, a laborer from the Bronx, articulated the sentiments of most Americans when he told LeBlanc, "Two wrongs don't make a right."[86] Unfortunately, this simple concept seemed to allude the Bush Administration and its right-wing war hawks who quickly shifted their focus to "regime change" and an endless "war on terror."

By early 2002, the party had begun to organize against the "continuing U.S. bombing of Afghanistan and the danger of expansion of the war into Iraq, [the] intensified Israeli aggression against the Palestinian people and [the] mounting danger of [the] use of nuclear weapons." That March Communists held a national meeting on *U.S. Imperialism and the Struggle for Peace in the 21st Century* attended by peace and justice activists from 14 states. Mobilizing party members and allies for the April 20 March on Washington for Peace and Justice was the focus of the conference called by the party's Peace and Solidarity Commission. "We must do everything we can to mobilize all who oppose the Bush administration['s] policies into the streets of D.C.," said Libero Della Piana, national coordinator of the Young Communist League, one of the initiating organizations. LeBlanc noted that the importance of the April 20 mobilization "has grown dramatically," especially after the revelations of the administration's Nuclear Posture Review, which contained "contingency plans to use tactical nuclear weapons." "The Bush administration's threat to use first-strike nuclear weapons will set off an alarm for millions of people in our country about the danger of nuclear war and the need to come to D.C. to take action to save our planet," LeBlanc added. Sarah Staggs, chair of the Commission, connected the fight for peace to domestic issues. "Whether it is the struggle for affordable housing, for immigrant rights, for nationalization of the steel industry or for a just foreign policy, none can make progress while the current administration pursues its unending 'war on terrorism,'" she said. This policy "has become the rationale for pursuing a militaristic, anti-democratic, anti-labor, anti-women and racist agenda against all peoples, while wrapping it in the flag of patriotism," she concluded, "which has become a roadblock in the path" of peace. Staggs also called on the assembled party members to "come together to develop winning strategies for removing this roadblock, for building peace and international solidarity."[87]

By mid-April, LeBlanc was on her way to the Middle East and the Occupied Territories, the West Bank, Gaza and Israel. She was part of a 16-person delegation organized by Fellowship of Reconciliation, described as "the largest interfaith pacifist organization" in the U.S. The group hoped to "learn first-hand about the conflict through staying in homes and meeting with Palestinian and Israeli activists and organizations" working for peace. LeBlanc interviewed Palestinian and Israeli trade unionists, elected officials and peace activists. She also met with representatives of the Communist Party of Israel and the Palestinian People's Party.[88] In a phone interview with *PWW* associate editor, Terrie Albano, LeBlanc noted, "It's hard to fathom the intensity of the conflict...[Palestinians] cannot go to work, cannot go to school, many people who are ill cannot go to the hospital, food is in short supply." She said, "The level of violence is unimaginable." LeBlanc reported on a standoff with Israeli Defense Forces outside of the Church of the Nativity, which had been under siege by Israeli soldiers. Palestinian Authority officials and Hamas activists, as well as "women, children, nuns and priests" said they would "rather starve than come out and be killed or arrested" – and likely tortured – by the Israeli army. "We went...to bring food to the church and we were immediately surrounded by Israeli Defense Forces. We had a stand off [sic] with them for a few hours. We had brought food and were asking for a chance to meet with the people in the church." LeBlanc also went to the Beach refugee camp, "which has a population of 75,000 people who were forced into that area in 1948. Many families who never left...have grown up in a situation of being refugees in their own land," LeBlanc noted.

An elderly Palestinian told LeBlanc that he lived with his family, "my brothers and my parents, [and] 12 children in three rooms. We are not terrorists. We are people who just want our land back. We want a peaceful settlement. But we want a settlement that guarantees we can have a state that lives side-by-side with the Israeli state." While in Israel, LeBlanc attended a 15,000 person rally calling for an "end to the occupation and a two-state solution," highlighting the fact that many Israelis also do not agree with their government's actions. The rally showed that "at the grassroots that people want peace, but peace in the sense that two states live together and respect each other's rights." LeBlanc said the Israeli military received $5 billion a year from the U.S., which supports the occupation and continues the "cycle of violence." "The only reason the Israeli government can do what they are doing is because they get money from the U.S. to do it," she concluded.[89]

Shortly after returning, LeBlanc embarked on a nationwide tour. She told comrades in Chicago, "I was witness to an enormous human [rights] crisis." She called the Israeli military occupation "a living nightmare." Palestinians were living under "economic strangulation," she added, as unemployment soared "to 75 or 80 percent." The Israeli military has "systematically destroyed the Palestinian infrastructure." In Ramallah, Israeli forces "destroyed every computer in the Ministry of Education, destroyed and flooded the Ministry of Finance, destroyed banks and ATMs and blew up the television stations." Symbols of capitalism weren't spared from the onslaught either. "They even tore up *Burger King, Toys R Us* [and] *Nike*...The message they wanted to send is: 'This is not a viable economy.'" While in Chicago, LeBlanc spoke with an audience of 400 people at an Islamic Association for Palestine banquet, listeners of a WPNA Arab-Language radio program and met with activists and journalists at the Burbank Arab Center. LeBlanc also spoke with audiences in San Francisco, Santa Cruz, Berkeley, Oakland, Seattle, Los Angeles, Baltimore, New

Haven, Philadelphia, Boston and New York.[90] In Northern California, she told audiences, this "is a crisis that is all-sided, and requires a political solution, including international intervention." She added, "it isn't enough to build a movement in solidarity with the Palestinian people alone...because U.S. foreign policy is an issue of democracy," which the 2002 domestic elections had the potential to impact.[91]

In mid-June, LeBlanc wrote a searing critique of the Bush Administration. She noted, as President Bush and Israeli Prime Minister Sharon met in D.C., the Israeli Defense Force "reoccupied Ramallah with a shoot-to-kill curfew, forcing the Palestinian Authority to cancel the first meeting of its new cabinet." She said, the IDF "has systematically attempted to destroy the PA infrastructure," which included "surrounding the presidential headquarters and bulldozing sections." The World Bank estimated that the damage of the first four weeks of the "military incursion at $361 million." The IDF even ransacked PA police stations and "seized all weapons."[92] As violence escalated in the Middle East, LeBlanc's speaking tour continued. She shared the podium with Mazin Qumsiyeh of Al-Awda, a Palestinian professor at Yale Medical School, and Yael Martin, a Jewish peace activist from the group Promoting Enduring Peace, while in New Haven, Connecticut. LeBlanc emphasized the role of domestic peace activists. She called on activists "to build a movement that can end the Bush administration's never-ending war policies," which was "a unifying conclusion." LeBlanc also spoke in Hartford.[93]

By October, LeBlanc was back in Israel and Palestine where she attended the Communist Party of Israel's Congress.[94] Reporting from Ramallah, LeBlanc discussed her meeting with Yasir Arafat, the President of the Palestinian Authority. She noted that the "compound" had been "under a 10-day siege by the Israeli army." She said the Israeli army had hoped to "ignite a conflict that would have caused the assassination of Arafat." The Palestinian National Authority headquarters was destroyed in the bombing. Signs of the attack were everywhere. "Now bombed buildings stand next to half built buildings with people trying to go on living under the occupation... People cannot work regularly, children cannot go to school regularly and they live with an incredible sense of uncertainty." Curfews and travel restrictions "caused the deaths of many," too. Palestinians were dying from "common illnesses because they cannot reach hospitals for treatment or medicines." LeBlanc emotionally added, that "they live with this fear every day," especially children. According to LeBlanc, President Bush's comments calling for the "reform of the PA" gave a "green light to step up the military actions on the West Bank and Gaza." Additionally, she argued that bringing "an end to the occupation" was the "only way for peace to be negotiated." While in the Mideast LeBlanc met with students from Haifa University, the deputy mayor – an Arab and a Communist – who told LeBlanc about the Israeli military's harassment of children there. She noted that of the 34 municipal council members, two were Communists. She also met with leaders of the Histradut, the Israeli labor federation, which was then in the "midst of a national strike of 150,000 workers, public and private, for cost of living increases." She added that she would soon participate in a solidarity action to form a human shield "to protect farmers." A Palestinian farmer had recently been killed by Israeli settlers.[95]

While LeBlanc was in Israel and Palestine, peace activists from across the United States met in Washington, D.C. to convene what would become United For Peace & Justice, an international coalition that grew to over 1,400 member groups from all across the world.[96] In an interview with the Australian *Guardian*, LeBlanc reflected on UFPJ's birth and said, it "grew out of the struggle to prevent the war in Iraq." The coalition brought together "traditional peace and disarmament groups nationally" with diverse local groups all with the goal of preventing war. Within a few years of its founding, LeBlanc would ascend to UFPJ's top leadership and in 2005 be elected

UFPJ national co-chair, along with Leslie Cagan, a long-time peace and LGBT rights activists. To LeBlanc, the war in Afghanistan, which started in fall 2001, "was initiated under the rubric of the global war on terror" by President Bush. The goal was to maintain "US military dominance by his [Bush's] pre-emptive strike policy and his endless war policy." After September 11, 2001, "there were people who felt that perhaps it [the attack on the Twin Towers] was an act of war. We in the peace movement," she continued, "of course raised our voices and said that September 11 was not a call to war but was in fact a time for our country to discuss in a broad national dialogue what...gave rise to acts of terror and attacks on civilians."[97]

During this time, LeBlanc recalled, "we [the CPUSA] made a decision that the party should work fulltime on peace. The party was involved in traditional peace movements all over the country. I was put in charge of mobilizing the labor movement and communities of color." LeBlanc and other Communists were welcomed with open arms by UFPJ.[98]

As part of its initial peace campaign, UFPJ called for rallies and protests on February 15, 2003[99] – less than four months after its founding conference. At a January CPUSA National Board meeting, LeBlanc noted, that "the list of international unions taking positions against the war on Iraq had two new additions," the Communications Workers Union of America and the United Farm Workers. She said, the unions had joined with "the National Council of Churches, with 140,000 congregations, MoveOn.org, over 40 U.S. cities, the Catholic Church and scores of labor, civil rights and other faith based organizations in opposing a unilateral, first-strike war against Iraq." She also emphasized the "upsurge of Gulf War veterans and military families against the war," and the founding of UFPJ in October. She added, "On Feb. 15 we will be in the streets, along with millions around the world to show that the American people are taking a stand against the war. Now we have to move from getting resolutions passed to getting buses on the highway to New York," she concluded. Adan Jesus Martin, the newly elected national co-coordinator of the YCL, mentioned the National Youth and Student Peace Coalition's call for a student strike on March 5. "It's hard to find a youth movement not against the war," he told fellow Communists. "We know thousands of youth will go to New York and San Francisco on Feb. 15 and come back to organize the student strike on March 5."[100] Both LeBlanc and Martin's comments proved prophetic as 790 demonstrations took place around the world on February 15, with 500,000 people participating in New York City alone.[101] Additionally, the NYSPC-led student strike resulted in an estimated 30,000 to 50,000 students walking out of college and university classes on March 5. That Jessica Marshall, also a YCL national co-coordinator, helped lead NYSPC served to highlight the role of young Communists in organizing mass protests against war,[102] something W.E.B. DuBois members had been adept at decades earlier.

That spring, LeBlanc reported on UFPJ's first national strategy conference held June 6-8. She noted, 550 delegates from 38 states representing 325 local and national peace groups converged and reflected on their early successes; i.e. the hugely successful protests held on February 15, "which mobilized millions around the U.S. with a half million in NYC alone." She called the day of action "a high point of resistance to the Bush administration's preemptive war strategy." The protests "brought together national peace organizations with newly-formed local peace coalitions, along with national civil rights, labor, religious, student and immigrant rights groups." "From that day on," LeBlanc added, "UFPJ helped to give voice to millions who stood in opposition to preemptive war on Iraq." The mass rally was characterized by *The New York Times* in its February 16 edition as the "other super power." For LeBlanc though, this was just the start. The June conference "drew diverse constituencies into action together, articulating the connections between foreign and domestic issues." According to LeBlanc, conference participants "came from communities where the policies of spending tax dollars for war and occupation is being felt every day in their schools, hospitals and senior centers." Participants "know from their own experience the interconnections between military spending and budget cuts, attacks on democratic rights and whipping up a war drive," as illustrated by the Patriot Act. As the conference convened, the White House and the right-wing on Capitol Hill "pushed through a Senate Bill to lift the ban on research and development of small nuclear weapons," which highlighted the "critical importance of an active and expanding peace movement." For LeBlanc, discussion of the "2004 elections dramatized the critical importance of turning back the far right control of the White House and Congress." With the demise of socialism in Eastern Europe and the Soviet Union, many feared U.S. imperialism would now have a free hand to unilaterally impose its will militarily around the world. The Middle East was a testing ground. The terrorist attacks on September 11 provided the spurious justification. "The priority for UFPJ of mass demonstrations, educational campaigns, lobbying and voter registration can be a powerful force in the 2004 elections," roughly 18 months away, and help "defeat the dangerous, strategic outlook of unending war of the Bush administration." LeBlanc was elected to the UFPJ steering committee at the 2005 conference,[103] which took place in St. Louis; this author attended.

Just a few weeks later thousands of activists, "stretching from 52nd to 48th streets in mid-Manhattan protested outside of George Bush's $2,000-a-plate campaign fundraiser." They "drew attention to the Bush administration's attacks on women's rights, health care, childcare, and worker's rights, and denounced Bush's policy of unending war." Carla Goldstein spoke for many of the protesters when she told this author, "We want to build a broad coalition of organizations who are connecting the dots between the issues." Goldstein, vice president of public affairs for Planned Parenthood of New York, added, "Bush's policies are dangerous to women's health," not just world peace. David Epstein, of the Union of Needletrades, Industrial and Textile Employees, said Bush "has done nothing to help American workers or workers overseas. He has taken away our civil liberties and started a war for no reason." LeBlanc told the assembled protesters, "The Bush administration has attacked women, attacked families...and took us to war on a lie." Some protesters held signs saying, "Drop Bush, not bombs!" LeBlanc noted, that "While Bush is lying, U.S. corporations are making profits." This was the real reason for the war. Despite the protests, the fundraiser "brought in around $4 million" for Bush's reelection campaign.[104]

By August, LeBlanc was in Japan attending the 2003 World Conference Against A and H Bombs representing UFPJ and the CPUSA. "To meet with the representatives of peace movements from here and around the world is not only an honor, but also a new opportunity to strengthen the movement for peace and justice in the United States," she told the assembled peace activists. While UFPJ's "efforts did not stop this senseless, illegal war...it gave birth to new levels of united political action by millions of people." She said, UFPJ "represents far more than these broad organizations," which had grown to over 600 groups by summer 2003. "Our coalition represents the emerging majority support for peace, justice and democracy." To her, the administration "defied the rising democratic upsurge," and pushed "ahead with its illegal war in the face of world opposition." Claims that Iraq had weapons of mass destruction proved false. Claims that Saddam Hussein was linked to Al-Qaeda was a lie. "The Bush administration took the real fears of the American people and went to war," she added. "Now they are sacrificing the lives of Iraqis and U.S. troops to satisfy their drive to control that region of the world." To many, this "drive" was nothing more than an effort to enrich oil companies and private contractors.

Of particular importance was the issue of nuclear weapons. "Our coalition takes a clear stand against the Bush administration's new nuclear weapon[s] posture, which, for the first time since the bombing of Hiroshima and Nagasaki, makes a first-strike nuclear attack a 'legitimate' option. We call on the U.S. to return to compliance with the ABM [Anti-Ballistic Missile] treaty and put an end to weapons in space." LeBlanc called for "a strong unified movement involving a broad cross section of the people," if peace was to be won. However, "in the final analysis, the way to break the Bush administration's pre-emptive, first strike foreign policy is by defeating Bush and the right wing in the 2004 election," LeBlanc added connecting militarism abroad with electoral politics domestically. "Without strong ties of solidarity with the world peace movement, we cannot succeed," she concluded.[105]

LeBlanc also met with Nishiguchi Hikaru, of the International Bureau of the Japanese Communist Party, "to discuss their common struggle against the Bush foreign policy doctrine of first strike nuclear war." This was the first official meeting of the two Communist Parties since the early 1980s; the CPUSA had attacked the JCP, calling it "anti-Soviet, anti-working class and anti-Marxism-Leninism." The rapprochement was initiated by CPUSA national chair, Sam Webb, and international secretary, Marilyn Bechtel. "We believe the unity of the world communist movement is more important than ever," LeBlanc said. "Our parties are each working urgently to avert U.S. imperialism's rampant drive for world domination and its doctrine of perpetual pre-emptive warfare." At the JPC's 22nd Congress in 2000, the party claimed over 380,000 members; its newspaper had two million subscribers. The JPC also has "significant representation" in both houses of the national legislature and "has many assembly members." "We are excited to once again be linked with a very important party which is deeply involved in the struggle for a world free of the threat of nuclear weapons and closely connected to the daily struggles of the Japanese people," LeBlanc told the *People's Weekly World.*[106]

By spring 2004, UFPJ was organizing for another massive New York City rally and protest – this time at the Republican National Convention at Madison Square Garden. "There are two key moments this year when people throughout the United States will have the opportunity to send a resounding message of opposition to the Bush Agenda: Nov. 2, Election Day, and Aug. 29 in New York City," UFPJ said in a press release. According to the peace coalition "many thousands of individuals and hundreds of groups — antiwar, civil rights, immigrant, religious, labor, feminist, environmental, and many more — are planning to participate in this demonstration."[107] They hoped to send a clear message to the Bush administration and the right-wing's war hawks. On August 29, the opening day of the RNC, over "a half million people marched...to say 'No to the Bush agenda!'" According to organizers, the event "displayed a rising energy" and paved the way for "millions to have their say in the voting booth" on Election Day. LeBlanc noted, that UFPJ – and its coalition partners – were now shifting "to the precincts, where door-to-door work is already well underway." UFPJ "is busy making plans for mobilization of 1 million peace voters, with a focus on the battle ground states," she added. The march and rally "was a day to excite and inspire even greater efforts...to convince the 'maybe voter' that our future depends on their involvement in this year's elections. And it was a march heard around the world." She also made note of the bus full of protesters from the Ojibwe Indian Reservation in Wisconsin and the "peace trains" from Connecticut and New Jersey. She said, "On Aug. 29 we marched together, and now we're moving on to the next national action – Election Day."[108]

The Bush Administration proved more resilient than LeBlanc, the party or UFPJ had expected. Bush started his second term in January 2005 amidst growing protests, though, as "Over half of all Americans now believe the U.S. war in Iraq is not worth the human and financial cost." In fact, as LeBlanc noted, "Only 36 percent believe that maintaining current troop levels will ensure safety and stability in the country." To her, this was "a turning point moment for U.S. policy and the peace movement." "How can the peace movement meet the challenge," she asked? "Now is the time to build a massive, broad movement calling on Congress to set the date for removal of all U.S. troops and bases from Iraq," she wrote in the *PWW*. "The peace movement must work at the grassroots to show that the ongoing occupation of Iraq is the biggest barrier to rebuilding America's cities, from the Gulf Cost to neighborhoods across the nation." "The Iraq war price tag surpasses $200 billion," she added, as "nearly 2,000 U.S. soldiers have died" with "thousands more severely injured" and "veterans' hospitals are being closed." LeBlanc also noted the presidents "racist indifference in the days following Hurricane Katrina." Nearly 2,000 people perished during the flooding due to the administration's negligence and "distorted priorities." According to LeBlanc, "National Guard troops who should have been ready to respond to this natural disaster were in Iraq fighting a war based on lies." LeBlanc wasn't alone in this opinion, though. A *Wall Street Journal/NBC* poll found that "60 percent of Americans said rebuilding the Gulf Coast should be a higher priority than 'establishing democracy' in Iraq." The poll also reported that voters "top choice for paying for Gulf Coast recovery is [through] cutting funds for war." On top of UFPJ's ongoing and massive protests, LeBlanc also noted "shifting public opinion" against the Iraq war and "unprecedented criticism by military families and soldiers, most dramatically galvanized by Gold Star mother Cindy Sheehan's quest to meet with Bush in Crawford, Texas." LeBlanc also noted the anti-war sentiment among labor unions and the work of U.S. Labor Against the War that has "worked tirelessly over the last three years to pass antiwar resolutions in local unions, state federations and international unions...[USLAW] organized a national tour of Iraqi trade unionists." And their "activity culminated in...a historic antiwar resolution at the AFL-CIO's national convention in July," which, she added, was "the first time the labor federation has ever passed a resolution opposing a U.S. war." All this momentum was the "result of hard work by the peace movement...[UFPJ] organized some of the largest antiwar demonstration in the country's history, as well as countless peace actions in small towns in every state...[Its] multifaceted approach, including lobbying, massive mobilizations, grassroots education, civil disobedience and coalition-building," had built the "broadest movement possible to bring the troops home," LeBlanc concluded.[109]

On September 24, "300,000 antiwar demonstrators marched past the White House...chanting, 'End the war now – Bring the troops home!'" It was the largest peace protest since the invasion of Iraq in March 2003. Members of the Service Employees International Union, the American Federation of Teachers and the International Brotherhood of Electrical Workers, among others, participated. The demonstration was augmented by "mass lobbying" sponsored by UFPJ demanding that "lawmakers support an 'exit strategy' from Iraq and reconstruction at home." The tactic of mass civil disobedience was also used; "370 protesters sat down in front of the White House" and were arrested. LeBlanc and four other party members took part in the action.[110] By late October, LeBlanc was in Arizona speaking to comrades and allies about "Iraq, peace and U.S. imperialism."[111] In early December, she was in Chicago keynoting the "packed" 18th Annual *PWW* Banquet where she "described the dramatic growth of the peace movement." She noted, that the "legislative arena has become the key arena of the battle to end the occupation."[112]

Just a few days later, LeBlanc was in London; 1,200 people had gathered there for the international Stop the War Conference. In an interview with the *Morning Star*, she noted, "The endless spending on the military budget is increasingly making the [U.S.] economy unstable."

She added, "Huge numbers of people don't even have medical insurance. People are making the link. That frightens the right." She recalled a recent visit to the Pine Ridge Indian reservation. "It's one of the largest reservations in the country," she said. "There are 800 people from the reservation now serving in Iraq because of the predatory recruitment of the U.S. military...This reservation has the three poorest counties in the country with 85 percent unemployment. It is clear that the Bush administration made it a focus to go into the most impoverished communities — especially communities of color and immigrant communities — to press people who are in dire circumstances to join the military." This was a critique LeBlanc had been articulating for over 30 years. The London Conference called for "worldwide protests on the third anniversary of the invasion of Iraq [on] March 18-19."[113]

LeBlanc's leadership in UFPJ was instrumental throughout the first decade of the 21st century. Continuing to connect the struggle for peace to domestic issues and electoral politics was central to her activism as the decade neared its end. Leading up to the 2008 presidential elections, LeBlanc shifted her role somewhat and became UFPJ's organizing coordinator. The peace coalition had set a goal of mobilizing 25,000 volunteers to contact one million people on Saturday, September 20, 2008. They called it the "Million Doors for Peace" campaign. The goal: To "ask at least one million people throughout the country to sign petitions urging the next Congress to bring U.S. troops home from Iraq within one year." It was noted that the campaign was "unique in the history of anti-war movements. Instead of bringing tens of thousands of people together for one visible protest, participants will be organizing on the ground across the U.S., with an eye toward one-on-one public education and influencing members of Congress."[114]

In July 2009, LeBlanc toured Australia as a guest of the Communist Party of Australia, which was then helping to organize protests against the Talisman Sabre joint

U.S.-Australian military exercises then taking place.[115] In an interview with the *Guardian*, she noted the excitement then still resonating in the U.S. due to the election of Barack Obama. She said, "I think the peace movement scored an incredible victory with the election of Barack Obama." The new president kept his pledge that he "would set a deadline, a timetable for U.S. withdrawal from Iraq... Of course," she added, "the timetable that has been set by the new administration is not all that we would like. But you never win a total victory, you always win part and you continue to struggle," something the veteran Communist knew from experience. "Now we are trying to take that movement that rose in support of the Obama election and the majority opposition to the war in Iraq into a new national dialogue of the history and the impact of the war and the occupation of Afghanistan." Her optimism was apparent. We "are operating in a new environment, in a new political space in which perhaps we will have great success in helping people understand that you cannot solve issues around national security with war." She wasn't naive, though. She argued, "We also want to put a lot of pressure on the Obama administration to make good on a campaign promise that the leading edge of policy would be diplomacy first...[not] endless war."[116]

* * *

LeBlanc also began working fulltime for Peace Action, the nation's largest grassroots peace organization with chapters across the country. She would stay with Peace Action from 2009 until spring 2015 when she left to work for the Alliance for a Just Society "on a new project to create a national American Indian Leadership network."[117]

* * *

In winter 2016, roughly one month before Donald Trump was inaugurated as the 45th president of the

United States, LeBlanc was celebrating. The federal government, during the final days of the Obama administration, had announced that it would "not approve a permit for a segment of the Dakota Access Pipeline through the Standing Rock territory," which was "a landmark environmental justice and Native tribal sovereignty victory." As a Native American activist, LeBlanc had been fighting for indigenous peoples' rights, since at least 1973 with her involvement in the American Indian Movement and the stand-off at Wounded Knee. To her, this victory – though temporary – "laid bare the workings of systemic racism and its impact in Indian Country, reflected in militarized policing, racist agitation and the systemic denial of civil rights." To her, Native peoples were "perform[ing] their historic role as protectors of Mother Earth." And the victory was "a recognition of tribal sovereignty generated by an unprecedented, Native-led grassroots movement." She said, Native protesters "interrupted and disrupted the narrative" and fought back against "profit-hungry extractive industries [that] threaten the well-being of our land, water and air." As director of the NOA, LeBlanc argued that the "strategy and tactics of the Standing Rock movement were framed by the power of Native traditional beliefs and our special relationship with Mother Earth." Additionally, "water was the basis of unity across tribes, movements, generations and non-Native allies." The NOA's goal: To "build an infrastructure of close working relationships[,] to organize training sessions for Native community organizers[,] to strengthen the relationships...between Native nonprofits and tribes [and] to respond to the new dangers to land, air, and water that the GOP-controlled White House and Congress will present," which included the roll back of President Obama's order and the deregulation of environmental safeguards by the Trump Administration.

According to LeBlanc, "Never has there been such close collaboration between more than 300 tribes alongside

Native nonprofits and social movement activists. Standing Rock has changed everything."

Though President Trump opened the way for development of the pipeline, LeBlanc was still optimistic. "The victory no one can take back is the unprecedented unity of action of over 300 tribes, 22 municipalities, tens of thousands who have come to Standing Rock and the millions who have signed petitions, donated money, took divestment action or marched in their own towns and cities. Native-led direct action and solidarity are the foundation stones as we continue to protect our water and Mother Earth," she concluded.[118]

As the 2018 mid-term elections neared, Native Americans faced another assault – this time on their right to vote. The North Dakota Republican-controlled state legislature, still reeling from Democrat Heidi Heitkamp's 2012 Senate victory, passed a new law designed to suppress Native American votes. Heitkamp won with strong support from Native Americans, of which there are about 30,000 in North Dakota. Honest observers acknowledged that the law "disproportionately affects Native Americans," and put Heitkamp at even more of a disadvantage. With passage of the law, residential address were now required for voting. This proved to be a real obstacle, especially on reservations, where "Buildings lack numbers; streets lack signs. Even when a house has an address in official records, residents don't necessarily know what it is," it was noted in *The New York Times*; the article included a photo of LeBlanc helping with GOTV efforts.[119] Despite the additional hurdle, Native American voters "showed up to the polls in record numbers" on Election Day. Voting advocacy groups and Tribal leaders "worked overtime, down [to] the wire, and spent hundreds of thousands of dollars to get Native voters the tribal IDs needed to successfully cast a ballot," a clear rebuke of the GOP's voter suppression strategy. LeBlanc was one of those organizers. The press noted that she "helped organize an aggressive get-out-the-vote campaign in Standing Rock. She and other activists knocked on doors in the blistering cold throughout the reservation in the two weeks leading up to Election Day and on Tuesday, bused voters to the polls." According to LeBlanc, Native peoples "believed they had the right to vote and they want to make their right count." They "exercised their sovereign, civil, and inherent right to vote in this historic election." Though Heitkamp lost, 1,464 ballots were cast in Sioux County, where Standing Rock is located, an increase from the 1,257 ballots cast in the 2016 presidential elections; 84 percent of the ballots were cast for Heitkamp; there are only 2,752 eligible voters in Sioux County.[120]

Roughly 45 years after her participation in the standoff at Wounded Knee, LeBlanc was still fighting for Native rights. She was still challenging corporate control of natural resources and demanding that Native peoples have a voice at the table. As a Native American woman and Communist, she ran for public office, challenged police misconduct, helped build the Independent Media Movement and was instrumental in leading the largest U.S. peace coalition of the early 21st century.

In March 2017, LeBlanc was In Washington, D.C. speaking in front of thousands of Native American activists and their allies. At that rally she was introduced "as a powerhouse of a woman,"[121] an accurate description. Judith LeBlanc exemplifies the courage, moral and political fortitude, we desperately need as racism, sexism, corporate greed, and climate catastrophe plague our world.

Chapter 6

W. Alphaeus Hunton: The National Negro Congress, the Council on African Affairs and Black Liberation

It was early 1966. A coup led by a group of reactionary military leaders determined to stoke ethnic rivalries and build their "financial empires,"[1] had recently deposed of Kwame Nkrumah, the charismatic socialist first president of the newly independent African nation of Ghana. As an international leader of a "new, more militant generation of Pan-Africanists," Nkrumah was "determined to disprove those who doubted the ability of Africans to govern themselves."[2] This was a goal revolutionary leaders throughout the continent strove towards. The coup, backed by imperialist powers and supported by the CIA,[3] was a setback for liberation in Africa, an attempt to roll back the gains then being made by national liberation movements throughout the world – with the aid of ascendant socialism.[4]

In an "effort to attack notions of white superiority and black inferiority,"[5] Nkrumah – in late 1961 – invited the activist-scholar and now Communist Party, USA member, W.E.B. DuBois, to Ghana to oversee the "major work" of the *Encyclopedia Africana.* This was "a project Du Bois had contemplated and longed for for at least fifty years," and was considered by some to potentially be "the crowning achievement of his long life,"[6] a life full of tremendous accomplishments. As "head of a New Negro Encyclopedia," DuBois was "provided funds, a home and an office," a secretary and "at least five" research assistants.[7] However, DuBois - now 94 years old - needed more help with the monumental undertaking, which is why in early 1962 he asked the African American Communist intellectual, his friend and co-worker, William Alphaeus Hunton, to join him in Ghana. By July 1962 DuBois' health had declined dramatically, requiring hospitalization. He left Hunton in charge of the *Encyclopedia* as its Secretariat,[8] a position he would hold until the 1966 coup.

Hunton poured himself into the project. He "built the conceptual, human and material framework" for the projected 10 volume *Encyclopedia.* "He organized the staff, hammered out a list of entries, recruited contributors, and launched a monthly bulletin to keep all interested parties informed of the progress of the work." As James T. Campbell noted, the "actual business of getting the project up and running," fell on Hunton due to DuBois' declining health. Shortly after DuBois' death – in August 1963 – Hunton "embarked on an exhausting continental tour to organize corresponding secretariats in other decolonizing nations."[9] He had envisioned a project embraced and supported by the entire African diaspora. He told *Freedomways* readers in retrospect, "We of course had to start from zero, nothing comparable to what we planned ever having been published."[10] Unfortunately, as Hunton was working relentlessly, busily planning content entries and "organizing a committee of specialists from various parts of Africa,"[11] the coup ousted his patron Nkrumah and dashed his dream of completing DuBois' most ambitious work.

Writing from Ghana, Hunton's wife, Dorothy, told her friend, Esther Cooper Jackson, "A [Alphaeus] and I are both adjusting to our new way of life since the coup." She noted that many of their friends had left. "[O]ur circle has become a mere dot," she added dejectedly. "However, we are carrying on, hoping conditions will improve." She said, research on the *Encyclopedia* was progressing at a much "slower pace." "A is [now] only an area editor, and his new contract is for only one year, an unpleasant situation, but he's making the best of it."[12] Of course, the Hunton's had no way of knowing how things would soon change – and for the worse. "Right now I'm in a very depressed mood," she continued to Esther Cooper. "Three days ago the [Ghanaian] C.I.D. [Criminal Investigation Department] had a warrant to search our house. First they made a search of A's office and then came here...looking for what, I don't know." Somewhat jokingly Mrs. Hunton added, "it would take them weeks to go through all the [research] material we have," not the mere hours they had spent rummaging through papers.

Reflecting on the persecution they had experienced in the U.S. – a partial reason for accepting DuBois' invitation to relocate to Ghana – Dorothy commented, "I thought we were through with that when we left the states, but one never knows." With Nkrumah's ousting the Hunton's once again became subversive, though "we have done nothing but mind our business and work."[13] That their work supported national liberation and socialism served to make them enemies of U.S. imperialism and by default the post-coup Ghanaian ruling elite. Shortly thereafter, Mrs. Hunton was writing Esther Cooper again, "a hurried note to let you know that we have been deported." The Hunton's in a "mad scramble" packed. Due to Alphaeus' health, they were faced with the "nerve racking suspense" of jail or, hopefully, becoming passengers on a passing freight ship. Ghanaian officials quickly ordered a Farrell Lines freighter, the appropriately named *African Lightening*, to take on the Hunton's. "So ended our nearly five years in Ghana," Dorothy concluded. Reeling from the trauma, she added, "we are still a bit numb from the experience,"[14] an experience not unlike the political repression Alphaeus Hunton had faced throughout his activist life.

After a month long voyage, Alphaeus and Dorothy Hunton made their way to Staten Island where Alphaeus was interviewed by *The New York Times*. He called the expulsion, "unnerving and humiliating," but optimistically added that the *Encyclopedia* "was a pan-African project, not a Ghanaian one," which he hoped to continue working on. At the time of the coup, he continued, "articles were already being collected for the first volume" and the "board had hoped to enlarge the staff from 11 to 55." Hunton had asked the Nkrumah government to "double the $40,000 budget." However, since the coup funding had increasingly become a point of contention.[15] According to Nkrumah, who had been in China during the coup, the *Encyclopedia* was "being deliberately broken up because of the principles and ideology which inspired it,"[16] namely, national liberation and socialism, ideas Hunton had committed himself to three decades earlier. Hunton and Nkrumah, then a leader of the African Student Association, first met in April 1944, at a Council on African Affairs conference in New York.[17] Their meeting foreshadowed a coalescence of forces that resulted in a continent spanning drama for African American equality and national liberation.[18]

* * *

William Alphaeus Hunton, born in Atlanta, Georgia on September 18, 1903, was a scholar, political activist and life-long member of the CPUSA. While still young, he moved with his family to Brooklyn, where he finished high school. He graduated from Howard University in 1924 and Harvard University in 1926; afterward he taught English at Howard and led the effort to organize the university's faculty into the American Federation of Teachers Local 440.[19] After the faculty's victory, he urged the union and its members to engage in Washington's larger movements for social and economic justice. According to fellow Howard professor and Communist, Doxey A. Wilkerson, Hunton not only helped to organize the union, but also "fought to sustain [it] as a viable instrument for academic and social progress." Wilkerson added, the activities of the union "extended far beyond the campus, in support of working men's struggles in many places,"[20] an indicator of Hunton's leadership.

* * *

In 1936, Hunton attended the founding convention of the National Negro Congress in Chicago. Along with over "800 delegates representing 551 organizations and over 3 million people," Hunton helped build what eventually became "a broad federation of some 3,000 civic, religious and fraternal organizations"[21] committed to social, cultural, political and economic equality for African Americans.

Born out of a 1935 Howard University meeting between prominent African American leaders, including Socialist A. Phillip Randolph and Communist James W. Ford, the Congress reflected a "growing convergence of outlook between Communists and activist black intellectuals."[22] This was a convergence powerful enough to shake U.S. capitalism and its foundational cornerstone, white supremacy, to its core. Consequently, as a result of the 1935 meeting Howard University was put in the government's crosshairs. Anticommunists attempted to "silence and actually shut down the university."[23] John P. Davis, head of the Joint Committee for National Recovery and the person primarily responsible for sponsoring the initial conference, had been a CPUSA member since at least the fall of 1935, and possibly "for longer than generally believed."[24] This added fuel to the governments' investigative fire, especially, as he was "really [the person] running the National Negro Congress,"[25] not Randolph, the titular president. While at a meeting in the "citadel of the Party's Negro policies – the Central Committee's Negro Commission," Davis "characterized the building of a broad NNC as 'a paramount task of the Party.'" That Davis was the only fulltime NNC staff person with Communist secretaries, likely raised additional investigative eyebrows, as did his 1937 visit to the Soviet Union.[26] This visit served to highlight socialism's role in bolstering African American equality. As the Chicago area African American party leader, Claude Lightfoot, wrote, "The Communist Party threw all of its forces at the national and local levels to help him [Davis] put it [the NNC Convention] together," including mundane, organizational tasks like securing the actual convention hall.[27]

Despite government harassment, the NNC organized for workers' rights, against fascism and used "mass-protest tactics to challenge racial discrimination." Communists helped create a movement and organization "of national significance whose constituency and leadership extended considerably beyond the Party's ranks." Hunton was very proud of the NNC's successes, which he spent his life attempting to duplicate. As Mark Naison points out in *Communists in Harlem During the Depression*, while the NNC wasn't "promoted as a Communist initiative...[reds] played a significant, and possibly determinative role in setting the stage for the congress's creation."[28] Communists, like Hunton – who officially joined the party around this time[29] – "did not stand out politically." At the congress' founding convention the keynote argued, "the Negro must combine with white labor and overthrow the existing order in order to wrest their common rights from capitalism which exploits them both," a sentiment shared by Communists who focused on grunt work. They "arranged meetings, handled correspondences and organized fund raising." Basically, the CPUSA maintained a "low-keyed Party presence."[30] The NNC became "the embodiment"[31] of the party's Popular Front strategy, and quite possibly, as party member Harry Haywood later recalled, "the greatest Black united front movement of the period."[32]

According to James W. Ford, the NNC "was conceived" as a "rallying center for the Negro people to fight off greater oppression." It was an organizational center with the potential to align all "groupings among the Negro people," conservative, "middle-of-the-roaders," and leftists, including Communists. "We want, to the fullest extent," Ford continued, "to help make the [NNC] movement something that represents the broadest sections of the Negro people, an instrument for combatting the many evils which face the Negro people...We are interested in working with all who, like us want to reach the same goal,"[33] namely African American equality. For example, "Every Communist organization in Harlem, from the Young Liberators, to the Unemployed Council to the ILD [International Labor Defense],"[34] helped to build the NNC, while simultaneously organizing others – churches, fraternal groups, the YMCA and NAACP – around a shared Popular Front platform.

Strategically, the Popular Front was understood to mean that Communists should embrace anyone willing to help fight for workers' rights and African American equality. Advancing socialism was not then the main strategic goal. The party's acceptance "reached unprecedented heights."[35] Within five months of its founding, NNC councils existed in 26 cities and 70 chapters were formed across the country.[36] That many African Americans, like Hunton, simultaneously joined the NNC and CPUSA served to bolster an emerging Red-Black alliance.

Hunton quickly ascended to NNC leadership. As a member of its national executive board, he led the Washington, D.C. chapter and chaired the Labor Committee; his comrade, Wilkerson, chaired the Civic Affairs Committee. An "astute political journalist," Hunton also joined the editorial board of the NNC's journal, *Congress View*. He led campaigns to "Blast Jim Crow Out of Washington" and, as he put it, "make the district budget serve the human needs of the community" through boycotts, pickets, demonstrations, petitions and strikes. Hunton also "worked untiringly to bring Black workers into the trade unions."[37] The D.C. NNC directly challenged employment discrimination and police brutality. They were in many ways a precursor to today's #BlackLivesMatter movement.

It seemed like a new day with the birth of the NNC. A vibrant and energized organization was systematically exposing police violence and abuse, something Communists would continue to do throughout the 1950s and into the 1970s and 1980s with William L. Patterson's Civil Rights Congress [38] and Charlene Mitchell's National Alliance Against Racist and Political Repression, respectively. For example, when in late August 1936 Leonard Basey was shot dead by D.C. police, the NNC rallied and called for an indictment of the officer. The Black press screamed *KILLER-COP FREE.* It was reported that Basey was "the fortieth colored person shot to death by Metropolitan police since 1925" and that "Every officer involved has been exonerated." The *Daily Worker* published a list of the slain African Americans. The district attorney was indignant, telling Adam Lapin, the *Daily Worker* Washington bureau chief, he was "not interested in the case." By November, the officer was retired with a pension. The NNC was enraged. They saw the early retirement as a slap in the face to the Black community, perhaps a reward for maintaining the then prevailing racial order. The NNC lobbied for a House subcommittee investigation and formed the Joint Committee for Civil Rights in the District of Columbia, which sponsored a series of weekly radio broadcasts. John P. Davis told radio listeners, "A coroner's jury has held that an officer who has a mental fear for his life has a right to kill another person who has done nothing to cause that fear, who is not armed, and who has submitted peacefully to arrest." This is a scenario eerily similar to today's police killings. Like the #BlackLivesMatter movement, Hunton and the NNC dramatically brought public pressure to bear against institutionalized racism and the misuse and abuse of police power. They even organized a "public trial" condemning the "killer cops," demonstrating the effectiveness of "new-style tactics" designed to use "theatrics"[39] to garner public attention and support.

"Washington sets the pattern of discrimination against the Negro people," Hunton wrote. Its laws "establish the nation's unwritten laws by unofficial endorsement of, or passive indifference to practices of discrimination, segregation and brutal oppression."[40] That the "nation's unwritten laws" included a racial hierarchy designating African Americans as targets wasn't lost on Hunton or other Communists. These radicals would soon look abroad in their quest for allies[41] powerful enough to compel concessions away from Jim Crow and police terror. As Wilkerson would later recall, "there was one period of two or three months in which a Negro was shot by police on the average of once a week, usually in the back, and never with any punishment for the offending officers." Shortly thereafter, the NNC with the aid of local Communists led several marches and organized a conference of more than 100 organizations at the Lincoln Temple Congregational Church. At the conference, Hunton outlined several demands and announced a forthcoming mass meeting. The demands: removal of the police superintendent; denial of pension to the officer who shot and killed Basey; suspension and trial of other officers involved in recent shootings and police terror; and compensation for the victims. The next day 1,200 rallied.[42] As Erik S. Gellman points out in *Death Blow to Jim Crow: The National Negro Congress and the Rise of Militant Civil Rights*, Hunton "played an essential behind-the-scenes role in the police brutality campaign,"[43] and helped to build a broad based, Black and white, movement for social and economic justice. Wilkerson, added, "Alphaeus was in the thick of all these and related campaigns...He generally worked quietly, sensing and doing what needed to be done, seldom making big speeches, and never seeking the headlines; but those of us who worked with him knew very well that he was the mainstay of the struggle."[44]

In October 1937, the second NNC Convention was held in Philadelphia. Nearly 1,200 delegates attended.[45] The NNC's dramatic growth in the Black community centered on issues like police brutality and workers' rights and paralleled the growth of Black unionism generally. From

1936-1940 Black union membership increased from 100,000 to 500,000.[46] It was noted in the convention's *Official Proceedings* that the "past few months have witnessed the steady march forward of thousands of Negro workers into the progressive trade union movement," namely the CIO, which has "won new victories." As a result, "tens of thousands" have now "gained increased pay, shorter hours at work and improved living conditions."[47] The party-led NNC and the Southern Negro Youth Congress were in the vanguard of this upsurge.

The SNYC, which the NNC helped found earlier in 1937,[48] was led by Communists James E. Jackson, Esther Cooper,[49] Edward Strong and James Ashford, among others. Additionally, the NNC off-shoot was working class in character and eager to engage racism in the workplace, "adding a class content to the struggle for Black liberation."[50] SNYC members went directly "from the founding meeting" in Richmond, Virginia "to organizing local black tobacco workers into a new union – the Tobacco Stemmers and Laborers Industrial Union,"[51] a CIO affiliate of more than 5,000[52] Black female tobacco stemmers, organized and led by CPUSA member Christopher Alston.[53] After a three-day strike, employers agreed to their demands, invigorating the industrial union movement. Workers in other industries joined the CIO as a result of the SNYC's success.

One observer went so far as to call the Communist-led CIO-SNYC campaign, "the most significant thing that had happened to Richmond Negroes since Emancipation." Seven factories signed union contracts shortly thereafter. "For the first time, southern blacks would have a vehicle to take action and bring about change," Professor Johnetta Richards noted. "Nearly all of the established black civil rights organizations supported the creation of the SNYC," including "black newspapers, prominent clergy, and educational leaders."[54] At its peak, the SNYC counted more than 115 local councils,[55] many of which engaged in similar workers' rights campaigns and unionization drives. By 1938, African American Communists, like Hunton, would agree with the Communist International: reds were "a guiding force...in every phase of its [the NNC's] activities."[56] The same could be said about the SNYC, the NNC's "youth section,"[57] which was said to be "dominated by CP activists."[58]

In April 1940 the NNC held its third convention, which Hunton "was chiefly responsible" for organizing. At that convention, held in Washington, D.C. and attended by more than 1,300 people,[59] Hunton helped draft the NNC constitution and "delivered a major address," *Negroes and the War*, to a national radio audience.[60] Unfortunately though, unity was fractured when A. Philip Randolph – who was becoming increasingly "not happy"[61] about the growing and respected public Communist Party influence in the NNC – attacked the party from the podium for its "policies...program tactics and strategy," calling them "fitful, changeful and unpredictable," just like "the foreign policy and line of Moscow." Randolph was then "basically booed off the stage"[62] by the large Communist and CIO delegations. As Gellman noted, perhaps Randolph "felt like a second act" to John L. Lewis, head of the CIO who was then embracing Communists. That the CPUSA and the CIO helped fund the NNC probably irked Randolph, too; he relied on the generosity of the AFL to subsidize his Brotherhood of Sleeping Car Porters, which it was said, was "likely to disappear" without funds from the Federation.[63] Max Yergan, whose life would negatively intersect with Hunton's in a few short years, was elected the NNC's next president[64] after Randolph's departure.

Differing perspectives on the emerging war in Europe weren't the only issue driving a wedge between Randolph and the CPUSA-CIO-led NNC. At stake were differing views on how to organize workers, especially African Americans, into unions and the concomitant role of Communists in this upsurge.

Even though Randolph paid lip-service to industrial unionism and the work of the CIO, he chose to stay in the AFL – a Federation well known for its craft union traditions, lily white composition and segregated locals[65] – rather than join the CIO. In 1929, when the AFL begrudgingly agreed to charter the BSCP it was only as second-class, separate federal locals under the "authority of the national AFL leadership," not as a single international union. This maneuver "effectively subordinated organized black workers under the AFL's white leadership." Further, it wouldn't be until June of 1936 – just months after the NNC's founding – that the AFL granted an international charter to the BSCP.[66] In short, it was the Communist left-flank and the surging CIO that won concessions for African American's from the AFL's center, not Randolph. Viewed in isolation, Randolph's decision to align with the AFL seems odd. The CIO was a bastion of party activity since its founding and not nearly as resistant to Communist influence as the AFL,[67] and as a result considerably more welcoming to people of color, which Randolph well knew. Curiously, as the AFL's loyal opposition, Randolph's ideological summersaults justifying the continued subordinate role assigned to most Black AFL union members was largely based on his anticommunist alliance with the AFL's conservative white leadership – a leadership that begrudgingly gave him a platform and an audience,[68] while taking great pains to attempt to isolate the then ascendant red influence, an influence championing Black leadership. It was this racist status quo that Randolph was dependent upon as head of an African American union in the white AFL, hence a partial explanation for his resistance to Communist overtures, especially those made by Black Communists. Randolph's stature as a prominent Black labor leader wasn't preordained either. Arguably, several Communists could have eclipsed him as the foremost domestic Black labor leader. Ferdinand Smith, the Jamaican-born Communist and a leader of the National Maritime Union, would for a time cast somewhat of a red shadow over Randolph and be considered by many the most influential person of color in the U.S. labor movement. That Smith led a union that was majority white – the opposite of Randolph's BSCP – added to his considerable influence. As the tide turned towards Red Scare, Smith was unceremoniously ousted from the NMU in 1948 and eventually deported.[69] Additionally, Randolph's AFL – unlike Smith's CIO – refused to participate in international trade union conferences initiated and led by the World Federation of Trade Unions, a Federation less than hostile to Communists,[70] founded in fall 1945. The WFTU connected Pan-Africanism to the growing trade union movement and socialism. This put the CIO – not the AFL – in the mainstream of the then expanding international upsurge in workers' rights struggles backed by the Soviet Union. Randolph's rejection of the WFTU was a curious position to hold, as he was supposedly championing the defeat of racism, domestically and internationally. Further, it would not be until December 1949 that the International Confederation of Free Trade Unions – an anticommunist competitor of WFTU[71] – was founded. In short, Randolph's anticommunism effectively limited his and his union's avenues for international solidarity. State Department labor specialist, George McCray, no friend of the Communists, would remark that Randolph's shunning of the WFTU was "particularly stupid"[72] considering that organization's considerable representation among unions in the decolonizing nations of Africa. Further, within just a few short years it would be a Communist, Hunton, not Randolph, who would have decisive influence on DuBois – the leading Black intellectual and activist of the time – regarding union-based Pan-Africanism,[73] which undoubtedly irked the BSCP president. Randolph's disdain for Communists weakened his union domestically, while also serving to isolate it internationally. The well-known Communist councilman from Harlem, Benjamin Davis, Jr., would later call Randolph a "sheep in wolf's clothing...a pathological red-baiter, Soviet baiter and Wall Street bootlicker...constantly starting out like a lion and ending like a lamb."[74] Hunton's opinion of Randolph was probably not much different, especially when he used red-baiting scare tactics in an attempt to divide the CP-CIO-NNC coalition, a decisive moment for the NNC that proved difficult to recover from.

In 1943, John P. Davis resigned as NNC national secretary; his reasons were complicated. Ties with other prominent Communists had been strained due to the party's multiple shifts in foreign policy. Davis also felt "politically compromised" and did not want his CPUSA connections to "sabotage the NNC's need to reinvent itself."[75] The D.C. office closed, which "made the task of carrying on the Council's work extremely difficult and [too] much of a burden on Alphaeus," Dorothy Hunton wrote in retrospect. Further, in 1947 after "years of consistent struggle and effective work," the "beleaguered and harassed Congress" merged into the CRC, which itself had been created after a merger of the party-led ILD and National Federation of Constitutional Liberties.[76] The CRC was led by the well-known African American Communist, William L. Patterson,[77] who had spearheaded the party's defense of the Scottsboro Nine. Hunton would serve as a trustee of the CRC bail fund, a position for which he would be harassed and eventually jailed.

* * *

During the early 1940s Hunton also worked with American Peace Mobilization, which the House Committee on Un-American Activities called, "one of the most seditious organizations which ever operated in the United States."[78] This was a bold proclamation apparently only reserved for those organizations led by Communists. Of course, the Soviet Non-Aggression Pact with Germany signed in summer 1939, as well as the Communist Party's "ideological whiplash," as Gellman called it,[79] complicated matters. Anti-war sentiment was wide-spread; many Americans did not want to be entangled in another European war. However, the party's dramatic political shift justifying the Non-Aggression Pact was proof to some that the CPUSA was compromised and worked at the behest of a foreign power. Further, reds were often accused of trying to bring unions representing defense industry workers "under [the] leadership of the Communist party,"[80] an accusation that would soon be hurled at Hunton. Regardless, "preventing U.S. entry into the war [World War II]" was then considered "seditious," as Hunton personally found out. He and other peace activists were "assaulted" by "soldiers, sailors and marines" while picketing in front of the White House.[81] In May 1941, Hunton was called to testify before the committee due to his APM activism, a foreshadowing of the trials and travails that would soon hound Communists by 1948. Hunton responded to the committee's inquiries by asking why it "does not devote just one-tenth of its time to investigating the subversive undermining of American democracy" through "the varied form of discrimination and oppression practiced against Negro citizens," especially the "flagrant...denial of jobs to Negroes in certain defense industries." He added, "I see nothing subversive" in an organization "dedicated to the maintenance of peace and democracy," a sentiment then shared by most Americans. "You cannot make something bad by merely calling it a name," Hunton continued. Though he publicly denied CPUSA membership, he demanded "the right to testify" and to face his accusers – political cowards and sycophants who would later report that they were glad to have found nothing indicating Hunton "engaged in any activities...characterized as subversive or disloyal to our government." That Hunton "spearheaded the fight for 'all-out defense of democracy' in defense industry – right here at home," particularly by fighting for African Americans jobs at the Glenn L. Martin Aircraft Plant in Baltimore,[82] likely precipitated the witch hunt. Hunton's comrade, George Meyers, led the campaign to unionize and integrate the plant, which employed 37,000 workers. HUAC investigators argued, Communists were strategically positioned to cripple an industry essential for national security, hence the inquisition. Their goal, however, was actually considerably less conspiratorial. Hunton, Meyers and other party members helped to break down racist hiring practices at the plant, leading to 7,000 jobs for African American workers,[83] bolstering an alliance less susceptible to anticommunism, an alliance the entire weight of the U.S. government would soon try to destroy.

During the mid-1940s, Hunton also served as a director of the George Washington Carver School, the Harlem branch of the party's flagship adult education institution, the Jefferson School for Social Sciences.[84] Nearly 2,000 people attended classes and lectures at the Carver School during its first year with an additional 2,500 people attending its "I Am an American Day" meeting.[85]

* * *

Hunton resigned from Howard University in 1943 due to its increasingly restrictive political environment; Wilkerson resigned earlier to work fulltime for the CPUSA. Soon thereafter, Hunton became the educational director of the Council on African Affairs,[86] the domestic linchpin of the international Black liberation movement. It militantly promoted independence for African colonies and "the full freedom of colored peoples throughout the world."[87] The CAA began as the International Committee on African Affairs in 1937, funded by Paul Robeson and run by Max Yergan. Functioning primarily as an educational organization, the ICAA consisted of prominent Black lawyers, educators and artists. Reorganized in 1942, the CAA was "distinctly different," more adversarial than its predecessor with an emphasis on "militant black international diaspora consciousness" and "independent black leadership" with a Marxist-based analysis embracing "antiimperialist and anticapitalist politics." During World War II and the immediate post-war period, the CAA was part of "a second incarnation" of the Communist-led Popular Front, which endured through the early Cold War.[88] Hunton and other CAA leaders regularly met with officials of the U.S. State Department's Division of African Affairs,[89] providing insight and analysis. As Martin Duberman argued, the CAA fused "anticolonial and pro-Soviet sentiments" domestically,[90] a perspective held by its principle leaders, a perspective at odds with U.S. imperialism once Hitler and the Axis powers were defeated and the war time alliance with the Soviet Union was broken.

Historian Gerald Horne has called the CAA "the vanguard organization in the U.S. campaigning against colonialism."[91] Penny M. Von Eschen referred to the CAA as "vital and important,"[92] providing the connective tissue that brought together African Americans struggling for equality with Africans struggling for Black liberation, particularly in South Africa. Eric Arnesen termed the CAA, "hard-nosed and partisan in an emerging Cold War that rendered the Third World a crucial ideological and political battle-field."[93] In short, African Americans fighting for equality partnered with Black liberation movements in Africa. Further, both sought allies with ascendant socialism and advanced on multiple fronts.[94] In 1958 Hunton reflected on the CAA and its leading role, and noted, it "stood alone as the one organization in the United States devoting full-time attention to the problems and struggles of the peoples of Africa,"[95] a focus for which it would eventually be punished.

Hunton joined CAA chairman Paul Robeson,[96] and later W.E.B. DuBois, who would become vice chair, as they collectively articulated and fought for "radical internationalism" and "black nationalism, with [an] emphasis on racial consciousness and unity." As editor of the CAA's publications, *New Africa* and *Spotlight on Africa*, and through countless articles, pamphlets and booklets distributed globally, Hunton promoted "connections with Africa and concern for its problems." He placed the anticolonial struggle within a broadly defined history and "worldwide political economy." To many, the CAA was "in the vanguard of educating the general public about imperialism and its devastating effects on Africa."[97] Press releases, conferences and countless demonstrations, boycotts and marches highlighted domestic solidarity with Black liberation in Africa. Under Hunton's leadership, the CAA also "functioned as a press service," providing content to organizations, newspapers and journals, content largely unavailable elsewhere. *New Africa* became so influential that by 1950 it was banned in South Africa, Kenya and Belgian Congo.[98] Hunton provided content and analysis to 62 foreign papers and 67 U.S. newspapers and the CAA acted as "a liaison agency between the U.N. and the public, here and abroad, and particularly in Africa."[99] As Hunton noted, the CAA's "prime objective was to provide a sound basis of accurate information so that the American people might play their proper part in the struggle for African freedom."[100]

"Just as labor and the liberal forces of England recognized 180 years ago that their own interest lay in the overthrow of American slavery," Hunton told reporters, "so today it is necessary for Americans and all people of the anti-axis [sic] world to realize that their future security and peace must ultimately depend upon the abolition...of imperialism in Africa and throughout the world."[101] The CAA was the "central point of interaction between Africans' and African Americans' struggles for liberation."[102] International solidarity, especially with Black liberation movements in Africa, was seen as subversive, which led Attorney General Tom Clark to place the CAA on the list of subversive organizations that it claimed threatened to overthrow the U.S. government.[103] Though Max Yergan was then still the CAA's executive director, it was widely acknowledged that Hunton "single-handedly kept the organization afloat" and was considered the CAA's "leading figures at the height of... [its] influence."[104] This was high praise, especially since Hunton's co-workers included Robeson and DuBois. As others have written, CAA "activities and impact increased significantly after 1943" when Hunton joined the staff[105] and "1943 marked a turning point" for the CAA, as the "day-to-day work and policy was thereafter carried out by Hunton." It short, it was Hunton's leadership that made the CAA "a vital and important organization."[106] Hunton and the CAA established and maintained contacts with and aided Black liberation movements and leaders,[107] partly as an accredited UN observer.[108] As would become increasingly clear, the ruling class had hoped to contain African American activism safely within the bounds of domestic liberal anticommunism. Hunton and other Black Communists, like Ferdinand Smith, Benjamin Davis, Jr., and Paul Robeson, were pushed aside to make room for those more willing to acquiesce to this prerequisite. Ascendant socialism – and its domestic supporters – were labeled subversive. Support for liberation in Africa was the evidence.

As an organization that practiced international solidarity in a multiplicity of ways, the CAA, under Hunton's leadership, not only organized what amounted to "canned food drive[s] on behalf of hungry Africans,"[109] it merged humanitarian efforts with political activism geared towards Black liberation. Like the CRC[110] and the IWO,[111] among other party-led organizations, the CAA saw its role as both advocacy and activism. In January 1946, for example, 4,500 people attended a CAA sponsored meeting at Abyssinian Baptists Church to aid the "4,000,000 starving women and children in the Union of South Africa."[112] Every "available inch of space" was "jammed," the *Daily Worker* reported, as "10 tons of canned food and $1,730 in hard-earned money" was collected. Paul Robeson said, "freedom for the oppressed black peoples of Africa is inseparable from the struggle for freedom everywhere."[113] Hunton agreed and optimistically added, "Harlem will start the New Year, appropriately enough, with a demonstration of support for the oppressed victims of imperialism across the sea." He said the goal was to "collect a mountain of canned food and substantial funds for the relief...[of] famine-stricken Africans." Hunton saw "great wealth in South Africa's modern cities." But, he added, the "African's life is one of poverty, hunger and disease" due to the imperial theft of their lands. "Nine out of 10 African children are undernourished," while in "some areas the infant mortality rate is over 60 percent." To him, "chronic starvation" was a deliberate policy directed against Africans "in the land of gold and diamonds," which is "how the system of imperialism works."[114] Roughly one month earlier, in a December 1945 *Daily Worker* editorial, Hunton noted, "Outside pressure upon the South African government...must be developed." The CAA, he continued, is "the only organization in this country thus far to bring the starvation crisis in South Africa to the attention of the American public." The CAA "has constantly sought to mobilize such [public] pressure."[115] Additionally, in a *New York Times* letter to the editor, Hunton presented "a few facts...regarding the status of African people in the Union of South Africa." He decried the "deplorable health conditions and extremely high death rates," as well as the separate and unequal investments in education. The "present per capita expenditure for the education of the white child is about forty times that for the African child," he wrote. To Hunton, the logic of racism was simple. The "denial of adequate health, educational and other social services to the African majority" in South Africa "is the determination of the white ruling class of that country to keep the Africans from attaining a status of economic, social or political equality," i.e., to keep them subjugated. "The sole blame for the Africans' failure to become fully integrated in modern culture rests upon the European,"[116] he concluded. The ruling class was determined to stunt the growing demand for African American equality, Black liberation and socialism. South Africa would soon become a key battleground.

Just a few months later, the CAA filled Madison Square Garden with 15,000 people calling for Big Three (U.S., USSR and Great Britain) Unity for Colonial Freedom. The CAA protested the Truman Administration as it helped "bolster up crumbling European empires in Asia and in the Middle East." This was a "striking blow against the American people themselves," it was added. Max Yergan told the audience, "colonial imperialism stands indicted before the bar of world opinion today." He called "upon all Americans" to demand that "colonialism – that bankrupt, plundering and wasteful system of the past – be done away with" and be replaced by "a new relation amongst the peoples of the earth [sic] characterized by dignity." According to *The New York Times* the CAA was termed a "Communist-controlled organization supported mainly by Negroes,"[117] which highlighted two converging realities: One, that ruling elites tacitly acknowledged the growing and potent collaboration between Communists and Black radicals; and two, that the emerging Red Scare would soon focus laser-like on Communist-led organizations like the CAA and CRC to the detriment of African American equality, Black liberation and socialism.

The CAA coordinated actions with, for example, the African National Congress, urging politicians, businesses and others of influence to not support the racist regime in South Africa with "loans and other forms of aid."[118] The CAA-ANC relationship defied the prevailing winds of Red Scare and struggled to bring anti-apartheid into popular consciousness. The CAA organized a rally of 5,000 people in April 1952 that featured Congressman Adam Clayton Powell Jr. (D-New York), among others, to coincide with the ANC's Defiance Campaign. After the rally, the CAA picketed the South African consulate for 30 hours. It also started a petition drive in support of the ANC – with a goal of collecting 100,000 signatures. Hunton called for "redoubled efforts...to broaden the petition drive" and "translate into concrete and effective action the widespread bitterness and indignation of Americans, particularly black Americans, over the rampant racist barbarism" in South Africa. The CAA's legal defense fund, petition drives and campaigns to free political prisoners in South Africa foreshadowed the Free Mandela campaigns that emerged years later,[119] as well as the divestment movement, a campaign initiated and partly led by Communists like Henry Winston, Charlene Mitchell, Tony Monteiro, and the National Anti-Imperialist Movement In Solidarity with African Liberation. According to party leader Roberta Wood, the "relationship between Communists and these organizations is much more nuanced. True, we initiated [them], but with very real efforts to incorporate broader forces in real leadership."[120] This distinction is important and supports the party's continuing popular front approach. That Mitchell, and fellow Communist, Angela Davis, were invited to stay at Nelson Mandela's Soweto home in 1991,[121] however, meant domestic support organized by Communists for Black liberation in Africa was not forgotten – even as socialism retreated.

To the CAA, "the internationalization" of the Black freedom struggle meant civil rights at home and support for Black liberation abroad. It meant "material support" for "independence activists" and "striking trade unionists" in Nigeria, "unequivocal" support for the Land and Freedom Army in Kenya,[122] as well as African famine relief, generally, among other examples. The Nigerian Trades Union Congress in a letter to the CAA, noted, "To know that we have friends at the other end of the Atlantic is comforting and inspiring in our struggle for freedom from want and heartless exploitation."[123] As Hunton wrote, the CAA "was not content to function simply as an information agency. It sought to translate knowledge into action,"[124] which partly explains the attacks levied against it. In another letter, a white South African trade union leader thanked the CAA for its support and noted, "Progressive forces all over the world must take steps to see that South Africa does not become the Nazi Germany of the African continent."[125] The CAA promoted a "fundamental linkage" between the struggle for African American equality and the "fate of colonized peoples in Africa,"[126] thereby fostering a degree of internationalism largely absent from the civil rights organizations that would emerge after the near destruction of the domestic Communist left. Von Eschen put the matter this way,

"U.S. government prosecution of activists such as Robeson [and Hunton] and the CAA, fundamentally altered the terms of anticolonialism and effectively severed the black American struggle for civil rights from the issues of anticolonialism and racism abroad."[127] Horne forcefully articulates a similar sentiment. The emerging civil rights organizations, even those connected to Dr. Martin Luther King, Jr., "did not have the international ties of the CRC, nor the global reach of the CAA, which amounted to a net loss for African-Americans and their allies."[128] This is a qualitative loss the repercussions of which are still being felt to this day. In short, the CAA was the "most visible, vocal and vibrant African-American organization" that supported "African causes" in the 1940s and 1950s. Its "tactics, objectives and problems" were later "inherited"[129] by diasporic activists who emerged in the 1960s.

* * *

In addition to his many CAA responsibilities, Hunton also wrote regular columns for the *Daily Worker*, often highlighting Soviet socialism and its support of Black liberation in Africa. In July 1943, Hunton discussed a pamphlet published by the National Council of American-Soviet Friendship, of which he was a board member. The "common struggle against fascism" and the "strength of the Soviet Union" have "made possible the clearing away of the rubbish of falsehood and slander about that country" propagated by ruling elites. "There has developed a widespread and genuine appreciation" of "Soviet life," he wrote. For example, "the way in which, within a quarter of a century, many millions of people of different races, creeds and cultures, illiterate, impoverished and degraded victims of exploitation" were quickly "raised to full social, economic and political equality." Importantly, this is a "record of achievement... of special interest to those who are thinking about the problem of abolishing colonialism and semi-colonialism in all areas of the postwar world,"[130] particularly African Americans and Africans then attempting to build solidarity across the Atlantic with the aid of the CAA.[131] "Yes, Africans today are learning and talking about the Soviet Union," he continued in another column. "As the war [World War II] has made the whole world smaller, so it has brought Africans closer to the great land of the Soviets," a land where racism had been outlawed. "With their increasing knowledge" of Soviet socialism and its successes, "African leaders are more frequently citing the contrast between the failure of the European colonial administration." Its inability "to provide any appreciable social advancement for the masses of Africans" was contrasted with the "remarkable success of the Soviet government in bringing social well-being and economic efficiency to millions," "people who 25 years ago were in a state of colonial serfdom." According to Hunton, "people cannot develop until they have a goal which is in their own interests and of their own choosing," a challenge that required the elimination of the "outmoded system of imperialist exploitation and colonial tutelage,"[132] a system soon to be in decline as socialism advanced.

Hunton was also quick to point out the similarities between the racists at home and the fascists abroad. "The Hitlerite regime sought to prove that a super-race, a Herrenvolk [master-race], could rule the world." This was a proposition not unlike those advocating "'white supremacy' in America, together with the anti-Communists and anti-Semites, [who] propose to continue using Hitler's weapons and fighting Hitler's war even after Hitler is defeated," which unfortunately proved to be the case. Specifically, Hunton was then blasting reactionary, racist Mississippi Senator Theodore Bilbo, who – along with his ilk – "are becoming more and more desperate in their efforts to stop the Negro's march toward full citizenship rights."[133] By early September 1944, Hunton, along with numerous other "leaders of Negro organizations and trade unions" met in New York City to "map out plans for a mass non-partisan [voter] registration drive directed specifically to getting out the Negro vote" that fall,[134] a vote that would aid African Americans in their "march" toward equality. Domestically, Hunton continued, "The Negro is keenly aware of the stakes of freedom in this war." As African Americans reach a "higher level" in the struggle for equality, partly through the ballot box, they also "develop a closer relationship to the struggles of other oppressed peoples." Hunton's columns also focused on building international unity. He wanted to drive home "in graphic and inescapable terms the realization that no nation or group of people can find security and democracy today outside of a framework of world-wide security and democracy in which all groups and nations work together for their mutual benefit."[135]

Goodwill among colonial peoples, however, was not won simply with "good intentions," Hunton argued, "but [with] deeds." This reality left the so-called liberal, western democracies sorely lacking; their support of "colonial advancement" was "extremely limited and piecemeal," at best, and often perpetuated a racial hierarchy that found African Americans and Africans *both* relegated to the bottom rungs of society. An "entirely new approach to this problem of developing the colonies through broad and systematically planned undertakings" was required, Hunton wrote. He called for "a new vision and policy of cooperation," one based on equality and liberation, not continued racism and subjugation. "To ensure that deeds and not promises are the order of the day for colonial peoples, and to ensure that America plays its full part in accomplishing the deeds, Americans have their job cut out for them in the coming elections,"[136] Hunton concluded. He repeatedly connected the prospects for Black liberation in Africa with African American equality at home.

As a Marxist, Hunton saw the dialectic at work, too. "The more progressive" white trade unionists in South Africa "have taken a strong stand against the many Jim-crow [sic] disabilities inflicted upon African and other non-European workers," he argued. "As in our own

South, there is a growing recognition that the fight for Negro rights is an integral part of the fight for democratic rights in general." In the post-war period, the party would reevaluate its Black Belt thesis and refine its analysis; the centrality of the struggle for African American equality to democracy soon became a key component of its domestic strategic outlook. Regardless, the South African Communist Party was singled out as "a major force" for equality. That the "forces of extreme reaction in South Africa, which make a fetish of racialism and are even now still openly pro-Nazi," were "alarmed" by the growth and influence of the SACP was probably an understatement. That they were then "plotting to ride into power" during the post-war period with the aid of "Company unions" and "phony labor groups sponsored by fascist organizations" often aided by U.S. imperialism, was a tacit acknowledgement of the SACP's growing and considerable influence. That the goal was "to undermine the bona fide trade unions" in an effort "to intimidate the organized African workers," was clear. Similarly, the "South African equivalents of our poll-taxers and Hoover-Dewey Republicans are the enemy of both black and white workers," Hunton argued. However, he continued, "In the near future will come the showdown test," the decisive battle, "of whether organized labor and the liberal forces of South Africa...are strong enough and united enough to fight for and win the democratic prerequisites to prosperity" and "a more abundant life for the vast majority of its inhabitants,"[137] not just the minority, white ruling class.

In South Africa, Hunton continued, "There has been a growing tension" as "reactionary forces have attempted to block the Africans' increasingly organized efforts to gain justice," efforts often lead by Communists. Through "people's organization's" like the ANC and "supported by the Communist Party and a wide range of progressive elements," Africans demanded "better working conditions and trade union recognition, for abolition of the pass laws, [and] for better education." According to

Hunton, "disciplined and orderly" demonstrations were being "deliberately provoked" with "tear gas." The ruling class hoped to outlaw "public expressions of this sort" with the dubious justification of "protecting the public safety." The "South African counterparts of the Ku Klux Klan, Christian Front and other pro-fascist forces," were responsible for the violence, he added, not demonstrators seeking equality. To Hunton, "Racial discrimination whether in this country, Africa or elsewhere, is incompatible with any genuine concept of world security," a theme he had repeatedly articulated in his *Daily Worker* columns. In short, a "real and lasting victory over fascism" required that the emerging United Nations, "erase this evil [racism] wherever it exists."[138] Fortunately, this was a call backed by ascendant socialism, a call that created "ideological tensions" between the capitalist West and the socialist East, which ultimately forced concessions towards African American equality and Black liberation.

"Today the world is divided into two parts, unequal in size and in every other respect," Hunton wrote. While the United States, the Soviet Union and Western Europe were "highly industrialized" and enjoy "relatively high living standards," the "rest of the world including Asia, Africa, and Latin America, has an economy and living standards a hundred years or more behind the times." The "apologists for imperialism," he added, "would have us believe that the explanation is in the inherent 'primitive' character of the peoples in these territories," which "incidentally, also gives them the right, so these apologists claim, to rule over these people." This was nothing more than a spurious justification for continued subjugation. Conversely, the "real explanation" for the deliberate underdevelopment of Africa, Asia and Latin America was "to be found in the nature of colonialism itself." Colonialism was "a synonym for social stagnation," he added, as "colonies can only be profitable to a minority of foreign investors or immigrant settlers under conditions which are socially and economically disadvantageous to the native inhabitants," the indigenous peoples. "At one time Negro slaves represented the most profitable export commodity" in Africa, Hunton added. Capitalism's genesis was literally born on the backs of slave labor. "[L]ater it was such things as gold, diamonds, copper, oil and rubber," raw materials that then fed the growing western economies. "[S]elfish production for profit rather than the needs of the [indigenous] people...these are the inevitable, essential characteristics of colonialism," a system then in decline, thanks in part to the rise of socialism. According to Hunton, "these evils," colonialism and capitalism, must give way to "a new order of world-wide progress in place of the old imperialist regime of stagnation,"[139] which was a political paradigm favoring white supremacy and war over equality and peace. In short, domestically and internationally, "preserving the special privileges of a small clique of those white people who hold economic and political power"[140] was the goal of colonialism and imperialism, backed first and foremost by the United States. Of course, the still potent international Red-Black alliance Communists had spent decades building posed a considerable challenge, a challenge Hunton was then in the forefront of.

Domestically, Hunton wondered if "the employment gains we [African Americans] have made" during the war would be "maintained and extended" during the peace? Organized labor, he added, needs to "plan concretely for safeguarding the job status of Negroes as part of the larger task of maintaining democratic employment standards for all workers." Unfortunately, this task proved considerably more difficult with the passage of the Taft-Hartley Act in 1947, the coming Red Scare and the purging of Communists from the domestic labor movement. Again, Hunton focused on the international impact of domestic politics, and added, "the economic future of the Negro and the strength of the labor movement, when victory has been won, hinge on whether this country continues to play its proper role in developing and realizing a program of international collaboration for promoting a peaceful economy of abundance, world-wide in scope." Like other Communists, Hunton was optimistic that the war-time alliance with the Soviet Union would continue. In this alliance, he wrote, "lies the only real promise of security for the Negro and all other workers in America, as well as of liberation for peoples throughout the world from the chains of colonialism and feudalism."[141] An alliance with Soviet socialism was the only path toward African American equality and Black liberation in Africa, Hunton argued.

In early 1945, Hunton wrote optimistically of the coming end of World War II, the "finis to fascism." However, he added, "let's remember that many millions of colonial peoples all over the world are thinking, as 1945 begins, not only of the end of the war but of the time when they can be free from imperialist domination," fascism's not-so-distant cousin. Accordingly, he added, colonial peoples "understand that their liberation depends in the first place upon the defeat of the fascist enemy." However, he continued, "victory over the Axis will not of itself solve their problems," namely continued white supremacy and subjugation. Hunton again called for "a worldwide system of prosperity and peace," a call that would ultimately prove elusive. Further, the "planlessness [sic] of colonial administration" left much to be desired. Continued "talk of 'trusteeship' and 'preparing backward peoples for the management of their own affairs'" were little more than "modern paraphrases of 'the white man's burden.'" Left unanswered were the "practical questions of HOW and WHEN" colonial peoples would gain freedom, as "vague promises" juxtaposed "conscientious and systematic planning," which was required if "the democratic forces of the world" were to win "a real New Year and New Deal for the hundreds of millions of colonial peoples."[142] Even as western democracies refused to "yet admit it, it is nevertheless a fact that in order to survive today's world [they] must renounce colonialism, just as the world of a hundred years ago was compelled to renounce slavery. There is no other alternative," Hunton emphasized.

"[U]niversal economic ruin" brought on by "over-production and under-consumption,"[143] a by-product of capitalism in crisis, was predicted. Hunton continued, "It is necessary to decide, once and for all, whether the cake is to be kept or to be eaten! One can have unqualified imperial sovereignty," colonialism, "or collective security, but **not both together**" [**bold** in original],[144] he wrote. The specter of ascendant socialism coupled with the prospect of a shift in the balance of world power, haunted the ruling class. To Hunton, colonialisms defeat was coming; when was the question.

Hunton was far from naïve, though. Like his comrades, he called for unity and chastised forces who were unwilling to work with Communists. "The weakness of the progressive forces in South Africa," for example, isn't due to a "lack of program or lack of influence and following among the masses of the people." Rather, it was a result of "too much factionalism and division among those who should be fighting together. The [so-called] Labor Party, for example, will not collaborate with the Communist Party because of the latter's unqualified stand against all racial discrimination." "In South Africa as in the United States," he concluded, "the only way to lick reaction is through the **united** strength of all those on the side of democracy and progress" [**bold** in original],[145] including Communists, a lesson some have yet to learn. Though hard to imagine today, Hunton was in the mainstream of African radical thought. Radicals across the continent were not only discussing socialism. They were also discussing the possibility of leaping "the stage of capitalist development" and advancing "rapidly from feudalism to socialism" in the British West African colonies of Nigeria, Sierra Leone, the Gold Coast and Gambia. In "the most politically advanced sections of subject Africa" the "common struggle against the imperialist yoke has served to unite the workers," Hunton wrote. That "native African delegates" from these countries attended "the recent World Labor Conference in London," the first confluence in what would become the

WFTU in October 1945 representing 60 million workers, boded well for pro-worker, anti-racist alliances. "Even in their present early stage of development" these unions "are a major progressive and unifying force among the people...a politically developed and world-minded force," a force often led by Communists. Hunton also approvingly quoted a British trade union leader highlighting the similarities between "pre-Soviet Russia and Present-day Nigeria," and noted that "the Soviet Union would 'become a real model of twentieth century civilization,'"[146] as ascendant socialism aided Black liberation in Africa.

Hunton frequently sparred with apologists for imperialism in his columns. George S. Schuyler, a *Pittsburgh Courier* columnist, for example, "peddles his subversive poison...[his] made-in-Berlin propaganda...[which] specializes in redbaiting, parading before his readers every conceivable slander against the Soviet Union and against Communists." To Schuyler, "a dangerously large percentage of so-called thinking Negroes has swallowed the red propaganda," an explicit acknowledgement of the continued potency of a rising Black militancy comfortable with Red allies. Approvingly, Hunton quoted another *Pittsburgh Courier* columnist, Liu Liang-mo, who also shared a disdain for Schuyler. "Hitler's and Japan's last trump card is to split the unity of the United States with anti-communism and anti-sovietism [sic], and it looks like Mr. Schuyler is doing his best...to serve the purpose of our common enemy," a tactic many in Washington would soon emulate. Schuyler also attacked Black support for Roosevelt in the 1944 elections and paternalistically urged "really intelligent, informed" African Americans "interested in racial welfare" to vote for Norman Thomas and the Socialist Party, "to which the only alternative is ultimate slavery." "There you have it," Hunton exclaimed! "There couldn't be a better illustration of how the ultra-left and the ultra-right travel the same road of reaction." He likened Schuyler to Westbrook Pegler, a white conservative journalist who spent much of his career attacking unions, the New Deal, and Roosevelt.[147] According to Hunton, both sought to weaken democracy in a failed attempt to destroy Communists. Walter Lippmann, the dean of American journalists, was also on the receiving end of Hunton's broadsides. "Mr. Lippmann deliberately over-simplifies and distorts the program [then being] advanced by those calling for a colonial New Deal," Hunton wrote, as the United Nations and the Allied powers planned for a post-war world. Lippmann, like Schuyler and Pegler, "has apparently failed to grasp the fact that Yalta [where Roosevelt, Churchill and Stalin met] and the San Francisco meeting [where the United Nations was created] represent the emergence of a new kind of world – a world of collective security. Mr. Lippmann's eyes are on the past," he added. "He seems to be still thinking in the old terms of colonies as pawns in the imperialist game of power politics and spheres of influence."[148]

In his analysis of the April-May 1945 San Francisco meeting, Hunton criticized the American, British and French proposals regarding the post-war colonial "trusteeship problem." The Soviet delegates, on the other hand, "made the more specific and far-reaching proposal of 'progressive development toward self-government and self-determination, with active participation of the peoples of these territories having the aim to expedite the achievement of national independence.'" This was a goal Hunton continued to support. To Hunton, the "wording used in the revised draft of the American plan...fails to match the Soviet point of view" and was "even a qualification," a constraining, "of the original American formula." Apparently, this was "a concession to the wishes of the British" then preparing a "conveniently-timed" announcement of "plans for self-government in Burma." Complicating matters, however, was the lack of evidence, "for the very good reason that it can't be found," that the Burmese people "are satisfied with the self-government plans as proposed" by the British delegates. To Hunton, "A fundamental principle is at stake in this issue: It is no mere quibble over words." Former colonial peoples "cannot be said to be truly self-governing unless and until they have the right to independence," a reality then eluding the American, British and French delegations. Clearly, "withholding the right of independence makes the concept of self-determination, upon which the Big Five have already agreed, absolutely meaningless," Hunton argued. He then urged action. "The American people should insist," he concluded, "that their delegates...adhere to this policy in working out the final decision regarding trusteeship arrangements."[149] In another column, Hunton argued, "European powers will take their cues as to their colonial policies" from the U.S. delegation. Therefore, "the most progressive elements in this country" must "recognize and live up to their responsibility for mobilizing public opinion" in favor of "self-determination and independence for all colonial peoples, as demanded by the Soviet Union and other anti-imperialist states." This was a responsibility the CAA took seriously. The potential for a formidable Red-Black alliance continued to resonate, as a "serious and vigorous people's campaign" able to "counteract and negate the nationalist-imperialist currents" in the press and "in the very halls of Congress"[150] was then taking shape. Ultimately, Hunton would be disappointed by the U.S. delegation's proposals, which "fell woefully short" of CAA demands.[151]

Hunton called "all the fulsome adulation" bequeathed upon Gen. Jan Smuts, the prime minister of the Dominion of South Africa while in San Francisco, "wearisome, if not nauseating." He wrote that it would "be difficult to cite a better instance of these evils [racism and oppression] than the notorious case of South Africa itself." Smuts and the South African regime represented a "postwar fascist threat" where "8,000,000 non-white peoples and a large section of the white workers as well, are kept enslaved."[152] Conversely, he praised the SACP as "the only political party in South Africa which stands foursquare for the abolition of the entire system of exploitation," namely colonialism, imperialism and capitalism buttressed by racism. Despite the "cold shoulder" they received, Communists continued to build a "united front,"[153] thereby planting seeds resulting in their leading role in ending white minority rule and building a coalition government headed by the ANC.[154]

Hunton also took to task a House Naval Affairs Sub-Committee report released just weeks after the San Francisco meeting. The report suggested that the U.S. "should take out-right the Japanese mandated islands and the outlying Japanese islands" and "secure 'full title'" to the "other Pacific Islands,"[155] including the Philippine's. Another U.S. Communist, William Pomeroy, along with the Philippine Communist Party and the Huk guerillas [156] – after routing the Japanese – resisted U.S. imperialism and the puppet administration of Manuel Roxas. For Hunton, "Fine words and promises" were meaningless, and would "no longer suffice." "The time is now for actions," he continued, "and the first step in getting action – as far as this country is concerned – is for the American people to demand a clear and forthright statement" regarding "the future of the colonial peoples of Asia and the Pacific."[157] Hunton continued his critique of U.S. imperialism in the Pacific and noted that the "struggle of the Indonesians is the same at that of colonial peoples throughout Asia and Africa." He asked, "Why should Americans and the peoples of every other country be concerned about events in Java? Because that island is today the test of whether the imperialist powers have any solution other than brute force to offer," as "necessary radical adjustments of economic and political relations between themselves and those whom they govern as colonial 'dependents.'"[158] As far as U.S. imperialism was concerned, the "solution" was clearly "brute force." In 1965, over 500,000 Indonesian citizens were brutally massacred with the approval of U.S. imperialism.[159]

To Hunton, "The degree of intensity of the struggle varies...but the fundamental issue at stake is the same everywhere – freedom, freedom to live and order their own lives." Additionally, the ruling class knows "that the challenge to imperial domination," in Indonesia, the Philippines, South Africa and elsewhere, "means the weakening of imperial authority" everywhere. Once again connecting the domestic and international struggles for equality and liberation, Hunton added, "If brute force is to be the recourse of the imperialist powers for maintaining rule over their colonies, we may expect that brute force also will be used to silence the demands of underpaid and unemployed workers in this and other capitalist countries." Hunton continued, "the Indonesians' struggle for freedom is as much our fight as it is theirs." Hunton praised his comrades in the Longshore and Maritime unions, as they "have shown the way for labor to effectively oppose the imperialists by their practical action in halting the shipping of supplies, munitions and troops to the Dutch East Indies." He called on "all the trade unions – rank and file as well as leaders – [to] come forward, demonstrating the solidarity of white and non-white workers, of labor in the colonies with labor in the colony-holding countries, fighting together against imperialism." He then called on the WFTU to wield "its great power in the cause of democracy."[160]

"In attempting to block the march of millions of colonial and semi-colonial peoples toward freedom and progress, the imperialist powers are promoting, not good will, but an ever-increasing and explosively dangerous volume of ill will," Hunton added, as WWII turned to Cold War. Imperialist powers "aim at a 'peace' with all the old special privileges of race, nationality and class remaining intact,"[161] he concluded. South Africa was a case in point. There Africans "speak of the country as one gigantic concentration camp. Nowhere else in the world that I know of is the freedom of movement of people so restricted." The Pass Laws, "which the Nazis brought into use against the Jews of Europe," originated in 1817 in South Africa and have "been developed over the years into an elaborate technique for controlling the entry and movement of Africans," a less-than-subtle means of "maintaining a supply of cheap African labor," racist subjugation and oppression. According to Hunton, "The Pass is the African's badge of serfdom." For example, Black South Africans must use an identification pass, which "must be renewed monthly." To leave the segregated "reserve" a trek pass and a travel pass are required. "That makes three of these things to start with," though the District Commissioner can "simply refuse to grant these passes," if he so desires. Then "our African friend must immediately register" and get a six-day special pass, "the fourth pass, which allows him to seek work." After finding work, the "young African must acquire his fifth and sixth passes to prove that he has a job," a service contract pass and a daily laborer's pass. Both must be renewed monthly. "If he wants to visit someone who lives in another area...he must have his seventh and eighth passes," the one-day special pass and the location visitor's pass. If he is out past curfew, 9 p.m. for Africans, he must have a night special pass, the ninth pass. Additionally, he must also acquire a lodger's pass and a poll tax receipt pass. "That makes 11 of these dog tags," Hunton concluded indignantly. Though, he added that an additional pass, "exempting the bearer from carrying these other passes," had been granted to "only 12,300 [people] in 1940," a fraction of the then 8 million Black South Africans. That Africans "have been protesting against this humiliating and vicious Pass System, demanding its abolition,"[162] wasn't lost on Hunton or the domestic and international Red-Black alliance, an alliance then ascending despite the shifting of the political winds towards Red Scare and Cold War.

* * *

In a spring 1950 CAA pamphlet titled *Africa Fights for Freedom*, Hunton sarcastically noted that the "would-be exploiters of Africa have left just one thing out of their precise calculations and pat blueprints – the *people* of Africa. The 180 million of them are rising, organizing and fighting with increased strength to break the chains, and this spells the nemesis of colonial exploitation in the last continent left to the imperialist gang." He added, with "guns from the United States, [the] arsenal of world imperialism," a "brutal war of repression [is being waged] against the African people in a desperate effort to postpone their V-A Day." The Marxist academic also explored the complexity of fighting colonialism where a western-style capitalist economy did not yet exist. He added new context to the then emerging revolutionary situation in Africa. Throughout his writings, Hunton rejected a rigid Marxism rooted in the primacy of the working class. "Among the common characteristics of the African liberation movements," he wrote, "first to be noted is that it is the middle-class intellectuals – lawyers, business men [sic], journalists – who constitute the main leadership." However, he was careful to reconcile this seeming contradiction to Marxism-Leninism. "Africa has no class of wealthy and powerful indigenous land-holders and industrialists...therefore, at the present stage, the basic demands of the African middle class are in harmony with those of the workers and peasants." Later on, however, he notes that organized labor "spearheads the national liberation movement in the colonies, spurring the middle-class leaders and their organizations forward and showing through example how to fight the monopoly exploiters, the real enemy." There is a certain ambiguity in Hunton's writing. In some instances, he places "middle-class intellectuals" at the center of his analysis, while in other places the labor movement is emphasized. For example, he likened colonial workers as "the shock troops of the liberation movement," who along with the peasants, women, youth – and the Communists – are engaged in a struggle for life or death. To Hunton, the "imperialists are caught in their usual dilemma: they demand more and more black labor yet struggle desperately to prevent the development of a black proletariat," though one cannot be created without the other. In conclusion, Hunton articulated the dialectical relationship between Africans, African Americans, the Chinese, the Vietnamese, and other colonial peoples fighting for liberation. "The African people are on the side of democracy and world peace,"[163] he concluded.

The CAA didn't confine its activism to the struggle for African American equality and Black liberation, though. It also protested the emerging war in Korea and sponsored rallies calling for Hands Off Korea where prominent Communists like Benjamin Davis, Jr., and Ferdinand Smith spoke. At a July 1950 rally Paul Robeson said, "we want no war and there will be none." "All over the world we will impose the peace,"[164] he added. Shortly thereafter, however, Madison Square Garden refused rental to the CAA "pending action on the Mundt-Ferguson Communist-Control Bill,"[165] which was then in Congress. Though the Bill would not become law, the damage was done. The Red Scare and Cold War began to suffocate civil liberties. Communists like Hunton were sacrificed to make room for civil rights activists, like Randolph, more willing to acquiesce to liberal anti-communism in exchange for a retreat from Jim Crow. Regardless, Hunton, Robeson and the CAA "denounced the Garden's actions as a denial of free speech and the right of assembly." They also called for pickets,[166] which around 100 people took part in. Afterwards Hunton noted, "It is no accident that a progressive Negro organization [the CAA] and a great Negro leader like Paul Robeson, have [both] been made the first target of the proposed police state legislation."[167] Both – Robeson and the CAA – exemplified a still potent Red-Black alliance. Across the Atlantic, a similar trend was taking shape; Mandela, the SACP and the ANC alliance were likewise targeted.[168]

Hunton put the need for international solidarity succinctly in a response to a letter he received that spring. "Jim-Crowism, colonialism and imperialism are not separate enemies, but a single enemy with different faces and different forms," he wrote. He urged, "If you are genuinely opposed to Jim-Crowism in America, you must be genuinely opposed to the colonial, imperialist enslavement of our brothers in other lands."[169] Hunton was rearticulating a theme he would add to and expand upon for the remainder of his life, a theme bolstering a decades-long alliance then causing ruling elites to embrace thought control and political repression as legitimate means of isolating Communists and the organizations they led, organizations like the CAA and the CRC.

In the newly constituted February 1952 CAA newsletter, *Spotlight On Africa*, Hunton attacked the coalition of "imperialist over-lords" led by the United States, but noted resistance was mounting. He added, the CAA has "long foreseen" the "explosion of national resistance to foreign domination" as evidenced by the emerging Black liberation struggles then taking shape in Africa. To Hunton, the CAA's "job – more urgent and important today than ever before – is to help make the [domestic] opposition" to U.S. imperialism more "organized, vocal and effective," to "do the job which today requires doing." To that end, *Spotlight On Africa* was to be published twice monthly "to provide a digest of up-to-the minute news, and interpretation of what's behind the news, concerning the progress of the African peoples." Hunton urged CAA activists to "enlist hundreds of new members, and scores of representative organizations, especially among the Negro people" in this effort. As he put it, the CAA needed to "publish and disseminate more information in order to shatter the iron curtain of silence and hypocritical lies intended to conceal the drive for super-profits and war preparations in Africa and other enslaved lands."[170] Ultimately, the Red Scare would take a major toll on the CAA making its work increasingly difficult, and eventually its existence untenable.

In 1948 Max Yergan, the CAA's former executive director – turned FBI informant, who was suspended for "mal-feasance, mis-feasance, and non-feasance," as Hunton put it[171] – decided to exact revenge on the

CAA by "fully co-operating" and "supplying the FBI with information that would fuel the Bureau's relentless persecution"[172] of both the CAA as an organization, and its principal officers – Hunton, Robeson and Du Bois – as individuals. Yergan went so far as to later tour Europe and Africa defending U.S. foreign policy. He became an "extreme right-wing crusader," a vocal apologists for apartheid South Africa.[173] Doxey Wilkerson had warned party leaders as early as November of 1947 that Yergan had begun to "shift with the winds."[174] His concern proved well founded. According to historian Herbert Aptheker, then serving on the CAA executive board, Yergan was removed as executive director due to his inability to explain "very serious financial irregularities" and that it was only after his "financial irregularities" had been exposed that he turned to professional red-baiting.[175] At a five-hour February 1948 CAA executive board meeting, Yergan declared that the CAA was not "identified with any partisan ideology."[176] According to Robeson, Yergan's comment emboldened "red-baiters and would not help the Council"[177] as it struggled to fight off the assault. In March Yergan accused Robeson, Wilkerson and Hunton of trying to gain control of the organization. He told reporters, "this minority group" was part of a "unprincipled Communist-led effort to seize the organization, [its] prestige and property."[178] How Robeson could seize a group he founded, funded and led was left unanswered. Regardless, the meeting "marked a decisive defeat for Yergan" who abruptly left after being censured for his "financial transactions."[179] Yergan claimed the split was due to Robeson's support of the Henry Wallace presidential ticket,[180] a campaign backed by Communists. In April, Yergan's dramatics reached a crescendo. He and two supporters attempted to elect "a new set of officers to replace everyone except himself," while also unilaterally removing 23 leaders from the CAA's governing body.[181] On May 28, the CAA "business affairs" became "more tangled than ever," as *The New York Times* noted. Yergan then claimed that Hunton and Wilkerson broke into his office, a dubious claim at best, as the CAA executive board had removed him as executive director on May 26.[182]

Hunton saw Yergan's political turn as part of a larger assault on civil liberties. Just as the waters had begun to calm in the CAA with Yergan's removal, Hunton began defending his CPUSA comrades who had been rounded up and thrown in jail in July 1948, charged with advocating the overthrow of the U.S. government by force and violence. In an August 1949 letter to the *Daily Worker*, Hunton noted that the "odious legal proceeding" against the CPUSA's top leadership threatens civil liberties for two reasons. First, it "violates the basic American principle that guilt must be an overt act and not an opinion," which would "destroy the right of political advocacy," an "indispensable" right especially for African Americans "if we are to win our long and painful struggle for full freedom and equality." Second, he said, the "trial by judge [Harold] Medina bears the stench of the lynch-dominated court which daily convict[s] Negroes in the South of 'crimes' they have never committed." "In the fight which the Negro people are waging for their lives in the midst of unprecedented and mounting lynch terror in the South," Hunton continued, "they need the support and fraternal cooperation of every progressive force in America including the Communists." Hunton added, "The record will show that the fight for the freedom of the Communists is a fight for their right to fight for the rights of Negroes."[183]

In 1951, the House Un-American Activities Committee renewed its assault against the African American Communist and his main political outlets, the CAA and the CRC. Both had been branded Communist fronts. Hunton eventually received a six-month jail sentence – and was placed in a segregated Federal prison – for "refusing to divulge" the names of CRC contributors; Hunton served as a CRC trustee.[184] The CRC, a legal defense organization, then managed about $770,000 in donations, as well as a list of about 6,500 donors.[185] In summer 1951,

Donald H. Aiken, deputy superintendent of banks, questioned Hunton and other CRC trustees about the defense fund during a state banking inquiry. Aiken claimed his inquiry wasn't politically motivated. "We are interested only in violations of the banking law,"[186] he told reporters. Like the IWO, which was then being dissolved,[187] the CRC's books were beyond reproach. Additionally, the court hinted at recalling Hunton and the other defendants to "ask them the same questions they had previously refused to answer," thereby threatening possible additional contempt charges.[188] According to Illinois party leader, Gil Green – who, along with Gus Hall, Henry Winston and Robert Thompson, had been bailed out by the CRC and had gone underground precipitating the inquiry into the CRC bail fund – HUAC wanted "to cripple the entire [CPUSA] bail-raising effort,"[189] an effort largely spearheaded by African American radicals like Hunton, Robeson, DuBois and Patterson. The CRC was forced to comply. And Attorney General Nathaniel L. Goldstein eventually "turned over the list of [CRC] fund contributors" to the FBI in the "interest of national security." Grace Hutchins, author of the groundbreaking *Women Who Work*, fellow Communist and women's rights activist, became the "single trustee" of the CRC fund as it was being liquidated. She told reporters, she was "outraged and horrified." "In doing this," she declared, "the Attorney General has violated the confidential status of the fund records and exposed to possible persecution and harassment innocent people who did no more than exercise their constitutional rights in defense of a paramount constitutional right – the right to bail."[190] Ironically, the court's ruling took place just days before the 1952 4th of July celebrations.

According to Paul Robeson, the CAA – like the CRC – was "involved in a fight for its life." However, he added, we "must defend it and its work – against prosecution under the McCarran (thought control) Act." "This fight," he told his friend Ben Segal, "means heavy legal expenses," which required "substantial assistance" from donors. Segal was one of those donors. "It is true that the going is rough," Robeson concluded, "by deliberate design of the enemy,"[191] an enemy determined to crush what Robeson, DuBois and Hunton, as well as the CRC's Patterson, exemplified, i.e. Black militancy comfortable with red allies.

In 1954, the CAA turned the tables and put McCarthyism on trial. Hunton testified at a public trial called by the New York Trade Union Veterans Committee, a group of trade unionists and World War II veterans who came together to discuss the growing "menace of McCarthyism and what they could do to combat it." The trial was held at St. Nicholas Arena on West 66th Street. The Arena, better known for its boxing matches, would now be at the center of a different kind of pugilistic battle. Hunton – and other union and community leaders – testified against the Wisconsin Senator's attacks on democratic rights. As 5,000 people filled the arena and another 2,000 filled a separate, overflow hall, Hunton took the witness stand. He said, "It is my conviction that Senator McCarthy, as the agent and co-conspirator of the most corrupt and pro-fascist elements in America" intends to "stifle all expression of opposition to the imperialist, Jim-crow [sic], status quo." Hunton, no stranger to the witch-hunt, said the level of repression exacted upon Blacks and reds depends on the actions of the American people. "The people – and only the people – can stop fascism from coming to America," he concluded.[192]

This particular assault climaxed in 1955 when a federal grand jury ordered the CAA to "turn over all of its correspondence for the last decade." The government argued that the CAA violated the Foreign Agents Registration Act due to its work with the ANC. Financially crippled, the council, "on Hunton's recommendation, dissolved itself rather than release the records"[193] and face, as Horne put it regarding the 1951 CRC hearing, "the prospect of tireless inquisition."[194] Government harassment made continuing the CAA untenable, Hunton argued.[195] Herman P. Osborne, the American-based Caribbean activist, would later note that Max Yergan and those like him "wrecked" the CAA "and in so doing strengthened the hands of reactionary forces in this nation that eventually sent into exile and death" both Du Bois and Hunton.[196] The combined weight of McCarthyism, the Smith and McCarran Acts, cast a "blanket of fear and suspicion [which smothered] all free democratic expression," Hunton concluded.[197]

* * *

Just as the CAA was being dismantled representatives from 29 African and Asian nations came together in Indonesia to demand self-determination and independence. The Bandung Conference attendees claimed to represent "nearly a billion and a half people" in the decolonizing world. In the May 1955 CAA *Spotlight on Africa* newsletter, Hunton noted the conference "reflected the determination of Asian and African peoples at this stage of history to be done with Western dictation, guidance or 'tutelage.'" He said, decolonizing peoples were determined "to think for themselves and decide their own destiny." Hunton also criticized the small "anti-Communist faction" in Bandung, which included his one-time ally Adam Clayton Powell, Jr. He noted that "their attempt to picture 'Communist colonialism' as a greater present danger than Western colonialism" was a "favorite theme of the U.S. State Department." It has "the double value of focusing attention on what the Soviet Union and China are alleged to be doing while diverting attention from the expanding economic colonialism of the United States itself and from the colonial regimes, particularly in Africa, still retained by the European imperialist powers, allies all of them of the United States in its 'free world' crusade." Fortunately, as Hunton put it, "the forces of unity prevailed over the agents of disunity."

According to Hunton, the Bandung Conference "had a tremendous impact on all sections of the Negro people."

For Black Americans "the Conference had a special significance derived from their identification with the subject peoples in other lands and especially Africa," an identification born out of "a common experience of oppression and common striving for freedom." The domestic African American press agreed with Hunton's assessment. The Baltimore *Afro-American* called the conference a "clear challenge to white supremacy," as well as the U.S. government's "split personality approach to colonialism." The *Boston Chronicle* recognized Bandung as "an anti-imperialist conference," noting that "its formation strikes a blow at imperialism all around the globe." The Oklahoma *Black-Dispatch* editorialized: "We think it is about time that Western society awakens and does not set at naught the activities of a conference representing more than half the people on the globe. It is true these peoples are representatives of the colored race, but when they meet, as they are for the first time...they become like bees. Their sting can be terrible." The L.A. *Herald-Dispatch* saluted the conference and hoped that "the American Negro will learn a lesson from this historic meeting." Hunton agreed and added, African Americans should "derive greater strength from the knowledge of the kind of world colored peoples in other continents are trying to build."

Hunton saw Bandung as a sign of a shift in the worldwide balance of power, a shift precipitated by ascendant socialism and its embrace of self-determination and independence movements, including Black liberation in Africa. "If the Bandung Conference represented a new alignment of world forces, a fresh outlook toward achieving a world of equality, cooperation and peace among nations and peoples," then "the Negro people should be among the first in the United States to respond and orientate their thinking, organization and action in the new pattern," a pattern the ruling class was loath to welcome. "[African American's] interest in what transpired at Bandung must not be allowed to wane to die," Hunton argued. Additionally, African Americans must wield "their influence to place the Government of the United States on the side of the world's oppressed instead of their oppressors." Further, they must take "their proper place, along with all other sections of progressive America, at the side of the colored majority of mankind who have declared their determination to work together for PEACE,"[198] a sentiment at odds with the then raging Cold War.

* * *

Hunton spent 12 years of his life building and leading the CAA. With its dissolution, he was unemployed, blacklisted, and diligently looking for work that would both allow him to, in the words of his wife, "keep his self-respect and [his] sanity."[199] Hunton straddled optimism and despondence during this period in his life. He was fortunate to have "temporary employment," which provided "a weekly paycheck with my name on it for the first time in a long time." But he also lamented the fact that it also left him "little or no free time" for continued research or writing. However, he noted some "new opportunities," or political openings. He was jubilant about the "presentation of the Du Bois bust at the Schomburg Library"[200] celebrating his friend's pioneering work.

In 1957, Hunton published *Decision in Africa: Sources of Current Conflict*. His friend and co-worker, DuBois, called it a "brilliant exposition of the structure of the new imperial order in Africa and of the role of American capital, private and public, in underwriting it." In the foreword, DuBois praised Hunton's scholarly work. "I know of no one today who has a more thorough knowledge and understanding of that continent [Africa]" than Hunton. This was high praise indeed, as DuBois was considered "the most eminent of African scholars."[201] The *Pittsburgh Courier*'s review noted that *Decision in Africa* painted "a sorry picture of a continent being systematically and ruthlessly robbed" and added that "it is difficult if not impossible to controvert Mr. Hunton's thesis."[202] To Hunton, the project was a labor of love. He specifically dealt with issues "avoided by other writers," specifically the corporate interest in continuing colonialism. In a letter to a colleague he wrote, "The book is now out, and reviews will be appearing this month. Now comes the task of getting people to buy it and read it." While Hunton couldn't "afford any large-scale advertising" and while he didn't expect the book to "hit the best-sellers list," he was "convinced that a quite sizable audience...exist[ed] and can be reached if a few" colleagues and comrades "personally assume responsibility" for talking it up among friends, co-workers and allied organizations. "If I receive your consent," Hunton continued, "I would like to forward as quickly as possible three, five, ten books – whatever you specify."[203] Richard Morford accepted Hunton's challenge and wrote to the leadership of the National Council of American-Soviet Friendship, noting that the former NNC and CAA leader "has given unremitting attention, through many years, to developments in Africa, encouraging in every practicable way the struggle of the black men and women of Africa for freedom and equality. I do believe," Morford added, "the wide circulation of his book is a worthy project."[204] Hunton thanked Morford for his support, noting that seven people replied, nine books were sold and five were taken "on consignment." Hunton then urged that the book be brought to "the attention of Negroes not associated with the left,"[205] as their support was needed more than ever. Though locked out of the academic mainstream due to his political beliefs, Hunton pressed on.

Decision in Africa brought a Marxist analysis to the plunder of Africa, while highlighting a path forward aided by ascendant socialism. He noted that "the peoples of Asia, the Middle East and Africa" will no-longer "bend the knee by economic strangulation, for they now have an alternative to Western markets in the socialist sector of the world." He approvingly quoted Walter Lippman: "The emergence of the Soviet Union as a competitor is one of the great historic events of our times." To Hunton, "The *kind* of assistance given [by the Soviet Union] is of more significance than the quantity of it" [*italic* in original]. Further, since the "socialist countries do not normally make direct money loans," developing countries "do not have the problem of heavy interest rates or of being restricted to spending the money as the lender directs." Often "assistance takes the form of barter transactions that will enable the counties to industrialize themselves," thereby eliminating dependence on foreign markets. That ascendant socialism "came forward and offered economic assistance to the independent peoples of Africa" with "trade deals and technical knowhow," put imperialism back on its heels. The "offer of assistance" itself was a "threat to Africa and the 'free world,'" Cold War commentators insisted. Hunton noted, "what worries Washington is not so much the interests of the prospective recipients of Soviet aid as its *own* interests." Declining world imperialism "fears... the weakening or loss of its *exclusive* controlling influence...it fears giving these countries the chance to make choices and decisions of their own" [*italic* in original]. This fear, coupled with racist paternalism, was at the heart of the domestic Red Scare and international Cold War. Hunton also added, that this "expression" of racist paternalism "reflects the attitude (either unconscious or deliberate) of one talking about inferior people who *can't know* which way to go but must be pulled this way or that" [*italic* in original], lest their interests not align with U.S. imperialism. That these questions, like the 1956 nationalization of the Suez Canal, "could not be summarily resolved in the old ways of Western coercion and force, even though attempted, is proof of existence of a new equation of world power." Ascendant socialism was strategically positioned to force concessions on behalf of independence and self-determination, African American equality and Black liberation. That imperialism was "desperate and degenerate" wasn't lost on Hunton. "If the West's ideological and economic weapons cannot keep the African obedient to its dictation, will deadlier weapons be used...all in the name of saving Africa from Communism,"[206] he asked.

In 1958, Hunton attended the All-African People's Conference in Accra, the first convergence in Nkrumah's Pan-Africanists campaign for continental unity. Despite being treated like a criminal in the United States, while in Ghana Hunton was "treated like a visiting dignitary."[207] In an April 1959 *Political Affairs* article he wrote, "the African people, inspired by a new high level of confidence, determination and unity reflected at the Accra Conference...will persist in their struggle for full equality and freedom even if they have to fight alone."[208] Fortunately, however, they did not have to fight alone, as ascendant socialism "provided support as a genuine expression of its commitment to African liberation from European colonialism."[209] This reality is increasingly apparent now, nearly three decades after the collapse of the first socialist state. While in Accra, Hunton met with the director of the Institute on African Studies in Moscow who informed him that *Decision in Africa* had been translated into Russian and would soon be published in the Soviet Union. That Hunton would be invited to speak there and receive modest royalties for his book was just another example of ascendant socialism's commitment to African American equality and Black liberation, as well as its support for revolutionary movements and their cadre the world over. By spring 1961, *Decision in Africa* had been published in East Germany, Hungary, Romania and Bulgaria, as well. And that summer Hunton and his wife were again invited to the Soviet Union, this time for "a complete medical checkup," another source of aid to revolutionary leaders. For Hunton, the tireless worker, this wasn't a vacation, though, as radio and press interviews, university lectures and other speaking engagements were arranged throughout Eastern Europe.[210]

Central to Hunton's analysis of Black liberation was the question of political power. "The winning of political power is everywhere recognized as the first and fundamental requirement for African advancement." Africans "will be satisfied with nothing less than democratic self-government," he wrote in a February 1950 issue of *Masses & Mainstream.*[211] Hunton saw his life's work – especially his time with the CAA – as an expression of this idea. He was a domestic combatant in an international conflict for political power, African American equality, and Black liberation. Without reservation, Hunton criticized the "coalition of imperialist and pro-imperialist forces in the U.N. attempting to push aside" Patrice Lumumba, the first democratically elected prime minister of the Republic of the Congo. Lumumba was deposed by the dictator Joseph-Desire Mobutu in 1961 – with the aid of the CIA. That Lumumba "unquestionably enjoys the widest support among the Congolese" only added to the outrage when he was executed by firing squad. "It is a shame upon the United Nations! It is an insult against the Congolese and Africans generally," Hunton exclaimed.[212] As Hunton feared, "brute force" was used to roll back the gains then being made by national liberation movements, hence his emphasis on "winning political power."

In 1960, Hunton emigrated to Guinea before accepting DuBois' invitation in 1962 to work on the *Encyclopedia Africana* in Ghana. In Guinea, he boldly, perhaps optimistically, claimed, "The day is past where the poorer countries, for lack of any other source of aid, must obey the dictates of imperialist countries."[213] With socialism then in its ascendency, however, Hunton's optimistic view wasn't unrealistic. Black liberation in Africa, buoyed by ascendant socialism, was advancing on multiple fronts. "One of the good things about being in Guinea was the feeling that one was in the mainstream not only of African liberation forces but what was progressive globally," he added. The whirlwind of change in Africa provided Hunton with the intellectual and political freedom he was denied in the U.S. In Guinea, Hunton proposed to teach courses on, for example, *United Nations and*

African Administration and *United States Policy in Africa and Problems of Pan-African Unity and Cooperation.* Shortly after returning from the 1961 Eastern Europe trip, Hunton received a letter from DuBois asking him to help his former CAA co-worker embark on his most ambitious project, the creation of the *Encyclopedia Africana* in Ghana,[214] an invitation Hunton was excited to accept.

* * *

Hunton's ousting from Ghana in 1966 did not tame his scathing critique of colonialism, neo-colonialism and imperialism, though. He asserted, "colonial powers had yielded to popular self-government" in parts of Africa only to "strengthen their economic domination." He added that some leaders of "newly independent" African countries were nothing more than "the willing servants of their imperialist masters,"[215] as evidenced by post-coup Ghana. In early 1967 Zambian president Kenneth Kaunda invited Hunton to that country as his guest, where he worked on a history of the nationalist movement and wrote a column for *Mayibye*, the ANC bulletin,[216] thereby bringing full-circle a relationship given political substance with Hunton's initial work in the NNC 30 years earlier.

* * *

While in Africa, where there "is an openness, spacial [sic] as well as imaginative,"[217] Hunton watched as the civil rights movement back home grew in strength. As one of the intellectual and organizational architects of that movement, Hunton never gave up on the struggle for African American equality or Black liberation in Africa. He understood the dialectical unity between the national and international character of the struggle for equality. That Black liberation and African American civil rights movements both "evoke memories of a common heritage, of the experience of centuries of struggle against racist oppression," and both closely "parallel" each other because of this "heritage" is significant, as both are also the enemy of U.S. capitalism, which "would never passively reconcile itself" to "political independence in Africa or equality" at home. Hunton embodied, what the CPUSA national chair, Henry Winston called a "special affinity between Africans and [U.S.] Blacks...who are struggling against oppression on the home grounds of U.S. imperialism – one of the most powerful sources of oppression in Africa."[218]

William Alphaeus Hunton died in Lusaka, Zambia on January 13, 1970.[219] He lived life in service to African American equality, Black liberation and socialism. Writing to James and Esther Cooper Jackson shortly after Alphaeus' death, Dorothy Hunton noted, "I can't begin to tell you what a great consolation it has been to me in the darkest hours of my life to know that Alphaeus and I have so many wonderful friends all over the world, and that he was deeply loved, respected and admired for his contributions to the betterment of the human race. Such a gentle soul, humble and kind, unassuming and tireless in his dedication to his work." She added solemnly, "It wasn't an easy life," but it was one dedicated in service to the "human family." "I will be coming home in the spring," she concluded. "Africa without dear Alphaeus holds no place for me."[220]

Considered by some to be "one of the most neglected African American intellectuals"[221] of the 20th century, a consequence of his lifelong membership in the CPUSA, Hunton was nevertheless greatly admired within the African diaspora – like his good friends Paul Robeson and W.E.B. DuBois. Considered "A person with exceptional talent, rare personal integrity, a deep commitment to humanistic values, and an enormous capacity for hard work," Hunton was also modest, self-possessed and tenacious. One contributor to *Freedomways* would opine shortly after his death, for Hunton "there was no contradiction between scholarly pursuits and full participation by the scholar in all aspects of humankind's struggle for a better life,"[222] including the struggle for socialism. The *Daily World* commented that Hunton's passing was "an irreplaceable loss" to the struggles for African American equality and Black liberation.[223] Henry Winston and Gus Hall noted that Hunton's "contribution and dedication to the advancement of national liberation, peace and socialism won [him] the admiration and comradeship of people in all parts of the world."[224] *The New York Times* obituary was considerably more reserved, and simply recognized Hunton as "an American authority on Africa."[225] Members of the Alphaeus Hunton College Teacher's Club of the New York Communist Party argued in a spring 1975 issue of *Party Affairs* that "Nothing is more important for the Party than work in educating our people about the theory and practice of socialism,"[226] a project Hunton devoted his life to.

In April 1943, while Hunton was making the transition from Howard University professor and NNC leader to the CAA, *The Worker* noted, he is a "fine example of an intellectual that speaks the workers language,"[227] perhaps the highest praise possible for a Communist intellectual. As the political inquisitors questioned Hunton about the CRC trust fund in 1951, W.E.B. DuBois wrote, "I have come to know this fine man very well." DuBois called him, "Quiet, studious, conscientious and absolutely uncorruptible."[228] Eleven years later, in a September 1962 correspondence with Hunton, DuBois gently criticized his long-time co-worker and friend for his humility. Hunton had left his name out of a "splendid" report he had written regarding the *Encyclopedia Africana*.[229] DuBois' comments are sound advice to a new generation of activists and historians. Hunton's name should be revered – in the struggle for African American equality, Black liberation in Africa, and socialism.

Notes

Foreword

1) See e.g. Gerald Horne, *Confronting Black Jacobins: The U.S., the Haitian Revolution and the Origins of the Dominican Republic* (New York: Monthly Review Press, 2015)

2) The foregoing has been drawn heavily from Christine Ann Lutz, "'The Dizzy Steep to Heaven': The Hunton Family, 1850-1970," Ph.d. dissertation, Georgia State University, 2001. See also Gerald Horne, "Revolting Capital: Racism and Radicalism in Washington, D.C., 1918-1968," forthcoming

Author Introduction

1) Karl Marx and Friedrich Engels, *The Communist Manifesto* (International Publishers, 2014)

2) Philip S. Foner, ed., *The Bolshevik Revolution: Its Impact on American Radicals, Liberals, and Labor* (International Publishers, 2017), VIII

3) Kristen Ghodsee, *Second World, Second Sex: Socialist Women's Activism and Global Solidarity during the Cold War* (Duke University Press, 2018), 17

4) See: Gerald Horne, *Black and Red: W. E. B. DuBois and the Afro-American Response to the Cold War, 1944-1963* (University of New York Press, 1986), Gerald Horne, *Black Liberation/Red Scare: Ben Davis and the Communist Party* (University of Delaware Press, 1994), Gerald Horne, *Black Revolutionary: William Patterson and the Globalization of the African American Freedom Struggle* (University of Illinois Press, 2013) and Mary L. Dudziak, *Cold War Civil Rights: Race and the Image of American Democracy* (Princeton University Press, 2000)

5) NYU, TAM 347, Box 5, Folder 48: Memo from Winston to Jackson, February 10, 1966

6) "Kennedy Can End Bias, Davis Tells CCNY Students," The Worker, Sunday, May 14, 1961, 12

7) Taj Fraizier Robeson, *The East Is Black: Cold War China in the Black Radical Imagination* (Duke University Press, 2015)

8) Throughout its 100 year history, the CPUSA prioritized work among the African American community and was in the vanguard of the struggles for African American equality and Black liberation;

other Marxists groupings, particularly the Socialist Party, argued that the race question would be addressed once the class question had been solved. This pioneering aspect of the CPUSA's analysis and organizing made it unique. The courageous role of both Black and white Communists has been well documented and rightly celebrated. However, some argue that this unique focus proved detrimental to other struggles against racial and national oppression; while this is not my focus, it is worth noting. For example, in 1948 African American party leader William L. Patterson wrote, "He who has the leadership of the Negro people for equal rights, has the leadership of the whole American movement for constitutional liberties, civil and human rights...There is no problem, no issue, no project...that takes priority over the Negro question," (Gerald Horne, *Communist Front: The Civil Rights Congress, 1946-1956* (Associated University Presses, 1988), 330). Communists of other ethnicities may have disagreed. According to Enrique M. Buelna, "Despite the CP's claim that it welcomed all equally into its fold, it had problems. Prejudices based on race, ethnicity, and gender were not always cast aside. The fact that CP officials did not consistently regard Mexican Americans as on an equal plane with African Americans remained a sore point with [Ralph] Cuaron and other Mexican American [Communist] activists. A theoretical rigidity led the party to identify African Americans as a key component in the ultimate demise of American imperialism, and this resulted in the belief that this population mattered above all others." (Enrique M. Buelna, *Chicano Communists And The Struggle For Social Justice* (University of Arizona Press, 2019), 5) The party's "terrible position" supporting the internment of Japanese Americans during World War II is another case in point. (Tony Pecinovsky, "On 4th of July, remember CPUSA's commitment to patriotism," People's World, July 2, 2015, https://www.peoplesworld.org/article/on-4th-of-july-remember-cpusa-s-commitment-to-patriotism/) Party work among indigenous Hawaiians, and Asian-Pacific Islanders on the mainland was often underfunded, understaffed and deprioritized, despite organizing success. (Gerald Horne, *Fighting In Paradise: Labor Unions, Racism, And Communists In The Making Of Modern Hawai'i* (University of Hawaii Press, 2011)) Native Americans were also sometimes seen as lower on the ladder of priorities. Native American party leader Judith LeBlanc would criticize some comrades for viewing the struggle of Native peoples as a "side issue." (Judith LeBlanc, "On Native American Indians and the Anti-Monopoly Struggle," Political Affairs, July-August 1983, 53-54) CPUSA national co-chair Joe Sims said, "We made mistakes. We didn't fully grasp the significance of other struggles." Though, he added, "It would be a distortion to say that the Black question is the question; the party's attention to the issue was in relation to class unity and the fight for the leading role of the class as a whole. The role that racism plays, particularly against African Americans was formulated into those issues." (Sims, author interview, August 15, 2019) Regardless, the centrality of the struggles of African American equality and Black liberation was essential to the Party's analysis of capitalism, expanding democracy and struggling for socialism: from initiating and leading the Alabama Sharecroppers Union (Robin D.G. Kelley, *Hammer and Hoe: Alabama Communists During the Great Depression* (University of North Carolina Press, 1990)) to playing a foremost role in the creation and leadership of the National Negro Congress (Erik S. Gellman, *Death Blow to Jim Crow: The National Negro Congress and the Rise of Militant Civil Rights* (University of North Carolina Press, 2014)); to Communist leadership in the Council on African Affairs (Penny M. Von Eschen, *Race Against Empire: Black Americans and Anticolonialism, 1937-1957* (Cornell University Press, 1997)) and the Civil Rights Congress (Horne, *Communist Front...*, Ibid); as well as the campaign to free Angela Davis and the birth of the National Alliance Against Racist and Political Repression, etc. Communists viewed these formations, among others, as essential to the struggle for African American equality and Black liberation. That future Detroit mayor Coleman Young lived with well-known Communists James and Esther Cooper Jackson during his formative years (Tim Wheeler, "James Jackson: Communist leader and pioneer fighter for civil rights," People's World, June 7, 2019, https://www.peoplesworld.org/article/james-jackson-communist-leader-and-pioneer-fighter-for-civil-rights/); that white activists in the 1960s, Maoist no-less, recalled, "the CP was the best-integrated organization, by race, sex and age, that I've ever seen," (John F. Levin and Earl Silbar, ed., *You Say You Want a Revolution: SDS, PL, and Adventures in Building a Worker-Student Alliance* (1741 Press, 2019), 40); that Chicago party leader Ishmael Flory had a special relationship with Windy City Mayor Harold Washington despite red-baiting (Tim Johnson, discussion with author while at the CPUSA National Convention, June 21-23, 2019); and that this author would be introduced to the party through its leadership in the St. Louis chapter of the Coalition of Black Trade Unionists, then known as a Red Chapter, among countless other examples, illustrates the party's long affinity for African American equality and Black liberation, and the enduring relationships Communists built as part of this special focus. Additionally, this affinity partly explains why Samaria Rice – mother of the slain African American youth, Tamir Rice, from Cleveland, Ohio – proudly attended the CPUSA's 2019 National Convention. (Al Neal, "Behind the lens: A reflection on CP100," People's World, July 8, 2019, https://www.peoplesworld.org/article/behind-the-lens-a-reflection-on-cp100/) In short, this special affinity prioritizing the struggle for African American equality as central to the struggle for democracy is what I mean by the Red-Black alliance. To be clear this is not a CPUSA programmatic formulation, or formal partnership. It is shorthand for the context and history discussed above.

9) MSRC, Manuscript Division Howard University, "Patterson, William," https://dh.howard.edu/finaid_manu/152/

10) "500 at College Hear Patterson in Debate on Africa," The Worker, November 27, 1960, 10

11) Alphaeus Hunton, *Decision in Africa: Sources of Current Conflict* (International Publishers, 1957), 218-219

12) Bettina Aptheker "The Student Rebellion, Part 1," Political Affairs, March 1969, 15-24

13) NYU, TAM 132, Box 113, Folder 80: *Address by Dr. Claude Lightfoot To a Panel on International Coalitions at the National Black United Fund Conference,* June 29, 1979, Boston, MA. Re the NBUF, see: http://www.nbuf.org/overview/history

14) William Pomeroy, *The Forest: A personal record of the Huk guerilla struggle in the Philippines* (International Publishers, 1963) and William Pomeroy, *Bilanggo: Life as a Political Prisoner in the Philippines, 1952-1962* (University of the Philippines Press, 2009)

15) Michael A. Lebowitz, *The Contradictions Of Real Socialism: The Conductor And The Conducted* (Monthly Review Press, 2012)

16) NYU, TAM 132, Box 63, Folder 9: Letter from Pomeroy to Bechtel, August 12, 1990

17) Tony Pecinovsky, "Historians: History is more than an academic exercise," People's World, April 21, 2015, http://www.peoplesworld.org/article/historians-history-is-more-than-an-academic-exercise/

18) Harvey Klehr, John Earl Haynes and Kyrill M. Anderson, ed., *The Soviet World of American Communism* (Yale University Press, 1998), Sam Tanenhaus, "Gus Hall, Unreconstructed American Communist of 7 Decades, Dies at 90," The New York Times, October 17, 2000 and Francis X. Clines, "Kremlin Reportedly Gave $2 Million a Year to U.S. Communist Party," The New York Times, December 1, 1991. It is noted that Moscow gave about $4 billion to international Communist Party's and various left movements. It is estimated that the CPUSA received $40 million from the Soviet Union between 1971 and 1990. See, also: John Barron, *Operation Solo: The FBI's Man In The Kremlin,* (Regnery Publishing, Inc., 1996)

19) For example, see: Meredith L. Roman, *Opposing Jim Crow: African Americans And The Soviet Indictment Of U.S. Racism, 1928-1937* (University of Nebraska Press, 2012)

20) For example, see: Ghodsee, *Second World, Second Sex...,* Ibid and Julia L. Mickenberg, *American Girls In Red Russia: Chasing the Soviet Dream* (University of Chicago Press, 2017)

21) Foner, ed. *The Bolshevik Revolution...,* Ibid

22) See: Mark Naison, *Communists in Harlem during the Depression* (University of Illinois Press, 2005), Erik S. Gellman, *Death Blow To*

Jim Crow: The National Negro Congress and the Rise of Militant Civil Rights (University of North Carolina Press, 2012), Mark Solomon, *The Cry Was Unity: Communists and African Americans, 1917-1936* (University Press of Mississippi, 1998), Robin D. G. Kelley, *Hammer And Hoe: Alabama Communists During The Great Depression* (University of North Carolina Press, 1990), among other examples

23) V.J. Jerome, "Marxism-Leninism For Society and Science," The Communist, December 1937 (Vol. XVI, No. 12), 1,148

24) e.g. Lovett Fort-Whiteman. See: Klehr, Haynes and Anderson, ed., *Soviet World of American Communism*, Ibid, 218-219, Glenda Elizabeth Gilmore, *Defying Dixie: The Radical Roots Of Civil Rights, 1919-1950* (W.W. Norton & Co., 2008) and Meredith L. Roman, *Opposing Jim Crow: African Americans And The Soviet Indictment Of U.S. Racism, 1928-1937* (University of Nebraska Press, 2012)

25) Many Communists cut their political teeth in the Industrial Workers of the World, the Socialist Party, the Knights of Labor and other radical union movements prior to the birth of the Soviet Union and had a special affinity for the radical democratic traditions of this nation, especially the abolitionists and suffragists movements. "Communism Is 20th Century Americanism" wasn't simply rhetoric. Additionally, some, like suspected Communist Josephine Truslow Adams – "a unique kind of Communist" – emphasized their American revolutionary lineage; Adams was a descendent of President John Quincy Adams. See: "'Link' To Browder Retold At Inquiry," The New York Times, January 6, 1954

26) Mike Davidow, "Gus Hall at Yale and Benjamin Davis at Brown Present Communist Views on Main Issues," The Worker, Sunday, February 24, 1963, 2, 11

27) Frederick N. Rasmussen, "George Aloysius Meyers, 86, Communist Party member," Baltimore Sun, October 21, 1999, http://articles.baltimoresun.com/1999-10-21/news/9910210183_1_communist-party-meyers-party-members)

28) Aviva Chomsky, *Linked Labor Histories: New England, Colombia, And The Making Of A Global Working Class* (Duke University Press, 2008), 84, *Biographical Note*, Anne Burlak Timpson Papers, Five College Archives & Manuscripts Collections, http://asteria.fivecolleges.edu/findaids/sophiasmith/mnsss189.html#list-ser3. For more on Burlak, see: Quenby Olmsted Hughes, "Red Flame Burning Bright: Communist Labor Organizer Ann Burlak, Rhode Island Workers, and the New Deal," Rhode Island History, Summer/Fall 2009 (Vol. 67, Number 2)

29) William Minter, Gail Hovey and Charles Cobb Jr., ed., *No Easy Victories: African Liberation and American Activists over Half Century, 1950-2000* (Africa World Press, Inc., 2007), 69-72

30) Enrique M. Buelna, *Chicano Communists And The Struggle For Social Justice* (University of Arizona Press, 2019), 79

31) Wheeler, author interview, 10/2/2017

32) Paul L. Montgomery, "Communist Party Here Marks 50th Birthday Without Fanfare," The New York Times, September 2, 1969

33) NYU, TAM 347, Box 21, Folder 66: Gus Hall, untitled, no date

34) For example, see: Judith Stepan-Norris and Maurice Zeitlan, *Left Out: Reds and America's Industrial Unions* (Cambridge University Press, 2002), Clarence Taylor, *Reds At The Blackboard: Communism, Civil Rights, and the New York City Teachers Union* (Columbia University Press, 2011), Bruce Nelson, *Workers on the Waterfront: Seaman, Longshoremen, and Unionism in the 1930s* (University of Illinois Press, 1990), Roger Keeran, *The Communist Party and the Auto-Workers' Union* (International Publishers, 1986), Rosemary Feurer, *Radical Unionism In The Midwest, 1900-1950* (University of Illinois Press, 2006), James L. Lorence, *The Unemployed People's Movement: Leftists, Liberals, And Labor In Georgia, 1929-1941* (University of Georgia Press, 2011), Gerald Horne, *Fighting In Paradise: Labor Unions, Racism, And Communists In The Making Of Modern Hawaii* (University of Hawaii Press, 2011), Gerald Horne, *Class Struggle In Hollywood, 1930-1950: Moguls, Mobsters, Stars, Reds, & Trade Unionists* (University of Texas Press, 2001), Michael Dennis, *Blood On Steel: Chicago Steelworkers And The Strike Of 1937* (Johns Hopkins University Press, 2014)

35) For example, see: Penny M. Von Eschen, *Race Against Empire: Black Americans and Anticolonialism, 1937-1957* (Cornell University Press, 1997), Gerald Horne, *Communist Front: The Civil Rights Congress, 1946-1956* (Associated University Presses, 1998), Sara Rzeszutek Haviland, *James and Esther Cooper Jackson: Love And Courage In The Black Freedom Movement* (University Press of Kentucky, 2015) and Gerald Horne, *Paul Robeson: The Artist as Revolutionary* (Pluto Press, 2016). Horne forcefully notes, "However, these new groupings [organizations connected to Dr. Martin Luther King, Jr.] did not have the international ties of the CRC [Civil Rights Congress, headed by Communist William L. Patterson], nor the global reach of the CAA [Council on African Affairs, headed by Communist Alphaeus Hunton], which amounted to a net loss for African-Americans and their allies." Ibid, 150

36) For example, see: A. H. Raskin, "U.S. Communists Insist They Will Never Quit," New York Times, September 10, 1950, Scott Martelle, *The Fear Within: Spies, Commies, and American Democracy on Trial* (Rutgers University Press, 2001), John Somerville, *The Communist Trials and the American Tradition: Expert Testimony on Force, and Violence and Democracy* (International Publishers, 2000), *13 Communists Speak To The Court* (New Century Publishers, March 1953), Herbert Aptheker, *Dare We Be Free? : The Meaning of the Attempt to Outlaw the Communist Party* (New Century Publishers, 1961), and

Ellen Schrecker, *The Age of McCarthyism: A Brief History with Documents* (Bedford Books, 1994). Though Communists bore the brunt of the repression, between 1947 and 1956 "more than five million federal workers underwent loyalty screening, and about 25,000 were subject to the stigmatizing 'full field investigation' by the FBI." About 2,700 were dismissed, and 12,000 resigned. See: Landon R.Y. Storrs, *The Second Red Scare and the Unmaking of the New Deal Left* (Princeton University Press, 2013), p 2

37) "900 Mourn Foster At Carnegie Hall," The New York Times, September 19, 1961

38) John J. Abt with Michael Myerson, *Advocate and Activist: Memoirs of an American Communist Lawyer* (University of Illinois Press, 1993), 281

39) Nikolai Mostevets, *Henry Winston: Profile of a U.S. Communist* (Progress Publishers, 1983)

40) Mike Davidow, "Robert Thompson War Hero, Is Still McCarthyism Victim," The Worker, May 5, 1963, 12, Martelle, *The Fear Within...*, Ibid, 244 and Fred P. Graham, "Communist Denied Burial in Arlington," The New York Times, January 28, 1966

41) Philip Bart, ed., *Highlights Of A Fighting History: 60 Years of the Communist Party USA* (International Publishers, 1979), 6 and Philip S. Foner, *History of the Labor Movement In The United States, Vol 10* (International Publishers, 1994), 285, 286

42) Dennis, *Blood On Steel...*, Ibid, 59, 63

43) Fraser M. Ottanelli, *The Communist Party Of The United States: From the Depression to World War II* (Rutgers University Press, 1992), 34

44) "Law, Oliver (1900-1937)," BlackPast.org, http://www.blackpast.org/aah/law-oliver-1900-1937). There is a bit of a historical controversy regarding the actual events leading to Law's death. Over 30 years after his death, Cecil B. Eby, who also served in the Brigade, claimed that Law was killed by his own men. See: "Anatomy of an Anticommunist Fabrication: The Death of Oliver Law, An Historiographical Investigation," Grover Furr, Reconstruction 8.1 (2008), http://reconstruction.eserver.org/Issues/081/furr.shtml. See also: Claude Lightfoot, *Chicago Slums To World Politics* (New Outlook Publishers, no date), 81, 84

45) Harvey Klehr, John Earl Haynes and Fridrikh Igorevich Firsov, ed., *The Secret World Of American Communism* (Yale University Press, 1995), 152, 153

46) *The Age of McCarthyism...*, Ibid, 176. Eugene Dennis remarked: "Communists are second to none in our devotion to our people and to our country."

47) Fred Graham, "The Law: Communist Party Again on Trial," The New York Times, November 7, 1965

48) "Communist Party Convicted by U.S.; Is Fined $120,000," The New York Times, December 18, 1962

49) For example, see: Robert M. Zecker, *"A Road to Peace and Freedom": The International Workers Order and the Struggle for Economic Justice and Civil Rights, 1930-1954* (Temple University Press, 2018)

50) Elizabeth Gurley Flynn, *Horizons Of The Future For A Socialist Society*, Communist Party, 1959, 37

51) Horne, *Black Liberation / Red Scare...*, Ibid, 71

52) Bart, ed., *Highlights Of A Fighting History...*, Ibid, 80-81

53) Gilmore, *Defying Dixie...*, Ibid, 6

54) James W. Ford, "The Struggle For The Building Of The Modern Liberation Movement Of The Negro People," The Communist, September 1939 (Vol. XVII, No. 9), 817, 818, 829

55) Gerald Horne, *Ride & Fall Of The Associated Negro Press: Claude Barnett's Pan-African News and the Jim Crow Paradox* (University of Illinois Press, 2017), 86

56) Sims, author Interview, August 15, 2019

57) Arnold Johnson, "The Bill of Rights and the Twelve," Political Affairs, July 1949, 10-17

58) See: Gus Hall, "Paul Robeson: An American Communist," Communist Party, USA (text of a centennial tribute speech delivered on May 31, 1998, at the Winston Unity Auditorium, CP national office, 235 W. 23rd St., New York, NY), 3, 6, 8. Later reprinted as Gus Hall, "Paul Robeson: Artist, Freedom Fighter, Hero, American Communist," Political Affairs, July, 1998. Hall writes: "My own most precious moments with Paul were when I met with him to accept his dues and renew his yearly membership in the CPUSA. I and other Communist leaders, like Henry Winston...met with Paul to brief him on politics and Party policies and to discuss his work and struggles." See, also: Vijay Prashad, "Comrade Robeson: A Centennial Tribute to an American Communist," Social Scientist, Vol. 25, No. 7/8 (Jul.-Aug. 1997), 40, 41. Prashad, however, quotes from the above. Gerald Horne wondered if Robeson had been a member of the Communist Party of Great Britain, which was "more of a likelihood than U.S. membership." See: Gerald Horne, *Paul Robeson: The Artist as Revolutionary* (Pluto Press, 2016), 6. Martin Duberman notes that Robeson offered to publicly join the CPUSA in 1951 out of solidarity with his beleaguered comrades, but that the proposal was rejected by the Party's leadership. See: Martin Duberman, *Paul Robeson: A Biography* (The New Press, 1989), 420. While Robeson's membership in the CPUSA is contested, it is apparent he did not hesitate to align himself with the CPUSA, its leadership and its policies.

59) Paul Robeson, *For Freedom and Peace*, Council On African Affairs, 1949, 13, 14

60) William Z. Foster, *History of the Communist Party of the United States* (International Publishers, Inc., 1952), 562

61) C.J. Atkins, *People's World* opinion editor and friend of Lorch's, author interview. "He was a member of the CP of Canada here and

confirmed to me that he was indeed in the CPUSA before he left the U.S."

62) David Margolick, "Lee Lorch, Desegregation Activist Who Led Stuyvesant Town Effort, Dies at 98," The New York Times, March 1, 2014, https://www.nytimes.com/2014/03/02/nyregion/lee-lorch-desegregation-activist-who-led-stuyvesant-town-effort-dies-at-98.html

63) Fred Giman, "5,000 Mark May Day At Union Square Rally," The Worker, May 7, 1963, 3, 7

64) Gerald Horne, *Black Revolutionary: William Patterson and the Globalization of the African American Freedom Struggle* (University of Illinois Press, 2013) and Horne, *Communist Front...*, Ibid

65) Herbert Aptheker, "Racism And The Danger Of Fascism In The United States," in Racism And Reaction In The United States: Two Marxian Studies (New Outlook Publishers, 1971), 25

66) NYU, TAM 132, Box 110, Folder 13: 10,000 March On North Carolina – "Unity is Our Weapon," NAARPR, 1974

67) Ronald D. Cohen, ed., *Red Dust and Broadsides: A Joint Autobiography – Agnes 'Sis' Cunningham and Gordon Friesen* (University of Massachusetts Press, 1999), 336

68) Anthony Lewis, "U.S. Communists Have More Legal Troubles: Even Membership in the Party Is Subject to Attack in the Courts," The New York Times, April 1, 1956

69) See: Lightfoot, *Chicago Slums...*, Ibid, 84-86, "Millions in Chicago Hear Lightfoot and Worker Editor Hit High Court Actions," The Worker, Sunday, June 18, 1961 and "SACB Hearing on Lightfoot Bares FBI Bribery to Betray Negro People," The Worker, Sunday, February 3, 1963, 4

70) Klehr, Haynes and Firsov, ed *The Secret World Of American Communism*, Ibid, 13, 14. Klehr et al begrudgingly note just a few paragraphs later, that the Party "gained some respectability and some members," but "entered its death throes in 1989." However, contradicting his own statements, Klehr, in 1991, suggested that the Party "is the oldest, largest, wealthiest, best-organized, and most effective Marxist-Leninist group in America." See: Harvey Klehr, *Far Left Of Center: the American radical left today* (Transaction Publishers, 1991), 3; See also: Joseph R. Starobin, *American Communism In Crisis, 1943*-1957 (University of California Press, 1972), 224

71) "F.B.I. Infiltration Belittled By Hall," The New York Times, October 20, 1962. One former FBI agent, Jack Levine, bragged: from September 1960 to August 1961 the Bureau "had 1,500 paid informants in Communist ranks." For one account, see: Barron, *Operation Solo...*, Ibid

72) Abt, *Advocate and Activist...*, Ibid, 267-270

73) Peter Kihss, "U.S. Reds Weigh New Command," The New York Times, September 26, 1964

74) Michael Zagarell, "World Student Strike Against Vietnam War and Racism," Political Affairs, March 1968, 20

75) Re Johnson and Mora's membership in CPUSA (two of the Fort Hood Three): Elena Mora, long-time Party leader and niece of Dennis Mora, author interview, while in Chicago at a CPUSA National Board meeting, May 29-31, 2015 ; Marc Brodine, author interview, while in Chicago at a CPUSA Marxist Strategy and Tactics conference, February, 18, 2017: Brodine attended Party School with Johnson. Tim Wheeler, a fellow *Daily World* reporter who worked with Johnson in the NY office, author interview, October 2, 2017. See *The Fort Hood Three: The Case Of The Three G.I.'s Who Said "No" To The War In Vietnam* (Fort Hood Three Defense Committee, 1966). For obvious reasons (anticommunism) Mora and Johnson publicly denied membership in the CPUSA. See also: Martin Arnold, "3 Soldiers hold News Conference to Announce They Won't Go to Vietnam," The New York Times, July 1, 1966

76) "The Tet Offensive and the Media: United States Military Morale: Vietnam War," ABC-CLIO – history and the Headlines,

http://www.historyandtheheadlines.abc-clio.com/ContentPages/ContentPage.aspx?entryId=1199250¤tSection=1194544

77) Victor Devinatz, "The Antipolitics And Politics Of A New Left Union Caucus: 'The Workers' Voice Committee Of The UAW Local 6, 1970-1975," Nature, Society & Thought, Vol. 14, No. 3 (July 2001), 258-321, http://imid-ltd.com/devinatz.html

78) NYU, TAM 132, Box 110, Folder 14: *Remarks of Henry Winston At The Founding Conference of NAIMSAL, Chicago, October 1973,* Henry Winston, October 19-21, 1973

79) Charlene Mitchell, "For Freedom for Political Prisoners and Victims of Racism and Class Injustice," Party Affairs, Vol. VII, No. 1, January 1973, 32-40. The report is from a December 1972 meeting of the Party's central committee where Mitchell outlined the work of the National United Committee to Free Angela Davis, which she led, and made a proposal for a new national defense organization, which became the National Alliance at a founding conference in May 1973

80) Erik S. McDuffie, *Sojourning For freedom: Black Women, American Communism, and the Making of Black Left Feminism* (Duke University Press, 2011), 199-201 and Bettye Collier-Thomas and V.P. Franklin, ed., *Sisters in the Struggle: African American Women in the Civil Rights – Black power Movement* (New York University Press, 2001), 274

81) Scott Marshall, "Toward a National Movement of the Unemployed," Political Affairs, September 1983

82) Beatrice Lumpkin, *Always Bring A Crowd: The Story of Frank Lumpkin Steelworker* (International Publishers, 1999), "Frank and Beatrice Lumpkin papers, 1940-2013, bulk 1974-1986, Biographical / historical note," Chicago History Museum, http://explore.chicagocollections.org/ead/chicagohistory/123/0864c37/) and John Bachtell, "Frank Lumpkin, 'Saint of Chicago,' dies at 93,"

People's World, March 10, 2010, http://www.peoplesworld.org/article/frank-lumpkin-saint-of-chicago-dies-at-9/

83) James Strong, "Activist Call Daley Negligent In Probe Of Lozano Slaying," Chicago Tribune, January 1, 1985, http://articles.chicagotribune.com/1985-01-01/news/8501010165_1_richard-m-daley-jesus-garcia-charges) and John Bachtell, "Rudy Lozano remembered as fighter for immigrant rights," People's World, June 13, 2013, http://www.peoplesworld.org/article/rudy-lozano-remembered-as-fighter-for-immigrant-worker-rights/

84) Re Lozano and the CPUSA: Roberta Wood, CPUSA secretary-treasurer and friend of the Lozano's, author interview, while at a CPUSA Finance Committee meeting in New York City, November 16, 2016; Emile Schepers, chair of the CPUSA International Department and former Chicago area college professor, author interview in Washington D.C., June 25, 2017; Lozano was a student of Schepers

85) "Wilson Only Incumbent To Lose Seat In Primaries," St. Louis Post-Dispatch, March 9, 1983; Re Jones' ousting and Ozier, see: "Why did Mayor Slay fire Kenny Jones?," St. Louis American, June 16, 2005, http://www.stlamerican.com/news/political_eye/why-did-mayor-slay-fire-kenny-jones/article_0656c80c-31b5-55bf-a230-b530b5f73a74.html ; Re Jones' and Ozier's membership in the CPUSA: both belonged to the St. Louis area Party club and met regularly with the author

86) Judith Le Blanc, long-time CPUSA national board member, served as UFPJ's national co-chair from 2005 to 2008; Jessica Marshall served as the Young Communist League national coordinator and leader in the NYSPC: See, Tony Pecinovsky, "Out of the Classroom, Into the Battlefield," Alternet / Wire Tap, April 6, 2003, http://www.alternet.org/story/15549/out_of_the_classroom,_into_the_battlefield) and "Peace Movement and the 2008 Elections: Interview with Judith Le Blanc," Political Affairs, April 11, 2008, http://www.politicalaffairs.net/peace-movement-and-the-2008-elections-interview-with-judith-leblanc/. The author served on the YCL's national committee with Marshall

87) Barbara Palmer, "Students participate in national strike against war," Stanford Report, March 12, 2003, http://news.stanford.edu/news/2003/march12/strike-312.html), Lloyd Vries, "Students Cut Class To Protest War," CBS, March 10, 2003, http://www.cbsnews.com/news/students-cut-class-to-protest-war/ and Bryan Long, "Students pencil in Iraq protest," CNN, March 5, 2003, http://www.cnn.com/2003/US/03/04/sprj.irq.college.protest/

88) Farah Fazal, "Ferguson activist disappointed by visit with Obama," USA Today / KSDK-TV, December 3, 2014, https://www.usatoday.com/story/news/nation/2014/12/03/ferguson-activist-shares-experience/19815447/ and "Presidential Meeting with Community Leaders and Law Enforcement," C-SPAN, December 1,

2014, https://www.c-span.org/video/?322995-2/president-obama-meeting-community-leaders-ferguson-missouri

89) See: "Panel Discussion on Low Wage Workers," C-SPAN, June 13, 2014, https://www.c-span.org/video/?320055-2/panel-discussion-lowwage-workers. Re Aldridge and the CPUSA: Aldridge officially joined while at the June 2014 Convention. He, along with other Missouri Communists, including Nicholas James (SEIU-HC), James Raines and Mark Esters (both from CWA 6355), had gone for a walk, and when they returned, they announced Aldridge's membership to the author. Aldridge continues his activism with the Party locally and remains a leader of the Party-led St. Louis Workers' Education Society. Re Neal and James' membership: Neal was a member of the CP in Ohio prior to moving to St. Louis; James was a member of the CP in California also prior to coming to St. Louis

90) See: Gerald Horne, *Fighting in Paradise: Labor Unions, Racism, and Communists in the Making of Modern Hawaii* (University of Hawaii Press, 2102)

91) Jenny Carson, "Labor day celebration of struggle: Bea Lumpkin's 100th Birthday," People's World, http://www.peoplesworld.org/article/celebrating-the-joy-and-the-struggle-bea-lumpkins-100th-birthday/

92) "Most Democrats View Socialism Favorably," Rasmussen Reports, October 29, 2015, http://www.rasmussenreports.com/public_content/politics/general_politics/october_2015/most_democrats_view_socialism_favorably and Keith A. Spence, "The Democratic Socialist of America hit 25,000 members. Here's why this could mark a political turning point," Salon.com, August 5, 2017, http://www.salon.com/2017/08/05/the-democratic-socialists-of-america-hit-25000-members-heres-why-this-is-a-big-deal/)

93) Art Shields, "Will Fight for Bill of Rights, CP Leaders Tell Newsmen," The Worker, Sunday, June 18, 1961

94) Pecinovsky, *Historians...*, Ibid. The phrase comes from an Organization of American Historians workshop at the 2015 Annual Meeting in St. Louis, Missouri which the author attended. See, also: Tony Pecinovsky, "'Intersectional before it was cool': The women's movement under state socialism," People's World, October 3, 2019, https://www.peoplesworld.org/article/intersectional-before-it-was-cool-the-womens-movement-under-state-socialism/?fbclid=IwAR2Kmqt3j9ZjhNfPjf1zvhxOJcJGBBtLSHVbIIcfTS0NcGfp7tOcoS9HQ_8. Kristen Ghodsee notes, "There is still a strong 'red taboo,' but there are younger scholars who are challenging it in fascinating ways."

95) Edward P. Johanningsmeier, *Forging American Communism: The Life of William Z. Foster* (Princeton University Press, 1994)

96) James G. Ryan, *Earl Browder: The Failure of American Communism* (University of Alabama Press, 2005)

97) Carole Boyce Davies, *Left of Karl Marx: The Political Life of Black Communist Claudia Jones* (Duke University Press, 2008)

98) Gerald Horne, *Black Liberation/Red Scare: Ben Davis and the Communist Party* (University of Delaware Press, 1994)

99) Lara Vapnek, *Elizabeth Gurley Flynn: Modern American Revolutionary* (Westview Press, 2015)

100) Sara Rzeszutek Haviland, *James and Esther Cooper Jackson: Love And Courage In The Black Freedom Movement* (University Press of Kentucky, 2015)

101) Gerald Horne, *Black Revolutionary: William Patterson and the Globalization of the African American Freedom Struggle* (University of Illinois Press, 2013)

102) Gary Murrell, *"The Most Dangerous Communist in the United States": A Biography of Herbert Aptheker* (University of Massachusetts Press, 2015)

103) Robyn Spencer, *Angela Davis: Radical Icon* (Westview Press, 2020)

104) Nikolai Mostovets, *Henry Winston: Profile of a U.S. Communist* (Progress Publishers, 1983)

105) Claude Lightfoot, *Chicago Slums To World Politics* (New Outlook Publishers, no date)

106) Stepan-Norris and Zeitlan, *Left Out...*, Ibid, 4, 19

107) Daniel Rosenberg, "From Crisis to Split: The Communist Party USA," American Communist History, https://www.tandfonline.com/doi/full/10.1080/14743892.2019.1599627

108) Sam Roberts, "Metro Matters; Top Communist In U.S. Is Taking 'Fever' in Stride," The New York Times, December 8, 1988

109) Claude Lightfoot, *Racism and Human Survival: Lessons of Nazi Germany for Today's World* (International Publishers, 1972,) 15

110) Mark Potok, "The Year In Hate And Extremism," Intelligence Report (magazine of the Southern Poverty Law Center), Spring 2017 (February 15th), https://www.splcenter.org/fighting-hate/intelligence-report/2017/year-hate-and-extremism

111) John Bachtell, "Charlottesville and crisis of Trump administration," People's World, September 5, 2017, http://www.peoplesworld.org/article/charlottesville-and-crisis-of-trump-administration/

112) Ta-Nehisi Coates, "The First White President: The foundation of Donald Trump's presidency is the negation of Barack Obama's legacy," The Atlantic, October 2017, https://www.theatlantic.com/magazine/archive/2017/10/the-first-white-president-ta-nehisi-coates/537909/

113) Harry Fisher, *Comrades: Tales Of A Brigadista In The Spanish Civil War* (University of Nebraska Press, 1998), 14

114) Bill Bailey *The Kid from Hoboken: An AutoBiography of Bill Bailey: Book Two, Chapter XIV: Ripping the Swastika off the Bremen* (Bill

Bailey, 1993), http://www.larkspring.com/Kid/Book2/2-14.html), Studs Terkel, *The Good War: An Oral History Of World War II* (The New Press, 1984), 100 and Peter Duffy, *The Agitator: William Bailey and the First American Uprising against Nazism* (Public Affairs, 2019)

115) Bailey, *The Kid from Hoboken...*, Ibid, *Chapter* XIV and Chapter *XXII: Somewhere in Spain*, http://www.larkspring.com/Kid/Book2/2-22.html), *Chapter I: The Lonesome Ride Home*, http://www.larkspring.com/Kid/Book3/3-1.html) and *Chapter XII: The PT Boat*, http://www.larkspring.com/Kid/Book3/3-12.html)

116) Pomeroy, *The Forest...*, Ibid

117) Lightfoot, *Chicago Slums...*, Ibid, p 84-86

118) Gus Hall, "Talks With Students," Political Affairs, April 1962, 5-18

Chapter One

1) NYU, Tam 132, Box 113, Folder 44: *Memorial speech by Jim West*, no date, Arnold Johnson, "The Ohio Membership Campaign, "The Communist, April 1944, 319-326, http://www.unz.org/Pub/Communist-1944apr-00319 and Starobin, *American Communism in Crisis...*, Ibid, 71, 72. Note: the CPUSA dissolved itself at the May 1944 Convention and reconstitute as the Communist Political Association.

2) "Communists Off Ohio Ballot," The New York Times, May 30, 1942

3) NYU, TAM 132, Box 113, Folder 44: *Memorial Speech by Jim West*, no date and Horne, *Black Liberation/Red Scare...*, Ibid, 165

4) Guide to the Arnold Johnson Papers TAM.137: Historical/Biographical Notes, http://dlib.nyu.edu/findingaids/html/tamwag/tam_137/bioghist.html

5) *13 Communists Speak To The Court* (New Century Publishers, March 1953), 63

6) *Guide to the Arnold Johnson Papers...*, Ibid

7) Ottanelli, *The Communist Party of the United States...*, Ibid, 21 and John Gaventa, *Power and Powerlessness: Quiescence and Rebellion in an Appalachian Valley* (University of Illinois Press, 1982), 99

8) *The Kentucky Miners Struggle: The Record of a Year of Lawless Violence. The Only Complete Picture of Events Briefly Told* (The American Civil Liberties Union, 1932), 3

9) NYU, Tam 132, Box 113, Folder 44: *Memorial speech...*, Ibid

10) Gaventa, *Power and Powerlessness...*, Ibid, 100 and ACLU, *The Kentucky Miners Struggle...*, Ibid, 3

11) *Guide to the Arnold Johnson Papers...*, Ibid

12) See: Robert Jackson Alexander, *International Trotskyism, 1929-1985: A Documented Analysis of the Movement* (Duke university Press, 1991), 775, 776

13) William Z. Foster, *Little Brothers Of The Big Labor Fakers* (Trade Union Unity League, 1931), 8,9 and Harvey Klehr, *The Heyday of American Communism: The Depression Decade* (Basic Books, Inc., 1984), 15, 16

14) *Guide to the Arnold Johnson Papers..., Ibid* and Bart, ed., *Highlights of a Fighting History...*, Ibid, 58; Re Workers' Alliance, see: *Guides to Archive and Manuscript Collections at the University of Pittsburgh Library System: Summary Information – Title: Workers Alliance of America Records*, http://digital.library.pitt.edu/cgi-bin/f/findaid/findaid-idx?c=ascead&cc=ascead&rgn=main&view=text&didno=US-PPiU-ais200703

15) NYU, TAM 137, Box 2, Folder 1: *Statement By Arnold Johnson, National Legislative Director, On C.C.N.Y.s Refusal To Permit Him To Speak*, December 10, 1947

16) "Speech by Johnson, Communist, Is Barred by City College Dean," The New York Times, December 10, 1947

17) NYU, TAM 137, Box 2, Folder 1: "Students Protest Ban on Fast," Daily Worker, December 12, 1947, "100 At Columbia Hear Communist," The New York Times, December 18, 1947, "Columbia Will Let Communist Speak," The New York Times, December 16, 1947 and "Johnson Raps College Bans On Communists," Columbia Spectator, Vol. LXX, No. 59, December 18, 1947

18) "Two New England Colleges Hear Communist Spokesman," The Worker, April 30, 1963, 3, 7

19) "Bigger Role Urged For C.C.N.Y. Student," The New York Times, December 2, 1966

20) See: Libero Della Piana, "Communist Party head in historic debate at Univ of Georgia," People's World, February, 28, 2013, http://peoplesworld.org/communist-party-head-in-historic-debate-at-univ-of-georgia/ and *Phi Kappa Literary Society Debate*, Master Calendar: Happenings and Events at the University of Georgia, http://calendar.uga.edu/index.php/detail/the-debate-that-never-happened

21) NYU, TAM 137, Box 4, Folder 2: *Statement of Arnold Johnson, Vice-Chairman, New York State Communist Party, to hearing of Board of Education*, June 28, 1960; "School Board Urged to End Hysteria," The Worker, July 3, 1960, 12

22) NYU, TAM 188, Box 2, Folder 26A: Letter to Pittman from Mays, January 2, 1947

23) "Professors' Association Hits Job Witchhunts," The Daily Worker, March 22, 1956, 2

24) "350 Professors Urge End Of UnAmericans," The Worker, Sunday, March 26, 1961, 2

25) "Gets Award for Letting Gus Hall Speak," The Worker, May 1, 1962, 1

26) "Bigger Role Urged For C.C.N.Y. Students," The New York Times, December 2, 1966, "Swarthmore Campus Poll Hits McCarran Act," The Worker, May 22, 1962, 1 and Andrea London, "Jersey College Poll Opposes Ban on Gus Hall," The Worker, April 2, 1963, 3

27) "College Head Gets Liberties Award," The Worker, December 9, 1962, 2

28) See: Horne, Kelley, Solomon, Naison, Gellman, Davies, Johanningsmeier, Lewis, Gilmore, Howard, Ottanelli, et al

29) Arnold Johnson, "The Bill of Rights and the Twelve," Political Affairs, July 1949, 11

30) Foster, *History of the Communist Party...*, Ibid, 509 and Martelle, *The Fear Within...*, Ibid, XI

31) Time Magazine, October 24, 1949 (Vol. LIV, No. 17) and NYU, TAM 132, Box 112, Folder 80: *Medina Fans Now 50,000*, newspaper clipping, November 8, 1949

32) Johnson, *The Bill of Rights...*, Ibid, p 10, 11, 17

33) Maurice Isserman, *Which Side Were You On? : The American Communist Party During the Second World War* (Wesleyan University Press, 1982), 244. Though communists bore the brunt of the repression, between 1947 and 1956 "more than five million federal workers underwent loyalty screening, and about 25,000 were subject to the stigmatizing 'full field investigation' by the FBI." About 2,700 were dismissed, and 12,000 resigned: See: Landon R.Y. Storrs, *The Second Red Scare and the Unmaking of the New Deal Left* (Princeton University Press, 2013), 2

34) Johnson, *The Bill of Rights...*, Ibid, p 10, 11, 17

35) Joseph North, *Verdict Against Freedom: Your Stake in the Communist Trial* (New Century Publishers, November 1949), 3

36) Johnson, *The Bill of Rights...*, Ibid, p 10, 11, 17

37) See: Gus Hall, "Paul Robeson: An American Communist," Communist Party, USA (text of a centennial tribute speech delivered on May 31, 1998, at the Winston Unity Auditorium, CP national office, 235 W. 23rd St., New York, NY), 3, 6, 8. Later reprinted as Gus Hall, "Paul Robeson: Artist, Freedom Fighter, Hero, American Communist," Political Affairs, July, 1998. Hall writes: "My own most precious moments with Paul were when I met with him to accept his dues and renew his yearly membership in the CPUSA. I and other Communist leaders, like Henry Winston...met with Paul to brief him on politics and Party policies and to discuss his work and struggles." See, also: Vijay Prashad, "Comrade Robeson: A Centennial Tribute to an American Communist," Social Scientist, Vol. 25, No. 7/8 (Jul.-Aug. 1997), 40, 41. Prashad, however, quotes from the above. Gerald Horne wondered if Robeson had been a member of the Communist Party of Great Britain, which was "more of a likelihood than U.S. membership." See: Gerald Horne, *Paul Robeson: The Artist as*

Revolutionary (Pluto Press, 2016), 6. Martin Duberman notes that Robeson offered to publicly join the CPUSA in 1951 out of solidarity with his beleaguered comrades, but that the proposal was rejected by the Party's leadership. See: Martin Duberman, *Paul Robeson: A Biography* (The New Press, 1989), 420. While Robeson's membership in the CPUSA is contested, it is apparent he did not hesitate to align himself with the CPUSA, its leadership and its policies.

38) Paul Robeson, *For Freedom and Peace,* Council On African Affairs, 1949, 13, 14

39) "Robeson to Speak in Philadelphia," Daily Worker, October 6, 1949, 6

40) Alphaeus Hunton and Louis Burnham, "*'Fight for 12 Is Fight for Negroes,'*" Daily Worker, August 9, 1949, p 5

41) See: Horne, *Communist Front...,* Ibid; Re Johnson and the CRC, see: William L. Patterson, ed., *We Charge Genocide* (Civil Rights Congress, 1951), "The Petitioners"

42) Horne, *Black Revolutionary...,* Ibid, 125, 131

43) See: Mary L. Dudziak, *Cold War Civil Rights: Race and the Image of American Democracy* (Princeton University Press, 2000), 24

44) C.J. Atkins, *People's World* opinion editor and friend of Lorch's, author interview. "He was a member of the CP of Canada here and confirmed to me that he was indeed in the CPUSA before he left the U.S." See also: David Margolick, "Lee Lorch, Desegregation Activist Who Led Stuyvesant Town Effort, Dies at 98," The New York Times, March 1, 2014, https://www.nytimes.com/2014/03/02/nyregion/lee-lorch-desegregation-activist-who-led-stuyvesant-town-effort-dies-at-98.html

45) Claude Lightfoot, "Black Liberation Impossible Without Communists," Political Affairs, September-October 1969, 126

46) Horne, *Black Liberation/Red Scare...,* Ibid, 13, 14

47) Foster, *History of the Communist Party...,* Ibid, 518-521

48) "6 Camps For Reds Set Up, Then Closed," The New York Times, May 5, 1962 and C.P. Trussell, "Truman Won't Sign Subversive Curb; Red Roundup Ready," The New York Times, September 8, 1950

49) NYU, TAM 137, Box 2, Folder 3: "Vets Break Up Communist Rally," Associated Press, April 12, 1948, "Slug Speakers, Burn Books in Rochester," Daily Worker, April 13, 1948 and "Rochester Notables Score Mob Attack on CP Meet," publication unknown, April 16, 1948

50) Johnson, *The Bill of Rights...,* Ibid, 17

51) Foster, *History of the Communist Party...,* Ibid, 562

52) *13 Communists Speak...,* Ibid, 21, 25

53) See: "Judge Revokes Bail of 14 Reds: Must Get New Money Or Go to Jail," The Pittsburgh Press, July 16, 1951, 2, http://news.google.com/newspapers?nid=1144&dat=19510716&id=ADAbAAAAIBAJ&sjid=d00EAAAAIBAJ&pg=6156,19448

54) NYU, TAM 137, Box 2 Folder 8: *Arnold Johnson, Statement before Sentence, February 2, 1953* and *13 Communists Speak...*, Ibid, 62, 66, 67

55) Edward Ranzal, "Convicted Communists Snub Offer To Go to Russia Instead of Prison," The New York Times, February 3, 1953

56) "Judge Revokes...," Ibid, Russell Porter, "$875,000 Bail Asked For Indicted Reds," The New York Times, July 11, 1951 and Russell Porter, "Bail of 14 Reds Voided Again; New Bonds Required Today," The New York Times, July 17, 1951

57) "'Loyalty Test' for Bail," Daily Worker, July 12, 1951, 1

58) "Two Communists Freed In Bail Here," New York Times, August 17, 1951

59) "Judge Revokes...," Ibid, Porter, "$875,000 Bail Asked...," Ibid, and Porter, "Bail of 14 Reds...," Ibid

60) Harry Raymond, "Jail 15 Again As Court Bars CRC Bail Fund," Daily Worker, July 12, 1951, 1, 6

61) "China Unions Hit Jailing Hunton, Hammett, Field," Daily Worker, New York, July 25, 1951, 2

62) "Fur Locals Hit Jailing of Bail Fund Trustees," Daily Worker, New York, July 30, 1951, 2

63) "Urge Probe Of Saypol's Aid To Rackets: CRC Also Asks Inquiry into Persecution of Civil Rights Group," Daily Worker, August 6, 1951, 1

64) NYU, TAM 137, Box 2 Folder 6: Letters from Johnson to his wife, May 6, 1951, May 20, 1951, June 18, 1951 and June 21, 1951

65) Howard Eugene Johnson, Wendy Johnson, Mark D. Naison, ed., *A Dancer in the Revolution: Stretch Johnson, Harlem Communist at the Cotton Club* (Fordham University Press, 2014), 112

66) Johnson, "The Ohio Membership Campaign...," Ibid

67) NYU, TAM 137, Box 2, Folder 6: *Speech January 4, 1952*

68) NYU, TAM 137, Box 2, Folder 6: *Guest Colum By Arnold Johnson,* no date, no page

69) NYU, TAM 137, Box 2, Folder 10: Letter to Johnson from Hamilton, July 19, 1951

70) NYU, TAM 137, Box 2, Folder 10: Letter to Mrs. Johnson from Ripley Forbes, August 2, 1951

71) NYU, TAM 137, Box 2, Folder 10: Letter to Johnson from James K. More, August 3, 1951

72) NYU, TAM 137, Box 2, Folder 10: Letter to Johnson from Lee H. Ball, August 16, 1951

73) Re Rev. Frenyear, see: NYU, TAM 137, Box 2, Folder 10: "Church Upholds Woman Pastor," Religious News Service, October 9, 1951

74) NYU, TAM 137, Box 2, Folder 10: Letter to Johnson from Frank Heelen, April 4, 1964 and April 24, 1964

75) Bart, ed., *Highlights Of A Fighting History...*, Ibid, 267

76) Richard Fried, *Nightmare In Red: The McCarthy Era In Perspective* (Oxford University Press, 1990), 138

77) Edward Ranzal, "Anti-Red Witness Confesses He Lied," The New York Times, February 1, 1955

78) Simon Gerson, "Is America Returning To The Bill Of Rights," The Daily Worker, March 14, 1956, 4

79) NYU, TAM 137, Box 4, Folder 2: Arnold Johnson, "Halt The Tests! For A Summit Meeting For Peace!," Party Voice, No. 2, (November 2) 1958

80) "U.S. Communists Mark 39th Year," The New York Times, September 27, 1958

81) Arnold Johnson, "The 1958 Elections," Political Affairs, December 1958, 1, 8, 9

82) Holsaert, Noonan, Richardson, Robinson, Young and Zellner, ed., *Hands On The Freedom Plow: Personal Accounts By Women In SNCC* (University of Illinois Press, 2012), 55-61

83) NYU, TAM 132, Box 110, Folder 13: 10,000 March On North Carolina – "Unity is Our Weapon," NAARPR, 1974

84) *Testimony Of Arnold Johnson, Legislative Director Of The Communist Party, U.S.A.*, Hearing Before The Committee On un-American Activities House Of Representatives Eighty-Sixth Congress First Session, September 22, 1959 (U.S. Government Printing Office, Washington, 1959), 1108, 1109

85) *Guide to the Arnold Johnson Papers...*, Ibid

86) "Twin Communist Election Drive in Washington Heights," The Worker, August 14, 1960, 12, "Hit Bias in N.Y. Voter Registration," The Worker, August 28, 1960, p 12 and "Communists See Kennedy Victory," The New York Times, August 28, 1960

87) NYU, TAM 137, Box 3, Folder 3: Arnold Johnson, "The High Court and the McCarran Act," The Worker, March 19, 1961

88) Arnold Johnson, "CP Brief in High Court Defends Liberty," The Worker, Sunday, March 26, 1961, 3

89) Arnold Johnson, "HUAC Moves to Push McCarran Tyranny; Deadline Nov. 19," The Worker, November 19, 1961, 1

90) "Hamilton College Hears Communist," The Worker, April 24, 1962, 3

91) NYU, Tam 137, Box 3, Folder 3: Walter E. Orthwein, "On Washington U. Campus: Communism Debate Draws Yawns, Boos," St. Louis Globe Democrat, no date and "Hear Arnold Johnson In Collage in Midwest," The Worker, May 27, 1962, 2

92) NYU, TAM 137, Box 3, Folder 3: "Communist and Alton Lawyer In Debate on McCarran Law," St. Louis Post-Dispatch (no date)

93) "U.S. Acts To Label 10 As Communists," The New York Times, June 1, 1962

94) Art Shields, "Fight for Free Press Pledged at 'Worker' Rally," The Worker, March 11, 1962, 12

95) NYU, TAM 132, Box 109, Folder 53: James E. Jackson, *The First Amendment or The Last Liberty*, The Worker (tri-fold brochure), no date (circa 1961)

96) Arnold Johnson, "Editor Jackson Ordered Imprisoned, Wins Stay," The Worker, March 13, 1962, 1

97) "31 College Editors Hit McCarran Act, Urge JFK End Harassment of Press," The Sunday Worker, May 27, 1962, 2

98) Fred Gilman, "Jackson Lectures in College On Negroes' Freedom Struggle," The Worker, Sunday, June 9, 1963, 6, 8

99) "1,800 at Carnegie Rally Hail 39th Worker Birthday," The Worker, March 17, 1963, 3

100) NYU, TAM 137, Box 3, Folder 3: "Upsala College Hears Davis on McCarran Peril," Worker, April 15, 1962

101) Art Shields, "Tide Turning, Hall Tells Anti-McCarran Rally," The Worker, June 17, 1962, 1, 14

102) Peter Kihss, "Hall Says Party Will Stay In Open," The New York Times, December 6, 1961

103) "Gus Hall at Hunter," The New York Times, May 3, 1962

104) NYU, TAM 347, Box 21, Folder 66: Statement by Gus Hall, untitled, March 6, circa 1961-2

105) NYU, TAM 132, Box 150, Folder 13: *Press Release: Hall-Davis Defense Committee Alerts Americans To Current Attack Under McCarran Act* (Hall-Davis Defense Committee, September 4, 1962)

106) Oakley C. Johnson, "Struggle Is the Secret of Arnold Johnson's Optimism," The Worker, October 2, 1962, 4

107) "F.B.I. Infiltration Belittled By Hall," The New York Times, October 20, 1962. One former FBI agent, Jack Levine, bragged that from September 1960 to August 1961 that the Bureau "had 1,500 paid informants in Communist ranks."

108) "2 Newsmen Testify In Communist Case," The New York Times, October 5, 1962 and "FBI Pressures Newsmen To Act as Informers," The Worker, October 9, 1962, 1

109) NYU, TAM 137, Box, Folder 2: *Statement Of Arnold Johnson In Opposition to S.1194 and S.1196*

110) "Canada Officials Insist on Ban of Gus Hall and Arnold Johnson," The Worker, July 2, 1962, 3

111) Mary Helen Washington, *The Other Blacklist: The African American Literary and Cultural Left of the 1950s* (Columbia University Press, 2014), 137

112) Judy Kaplan and Linn Shapiro, ed., *Red Diapers: Growing Up In The Communist Left* (University of Illinois Press, 1998), 249, Amy Swerdlow, *Women Strike For Peace: Traditional Motherhood and Radical Politics in the* 1960s (University of Chicago Press, 1993) and Kathryn Cullen-Dupont, *Encyclopedia Of Women's History In America, Second edition* (Da Capo Press, 1998)

113) Guenter Lewy, *The Cause That Failed: Communism In American Political Life* (Oxford University Press, 1990), 185, 187

114) Roberta Wood's comment on manuscript; in author's possession

115) Re Wolins, see: Paul Kengor, *The Communist* (Threshold Editions/Mercury Ink – A division of Simon & Schuster, 2012), 114, Andrew L. Wang, "LeRoy Wolins, 1929-2005," Chicago Tribune, December 22, 2005, http://articles.chicagotribune.com/2005-12-22/news/z0512220100_1_cold-war-korean-war-vietnam-war and William J. Jorden, "Youth Is Accused Of Aiding Soviet," The New York Times, February 4, 1960

116) Esther Shield, "We Who Give Life Should Defend It, 'Says World Congress of Women," The Worker, July 2, 1963, 1

117) Lewy, *The Cause That Failed...*, Ibid, 185, 187

118) "Senate Witchhunters' Target Is – Peace, Says Arnold Johnson," The Worker, September 4, 1960, 3

119) "National Committee Formed To End House UnAmericans," The Worker, September 4, 1960, 3

120) Arnold Johnson, "Victims of the UnAmericans," The Worker, April 16, 1961, 10

121) NYU, TAM 137, Box 4, Folder 5: Arnold Johnson, *May Day Speech at Union Square*, May 1, 1964,

122) *National Coordinating Committee to End the War in Vietnam Records*, Appendix II: NCC Steering Committee Members (University of Wisconsin Digital Collections),

http://digicoll.library.wisc.edu/cgi/f/findaid/findaid-idx?c=wiarchives;cc=wiarchives;view=text;rgn=main;didno=uw-whs-mss00278) and Lewy, *The Cause That Failed...*, Ibid, 266

123) NYU, TAM 132, Box 133, Folder 13: Arnold Johnson, *On the November Peace Demonstrations*, no date

124) NYU, TAM 132, Box 110, Folder 38: *The Peace Movement – 11/11/65,* Memorandum

125) Niebyl-Proctor Marxist Library: National Executive of the W.E.B. DuBois Clubs of America, *Report On The Convention Of The National Coordinating Committee To End The War In Vietnam* (in Washington, D.C. from Nov. 25-28, 1965)

126) Wheeler, author interview 10/2/2017

127) NYU, TAM 137, Box 4, Folder 6: *Documents From Cleve.*, Mobilizer (bulletin of the Spring Mobilization Committee to End the War in Vietnam), Vol. 1, No. 1 (December 19), 1966, New York

128) NYU, TAM 137, Box 3, Folder 14: Letter to Mr. Leslie Paffrath from Johnson, February 18-20, 1965

129) NYU, TAM 137, Box 3, Folder 14: Memo from Johnson, February 23, 1965

130) NYU, TAM 137, Box 3, Folder 14: Gus Hall, Hyman Lumer, Arnold Johnson, "The Substantive Dialogue," Continuum, Vol. 3, No. 3, Autumn 1965, 345-353

131) "New England Hears Marxists," The Worker, April 23, 1963, 3

132) "Benjamin Davis' Negro Unity Plan Greeted at Forums in Los Angeles," The Worker, Sunday, March 10, 1963, 2

133) Arnold Johnson, "Guest Column: Election showed no swing to right," Daily World, November 21, 1968, 6

134) NYU, TAM 132, Box 110, Folder 38: *What Next in the Peace Fight????: A Statement by the Communist Party* (Communist Party, USA, 1968)

135) NYU, TAM 132, Box 110, Folder 38: Memo by the CPUSA Peace Commission (likely written by Johnson), *The Demonstration On November 15th And The Job Ahead*, circa 1969

136) "Meet the Communists," Daily World, November 12, 1969, 8 and "Communist Party figures march in united parade," Daily World, November 18, 1969, 9

137) Roberta Wood's comment on the manuscript; in author's possession

138) NYU, TAM 132, Box 110, Folder 38: *The Demonstration On November 15th...*, Ibid

139) Arnold Johnson, "Peace Can Be Won," World Magazine, March 14, 1970, M-5, M-8

140) "Youth leads at 'World' fete," Daily World, April 14, 1970, 9

141) Arnold Johnson, "The confrontation ahead and ideas on meeting it," Daily World, April 16, 1970, 6

142) Walter Goodman, "The New Mobe (I): Who's Who? What's What?," The New York Times, November 30, 1969

143) "U.S. Communist Party Aide Is Indicted in Contempt," The New York Times, November 11, 1970

144) NYU, TAM 137, Box 3, Folder 21: Arnold Johnson, Memo to All of the Steering Committee of New Mobilization with Statement, June 15, 1970

145) NYU, TAM 137, Box 3, Folder 21: A Legal Memo on HISC Has No Authority to Investigate MOBE, June 26, 1970

146) Amadeo Richardson, "Honor Arnold Johnson, freedom fighter," Daily World, May 4, 1974, 2

147) NYU, TAM 137, Box 3, Folder 21: letter from Norma Spector, "To Protest The Contempt Citation Of Arnold Johnson," no date

148) NYU, TAM 137, Box 3, Folder 21: Letter to Attorney General John Mitchell, September 23, 1970

149) NYU, TAM 137, Box 3, Folder 21: *Press Release: Statement By National Committee, Communist Party, U.S.A. On The Indictment Of Arnold Johnson...*, November 11, 1970

150) NYU, TAM 132, Box 113, Folder 44: *Monsignor Charles Owen Rice Tells Why...Nixon's Plan To Silence Arnold Johnson – Communist... Is Nixon's Plan To Silence You* (no publisher, tri-fold brochure, no date)

151) Abt, *Advocate and Activist...*, Ibid, 267-270

152) NYU, TAM 132, Box 113, Folder 44: *Monsignor Charles Owen Rice...*, Ibid

153) "Communist Slate Is State's First Since '46," The New York Times, October 25, 1970

154) "Suit Here Calls for Destruction Of Secret Passport Office File," The New York Times, February 25, 1971

155) James William Coleman, *The Criminal Elite: Understanding White-Collar* Crime, Sixth Edition (Worth Publishers, 2006), 69

156) Penny Lewis, *Hardhats, Hippies, And Hawks: The Vietnam Antiwar Movement as Myth and Memory* (Cornell University Press, 2013), 134

157) John Gilman, *Footsoldier for Peace and Justice: The Story of John Gilman* (iUniverse Inc., 2009), 153

158) *Vote for a Fighter against War and Racism: Jarvis Tyner Communist Candidate for Vice President* (Hall-Tyner Election Campaign Committee, four page leaflet, 1972)

159) NYU, TAM 137, Box 3, Folder 21: Arnold Johnson, *For A Majority Peace Movement*

160) Michael Zagarell, "World Student Strike Against Vietnam War and Racism," Political Affairs, March 1968, 20

161) Bettina Aptheker, *Big Business And The American University* (New Outlook Publishers, 1966), 2, Bart, ed., *Highlights Of A Fighting History...*, Ibid, 324-328, Bettina Aptheker, *Intimate Politics: How I Grew Up Red, Fought for Free Speech, and Became A Feminist Rebel* (Seal Press, 2011) and Aptheker, author interview, 1/29/2018

162) NYU, TAM 132, Box 108, Folder 20: *International Student – Faculty STRIKE, April 26 To: Bring The Troops Home From Vietnam Now, End Racial Oppression, Stop The Draft* (The Student Mobilization Committee, tri-fold brochure)

163) Wilber W. Caldwell, *1968: Dreams of Revolution* (Algora Publishing, New York, 2009), 124

164) Bart, ed., *Highlights Of A Fighting History...*, Ibid, 487

165) Robert Greenblatt, *National Mobilization Committee to End the War in Vietnam, Fact Sheet on the New McCarran Act* (5 page letter), Mennonite Church USA Archives, Goshen IN; I-3-5.16 Box 75 Folder 1, http://palni.contentdm.oclc.org/cdm/ref/collection/gopplow/id/631 ; Re Vizard, see: Doug Rossinow, *The Politics of Authenticity: Liberalism, Christianity, and the New Left in America* (Columbia University Press, 1998), 176; Re bombing DBC, see: Seth Rosenfeld, *Subversives: The FBI's War on Student Radicals, and Reagan's Rise to Power* (Farrar, Straus and Ciroux, 2012), 318-319

166) Douglas Robinson, "Du Bois 'Duplicity' Decried By Nixon," The New York Times, March 9, 1966, https://archive.nytimes.com/www.nytimes.com/books/00/11/05/specials/dubois-nixon.html

167) Jim Sayre, "The Commie-Chasers Get W.E.B. DuBois And Boys," The Stanford Daily, March 30, 1966, 6

168) Peter Kihss, "Subversives Unit Seeks Proof Red Front Is Red," The New York Times, February 8, 1972

169) Tim Wheeler, "DuBois Clubs reunion: Memories, battles yet to be fought and won!," People's World, June 18, 2013,

http://peoplesworld.org/dubois-clubs-reunion-memories-battles-yet-to-be-fought-and-won/

170) Greenblatt, *National Mobilization Committee to End the War in Vietnam, Fact Sheet...*, Ibid, 1

171) M.S. Handler, "Marxists Join Antiwar Drive but Deny Inspiring It," The New York Times, October 23, 1965

172) John F. Levin and Earl Silbar, ed., *You Say You Want a Revolution: SDS, PL, and Adventures in Building a Worker-Student Alliance* (1741 Press, 2019), 40

173) Niebyl-Proctor Marxist Library: W.E.B. DuBois Clubs, recruitment brochure, no date (circa summer 1966), Greenblatt, *National Mobilization Committee to End the War in Vietnam, Fact Sheet...*, Ibid, 1 and "Bomb Thrown in Window Damages Communist Offices," The New York Times, May 3, 1966

174) "The Tet Offensive and the Media: United States Military Morale: Vietnam War," ABC-CLIO – history and the Headlines, http://www.historyandtheheadlines.abc-clio.com/ContentPages/ContentPage.aspx?entryId=1199250¤tSection=1194544

175) Re Johnson and Mora's membership in CPUSA (two of the Fort Hood Three): Elena Mora, long-time Party leader and niece of Dennis Mora, author interview, while in Chicago at a CPUSA National Board meeting, May 29-31, 2015 ; Marc Brodine, author interview, while in Chicago at a CPUSA Marxist Strategy and Tactics conference, February, 18, 2017: Brodine attended Party School with Johnson. Tim Wheeler, a fellow *Daily World* reporter who worked with Johnson in the NY office, author interview, October 2, 2017. See *The Fort Hood Three: The Case Of The Three G.I.'s Who Said "No" To The War In Vietnam* (Fort Hood Three Defense Committee, 1966). For obvious reasons (anticommunism) Mora and Johnson publicly denied membership in the CPUSA. See also: Martin Arnold, "3 Soldiers hold News Conference to Announce They Won't Go to Vietnam," The New York Times, July 1, 1966

176) Norman Markowitz, "Old Struggles in a 'New Age': The CPUSA and the 1960s," Political Affairs, April 2010,

http://politicalaffairs.net/old-struggles-in-a-new-age-the-cpusa-and-the-1960s/

177) Tim Wheeler, "DuBois Clubs Convention Cheers Soldiers 'Hell No, I Won't Go,'" The Worker, September 12, 1967

178) "Communist Slate Is State's First Since '46," The New York Times, Sunday, October 25, 1970

179) "Anti-war vets feted on Veteran's Day," Daily World, November 13, 1968, 10

180) Paul Friedman, "Draft Resistance Movement," Political Affairs, April 1968, 59

181) NYU, TAM 132, Box 108, Folder 20: Vietnam Summer, letter dated May 8, 1967 (3 pages)

182) Herbert Aptheker, *Mission To Hanoi* (International Publishers, 1966) and Gary Murrell, *"The Most Dangerous Communist in the United States": A Biography Of Herbert Aptheker* (University of Massachusetts Press, 2015)

183) Wheeler, author interview, 10/2/2017

184) NYU, TAM 347, Box 13, Folder 50: *Statement: On the Events in Vietnam by the Communist and Workers' Parties, Participating in the Consultative Meeting,* (James E. Jackson attended in Moscow, March 1-5, 1965), document dated March 3, 1965

185) NYU, TAM 132, Box 110, Folder 38: Gus Hall, Jarvis Tyner, Rasheed Story and Joseph North, *We Saw Hanoi Bombed! An Appeal To People Of U.S. By Eyewitnesses To Slaughter & Destruction By Nixon's Planes* (Hall-Tyner Election Campaign Committee, 1972)

186) Bart, ed., *Highlights Of A Fighting History...*, Ibid, 375, 376

187) Daniel Rubin, *For A Party Of Mass Action: New conditions, new tasks of the Party in the '70s* (New Outlook Publishers, April 1972), 2, 3, 12, 18, 19

188) NYU, TAM 137, Box 4, Folder 7: Hand-written note by Johnson: "Thirty years ago..." and "Winston In Moscow En Route To Vietnam," Daily World, August 30, 1975, 2

189) NYU, TAM 137, Box 4, Folder 7: Hand-written note by Johnson: For an American-Vietnamese Friendship Society

190) Joseph North, "Winston describes joy of Hanoi's celebration," Daily World, September 10, 1975, 2, 10

191) Ronald Tyson, "The First Congress of the Communist Party of Cuba: Firm foundation for socialism," World Magazine, January 24, 1976, M-2, M-3

192) "YWLL pledges more support for Angolans," Daily World, February 18, 1976, 2, "World meet opens to support Angola," Daily World, February 3, 1976, 4, Tom Foley, "MPLA able to defend gains, says Monteiro," Daily World, March 16, 1976, 3 and "Chicago to hear Monteiro Sunday," Daily World, March 16, 1976, 3

193) Tom Foley, "400 at DW forum hear Cuba CP meet report," Daily World, February 3, 1976, 2

194) *Guide to the Arnold Johnson Papers...*, Ibid and Joan Cook, "Arnold Johnson Is Dead at 84," The New York Times, September 28, 1989

195) Arnold Johnson, "How To Reach Millions," Party Affairs, Vol. 11, No. 1 (February 1977), 37

196) Arnold Johnson, “End the McCarran Era!,” Political Affairs, April 1967, 17, 23

197) Flynn, *Horizons Of The Future...*, Ibid, 37

198) Johnson, “End the McCarran Era!,” Ibid, 17, 23

199) Abt, *Advocate and Activist...*, Ibid, 281

200) S. K. Davis, “Twin Cities Hear John Abt Tell of McCarran Menace,” The Worker, Sunday, February 4, 1962, 2

201) Horne, *Communist Front...*, Ibid, 124

202) NYU, TAM 132, Box 113, Folder 44: “Old Reds Enjoy Last Laugh At Generation of Persecution,” Washington Post, September 24, 1973

Chapter Two

1) Mark Bowden, *Hue 1968: A Turning Point of the American War in Vietnam* (Atlantic Monthly Press, 2017)

2) James E, Jackson, *Revolutionary Tracings in World Politics and Black Liberation* (International Publishers, 1974), 17

3) “1968: A Year Of Upsets And ‘Impossible’ Victories,” Freedomways, Summer, 1968, Vol. 8, No.3, 205

4) Lynn Langway, “From hustings to hustings,” World Magazine, October 5-6, 1968, M-8

5) Nora North, “Fisk students put searching queries to Mrs. Mitchell,” Daily World, October 29, 1968, 10

6) *Charlene Mitchell on 1968 Presidential Election Laws* (KTVU, 7/16/1968, San Francisco Bay Area Television Archive), https://diva.sfsu.edu/collections/sfbatv/bundles/220770) and Bruce A. Glasrud and Cary D. Wintz, ed., *African Americans and the Presidency: The Road to the White House* (Routledge, 2010), 2, 39

7) NYU, TAM 132, Box 123, Folder 13: Charlene Mitchell, *Communist Candidate Speaks On Black Liberation* (CPUSA tri-fold brochure, 1968)

8) See: Mark Naison, *Communists in Harlem during the Depression* (University of Illinois Press, 2005), Erik S. Gellman, *Death Blow To Jim Crow: The National Negro Congress and the Rise of Militant Civil Rights* (University of North Carolina Press, 2012), Mark Solomon, *The Cry Was Unity: Communists and African Americans, 1917-1936* (University Press of Mississippi, 1998), Robin D. G. Kelley, *Hammer And Hoe: Alabama Communists During The Great Depression* (University of North Carolina Press, 1990), among other examples

9) Re Johnson and Mora’s membership in CPUSA (two of the Fort Hood Three): Elena Mora, long-time Party leader and niece of Dennis Mora, author interview, while in Chicago at a CPUSA National Board meeting, May 29-31, 2015 ; Marc Brodine, author interview, while in Chicago at a CPUSA Marxist Strategy and Tactics conference,

February, 18, 2017: Brodine attended Party School with Johnson. Tim Wheeler, a fellow *Daily World* reporter who worked with Johnson in the NY office, author interview, October 2, 2017. See *The Fort Hood Three: The Case Of The Three G.I.'s Who Said "No" To The War In Vietnam* (Fort Hood Three Defense Committee, 1966). For obvious reasons (anticommunism) Mora and Johnson publicly denied membership in the CPUSA. See also: Martin Arnold, "3 Soldiers hold News Conference to Announce They Won't Go to Vietnam," The New York Times, July 1, 1966

10) Norman Markowitz, "Old Struggles in a 'New Age': The CPUSA and the 1960s," Political Affairs, April, 2010, http://politicalaffairs.net/old-struggles-in-a-new-age-the-cpusa-and-the-1960s/

11) Michael Zagarell, "World Student Strike Against Vietnam War and Racism," Political Affairs, March 1968, 20. Re Aptheker's leadership in the Du Bois Clubs, the FSM and Student Mobe, see: Bettina Aptheker, *Big Business And The American University* (New Outlook Publishers, 1966), 2, Bart, ed., *Highlights Of A Fighting History...*, Ibid, 324-328, Bettina Aptheker, *Intimate Politics...*, Ibid and Aptheker, author interview, 1/29/2018

12) Paul Friedman, "Draft Resistance Movement," Political Affairs, April 1968, 59-61 and Will Lissner, "U.S. Reds Score New Left's Ideas," The New York Times, July 5, 1968

13) Mike Davidow, "CP candidates bring new life to campus," Daily World, October 15, 1968, 3

14) "Twin Cities TV, press get Charlene's message," Daily World, October 18, 1968, 9

15) "Anti-war vets feted on Veterans Day," Daily World, November 13, 1968, 10

16) John Abt, "The Revised McCarran Act," Political Affairs, March 1968, 10-19

17) Nicholas Gagarin, "Charlene Mitchell: Silhouette," The Harvard Crimson, November 5, 1968, http://www.thecrimson.com/article/1968/11/5/charlene-mitchell-pbtbhe-frederick-douglas-book/

18) James Perloff, "Communist Party Candidate Raps 'Capitalist University,'" The Stanford Daily, Wednesday, October 30, 1968, 4

19) Robert S. Browne, "The Challenge Of Black Student Organizations," Freedomways, Fall, 1968, Vol. 8, No. 4, 325

20) Re Esther-Cooper, see: Haviland, *James and Esther Cooper Jackson...*, Ibid; Re Hunton, see: *William Alphaeus Hunton papers, 1926-1967*, The New York Public Library: Archives & Manuscripts, http://archives.nypl.org/scm/20646; Re Strong, see: Horne, *Black Liberation/Red Scare...*, Ibid, 271; Re Jones, see: Davie, *Left Of Karl Marx...*, Ibid; Re Wilkerson, see: *Doxey A. Wilkerson papers, 1927-1993 [bulk 1950's-1980's]*, The New York Public Library: Archives & Manuscripts, http://archives.nypl.org/scm/20928. Wilkerson left

the party in 1957. Re Graham Du Bois, see: Gerald Horne, *Race Woman: The Lives Of Shirley Graham Du Bois* (New York University Press, 2000)

21) Horne, *Race Woman...*, Ibid, 217-220

22) Olivia Vassell and Todd Steven Burroughs, "No Common Ground Left: Freedomways, Black Communists vs. Black Nationalism/Pan-Africanism," Afrocology: The Journal of Pan African Studies, Vol. 8, No. 10, March 2016, 22

23) Cliff Kincaid, "Soviet Funded Black 'Freedom' Journal," Accuracy in Media, https://www.aim.org/aim-column/soviets-funded-black-freedom-journal/

24) Brian Dolinar, *The Black Cultural Front: Black Writers and Artists of the Depression Generation* (University of Mississippi, 2014)

25) Gagarin, *Charlene Mitchell: Silhouette...*, Ibid and Mitchell, *Communist Candidate Speaks...*, Ibid

26) Mitchell, *Communist Candidate Speaks...*, Ibid and Arnold Johnson, "The Elections of 1968," Political Affairs, October 1968, 42

27) Langway, "From the hustings...," Ibid

28) Sam Kushner, "Charlene wowed 'em in LA with her cool," Daily World, October 3, 1968, 3

29) "CUNY students hear Charlene," Daily World, October 22, 1968, 9

30) "Texan youths hear Charlene Mitchell," Daily World, October 25, 1968, 5

31) North, "Fisk students put...," Ibid

32) "Mrs. Mitchell stumps NE colleges," Daily World, November 2, 1968, 10

33) Nicholas Gagarin, "Black Communist Leader Predicts Liberalism's End," The Harvard Crimson, November 1, 1968,
http://www.thecrimson.com/article/1968/11/1/black-communist-leader-predicts-liberalisms-end/

34) "Charlene Mitchell to top record tour with Daily World fete Nov. 3," Daily World, October 29, 1968, 10

35) "Black Americans on long road to political equality," Reuters, Monday, June 30, 2008, http://www.reuters.com/article/us-usa-politics-history-idUSN1735279520080630), Glasrud and Wintz, ed., *African Americans and the Presidency...*, Ibid, 39 and "Final 1968 Presidential Returns Show 499,704-Vote Nixon Lead," The New York Times, December 12, 1968

36) Richard Loring, "A Communist Candidacy in Los Angeles," Political Affairs, September 1966, 10-18

37) Gus Hall, *Gus Hall Speaks: For a Meaningful Alternative* (New Outlook Publishers, 1967), 40-41, 53

38) NYU, TAM 132, Box 123, Folder 13: *WHY?* (Communist Party Campaign Committee, folded flier, no date)

39) Henry Winston, "The 1968 Elections," Political Affairs, August 1968, 3-4, 11-14

40) Kendra Alexander, "Communist Theory and Practice for Black Liberation," Political Affairs, August / September 1979, 18

41) Glasrud and Wintz, ed., *African Americans and the Presidency...*, Ibid, 39

42) Clara Colon, "Equality For Working Women," Political Affairs, November 1968, 32

43) See: Joseph North, James Jackson and George Meyers, *Gus Hall: The Man and The Message* (New Outlook Publishers, 1970), 31, Mike Davidow, "12,000 Listen to Gus Hall In Oregon Football Field," The Worker, Sunday, February 18, 1962, 3, 11, Rob Royer, "Gus Hall Rides a Golf Cart Into Eugene and the Demise of the Commonwealth Federation," The Cascadia Courier, April 9, 2012, http://www.thecascadiacourier.com/2012/04/gus-hall-invades-eugene-and-demise-of.html and Bart, ed., *Highlights Of A Fighting History...*, Ibid, 329. Re Aptheker, see: Murrell, *"Most Dangerous Communist...,"* Ibid

44) North, "Fisk students put...," Ibid

45) Winston, "The 1968 Elections," *Ibid* and Arnold Johnson, "The Crucial Elections Of 1968," Political Affairs, October 1968, 41, 42

46) NYU, TAM 132, Box 123, Folder 13: Charlene Mitchell, *We Come Forward: Text of acceptance speech...*(CPUSA poster, 1968)

47) Matthew Hallinan, "The Party Campaign: A New Dawn," Political Affairs, September 1968, 43 and Bruce Lambert, "Vincent Hallinan Is Dead at 95; An Innovative Lawyer With Flair," The New York Times, October 4, 1992

48) Aptheker, author interview, 1/29/2018

49) See: "Dr. Spock urges vote for Gregory," Daily World, October 29, 1968, 10, "Gregory speaks at school 271," Daily World, November 1, 1968, 3, Ken Bailey, "Dick Gregory stars in city windup," Daily World, November 5, 1968, 3, Mike Davidow, "Pollsters puzzled as race narrows, old lines crumble," Daily World, November 5, 1968, 3 and Mike Davidow, "Voters' independence vast but fragmented," Daily World, November 1, 1968, 3

50) Johnson, "The Crucial Elctions...," Ibid, 41, 42

51) NYU, TAM 132, Box 218, Folder 25: Michael Myerson, *On The Crisis In The Party* (June 1990)

52) Gus Hall, *Make This Election Count: the aims of Communists in '72* (New Outlook Publishers, 1972), 44

53) Betty Gannett, "Relation of Fight for Democracy to Socialism," Political Affairs, December 1968, 12

54) Editorial Comment, "The 1968 Presidential Elections," Political Affairs, January 1969, 7

55) McDuffie, *Sojourning For freedom...*, Ibid, 140, William Minter, Gail Hovey and Charles Cobb Jr., ed., *No Easy Victories: African*

Liberation and American Activists over Half Century, 1950-2000 (Africa World Press, Inc., 2007), 69-72, *Interviews for 'No Easy Victories': Charlene Mitchell*, http://www.noeasyvictories.org/interviews/int04_mitchell.php, Amber Cortes, *An Interview With Charlene Mitchell* (PRX.org, March 8, 2006), https://beta.prx.org/stories/10346 and "Angela Davis Tribute to Charlene Mitchell," video from a panel at the *Black Women and the Radical Tradition* conference held at the Graduate Center for Worker Education of Brooklyn College, March, 28, 2009, https://vimeo.com/10354190

56) See: Bart, ed., *Highlights Of A Fighting History...*, Ibid, 465, *Communist Youth in America*, Online Archive of California, http://www.oac.cdlib.org/view?docId=kt4w1003q8;NAAN=13030&doc.view=frames&chunk.id=d0e722&toc.id=d0e97&brand=oac4, William Strand, "Probers Assail American Youth For Democracy: Schools Asked to Fight Red Front Group," Chicago Daily Tribune, April 16, 1947, 18 and "Columbia Will let Communist Speak," The New York Times, December 16, 1947

57) Minter, Hovey and Cobb Jr., ed., *No Easy Victories...*, Ibid, 69-72, *Interviews for...*, Ibid and John Hart, "Unity + struggle + organization = victory," Daily World, May 29, 1980, 16

58) Horne, *Black Revolutionary...*, Ibid, 88

59) Minter, Hovey and Cobb Jr., ed., *No Easy Victories...*, Ibid, p 69-72 and *Interviews for...*, Ibid

60) Thomas W. Devine, *Henry Wallace's 1948 Presidential Campaign and the Future of Postwar Liberalism* (University of North Carolina Press, 2015) and Bart, ed., *Highlights Of A Fighting History...*, Ibid, 230

61) Minter, Hovey and Cobb Jr., ed., *No Easy Victories...*, Ibid, 69-72 and *Interviews for...*, Ibid

62) See: Paul Robeson, Jr., *The Undiscovered Paul Robeson: Quest for Freedom, 1939 – 1976* (John Wiley & Sons, Inc., 2010), 10, Horne, *Paul Robeson...*, Ibid, 103 and Von Eschen, *Race Against Empire...*, Ibid

63) Minter, Hovey and Cobb Jr., ed., *No Easy Victories...*, Ibid, p 69-72 and *Interviews for...*, Ibid

64) Alexander, "Communist Theory and Practice...," Ibid, 18 and Sanford J. Ungar, "Angela Davis Acquitted of All Charges," Washington Post, June 5, 1972

65) Charlene Mitchell, *For Freedom for Political Prisoners and Victims of Racism and Class Injustice*, Party Affairs, Vol. VII, No. 1, January 1973, 32-40

66) Horne, *Communist Front...*, Ibid, 102

67) Mitchell, *For Freedom for Political Prisoners...*, Ibid, 32-40

68) Horne, *Communist Front...*, Ibid, 99

69) Mitchell, *For Freedom for Political Prisoners...*, Ibid, 32-40

70) Joy James, *Transcending the Talented Tenth: Black Leaders and American Intellectuals* (Routledge, 1997), 179-180

71) NYU, TAM 132, Box 110, Folder 17: *A Call to a Founding Conference For A National Defense Organization Against Racist And Political Repression*, May 11-13, 1973

72) NYU, TAM 132, Box 110, Folder 13: *10,000 March On North Carolina* – "Unity is Our Weapon," National Alliance, 1974 and "Justice Assailed In North Carolina," The New York Times, July 5, 1974

73) Jose Perez, "Workshop denounces raids on foreignborn," Daily World, January 28, 1975, 3

74) John Franklin, "Parley maps citywide police crime hearing," Daily World, January 28, 1975, 3

75) NYU, Tam 132, Box 110, Folder 13: National Alliance Against Racist and Political Repression 2nd Annual Conference, May 10-12, 1975

76) *United States of America Congressional Record: Proceedings And Debates of the 93rd Congress Second Session* – Vol. 120 – Part 17, July 2, 1974 to July 15, 1974 (U.S. Government Printing Office, Washington, 1974), Congressional Record – House, July 11, 1974, 22,985

77) McDuffie, *Sojourning For Freedom...*, Ibid, 199-201

78) NYU, TAM PE.043, Box 70, Folder 2: Angela Davis, *JoAnne Little: The Dialectics of Rape* (NAARPR, no date), and Bettye Collier-Thomas and V.P. Franklin, ed., *Sisters in the Struggle: African American Women in the Civil Rights – Black power Movement* (New York University Press, 2001), 269, 274

79) NYU, TAM 132, Box 250, Folder 1: Charlene Mitchell, *Opening Report to Conference of Lawyers and Law Students,* January 1975

80) NYU, TAM 132, Box 110, Folder 13: "Wilmington 10 Day in D.C. Hits Federal Complicity in N. Carolina Repression," The Organizer: Newsletter Of The National Alliance Against Racist And Political Repression, Vol. 2, No. 3, 1975

81) Gene Tournour, "Charlene Mitchell points to new struggles," Daily World, November 6, 1975, 3

82) NYU, TAM 132, Box 110, Folder 13: National Alliance Against Racist and Political Repression: 3rd Annual Conference (conference program, November 14-16, 1976) and NYU, TAM 132, Box 110, Folder 13: *We Can Fight Back and Win: The Program of the National Alliance Against Racist & Political Repression* (NAARPR, 1978, folded brochure)

83) NYU, TAM 132, Box 110, Folder 13: Charlene Mitchell, "Tipping the scales – for justice," World Magazine, August 20, 1977

84) NYU, TAM 132, Box 110, Folder 13: The Organizer, NAARPR, Vol. 4, No.1, 1977

85) Claude Lightfoot, *Ghetto Rebellion To Black Liberation* (International Publishers, 1968), 184

86) Horne, *Paul Robeson...*, Ibid, 150

87) Charlene Mitchell, "A strategy to defeat the ultra-right," Daily World, May 10, 1980, 12-13

88) Charlene Mitchell, "Terrorism in the U.S.," Daily World, March 26, 1981, 12-13

89) NYU, TAM 132, Box 110, Folder 13: Proposal to the William L. Patterson Foundation for Southern Human Rights Writing Project (NAARPR, 4 pages, no date (circa 1982))

90) See: Kenneth Robert Janken, *The Wilmington Ten: Violence, Injustice, and the Rise of Black Politics in the 1970s* (University of North Carolina Press, 2016) and Antar Mberi, "Spying revealed on rights leader," Daily World, February 9, 1982, 2

91) "Winston slams police frameup," Daily World, March 20, 1982, 2

92) Romulo Fajardo, "Angela Davis slams frameup," Daily World, March 24, 1982, 2

93) NYU, TAM 132, Box 110, Folder 13: Proposal to the William L. Patterson Foundation for Southern Human Rights Writing Project, Ibid. For more on the founding of the William Patterson Foundation see: Victoria Missick, "'William Paterson Foundation' called for at birthday fete," Daily World, August 30, 1975, 2

94) NYU, TAM 132, Box 110, Folder 13: "Mitchell/Welch: Struggle For Justice," The Organizer, NAARPR, Vol. IX, No. 2 (May/June 1982)

95) See: Frank Edgar Chapman, Jr., *The Damned Don't Dry* (Lulu Press, 2019) and Rosalie Chan, "TCR Talks: Fighting the 'new Jim Crow,'" The Chicago Reporter, July 7, 2014, https://www.chicagoreporter.com/tcr-talks-fighting-new-jim-crow-0/

96) NYU, TAM 132, Box 110, Folder 13: National Alliance Against Racist and Political Repression – Report Back (NAARPR, 1983)

97) NYU, TAM 132, Box 110, Folder 13: Memo from Haywood Burns, Angela Davis and Pete Seeger, April 1984

98) "Amtrak settlement a 'victory,'" Daily World, June 14, 1984, 3-D

99) Charlene Mitchell and Michael Myerson, "The Death Penalty: A Class Weapon," Political Affairs, February 1977, 22, 24

100) Charlene Mitchell, "Afro-American Equality vs. Reaganite Racism," Political Affairs, June 1982, 15-17

101) "Editorials: Now, more than ever," Black Liberation Journal, Vol. 5, No. 2, Fall 1982, 3

102) Charlene Mitchell, "New Levels of Struggle – New Levels of Unity," Black Liberation Journal, Vol. 6, No. 1 (Fall 1983), 6, 11

103) Charlene Mitchell, "Black Voters: A Greater Force in '84," Political Affairs, July 1984, 29-31

104) "Wilson Only Incumbent To Lose Seat In Primaries," St. Louis Post-Dispatch, March 9, 1983. Re Jones' membership in the CPUSA:

he belonged to the St. Louis area party club and met regularly with the author

105) Charlene Mitchell, "The Triple-Layered Crisis And the Sharpened Edge of Racism," Political Affairs, August 1985, 21

106) Charlene Mitchell, "The Fight for Socialism Includes the Struggle for Democracy," Political Affairs, February 1991, 17

107) Mike Giocondo, "Spirited rally kicks off weekend," Daily World, May 22, 1990, 12 and Mike Giocondo, "Mapping a decade of struggle for human rights," Daily World, May 22, 1990, 12

108) Colin Freeman and Jane Flanagan, "Nelson Mandela 'proven' to be a member of the Communist Party after decades of denial," The Telegraph, December 8, 2012, https://www.telegraph.co.uk/news/worldnews/nelson-mandela/9731522/Nelson-Mandela-proven-to-be-a-member-of-the-Communist-Party-after-decades-of-denial.html

109) "Home from South Africa: Angela Davis, Charlene Mitchell plan national report-back tour," Daily World, September 21, 1991, 2

110) Charlene Mitchell, "'This country desperately needs socialism,'" Daily World, November 30, 1990, 21

111) Charlene Mitchell, "A Communist Examines the Past Decade," Political Affairs, December 1990, 25-28

112) Raymond Suttner, "Crisis in the CPUSA: Interview with Charlene Mitchell," The African Communist, No. 135, Fourth Quarter, 1993 (7/23/1993), https://www.nelsonmandela.org/omalley/index.php/site/q/03lv02424/04lv02730/05lv03005/06lv03006/0wlv03075/08lv03082.htm#

113) James, *Transcending the Talented Tenth...*, Ibid, 176. For an analysis of the 1991 split, see: Daniel Rosenberg, "From Crisis to Split: The Communist Party USA," American Communist History, https://www.tandfonline.com/doi/full/10.1080/14743892.2019.1599627

114) Madeleine Provinzano, "Liberation fighters hail award to Charlene Mitchell," Daily World, April 3, 1974, 10

115) Pat Fry, "National forum on police crimes calls for civilian police accountability councils," People's World, May 28, 2014, http://peoplesworld.org/national-forum-on-police-crimes-calls-for-civilian-police-accountability-councils/

Chapter Three

1) Mike Davidow, "Gus Hall Speaks to Overflow Crowd At University of Virginia," The Worker, Sunday, February 12, 1963, 8, 11

2) In the early 1960s, Young Communists Mike Stein and Alva Buxenbaum, among others, served as leaders in the party-led Advance Youth Organization and the Progressive Youth Organizing

Committee, respectively; Buxenbaum later became CPUSA Women's Commission chair. Advance included among its membership Angela Davis and Bettina Aptheker and worked with various other student groups, including the National Student Association, Students for a Democratic Society, and the Student Nonviolent Coordinating Committee. Advance and PYOC members defiantly challenging HUAC and McCarran Act thought control. They were very much a part of the youth and student upsurge and campus free speech movements. In March 1964 the W.E.B. DuBois Clubs was founded, which included working class youth leaders like Jarvis Tyner. In September 1964, the Berkeley Free Speech Movement (*The FSM*) emerged and propelled Communist and DBC leader Bettina Aptheker into the spotlight. Daughter of Marxist historian Herbert Aptheker, she would publicly announce her membership in the CPUSA during the height of *The FSM*. In response to a *People's World* article (Tony Pecinovsky, "On 4th of July, remember CPUSA's commitment to patriotism," People's World, July 2, 2015, http://peoplesworld.org/on-4th-of-july-remember-cpusa-s-commitment-to-patriotism/) Aptheker remarked that Jarvis Tyner and Alva Buxenbaum had nothing to do with the Free Speech Movement. Both lived in the New York area at the time; however, both were involved with the DuBois Clubs, which was a national organization." (See: FSM-A http://btstack.com/btstackfsmpressbib.html). Aptheker's remarks, as they relate to *The FSM* – a movement located on the University of California-Berkeley campus in 1964-65 – are correct. However, regarding the considerably broader (lower case) student free speech movement, which preceded *The FSM* by several years, a different picture has emerged. Young Communists – like Stein and Buxenbaum – led campus organizations (Advance, the PYOC, and later the W.E.B. DuBois Clubs, and YWLL) that challenged the confines of intellectual permissibility with Communist speakers and acted as a bulwark against censorship, thereby helping to spur campus free speech movements on numerous universities across the country. They organized to "Ban the Ban" of Communist speakers. Students – in revolt – challenged faculty, administration and right-wing community leaders; they fought censorship to have Communists speak; they were a free speech movement. To be clear, they were not *The FSM*. Aptheker herself noted in 1968, "Not infrequently, therefore, the [student] movement has challenged the basic structure of power in the universities and in society." Adding, "the movement" began in spring 1960 and "reached its first plateau in the fall of 1964 with the Berkeley Free Speech movement," indicating that its growth was cumulative, a quantitative swell of activity, often with students fighting for the right to hear Communists speak. (See: Bettina Aptheker, *Columbia, Inc.* (W.E.B. DuBois Clubs, 1968), Introduction.) Further, as this chapter argues, the organizing of Communist speaking engagements on college campuses was often a catalyst for youth and students inclined to challenge campus faculty, administration and community censorship, i.e. a free speech movement. Historian Gerald Horne noted, "Because the FBI was prone to ascribe student protest of the 1960s to party manipulation, a tendency of historians has been to ignore the party's role. In fact, the party had a major role in igniting these protests insofar as an initial grievance of students was the effort to bar them from hearing Reds on campuses." (See, Horne, *Black Liberation / Red Scare...*, Ibid, 311) Gus Hall was one of the Communists they tried to bar. (See: Bart, ed., *Highlights Of A Fighting History...*, Ibid, 324-331)

3) Mike Davidow, "Gus Hall at Yale and Benjamin Davis at Brown Present Communist Views on Main Issues," The Worker, Sunday, February 24, 1963, 2, 11

4) George C. Kohn, *Thomas Dodd: censured senator*, in The New Encyclopedia of American Scandal (Facts On File, Inc., 2000), 110

5) Arnold Johnson, "Boston Areas Get an Earful on Communist Ideas, Goals," The Worker, Sunday, March 17, 1963, 2 and Arnold Johnson, "Brandeis Students Overflow Auditorium to Hear Gus Hall," The Worker, Sunday, March 26, 1963, 4

6) "Aptheker at Michigan State," The Worker, Sunday, January 27, 1963, 4, "Michigan Parleys Hear Dr. Aptheker," The Worker, March 26, 1963, 6, "More Colleges Hear Aptheker," The Worker, April 2, 1963, 7

7) "Hear Aptheker," The Worker, June 30, 1963, 8 and "Cambridge Memorial for Dr. DuBois," The Worker, December 3, 1963, 3

8) Davidow, "Gus Hall at Yale and Benjamin Davis at Brown...," Ibid

9) Douglass Archer, "Students at City College Fill Hall to Hear Davis," The Worker, Sunday, November 10, 1963, 2

10) Harry Golden, Jr., "The Ben Davis Interview," Detroit Free Press, May 3

11) Foster, *History of the Communist Party...*, Ibid, 562

12) "1,500 Rhode Island College Students Hear Hyman Lumer on 'Capitalism and Socialism,'" The Worker, April 14, 1963, 2,11

13) "2,500 at Colorado State College Hear Communist Youth Leader," The Worker, April 23, 1963, 3

14) "Michigan U. Students Hear Carl Winter," The Worker, Sunday, June 9, 1963, 4

15) "UCLA Students Hear Dorothy Healey," The Worker, November 10, 1963, 3 and "A Communist Talks To Students," Communist Party of SO. California, October 1963, 5

16) "Ban Against Communists to End," The Worker, July 16, 1963, 8

17) Wallace Turner, "Red Speaks on Coast Campus Despite Protests," The New York Times, May 1, 1964

18) Gus Hall, "Talks With Students," Political Affairs, April, 1962, 5-18, Mike Davidow, "12,000 Listen to Gus Hall In Oregon Football Field," The Worker, February 18, 1962, 3, 11, Mike Davidow, "Gus Hall's 37 Speeches Stir the West Coast," The Worker, March 11, 1962, 6, 7, Rob Royer, "Gus Hall Rides a Golf Cart Into Eugene and the Demise of the Commonwealth Federation," The Cascadia Courier, April 9, 2012, http://www.thecascadiacourier.com/2012/04/gus-hall-invades-eugene-and-demise-of.html, North, Jackson, Meyers, *Gus Hall: The Man...*, Ibid, 31, and Bart, ed., *Highlights Of A Fighting History...*, Ibid, 329

19) Mike Davidow, "Gus Hall's Coast Visit Helps Deliver Blow to Ultra Right," The Worker, Sunday, February 11, 1962, 3, 10

20) "College Students Hear Hall, Bart and Aptheker," The Worker, Sunday, February 25, 1962, 2

21) "Hamilton College Hears Communist," The Worker, April 24, 1962

22) "College Students Hear Hall, Bart and Aptheker," The Worker, February 25, 1962, 2

23) "250 at Pennsylvania U. Hear Aptheker on McCarran Act," The Worker, April 3, 1962, 4

24) Mike Davidow, "Ben Davis at Harvard, His Alma Mater, Speaks on CP and the Constitution," The Worker, April 29, 2

25) James E. Jackson, *The Philosophy Of Communism* (New Century Publishers, 1963), 10

26) Davidow, *Gus Hall's 37 Speeches...*, Ibid

27) "Gus Hall at CCNY Warns His trial Is Meant As Wedge," The Worker, April 10, 1962, 1, 7

28) Arnold Johnson, "1,000 Swarthmore Students Hear Gus Hall," The Worker, May 6, 1962, 2

29) "Gets Award for Letting Gus Hall Speak," The Worker, May 1, 1962, 1

30) Art Shield, "7,000 in Biggest May Day Rally in Years," The Worker, May 6, 1962, 16

31) "400 at Hunter Hear Gus Hall," The Worker, May 12, 1962, 2

32) Sam Kushner, "Gus Hall in Chicago, Ben Davis in Minneapolis Heard on McCarran Act," The Worker, May 13, 1962, 2

33) "Midwest Campuses To Hear Gus Hall," The Worker, May 6, 1962, 4 and "Wisconsin Hears Gus Hall In College, on Air, in Press," The Worker, May 20, 1962, 2

34) Art Shields, "Tide Turning, Hall Tells Anti-McCarran Rally," The Worker, June 17, 1962, 1

35) "Carl Winter Explains CP Views to Campus," The Worker, December 9, 1962, 4

36) Gus Hall, *Main Street to Wall Street: End The Cold War* (New Century Publishers, 1962), 31-32

37) Davidow, *12,000 Listen to Gus Hall...*, Ibid

38) Hall, *Talks With Students*, Ibid, 5-18

39) Wheeler, author interview, 10/2/2017

40) Art Shields, "Will Fight for Bill of Rights, CP Leaders Tell Newsmen," The Worker, Sunday, June 18, 1961

41) "Gus Hall Reviews Role Of Reds In U.S.," The New York Times, December 8, 1961

42) On the lower case free speech movement in 1963 (not the *FSM*, which did not emerge until summer/fall 1964), for example, see: "Jersey College Poll Opposes Ban on Gus Hall," The Worker, April 2, 1963, 3, "Hit Ohio Bill to Curb Campus Speakers," The Worker, Sunday, June 16, 1963, 4, "N.C. College Heads Assail Speakers Curb," The Worker, July 2, 1963, 6, "Ban Against Communists End," The Worker, July 16, 1963, 8, James Dolsen, "Student Picket HUAC Inquisitors in Phila.," The Worker, October 8, 1963, 4, "Students Hit SACB Hearing," The Worker, October 15, 1963, 3, "300 at Rally Defend Advance Youth Group," The Worker, November 5, 1963, p 3, among other examples

43) "Bigger Role Urged For C.C.N.Y. Student," The New York Times, December 2, 1966

44) "Swarthmore Campus Poll Hits McCarran Act," The Worker, May 22, 1962, 1 and Andrea London, "Jersey College Poll Opposes Ban on Gus Hall," The Worker, April 2, 1963, 3

45) Peter Kihss, "U.S. Reds To Join Civil Rights Drive," The New York Times, June 25, 1966

46) Horne, *Black Liberation / Red Scare...*, Ibid, 311

47) Kihss, "U.S. Reds To Join Civil Rights Drive," Ibid

48) "F.B.I. Chief Reports Reds Aim At Youth," The New York Times, January 3, 1964

49) Kathlyn Gay, ed., "Hall, Gus (1910-2000)," in American Dissidents: An Encyclopedia of Troublemakers, Subversives, and Prisoners of Conscience (ABC-CLIO, LLC, 2012), 267, North, Jackson, Meyers, *Gus Hall: The Man...*, Ibid, 4-10, 13, 15, 57, Gus Hall, *Working Class USA: The Power And The Movement* (International Publishers, 1987), 9 and Rodney P. Carlisle, ed., *Encyclopedia of Politics: The Left and the Right* (Sage Publications, Inc., 2005), 207. Re Davis, see: Michael K. Honey, *Southern Labor and Black Civil Rights: Organizing Memphis Workers* (University of Illinois, 1993)

50) Stepan-Norris and Zeitlan, *Left Out...*, Ibid, 42 and Ottanelli, *The Communist Party...*, Ibid, 143. However, Stepan-Norris, Zeitlin and Ottanelli all site Foster, *History of the Communist Party...*, Ibid, 349

51) Victor G. Devinatz, "A reevaluation of the Trade Union Unity League, 1929-1934," Science & Society, Vol. 71, No. 1, January 2007, 36, 55

52) Dennis, *Blood On Steel...*, Ibid, 17

53) Stepan-Norris and Zeitlan, *Left Out...*, Ibid

54) Bart, ed., *Highlights Of A Fighting History...*, Ibid., 150, 151

55) North, Jackson, Meyer, *Gus Hall: The Man...*, Ibid, 15

56) "Testify Reds Led Ohio Steel Strike," The New York Times, November 5, 1963 and "Hunt C.I.O. Leader As Bombing Chief," The New York Times, June 30, 1937

57) Dennis, *Blood On Steel...*, Ibid., 24, 25, 63, 66 and Michael Dennis, *The Memorial Day Massacre And The Movement For Industrial Democracy* (Palgrave Macmillan, 2010), 95. Re Johnson, see: Ruth Needleman, *Black Freedom Fighters In Steel: The Struggle For Democratic Unionism* (Cornell University Press, 2003) and Rick Halpern, *Down on the Killing Floor: Black And White Workers In Chicago's' Packinghouses, 1904-54* (University of Illinois Press, 1997)

58) Abt, *Advocate and Activist...*, Ibid, 67-68

59) Bart, ed., *A Fighting History...*, 141

60) Wyndham Mortimer, *Organize: My Life as a Union Man* (Beacon Paperback, 1972)

61) North, Jackson, Meyer, *Gus Hall: The Man...*, Ibid, 16, 17, 49

62) "Gus Hall Is Ousted In 'Purge' Of C.I.O.," The New York Times, July 4, 1937

63) *Gus Hall Memorial*, brochure issued at Hall Memorial service, Cooper Union, November 19, 2000, 4; Re Local 1375: Rick Nagin, author interview, at the Chicago Workers' Education Society, PW/CP offices on March 12, 2016

64) Judith LeBlanc, "Warren, Ohio says 'Welcome Home, Gus Hall!,'" People's Weekly World, June 17, 1995, 3

65) *Gus Hall Memorial*, Ibid. Re SOAR, see: Scott Marshall, former CPUSA Labor Commission chair, served on the SOAR International Executive Board from District 7, http://myuswlocal.org/sites/US/SOAR/index.cfm?action=albumPhoto&photoId=ca63badb-c304-414d-b6ac-8f80b201e540

66) Fred Gaboury, "AFL-CIO Convention charts path to future," People's Weekly World, October 4, 1997, http://www.hartford-hwp.com/archives/45b/095.html

67) For examples, see: Mark Esters was lead organizer for CWA 6355, the Missouri State Workers' Union and president of the St. Louis Coalition of Black Trade Unionists; he also served on the executive board of the Greater St. Louis Central Labor Council. Josh LeClair is currently the CP Florida District Organizer. Prior to his current position he served as the Florida AFL-CIO State-Wide Community Organizer and as an organizer for the American Federation of State, County and Municipal Employees Council 79; he also serves on the executive boards of the Florida AFL-CIO. Prior to his retirement as business manager of the Operating Engineers International Union Local 148 (which he served as for 27 years), Don Giljum also served on the Missouri AFL-CIO and the Greater St. Louis Central Labor Council executive boards; he is currently the organizing and collective

bargaining co-chair of the St. Louis Jobs with Justice Workers' Rights Board and secretary-treasurer of the St. Louis Workers' Education Society. Mark Froemke is president of the Western Minnesota Area AFL-CIO Labor Council, a long-time member of the party's National Committee. John Wojick serves as vice president of the International Labor Communications Association, as labor editor of the *People's World.* Michelle Artt serves as the Metro Detroit AFL-CIO Civil Rights Committee chair, and on the Metro AFL-CIO and Detroit Federation of Teachers' executive board. Al Neal served as the mid-west coordinator of the fast food workers 'Fight for $15' and bargaining rep. for the Service Employees International Union-Health Care, along with St. Louis party members Nicholas James and Bryan Evans.

68) "Joins Red Secretariat," The New York Times, May 17, 1950 and North, Jackson, Meyer, *Gus Hall: The Man...*, Ibid., 17-20, 49

69) Schrecker, *The Age of McCarthyism...*, Ibid, 176 and Isserman, *Which Side Were You On...*, Ibid, 180. Isserman writes that nearly 1/5 of male communists were serving in the armed forces by January 1943

70) North, Jackson, Meyer, *Gus Hall: The Man...*, Ibid

71) Foster, *History of the Communist Party...*, Ibid, p 509 and Martelle, *The Fear Within...*, Ibid

72) Gus Hall, *Which way for young Americans* (Labor Youth League, October 1950)

73) "Draft Dodger Sentenced," The New York Times, September 11, 1951

74) "Truman Assailed On Move In Korea," The New York Times, June 19, 1950

75) "Hall, Fugitive Red, Seized In Mexico, Deported To U.S.," The New York Times, October 10, 1951, "Gus Hall To Face Contempt Action," The New York Times, November 1, 1951, "A New Gus Hall Appears In Court," The New York Times, November 3, 1951, Gus Hall, "Some Thoughts on Returning," Political Affairs, June 1959, 20-24

76) *Communist Party Oral Histories (Danny Rubin: Part 3)*, part of the oral histories collection, Tamiment Library, NYU, https://wp.nyu.edu/tamimentcpusa/collections/tamoh/danny-rubin/part3/

77) Niebyl-Proctor Marxist Library: Bob Thompson, *Eastern Seaboard Conference Of Communist Youth,* October 1958

78) Mike Davidow, "Robert Thompson War Hero, Is Still McCarthyism Victim," The Worker, May 5, 1963, 12 and Fred P. Graham, "Communist Denied Burial in Arlington," The New York Times, January 28, 1966

79) Niebyl-Proctor Marxist Library: *Eastern Seaboard Conference...*, Ibid

80) Harry Schwartz, "New Strain Seen Dividing U.S. Reds," The New York Times, December 15, 1959, Hall, *Working Class USA...*, Ibid, 48

81) *Communist Party Oral Histories (Danny Rubin: Part 3)*, Ibid

82) Benjamin J. Davis, *Upsurge In The South: The Negro People Fight For* Freedom (New Century Publishers, 1960)

83) "500 at College Hear Patterson in Debate on Africa," The Worker, Sunday, November 27, 1960, 10

84) See: Frazier, *The East Is Black...*, Ibid.

85) "Kennedy Can End Bias, Davis Tells CCNY Students," The Worker, Sunday, May 14, 1961, 12

86) Re Aptheker, Davis and Burnham: Aptheker, author interview, 1/29/2018

87) *Communist Party Oral Histories (Danny Rubin: Part 4)*, Ibid, https://wp.nyu.edu/tamimentcpusa/collections/tamoh/danny-rubin/part4/

88) "Gus Hall and Ben Davis Face Arraignment," The Worker, April 1, 1962, 1, 10

89) Andrea London, "Youth Pledge Drive To End McCarran Act," The Worker, January 20, 1963, 2

90) "McCarran Act Information Kit Sent to Student Leaders," The Worker, March 17, 1963, 3, "Woman Here Is Ordered To Register as Communist," The New York Times, November 6, 1962 and Sewell Chan, "Miriam Friedlander, Former Councilwoman, Dies at 95," The New York Times, October 8, 2009, https://cityroom.blogs.nytimes.com/2009/10/08/friedlander-former-councilwoman-dies-at-95/

91) "Debate on McCarran Act Heard by CCNY Students," The Worker, March 12, 1963, 8

92) "Advance Youth Group Asks Unity Against Persecution," The Worker, September 8, 1963, 9

93) "Student Groups Unite To Picket Wtchhunters," The Worker, September 29, 1963, 2

94) "300 at Rally Defend Advance Youth Group," The Worker, November 5, 1963, 3

95) Sam Kushner, "Not Intimidated: Youth Organizing Conference Vows Convention within Year," The Worker (Midwest Edition), January 8, 1961, 1 and "Youth Bill of Rights," The Worker (Midwest Edition), January 8, 1961, MW 4

96) Fulton Lewis, Jr., "Washington Report," Reading Eagle, August 23, 1961, 12

97) Hall, *Working Class USA...*, Ibid

98) Horne, *Black Liberation / Red Scare...*, Ibid, 311

99) "Red Ban Decried At City College," The New York Times, November 3, 1961

100) Horne, *Black Liberation / Red Scare...*, Ibid, 313

101) "Urge Youth Committee 'Create Jobs,'" The Worker, December 3, 1961, 12

102) "Davis Hails Bid to Speak at City College," The Worker, December 24, 1961, 12

103) Donald Janson, "Red Drive Found In U.S. Colleges," The New York Times, January 27, 1962

104) Horne, *Black Liberation / Red Scare...*, Ibid, 314

105) NYU, Tam 137, Box 3, Folder 3: Walter E. Orthwein, "On Washington U. Campus: Communism Debate Draws Yawns, Boos," St. Louis Globe Democrat, No date and "Hear Arnold Johnson In Collage in Midwest," The Worker, May 27, 1962

106) "Hamilton College Hears Communist," The Worker, April 24, 1962

107) NYU, TAM 137, Box 3, Folder 3: "U.S. Red Claims Americans Some Day Will Be Socialist," The Trinity Tripod, December 7, 1962

108) NYU, TAM 137, Box 3, Folder 3: Arnold Johnson, "1,000 Swarthmore Students Hear Gus Hall," The Sunday Worker, May 6, 1962

109) NYU, TAM 137, Box 3, Folder 19: Lecture & Information Bureau – To Editors of College Papers, To Student Councils, September 1962

110) Hall, *Main Street to Wall Street...*, Ibid, 6, 23, 25

111) Al Richmond, *Campus Rebels* (Pacific Publishing Foundation, no date, circa 1960), 31

112) Daniel Rubin, "Youth and America's Future," Political Affairs, October 1962, 1-12 and *Communist Party Oral Histories (Danny Rubin: Part 7,* Ibid, https://wp.nyu.edu/tamimentcpusa/collections/tamoh/danny-rubin/part7/

113) Daniel Rubin, "1,000 Attending National Student Parley in Ohio," The Worker, August 28, 1962, 3

114) Daniel Rubin, "Student Congress Hits Perils in McCarran Act," The Worker, September 9, 1962, 2, 11

115) Rubin, "Youth and America's Future...," Ibid

116) Communist Party, USA, "On The Arrest Of Gus Hall And Benjamin J. Davis," Political Affairs, April 1962, 1-4

117) "Gus Hall at Hunter," The New York Times, May 3, 1962

118) Jackson, *The Philosophy Of Communism...*, Ibid, 15

119) NYU, TAM 132, Box 153, Folder 21: Gus Hall, *An Open Letter to the Socialist Party from Gus Hall* (Communist Party, 1962)

120) See: Murrell, *'The Most Dangerous Communist...*, Ibid, Herbert Aptheker, "Is the Soviet Union A Progressive Society," Political Affairs, April 1963, 45 and Herbert Aptheker, "Though Crushed, It Rises Again," Political Affairs, December 1963, 40

121) Gus Hall, "For a Campaign Of Party Renewal," The Worker, Sunday, November 17, 1963, 5, 9

122) NYU, TAM 132, Box 150, Folder 13: Letter from Jackson to Winston, no date (circa fall 1963)

123) *Communist Party Oral Histories (Danny Rubin: Part 7),* Ibid

124) Niebyl-Proctor Marxist Library: Phil Davis, *Memo From The National Office,* no date (circa summer 1964)

125) Niebyl-Proctor Marxist Library: *Spur newsletter – w.e.b. dubois clubs of America,* October 16, 1964. For more on the murder of Chaney, Goodman and Schwerner, see: William Bradford Huie, *Three Lives for Mississippi* (University of Mississippi Press, 2000)

126) *Communist Party Oral Histories (Danny Rubin: Part 9,* https://wp.nyu.edu/tamimentcpusa/collections/tamoh/danny-rubin/part9/ and Joe Atkins, "SNCC veterans and young activists testify to workers' rights as civil rights at Mississippi Freedom Summer 50th Anniversary Conference," Facing South, June 30, 2014, https://www.facingsouth.org/2014/06/sncc-veterans-and-young-activists-testify-to-worke.html

127) Niebyl-Proctor Marxist Library: Davis, *Memo From The National Office,* Ibid

128) Peter Kihss, "U.S. Reds Weigh New Command," The New York Times, September 26, 1964

129) Arnold Johnson, "The American Peace Movement," Political Affairs, March 1963, 10

130) NYU, TAM 137, Box 4, Folder 5: Arnold Johnson, 1964 Elections (hand-written), 18, 19

131) Gus Hall, *Communism, Mankind's Bright Horizon* (New Outlook Publishers, 1966), 5 and Christopher Friedrichs, "Hall Says Vietnam Escalation Might Result in Nuclear War," Daily Columbia Spectator, December 16, 1965, 1

132) Niebyl-Proctor Marxist Library: *Youth and the Communist Party* (National Youth Commission, CPUSA, no date, circa fall/winter 1965)

133) Peter Kihss, "Leaders Urge U.S. Communists to Work 'in and Around the Orbit of the Democratic Party,'" The New York Times, June 26, 1966

134) Peter Kihss, "U.S. Reds Will Press Fort Left-Wing Unity," The New York Times, February 24, 1966

135) "Communism Hailed By Young Delegates," The New York Times, July 7, 1968

136) Henry Winston, *Build The Communist Party – The Party Of The Working Class* (New Outlook Publishers, 1969), 28

137) A. Brychkov, *American Youth Today* (Progress Publishers, 1973), 208

138) Levin and Silbar, ed., *You Say You Want a Revolution...,* Ibid, 40

139) For example, see: Holsaert, Noonan, Richardson, Robinson, Young and Zellner, ed., *Hands On The Freedom Plow: Personal Accounts By Women In SNCC* (University of Illinois Press, 2012), 55-61. Also, Cassie (Weaver / Davis) Lopez, author interview, 4/28/2019. Lopez worked for SNCC in Detroit before joining the DBC, as did her then husband, Phillip Davis, who would become DBC national chair. See also, Terrence Hallinan, *Mississippi: Winds*

of Change (W.E.B. DuBois Club, February 1964). Hallinan spent summer 1963 "engaged in voter registration work with the Student Nonviolent Coordinating Committee in the Mississippi Delta... during those two months he was arrested twice, beaten by the police, attacked with electric cattle prodders and chased out of town by the White Citizens Council. Thus, he was able to feel something of the terror which the Negro people face in Mississippi."

140) For example, see: Niebyl-Proctor Marxist Library: *Spur newsletter – w.e.b. dubois clubs of America,* no date (circa spring/summer 1965). It was noted in the Local Club News section that the Washington, D.C. DuBois Clubs "played a leading role" in the March on Washington to End the War in Vietnam. "Large contingents organized by the DBCs arrived in Washington from throughout the East Coast, New England and from the Midwest." The New York DuBois Club alone "organized 17 bus loads for the capitol rally." Additionally, Robert Greenblatt, the national coordinator of the National Mobilization Committee to End the War in Vietnam, would note in 1968 that the SACB attack on the DBC was a "new witch hunt... designed to destroy [the] movement and pick off its leadership," of which Communists were a part. *National Mobilization Committee to End the War in Vietnam, Fact Sheet...,* Ibid

141) Aptheker, author interview, 1/29/2018 and Aptheker, *Intimate Politics...,* Ibid

142) Richard Loring, "A Communist Candidacy in Los Angeles," Political Affairs, September 1966, 10-18 and Arthur Herzog, "A Specter Haunts The American Communist Party," New York Times, October 25, 1964

143) Niebyl-Proctor Marxist Library: W.E.B. DuBois Clubs, recruitment brochure, no date (circa summer 1966)

144) Robert Greenblatt, *National Mobilization Committee to End the War in Vietnam, Fact Sheet on the New McCarran Act,* 5 pages, Mennonite Church USA Archives, Goshen IN; I-3-5.16 Box 75 Folder 1: http://palni.contentdm.oclc.org/cdm/ref/collection/gopplow/id/631

145) Niebyl-Proctor Marxist Library: *Opening Report on Review of Youth Work,* San Francisco – February 1967, BA – for District Board

146) Niebyl-Proctor Marxist Library: *Northern California District: Preparation For Review Of Youth Work,* N CA Youth Commission, CPUSA, no date (circa fall 1966 / winter 1967)

147) Niebyl-Proctor Marxist Library: Mike Zagarell, *A Critical Moment – a Six-Month Perspective (Report to a National Youth Conference of C.P.U.S.A.),* no date (circa 1967)

148) Langway, *From hustings...,* Ibid

149) NYU, TAM 132, Box 218, Folder 25: Michael Myerson, *On The Crisis In The Party* (June 1990)

150) Rosenberg, *From Crisis to Split...,* Ibid

151) Bettina Aptheker, *Columbia, Inc.* (W.E.B. DuBois Clubs, 1968), Introduction

152) Bettina Aptheker, *Big Business And The American University* (New Outlook Publishers, 1966), 27-28, Aptheker, author interview, 1/29/2018 and *Youth and the Communist Party...*, Ibid

153) Peter Kihss, "U.S. Reds Cite Gain In Youth Members," The New York Times, Friday, June 24, 1966

154) Gus Hall, *The Eleventh Hour – Defeat The New Fascist Threat!* (New Century Publishers, 1964), 8, 9, 13

155) Friedrichs, *Hall Says Vietnam Escalation...*, Ibid

156) "U.S. Reds Identify Five More Leaders," New York Times, March 16, 1967

157) Gus Hall, *Toward Unity Against World Imperialism* (New Outlook Publishers, 1969), 7, 8

158) Deborah Nelson, *The War Behind Me: Vietnam Veterans Confront The Truth About U.S. War Crimes* (Basic Books, 2008) and *Crimes of War: Commentary by Nelson*, http://www.crimesofwar.org/commentary/the-war-behind-me-vietnam-veterans-confront-the-truth-about-us-war-crimes-in-vietnam/

159) Hall, *Toward Unity...*, Ibid

160) Kendrick Oliver, *The My Lai massacre in American history and memory* (Manchester University Press, 2006) and Seymour M. Hersh, "The Scene Of The Crime: A reporter's journey to My Lai and the secrets of the past," The New Yorker, March 30, 2015, http://www.newyorker.com/magazine/2015/03/30/the-scene-of-the-crime

161) Charles Hirschman, Samuel Preston and Vu Manh Loi, "Vietnamese Casualties During the American War: A New Estimate," Population and Development Review, Vol. 21, Issue 4 (Dec. 1995), 790, 807

162) Hall, *Toward Unity...*, Ibid, p 8

163) Herbert Aptheker, *Mission To Hanoi* (International Publishers, 1966)

164) Herbert Aptheker, "Vietnam: Life Or Death," Political Affairs, April 1965, 30 – 32

165) Gus Hall, "Anti-Monopoly Movements," Political Affairs, May 1965, 33-38

166) Gus Hall, "The World Scene," Political Affairs, March 1970, 3-10

167) NYU, TAM 137, Box 4, Folder 6: Cleveland, Ohio – Special to Daily World, no date

168) Gus Hall, *Out Of Indo-China! Freedom For Angela Davis! – Our Goals For 1971 And How To Win Them: The Sharpening Crisis of U.S. Imperialism and the Tasks of the Communist Party* (New Outlook Publishers, 1971), 7, 12

169) "Hall Finds Communist Gain," The New York Times, October 31, 1972

170) Arnold Johnson, "On To The Chicago Amphitheatre June 29!," Preconvention Discussion Issue No. 4, Party Affairs, Vol. 9, No. 4 (May 1975), 1-2

171) Roslyn Riddle, "Angela Davis Highlights Chicago Rally," Ann Arbor Sun, July 4, 1975, "A Memorable Convention," Political Affairs, August 1975, 1 and Arnold Becchetti, "The 21st National Convention: Toward A Mass CP," Political Affairs, September 1975, 35

172) See: Preconvention Discussion Issue No. 6, Party Affairs, Vol. 9, No. 6 (June 1975), back cover. Re USSA and Communists in the 2000s, see: Tony Pecinovsky, "Says USSA aim is to 'alter power relations on campuses,'" People's World, August 11, 2014, http://peoplesworld.org/says-ussa-aim-is-to-alter-power-relations-on-campuses/, and Tony Pecinovsky, "An interview with USSA's Maxwell Love," People's World, August 12, 2014, http://peoplesworld.org/an-interview-with-ussa-s-maxwell-love/. Additionally, Athena Matyear, the USSA then (2014) training director was a member of the YCL. Julia Beatty, former USSA president (2002), and Kristy Ringor, USSA's communications director, were both active in the YCL for several years. Ringor served on the YCL's national committee and on the editorial board of *Dynamic*, the magazine of the YCL. See: *Dynamic* (YCL, Winter, 2005) and Julie Beatty and Kristy Ringor, "Students Dissent to War," Dynamic, Winter/Spring, 2002, 11. For a brief history of the NSA, see: http://usstudents.org/who-we-are/history/

173) Kathy Kelly, *United States National Student Association: Report Of The Officers*, prepared for the 28th National Student Congress, August 17-24, 1975, 30

174) Gus Hall, *Gus Hall Speaks on Youth Rights* (Hall-Tyner Election Campaign Committee, 1976)

175) NYU, TAM 347, Box 5, Folder 48: *Speech by James Steele,* National Chairman of the Young Workers Liberation League, Tuskegee Institute, Tuskegee, Alabama, October 27, 1976

176) Aptheker, AUTHOR INTERVIEW, 1/29/2018

177) "The Tet Offensive...," Ibid and Markowitz, "Old Struggles in a 'New Age'...," Ibid

178) Re Johnson and Mora's membership in CPUSA (two of the Fort Hood Three): Elena Mora, long-time Party leader and niece of Dennis Mora, author interview, while in Chicago at a CPUSA National Board meeting, May 29-31, 2015. Marc Brodine, author interview, while in Chicago at a CPUSA Marxist Strategy and Tactics conference, February 18, 2017: Brodine attended Party School with Johnson. Tim Wheeler, a fellow *Daily World* reporter who worked with Johnson in the NY office, author interview, October 2, 2017. See *The Fort Hood Three: The Case Of The Three G.I.'s Who Said "No" To The War In Vietnam* (Fort Hood Three Defense Committee, 1966). For obvious reasons (anticommunism) Mora and Johnson publicly

denied membership in the CPUSA. See also: Martin Arnold, "3 Soldiers hold News Conference to Announce They Won't Go to Vietnam," The New York Times, July 1, 1966

179) Bart, ed. *Highlights Of A Fighting History...*, Ibid, 373

180) Zagarell, *World Student Strike Against Vietnam War...*, Ibid, p 20, Aptheker, *Big Business And The American University*, Ibid, 2, Bart, ed., *Highlights Of A Fighting History...*, Ibid, 324-328 and Aptheker, *Intimate Politics...*, Ibid

181) Aptheker, author interview, 1/29/2018

182) Suttner, "Crisis in the CPUSA: Interview with Charlene Mitchell...," Ibid

183) Charlene Mitchell, "For Freedom for Political Prisoners and Victims of Racism and Class Injustice," Party Affairs, Vol. VII, No. 1, January 1973, 32-40. The report is from a December 1972 meeting of the party's central committee. There Mitchell outlined the work of the National United Committee to Free Angela Davis, which she led, and made a proposal for a new national defense organization, which became the National Alliance at a founding conference in May 1973

184) NYU, TAM 132, Box 110, Folder 14: Henry Winston, *Remarks of Henry Winston At The Founding Conference of NAIMSAL, Chicago, October 1973,* October 19-21, 1973

185) Devinatz, "The Antipolitics And Politics Of...," Ibid

186) "Communist Doctrine: Red Leader Advises U.S. Youth," The Spokesman Review, March 15, 1970, 5

187) Brian Rubinsky, "Working Class Internationalism: The American Communist Party and Anti-Vietnam War Activism 1961-1971" (Doctoral Dissertation, Rutgers University, October 2014), 58

188) Danny Spector, "The Founding of the Young Workers Liberation League: Combining theory with youthful style," People's Daily World, February 7, 1990, 10

189) *The Anti-Defense Lobby: Part II "The Peace Movement, Continued,"* Executive Summary, Institution Analysis (The Heritage Foundation), No. 11, September 1979

190) Peter Kihss, "Subversives Unit Seek Proof Red Front Is Red," The New York Times, February 8, 1972

191) Gus Hall, "Gus Hall: The Working Class Answer to the Deepening Crisis" (New outlook Publishers, 1979), 6

192) "New York salutes women in struggle," People's Weekly World, March 21, 1998, 4

193) "300 celebrate opening of NYC Marxist school," Daily World, November 16, 1978, 2

194) See: Marvin E. Gettleman, "'No Varsity Teams': New York's Jefferson School of Social Science, 1943-1956," Science & Society, Vol. 66, No. 3 (Fall 2002)

195) "300 celebrate opening...," Ibid

196) "Youth leaders to discuss perspectives for the 80's," Daily World, December 27, 1979, 4

197) Sims, author interview, August 21, 2019 and "Communist to take office as UMass student President," UPI, December 29, 1988, https://www.upi.com/Archives/1988/12/29/Communist-to-take-office-as-UMass-student-president/3715599374800/

198) Gus Hall, *The Youth Reservoir: How To Tap It (opening remarks: Party Conference on work among youth, June 18, 1984)* (Communist Party, USA, 1984)

199) James Steele, "Festival of Youth and Peace," Political Affairs, October 1985

200) Gus Hall, "The Caricature of 'Communism,'" Political Affairs, January 1989, 2-5

201) Sam Tanenhaus, "Gus Hall, Unreconstructed American Communist of 7 Decades, dies at 90," The New York Times, October 17, 2000

202) Rubinsky, "Working Class Internationalism...," 60

203) "On U.S. Campuses...Gus Hall Provokes 'Right to Speak' Battles," The Cornell Daily Sun, February 16, 1962, 10

204) Davidow, "Gus Hall's 37 Speeches...," Ibid

205) Pecinovsky, "Historians...," Ibid and : Tony Pecinovsky, "'Intersectional before it was cool': The women's movement under state socialism," People's World, October 3, 2019, https://www.peoplesworld.org/article/intersectional-before-it-was-cool-the-womens-movement-under-state-socialism/?fbclid=IwAR2Kmqt3j9ZjhNfPjf1zvhxOJcJGBBtLSHVbIIcfTS0NcGfp7tOcoS9HQ_8. Kristen Ghodsee notes, "There is still a strong 'red taboo,' but there are younger scholars who are challenging it in fascinating ways."

206) Tanenhaus, "Gus Hall, Unreconstructed...," Ibid

207) Jose A. Cruz, "500 New Yorkers celebrate life of Gus Hall," People's Weekly World, December 2, 2000, 2

208) John Bachtell, "Ideology And Youth Today," Political Affairs, July 1989, 8-32

209) *May 18, 1999: School Violence*, Baltimore City School Board member and YCL leader, Anita Wheeler speaking before the House Education and Workforce Subcommittee on Early Childhood, Youth and Families, CSPAN, http://www.c-span.org/video/?123417-1/school-violence

210) Anita Wheeler, "From the Editor...," Dynamic, Winter/Spring 2000, 2

211) NYU, TAM 347, Box 21, Folder 66: Gus Hall, *From the desk of Gus Hall* (January 2000)

212) Re Marshall and Le Blanc: Le Blanc, CPUSA national board member, served as UFPJ's national co-chair from 2005 to 2008. Marshall served as the YCL national coordinator and leader in

NYSPC. See: Tony Pecinovsky, "Out of the Classroom, Into the Battlefield," Alternet / Wire Tap, April 6, 2003, http://www.alternet.org/story/15549/out_of_the_classroom,_into_the_battlefield and "Peace Movement and the 2008 Elections: Interview with Judith Le Blanc," Political Affairs, April 11, 2008, http://www.politicalaffairs.net/peace-movement-and-the-2008-elections-interview-with-judith-leblanc/. The author served on the YCL's national committee during this time with Marshall.

213) Barbara Palmer, "Students participate in national strike against war," Stanford Report, March 12, 2003, http://news.stanford.edu/news/2003/march12/strike-312.html, Lloyd Vries, "Students Cut Class To Protest War," CBS, March 10, 2003, http://www.cbsnews.com/news/students-cut-class-to-protest-war/ and Bryan Long, "Students pencil in Iraq protest," CNN, March 5, 2003, http://www.cnn.com/2003/US/03/04/sprj.irq.college.protest/

214) Tony Pecinovsky, "Victory for Wash U students in living wage," People's Weekly World, April 29, 2005, http://www.peoplesworld.org/article/victory-for-wash-u-students-in-living-wage/. The author met regularly with Uzoma, Christmas and Castellano; all were part of the local YCL chapter

215) Eric Larson, ed., *Jobs With Justice: 25 Years, 25 Voices* (PM Press, 2013). Smiley served as YCL national coordinator while the author was part of the YCL national committee; Faulkner was also on the YCL NC; both traveled to Venezuela in 2005 along with the author.

216) Gus Hall, "Curb The Corporate Military Dogs!," Party Organizer, Vol. XIV, No. 1, Jan-March 1980, 24, 25

217) Jarvis Tyner, "League / Party Relationship," Party Organizer, Vol. XIV, No. 1, Jan-March 1980, 36

218) North, Jackson, Meyer, *Gus Hall: The Man...*, Ibid, 31-34

219) "Gus Hall on TV Interview Declares New Problems Need New Answers," The Worker, Sunday, January 17, 1961, 4

220) Eillie Anzilotti, "For young people, socialism is now more popular than capitalism," Fast Company, August 13, 2018, https://www.fastcompany.com/90218064/for-young-people-socialism-is-now-more-popular-than-capitalism and Keith A. Spence, "The Democratic Socialist of America hit 25,000 members. Here's why this could mark a political turning point," Salon.com, August 5, 2017, http://www.salon.com/2017/08/05/the-democratic-socialists-of-america-hit-25000-members-heres-why-this-is-a-big-deal/

Chapter Four

1) Harry Raymond, "Manhandle Winston in Court Appearance," Daily Worker, New York, March 6, 1956, 1, 8

2) James Jackson, "Winston's Condition is 'Serious'; Jail Guards Patrol Operating Room," The Worker, Sunday, February 7, 1960, 1, 14 and "Save Winston from the Heartless," The Worker, Sunday, February 7, 1960, 2

3) Jack Stachel, "Henry Winston Not Yet Out Of Danger," The Worker, Sunday, February 14, 1960, 1, 4 and Benjamin Davis, "Intensify Fight To Free Winston," The Worker, Sunday, April 24, 1960, p 2

4) See: Gus Hall, "Paul Robeson: An American Communist," Communist Party, USA (text of a centennial tribute speech delivered on May 31, 1998, at the Winston Unity Auditorium, CP national office, 235 W. 23rd St., New York, NY), 3, 6, 8. Later reprinted as Gus Hall, "Paul Robeson: Artist, Freedom Fighter, Hero, American Communist," Political Affairs, July, 1998. Hall writes: "My own most precious moments with Paul were when I met with him to accept his dues and renew his yearly membership in the CPUSA. I and other Communist leaders, like Henry Winston...met with Paul to brief him on politics and Party policies and to discuss his work and struggles." See, also: Vijay Prashad, "Comrade Robeson: A Centennial Tribute to an American Communist," Social Scientist, Vol. 25, No. 7/8 (Jul.-Aug. 1997), 40, 41. Prashad, however, quotes from the above. Gerald Horne wondered if Robeson had been a member of the Communist Party of Great Britain, which was "more of a likelihood than U.S. membership." See: Gerald Horne, *Paul Robeson: The Artist as Revolutionary* (Pluto Press, 2016), 6. Martin Duberman notes that Robeson offered to publicly join the CPUSA in 1951 out of solidarity with his beleaguered comrades, but that the proposal was rejected by the Party's leadership. See: Martin Duberman, *Paul Robeson: A Biography* (The New Press, 1989), 420. While Robeson's membership in the CPUSA is contested, it is apparent he did not hesitate to align himself with the CPUSA, its leadership and its policies.

5) See: Horne, *Paul Robeson...*, Ibid, *Black Liberation / Red Scare...*, Ibid and *Black Revolutionary...*, Ibid

6) "500 at Rally Call for Winston's Freedom," The Worker, Sunday, July 3, 1960, 14

7) See: Horne, *Fighting In Paradise...*, Ibid, 4, 16

8) Frederick N. Rasmussen, "A half-century ago, new 50-star American flag debuted in Baltimore," The Baltimore Sun, July 2, 2010, http://articles.baltimoresun.com/2010-07-02/news/bs-md-backstory-1960-flag-20100702_1_48-star-flag-blue-canton-fort-mchenry

9) Christopher Woolf, "Historians disagree on whether 'The Star-Spangled Banner' is racist," PRI, August, 20, 2016, http://www.pri.org/stories/2016-08-30/historians-disagree-whether-star-spangled-banner-racist. Gerald Horne answers in the affirmative. "Pledging Allegiance to the Denial of the Racist History of America,"

The Real news Network, July 4, 2016, http://therealnews.com/t2/index.php?option=com_content&task=view&id=31&Itemid=74&jumival=16668#newsletter1. Re the 'slaveholding republic,' see: Gerald Horne, *Negro Comrades of the Crown: African Americans and the British Empire Fight the U.S. Before Emancipation* (New York University Press, 2012) and Gerald Horne, *The Counter-Revolution of 1776: Slave Resistance and the Origins of the United States of America*, Gerald Horne (New York University Press, 2014)

10) "Winston, Blind, Is Shifted from Hospital to Jail," The Worker, Sunday, October 9, 1960, 12

11) Benjamin J. Davis, *Upsurge In The South: The Negro People Fight For* Freedom (New Century Publishers, 1960), 22

12) Mostevets, *Henry Winston: Profile...*, Ibid, 62

13) "World Appeal Issued to Help Free Winston," The Worker, Sunday, September 25, 1960, 4

14) "Winston Case to Be Brought to UN Human Rights Commission," The Worker, Sunday, October 23, 1960, 12

15) Mike Newberry, *The Cruel And Unusual Punishment Of Henry Winston* (Harlem Committee To Free Henry Winston, No date), 16

16) "Winston Files Suit, Asks Million Dollars Damage," The Worker, Sunday, November 13, 1960, 3 and "Red Leader in Prison Sues U.S. For $1,000,000 Over Lost Sight," The New York Times, November 8, 1960

17) "Foster Urges Protest On Winston," The Worker, Sunday, October 23, 1960, 8

18) "Winston, Blind...," Ibid

19) Horne, *Black Liberation / Red Scare...*, Ibid, 305-306, 315

20) See: Jarvis Tyner, *Henry Winston Presente! Henry Winston Is In The House!* (Henry Winston 100th Anniversary Tribute program booklet, 2012, no page), text of a speech by Tyner delivered February 19, 2012, at Winston Unity Hall, CPUSA national office, 235 W. 23rd St., New York

21) Esther Cooper Jackson, ed., *Freedomways Reader: Prophets in Their Own Country* (Westview Press, 2000), Introduction, XXX

22) NYU, TAM 347, Box 21, Folder 9: James E. Jackson, *James E. Jackson Tribute at the Memorial to Henry Winston,* January 10, 1987

23) Mostevets, *Henry Winston: Profile...*, Ibid, 63-67

24) Arnold Johnson, "Winston Returned To Prison Hospital," The Worker, Sunday, April 30, 1961, 3

25) "Kennedy Orders Winston Freed; Red Leader Is Blind and Ailing," The New York Times, July 1, 1961

26) Mostevets, *Henry Winston: Profile...*, Ibid, 67

27) Mike Newberry, "Winston Says Socialist Faith Conquered Ordeal," The Worker, Sunday, July 16, 1961, 3

28) "350 Professors Urge End Of UnAmericans," The Worker, Sunday, March 26, 1961, 2

29) See: Rosemary Feurer, *Radical Unionism in the Midwest, 1900-1950* (University of Illinois Press, 2006)

30) Mike Davidow, "1,200 at Rally Call for End Of McCarran, *Smith Acts*," The Worker, Sunday, August 6, 1961, 12

31) "Oil, Chemical Workers Hit UnAmericans," The Worker, Sunday, September 3, 1961, 10

32) "Pete Seeger to Address Anti-HUAC Rally Dec. 6," The Worker, December 3, 1961, p 12

33) See: Joseph North, James Jackson and George Meyers, *Gus Hall: The Man and The Message* (New Outlook Publishers, 1970), 31, Mike Davidow, "12,000 Listen to Gus Hall In Oregon Football Field," The Worker, Sunday, February 18, 1962, 3, 11, Rob Royer, "Gus Hall Rides a Golf Cart Into Eugene and the Demise of the Commonwealth Federation," The Cascadia Courier, April 9, 2012, http://www.thecascadiacourier.com/2012/04/gus-hall-invades-eugene-and-demise-of.html and Bart, ed., *Highlights Of A Fighting History...*, Ibid, 329.

34) Art Shields, "Will Fight for Bill of Rights, CP Leaders Tell Newsmen," The Worker, Sunday, June 18, 1961

35) Mostevets, *Henry Winston: Profile...*, Ibid, p 70, 79 and "Winston Starts Home Today," New York Times, February 27, 1964

36) Mostevets, *Henry Winston: Profile...*, Ibid, p 11-14, 17, 20-28

37) NYU, TAM 132, Box 110, Folder 19: *Official Proceedings: Second National Negro Congress, October 15-17, 1937* (NNC, 1937)

38) Klehr, Haynes and Firsov, ed *The Secret World Of American Communism*, Ibid, 152-153

39) Henry Winston, "Dimitrov and Our Fight for Peace," Political Affairs, August 1982, 2 and "Young Reds Open Parley In Moscow," The New York Times, September 27, 1935

40) Mostevets, *Henry Winston: Profile...*, Ibid, 31

41) Max Hastings, *Inferno: The World At War, 1939-1945* (Vintage Books, 2012) and John Lukacs, *June 1941: Hitler and Stalin* (Yale University Press, 2006)

42) Schrecker, *The Age of McCarthyism...*, Ibid, 176

43) Henry Winston, *Old Jim Crow Has Got To Go!* (New Age Publishers, 1941), 10, 13

44) James West, "Communists in World War II," Political Affairs, September / October 1969, 94

45) Mostevets, *Henry Winston: Profile...*, Ibid, 36-38 and Martelle, *The Fear Within...*, Ibid

46) Hyman Lumer, *The Professional Informer* (New Century Publishers, 1955), 5

47) Mostevets, *Henry Winston: Profile...*, Ibid., 41, 42

48) Martelle, *The Fear Within...*, Ibid, 82, 83

49) Henry Winston, "Building the Party – Key to Building the United Front of Struggle," Political Affairs, May 1950, 59-82

50) NYU, TAM 137, Box 2, Folder 2: *Statement of Arnold Johnson In Opposition to S1194 and S.1196*

51) "Rally In Garden Barred," The New York Times, August 29, 1950

52) A. H. Raskin, "U.S. Communists Insist They Will Never Quit," The New York Times, September 10, 1950

53) "2,000 Here Attend Three Red Rallies," The New York Times, December 28, 1950

54) Winston, *Building the Party...*, Ibid

55) Stepan-Norris and Zeitlan, *Left Out...*, Ibid, 4, 19

56) Winston, *Building the Party...*, Ibid

57) Roy Hudson, "The I.L.W. U. Convention – A Victory For All Labor," Political Affairs, July 1949, 45-57

58) Winston, *Building the Party...*, Ibid; Re Smith, the NMU and Curran, see: Gerald Horne, *Red Seas: Ferdinand Smith and Radical Black Sailors in the United States and* Jamaica (New York University Press, 2009)

59) Winston, *Building the Party...*, Ibid

60) Peter Kihss, "U.S. Reds Confess Party Mistakes; Draft Reforms," The New York Times, September 23, 1956

61) NYU, TAM 137, Box 3, Folder 3: Arnold Johnson, *Rebuild the Party!,* Party Voice, April 1958

62) NYU, TAM 132, Box 109, Folder 1: *Communist Party, USA, Organizational Apparatus: Declassified FBI Report,* April 1, 1949

63) "Reds' Rally Fails To Fill The Garden," The New York Times, September 20, 1950

64) "Rally In Garden Barred," The New York Times, August 29, 1950

65) Robert C. Thompson, "The Struggle for Peaceful Co-Existence and Party Mass Ties," Political Affairs, March 1961, 27

66) Isserman, *Which Side Were You On?...*, Ibid, 244

67) Harry Raymond, "3,200 Crowd Into Our Happy Birthday Party," The Daily Worker, January 23, 1956, 1

68) NYU, TAM 137, Box 4, Folder 1: Roy Finch, "An Observer Reports On The Communist Convention," Liberation, March 1957, 4-6

69) "U.S. Communists Mark 39th Year," New York Times, September 27, 1958

70) "Communists Ask 'hands Off Cuba,'" The New York Times, Sunday, December 13, 1959

71) See: Horne, *Communist Front...*, Ibid and Peter Kihss, "Red Bail Jumpers Wreck Fund; State Takes Over to Liquidate It," The New York Times, April 15, 1952. Re the CAA, see: Von Eschen, *Race Against Empire...*, Ibid, 141-144 and Horne, *Paul Robeson...*, Ibid. Horne called the demise of the CAA a "forced liquidation,"185

72) Mostevets, *Henry Winston: Profile...*, Ibid, 53

73) NYU, TAM 132, Box 150, Folder 13: Letter from Flynn to Winston, February 4, 1962

74) NYU, TAM 132, Box 150, Folder 13: Letter from Flynn to Winston, April 17, 1962

75) NYU, TAM 132, Box 150, Folder 13: Letter from Flynn to Winston, April 26, 1962

76) NYU, TAM 132, Box 150, Folder 13: Letter from Flynn to Winston, March 23, 1963

77) NYU, TAM 132, Box 150, Folder 7: Letter from Smith to Winston, February 23, 1961

78) NYU, TAM 132, Box 150, Folder 13: Letter from Flynn to Winston, March 23, 1963

79) NYU, TAM 132, Box 150, Folder 13: Letter from Flynn to Winston, September 6, 1963

80) NYU, TAM 132, Box 150, Folder 30: Letter from Colon to Winston, September 27, 1963

81) NYU, TAM 132, Box 150, Folder 1: Letter from Bart to Winston, August 20, 1963

82) NYU, TAM 132, Box 150, Folder 1: Letter from Bart to Winston, October 15, 1963

83) NYU, TAM 132, Box 150, Folder 13: Letter from Jackson to Winston, no date (circa 1963)

84) NYU, TAM 132, Box 150, Folder 18: Letter from Lightfoot to Winston, April 29, 1962

85) NYU, TAM 132, Box 150, Folder 13: Letter from Flynn to Winston, September 6, 1963

86) NYU, TAM 132, Box 150, Folder 2: Letter from Grossman to Winston, February 10, 1964

87) NYU, TAM 132, Box 150, Folder 7: Letter from Abt to Winston, April 9, 1963

88) NYU, TAM 132, Box 150, Folder 30: Letter from Winston to Abt, no date (circa 1963)

89) NYU, TAM 132, Box 150, Folder 7: Letter from Abt to Winston, October 15, 1963

90) NYU, TAM 132, Box 150, Folder 13: Letter from Jackson to Winston, no date (circa 1963)

91) NYU, TAM 132, Box 150, Folder 7: Letter from Winston to Abt, September 30, 1963

92) NYU, TAM 347, Box 5, Folder 48: Letter from Winston to Jackson, August 28, 1963

93) NYU, TAM 347, Box 5, Folder 48: Letter from Winston to Jackson, October 8, 1963

94) Henry Winston, *New Colonialism: U.S. Style* (New Outlook Publishers, 1965)

95) Gerald Horne, *White Supremacy Confronted: U.S. Imperialism and Anti-Communism vs. the Liberation of Southern Africa, from Rhodes to Mandela* (international Publishers, 2019)

96) NYU, TAM 347, Box 5, Folder 48: Memo from Winston to Jackson, February 10, 1966

97) See: David Levering Lewis, Michael H. Nash, Daniel J. Leab, ed., *Red Activists and Black Freedom: James and Esther Jackson and the Long Civil Rights Revolution* (Routledge, 2010)

98) NYU, TAM 347, Box 13, Folder 11: *A Call To All Afro-Americans, To All Americans – To A National Conference Of Support For Africa Freedom* (no publisher, no date; circa 1966/1967)

99) NYU, TAM 347, Box 13, Folder 5: *Ad Hoc Bulletin,* Ad Hoc Committee For A Scientific Socialist Line, November 1963 (Vol. 1, No. 6)

100) Henry Winston, "Unity and Militancy For Freedom and Equality," Political Affairs, February 1968, 1-9

101) Peter Kihss, "U.S. Reds To Join Civil Rights Drive: Convention Here Warned of 'White Chauvinism,'" New York Times, June 25, 1966 and Kelley, *Hammer and Hoe...,* Ibid

102) See: Von Eschen, *Race Against Empire...,* Ibid, Horne, *Communist Front...,* Ibid, Haviland, *James and Esther Cooper Jackson...,* Ibid, and Horne, *Paul Robeson...,* Ibid, 150. Horne forcefully notes, "However, these new groupings [organizations connected to Dr. Martin Luther King, Jr.] did not have the international ties of the CRC [Civil Rights Congress, headed by communist William L. Patterson], nor the global reach of the CAA [Council on African Affairs, headed by communist Alphaeus Hunton], which amounted to a net loss for African-Americans and their allies."

103) Peter Kihss, "U.S. Communist Party Supports Negro Violence," New York Times, October 23, 1967

104) "Reds in U.S. Urged to Give More Support to Negroes," New York Times, May 5, 1969

105) Gil Green, *Terrorism – Is It Revolutionary* (New Outlook Publishers, 1970), 4

106) Horne, *White Supremacy Confronted...,* Ibid, 586

107) NYU, TAM 132, Box 110, Folder 14: Henry Winston, *Remarks of Henry Winston At The Founding Conference of NAIMSAL, Chicago, October 1973,* October 19-21, 1973

108) Ron Tyson, "7500 Demonstrate In Washington For African Liberation," Daily World, May 29, 1974, 1

109) "World meet opens to support Angola," Daily World, February 3, 1976, 4

110) Tom Foley, "MPLA able to defend gains, says Monteiro," Daily World, March 16, 1976, 3 and "Chicago to hear Monteiro Sunday," Daily World, March 16, 1976, 3

111) Victoria Missick, "South Africa condemned at special UN hearings," Daily World, June 25, 1976, 3

112) Alicia Weissman, "UN rally protests visit by Ian Smith," Daily World, October 10, 1978, 1, 11

113) "Protest wins review on visa for Nokwe," Daily World, June 25, 1976, 3

114) "Philly protest tomorrow to hit racist tennis tourney," Daily World, August 28, 1976, 9

115) "R.I. committee is building African liberation support," Daily World, March 30, 1978, 9

116) "Freedom fighter from Africa to talk at Chicago dinner," Daily World, November 2, 1978, 5 and "ZAPU leader to speak at Naimsal dinner," Daily World, December 6, 1978, 5

117) "ANC representative notes connection of struggles," Daily World, March 9, 1979, 3

118) Arlene Tyner, "Phila. Affair backs African liberation," Daily World, March 30, 1979, 10

119) Cindy Hawes, "A talk with an African labor leader," Daily World, July 31, 1979, 6

120) Mike Giocondo, "African freedom fighter links Zimbabwean-U.S. struggles," Daily World, November 7, 1979, 4

121) Re Lozano and the CPUSA: Roberta Wood, CPUSA secretary-treasurer and friend of the Lozano's, author interview, while at a CPUSA Finance Committee meeting in New York City, November 16, 2016; Emile Schepers, chair of the CPUSA International Department and former Chicago area college professor, author interview in Washington D.C., June 25, 2017; Lozano was a student of Schepers

122) Ron Johnson, "South African women seek assistance," Daily World, May 8, 1980, 7

123) Sims, author interview, August 21, 2019

124) NYU, TAM 132, Box 110, Folder 14: *Statement By John Gaetsewe, General Secretary Of The South African Congress Of Trade Unions,* March 7, 1978 and Ronald Tyson, "S. Africa unionist: 'Cut apartheid ties,'" Daily World, March 14, 1978, 3, 11

125) NYU, TAM 132, Box 110, Folder 14: *Soviet Union, Cuba & Viet Nam To Speak Out On Southern Africa At Cooper Union's Great Hall March 10,* Press Release, March 2/7, 1979 and Amadeo Richardson, "Vietnamese aide to join March 10 S. Africa fete," Daily World, February 27, 1979, 5

126) Henry Winston, "The Communist Party, Now More Than Ever," Political Affairs, September 1975, 15, 16

127) Roslyn Riddle, "Angela Davis Highlights Chicago Rally," Ann Arbor Sun, July 4, 1975, and "A Memorable Convention," Political Affairs, August 1975, 1

128) NYU, TAM 132, Box 218, Folder 25: Michael Myerson, *On The Crisis In The Party* (June 1990)

129) Arnold Becchetti, "The 21st National Convention: Toward A Mass CP," Political Affairs, September 1975, 26, 35

130) Henry Winston, "SUMMARY: Comrade Henry Winston's SPECIAL REPORT ON PARTY BUILDING," Party Organizer, June-July-August, Vol. 12, No. 4, 1978, 19-22

131) NYU, TAM 347, Box 5, Folder 48: Winston memo to Hall and Jackson, December 19, 1978

132) Henry Winston, "Marxism-Leninism: A Science for Our Time," Political Affairs, June 1983, 17

133) "1980: Year of Unity and Advance [interview with Henry Winston]," Political Affairs, January 1980, 1-2

143) Rick Nagin, "Ohio – CP Senate Vote Grows," Political Affairs, January 1981, 22

135) Ted Pearson, "Illinois – Growing Voter Independence," Political Affairs, January 1981, 13

136) Maurice Jackson, "D.C. – Municipal Elections and the Statehood Question," Political Affairs, January 1981, 26

137) Gus Hall, "Assessment of the 1982 Anti-Reagan Election Wave," Political Affairs, December 1982, 2

138) The author was part of the St. Louis, Missouri party club and met regularly with CBTU-Party leaders like Jim Wilkerson, Steve Lucius, Kenny Jones, etc., all of whom, among others, served on the St. Louis CBTU executive board

139) "Wilson Only Incumbent To Lose Seat In Primaries," St. Louis Post-Dispatch, March 9, 1983. Re Jones and the CPUSA: Jones belonged to the St. Louis area party club and met regularly with the author; he was also a long-time leader in the St. Louis Coalition of Black Trade Unionists

140) Evelina Alacron, "California Communists in Statewide Electoral Coalition," Political Affairs, January 1991, 14

141) Scott Marshall, "Toward a National Movement of the Unemployed," Political Affairs, September 1983, 3-5, 9

142) Beatrice Lumpkin, *Always Bring A Crowd: The Story of Frank Lumpkin Steelworker* (International Publishers, 1999), "Frank and Beatrice Lumpkin papers, 1940-2013, bulk 1974-1986, Biographical / historical note," Chicago History Museum, http://explore.chicagocollections.org/ead/chicagohistory/123/0864c37/) and John Bachtell, "Frank Lumpkin, 'Saint of Chicago,' dies at 93," People's World, March 10, 2010, http://www.peoplesworld.org/article/frank-lumpkin-saint-of-chicago-dies-at-9/

143)) James Strong, "Activist Call Daley Negligent In Probe Of Lozano Slaying," Chicago Tribune, January 1, 1985, http://articles.chicagotribune.com/1985-01-01/news/8501010165_1_richard-m-daley-jesus-garcia-charges and John Bachtell, "Rudy Lozano remembered as fighter for immigrant rights," People's World, June 13, 2013, http://www.peoplesworld.org/article/rudy-lozano-remembered-as-fighter-for-immigrant-worker-rights/. Re Lozano and the CPUSA: Roberta Wood, CPUSA secretary-treasurer and friend of the

Lozano's, author interview, while at a CPUSA Finance Committee meeting in New York City, November 16, 2016; Emile Schepers, chair of the CPUSA International Department and former Chicago area college professor, author interview in Washington D.C., June 25, 2017; Lozano was a student of Schepers

144) Marshall, "Toward a National Movement...," Ibid

145) Henry Winston, "The Draft Document and Some Tactical and Strategic Questions," Political Affairs, July-August 1983, 36-38

146) NYU, TAM 132, Box 150, Folder 3: Letter to Hall from Nagin, February 21, 1985

147) Central Committee, CPUSA, "Henry Winston, 1911-1986," Political Affairs, January 1987, 2

148) Jarvis Tyner, "I remember Winnie," People's Weekly World, May, 7, 2004, http://www.peoplesworld.org/article/i-remember-winnie/

149) NYU, TAM 347, Box 21, Folder 9: James E. Jackson, *James E. Jackson Tribute at the Memorial to Henry Winston,* January 10, 1987

150) Speech by Angela Davis, Sunday, February 19, 2012 at the Henry Winston Centennial Celebration, Henry Winston Unity Hall, 235 W. 23rd St., New York, NY 10011. Published in the Henry Winston 100th Anniversary Tribute program booklet, no page

Chapter Five

1) Ben Mathis-Liley, "Trump Was Recorded in 2005 Bragging About Grabbing Women 'by the Pussy,'" Slate, October 7, 2016, http://www.slate.com/blogs/the_slatest/2016/10/07/donald_trump_2005_tape_i_grab_women_by_the_pussy.html and Penn Bullock "Transcript: Donald Trump's Taped Comments About Women," The New York Times, October 8, 2016, https://www.nytimes.com/2016/10/08/us/donald-trump-tape-transcript.html?_r=0

2) Melissa Chan, "Donald Trump's 'Nasty Woman' Comment at the Presidential Debate Sets Off Social Media Firestorm," Fortune, October 20, 2016, http://fortune.com/2016/10/19/presidential-debate-nasty-woman-donald-trump and Janell Ross, "Trump's 'such a nasty woman' comment has sparked something," The Washington Post, October 20, 2016, https://www.washingtonpost.com/news/the-fix/wp/2016/10/20/trumps-such-a-nasty-woman-comment-has-sparked-something/?utm_term=.14eabf511c59

3) Aamna Mohdin, "American women voted overwhelmingly for Clinton, except the white ones," Quartz, November 9, 2016, https://qz.com/924433/ibm-thinks-its-ready-to-turn-quantum-computing-into-an-actual-business/ and Kenneth T. Walsh, "Clinton Wins Popular Vote by Nearly 3 Million Ballots," U.S. News & World Report, December 21, 2016, https://www.usnews.com/news

/ken-walshs-washington/articles/2016-12-21/hillary-clinton-wins-popular-vote-by-nearly-3-million-ballots

4) Rebecca Sinderbrand, "How Kellyanne Conway ushered in the era of 'alternative facts,'" The Washington Post, January 22, 2017, https://www.washingtonpost.com/news/the-fix/wp/2017/01/22/how-kellyanne-conway-ushered-in-the-era-of-alternative-facts/?utm_term=.65083939f5a2

5) Judith Leblanc, "Judith LeBlanc – We March for Mother Earth," C-SPAN, January 21, 2017, https://www.c-span.org/video/?422332-1/womens-march-washington-protests-new-trump-administration&start=12442

6) Sara Jeffe, "Standing Rock is everywhere, with Judith LeBlanc," February 7, 2017, https://sarahljaffe.com/2017/02/07/standing-rock-is-everywhere-with-judith-leblanc/

7) Mark Taylor-Canfield, "Seattle Divests $3 Billion From Wells Fargo as Army Approves Construction of Dakota Access Pipeline," Truthout, February 8, 2017, http://www.truth-out.org/news/item/39410-seattle-divests-3-billion-from-wells-fargo-as-army-approves-construction-of-dakota-access-pipeline

8) Jeffe, *Standing Rock is everywhere...*, Ibid

9) NYU, TAM 132, Box, 110, Folder 21: *National Conference on Indian Liberation of the Communist Party: News Release,* October 11, 1969

10) Gus Hall, *Ecology: Can we survive under capitalism* (International Publishers, 1972)

11) Judith LeBlanc, "Wounded Knee, 1973-1998: In the struggle continues," People's Weekly World, April 25, 1998 and "Upsetting Billionaires at Standing Rock [Interview with LeBlanc]," Inequality.org, September 28, 2016, http://inequality.org/standing-standing-rock/

12) "New York salutes women in struggle," People's Weekly World, March 21, 1998 and LeBlanc, author interview, 10/29/2019

13) LeBlanc, author interview, 10/29/2019

14) *Seattle Civil Rights & Labor History Project: Lonnie Nelson – Communist Party,* University of Washington, http://depts.washington.edu/civilr/nelson.htm

15) LeBlanc, "Wounded Knee...," Ibid

16) "Upsetting Billionaires...," Ibid

17) Ralph Rinaldi, "Springfield YWLL pair beat police frame-up," Daily World, October 22, 1975, 9

18) "CP announces drive for Mass. State senate," Daily World, September 21, 1976, 2, 4 and LeBlanc, author interview, 10/29/2019

19) Judith LeBlanc, "Native American Indians and Nov. 2," Daily World, October 21, 1976, 7

20) Gail Halfkenny, "CP candidate in Boston fights for rights of youth," Daily World, August 28, 1976, 9

21) "CP announces drive for Mass. State senate," Daily World, September 21, 1976, 2, 4

22) Judith LeBlanc, "Native American Indians and Nov. 2," Daily World, October 21, 1976, 7

23) Nathaniel Hibben, "Judith LeBlanc brings campaign to South Boston and Dorchester," Daily World, October 30, 1976, p 2 and Kristen Ghodsee, *Second World, Second Sex: Socialist Women's Activism and Global Solidarity during the Cold War* (Duke University Press, 2018)

24) Mike Zagarell and Mike Giocondo, "The election results – Independents Gain; No Carter Mandate," Daily World, November 4, 1976, 1, 3 and LeBlanc, author interview, 10/29/2019

25) WM. Heineken, "CP State Senate candidate in Boston gets 7.5% of vote," Daily World, November 10, 1976, 3

26) "Patrinos weighs suit for new Philly election," Daily World, May 25, 1974, 2

27) LeBlanc, author interview, 10/29/2019

28) "Polly Halfkenny gets 4,363 votes in Boston," Daily World, September 29, 1977, 3

29) Will McQuill, "Boston forum hears reports on USSR," Daily World, March 22, 1977, 9 and LeBlanc, author interview, 10/29/2019

30) Judith LeBlanc, "On Native American Indians and the Anti-Monopoly Struggle," Political Affairs, July-August 1983, 53-54

31) For a contemporary example, see: LIUNA letter (*LIUNA Joins Pipeline Crafts in Letter to the White House*) to President Obama, October 3, 2016, http://www.liuna.org/news/story/liuna-fights-for-good-jobs-building-dakota-access-pipeline and Sean Sweeney, "Standing Rock Solid with the Frackers: Are the Trades Putting Labor's Head in the Gas Oven?," New Labor Forum, March 25, 2015, http://newlaborforum.cuny.edu/2015/03/25/standing-rock-solid-with-the-frackers-is-labor-putting-its-head-in-the-gas-oven/

32) LeBlanc, "On Native American Indians...," Ibid and LeBlanc, author interview, 10/29/2019

33) "Communist women on TV: May 28 channels & times," Daily World, May 22, 1986, 12-D

34) Ron Johnson, "Learning from each other for the fightback," People's Daily World, August 7, 1986, 18-A

35) Judith LeBlanc, "On the Preconvention Party-Building Campaign," Political Affairs, May 1987, 33

36) Judith LeBlanc, "Anti-Communism, Left Unity and the Communist Party," Political Affairs, January 1989, 5-7

37) Cindy Hawes, "L.A. PDW picnic – fun, food and funds," People's Daily World, August 11, 1988, 2-A

38) Cindy Hawes, "130 parties demand end to war on Nicaragua," People's Daily World, November 14, 1988, 7-A

39) Pat Fry, "CP leader sees battle over economy," People's Daily World, November 30, 1988, 2-A

40) Judith LeBlanc, "The Communist Party and Its Ideology," Political Affairs, August 1989, 14-18

41) Judith LeBlanc, "A Communist Party for the 90s," Political Affairs, January 1992, 25-36

42) Judith LeBlanc, "Rebuild America: Jobs and Equality Campaign," Political Affairs, November 1993, 19, 20

43) "New CPUSA officers will aid people's struggles," People's Weekly World, June 27, 1992, 13

44) John Rummel, "Communist Party's equality commission maps plans," December 18, 1993, 5

45) Les Bayless, "Congress at mid-sem...," People's Weekly World, December 18, 1993, 12

46) "NY Communists explore fight against racism," People's Weekly World, January 22, 1994, 5

47) Tim Wheeler, "Communist Party leaders meet – Urge class unity, action for jobs," People's Weekly World, January 29, 1994, 4

48) Tim Wheeler, "Hook up with the World: Weeks events finalized," People's Weekly World, April 2, 1994, 3

49) "Remember Dr. King: Demand jobs & equality now! Call, fax, E-mail the White House, Congress," People's Weekly World, April 2, 1994, 3

50) "Let's talk, modem to modem," People's Weekly World, April 2, 1994, 3

51) Judith LeBlanc, "American Indians: What path to equality," People's Weekly World, May 7, 1994, 18

52) Re *People Before Profits* show, see: Guide to the Communist Party of the United States of America Records TAM.132, Tamiment Library, New York University, http://dlib.nyu.edu/findingaids/html/tamwag/tam_132/dscaspace_ccecad241e3a53e737ce984bc51d3e9e.html

53) "Communist Party national leaders meet," People's Weekly World, January 30, 1999, 2 and LeBlanc, author interview, 10/29/2019

54) Michael Cooper, "Officers in Bronx Fire 41 Shots, And an Unarmed Man Is Killed," The New York Times, February 5, 1999, https://www.nytimes.com/1999/02/05/nyregion/officers-in-bronx-fire-41-shots-and-an-unarmed-man-is-killed.html

55) Changing America, Episode 1, Chelsea Fund for Education, Released March 3, 1999

56) Changing America, Episode 2, Chelsea Fund for Education, Released April 30, 1999

57) Campbell Robertson, "Texas Executes White Supreamist for 1998 Dragging Death of James Byrd Jr," New York Times, April 24,

2019, https://www.nytimes.com/2019/04/24/us/james-byrd-jr-john-william-king.html

58) "Virginia shipyard struck," CNNMoney, April 5, 1999, https://money.cnn.com/1999/04/05/companies/shipping/

59) Changing America, Episode 4, Chelsea Fund for Education, Released April 30, 1999

60) "Striking shipyard workers confront CEO," People's Weekly World, July 3, 1999, 1, 3

61) Changing America, Episode 13, Chelsea Fund for Education, Released June 22, 1999

62) Changing America, Episode 15, Chelsea Fund for Education, Released July 6, 1999

63) "Shipyard strikers to march in D.C.," People's Weekly World, July 3, 1999 and Changing America, Episode 5, Chelsea Fund for Education, Released April 30, 1999

64) "National News; Shipyard Strike Is Settled," The New York Times, July 31, 1999, https://www.nytimes.com/1999/07/31/us/national-news-briefs-shipyard-strike-is-settled.html

65) Alexa Dimick, "A "Change" for the better on the air," People's Weekly World, July 24, 1999, 2

66) Changing America, Episode 7, Chelsea Fund for Education, Released May 11, 1999

67) Dennis McLellan, "John Randolph, 88; Tony-Winning Character Actor Was Blacklisted," The Los Angeles Times, February 27, 2004, https://www.latimes.com/archives/la-xpm-2004-feb-27-me-randolph27-story.html and Changing America, Episode 8, Chelsea Fund for Education, Released July 7, 1999

68) Changing America, Episode 10, Chelsea Fund for Education, Released June 1, 1999

69) Changing America, Episode 11, Chelsea Fund for Education, Released July 7, 1999

70) Changing America, Episode 9, Chelsea Fund for Education, Released May 25, 1999 and Steven Greenhouse, "After Scandals, New Union Leaders Turn More Aggressive," The New York Times, March 22, 1999, https://www.nytimes.com/1999/03/22/nyregion/after-scandals-new-union-leaders-turn-more-aggressive.html

71) Changing America, Episode 12, Chelsea Fund for Education, Released June 15, 1999

72) Changing America, Episode 14, Chelsea Fund for Education, Released June 29, 1999

73) Mike Quinn, "Changing America preview: 'The Empire Strikes Back,'" People's Weekly World, September 25, 1999, 16

74) Mike Quinn, "'Changing America' New season features Chavez-Thompson, Huerta," People's Weekly World, October 2, 1999, 3

75) Changing America, Season 2, Episode 1, Chelsea Fund for Education, Released September 28, 1999

76) Changing America, Season 2, Episode 2, Chelsea Fund for Education, Released October 6, 1999

77) Changing America, Season 2, Episode 9, Released November 23, 1999

78) Changing America: Battle in Seattle Special, Released January 24, 1999

79) Changing America, Texas Trail: First-Hand in Bush Land, October 10, 2000

80) LeBlanc, author interview, 10/29/2019

81) "CPUSA new leadership for a new century," People's Weekly World, March 11, 2000, 3, 15

82) Evelina Alarcon, "U.S. Communist leaders visit China," People's Weekly World, March 8, 2002, https://www.peoplesworld.org/article/u-s-communist-leaders-visit-china/

83) Jim Lane, "Texans hear CPUSA leader," People's Weekly World, March 17, 2001, 9

84) Judith LeBlanc, "Vanguard – as radical as reality," People's Weekly World, March 17, 2001, 13

85) Sam Webb, "Stopping the right-wing is still key," People's Weekly World, March 17, 2001, 13

86) Judith LeBlanc, "From our September 11, 2001 archives: Facing the future from Ground Zero," People's Weekly World, digitally published September 8, 2011, https://www.peoplesworld.org/article/from-our-september-11-2001-archives-facing-the-future-from-ground-zero-3/

87) Evelina Alarcon, "CPUSA conference urges all-out mobilization Apr. 20 march for peace and justice," People's Weekly World, March 22, 2002, https://www.peoplesworld.org/article/cpusa-conference-urges-all-out-mobilization-apr-20-march-for-peace-and-justice/

88) Evelina Alarcon, "PWW writer goes to Mideast," People's Weekly World, April 19, 2002, https://www.peoplesworld.org/article/pww-writer-goes-to-mideast/

89) Evelina Alarcon, "Eyewitness to occupation: Funds must be frozen to end conflict," People's Weekly World, April 26, 2002, https://www.peoplesworld.org/article/eyewitness-to-occupation-funds-must-be-frozen-to-end-conflict/

90) Sue Webb and John Bachtell, "Speakers say Israel and Palestine both in crisis," People's Weekly World, May 11, 2002, 16 and "Judith LeBlanc Tour 2002," People's Weekly World, May 14, https://www.peoplesworld.org/article/judith-le-blanc-tour-2002/

91) Juan Lopez, "Building Middle East peace and justice," People's Weekly World, May 31, 2002, https://www.peoplesworld.org/article/building-middle-east-peace-with-justice/

92) Judith LeBlanc, "Bush maneuvers in the Mideast," People's Weekly World, June 14, 2002, https://www.peoplesworld.org/article/bush-maneuvers-in-the-mideast/

93) John Pappademos and Evelina Alarcon, "'Eyewitness to Occupation' events," People's Weekly World, June 14, 2002, https://www.peoplesworld.org/article/eyewitness-to-occupation-events/

94) John Pappademos and Evelina Alarcon, "World reporter goes back to Israel and Palestine," People's Weekly World, October 10, 2002, https://www.peoplesworld.org/article/world-reporter-goes-back-to-israel-and-palestine/

95) Judith LeBlanc, "Reporters notebook: Occupation hurts both Palestinians, Israelis," People's Weekly World, October 24, 2002, https://www.peoplesworld.org/article/reporter-s-notebook-occupation-hurts-both-palestinians-israelis/

96) "About UFPJ," United For Peace and Justice http://www.unitedforpeace.org/about/

97) "The peace movement in the USA," Guardian: The Worker's Weekly, July 8, 2009, https://www.cpa.org.au/guardian/2009/1418/16-peace-movement-usa.html

98) LeBlanc, author interview, 10/29/2019

99) "History," United For Peace & Justice, http://www.unitedforpeace.org/about/get-involved/history/

100) Roberta Wood, "Communist meet heats up Chicago," People's Weekly World, January 30, 2003, https://www.peoplesworld.org/article/communist-meet-heats-up-chicago/

101) *History,* United For Peace & Justice (visited on 8/6/2019: http://www.unitedforpeace.org/about/get-involved/history/

102) Barbara Palmer, "Students participate in national strike against war," Stanford Report, March 12, 2003, http://news.stanford.edu/news/2003/march12/strike-312.html, Lloyd Vries, "Students Cut Class To Protest War," CBS, March 10, 2003, http://www.cbsnews.com/news/students-cut-class-to-protest-war/ and Bryan Long, "Students pencil in Iraq protest," CNN, March 5, 2003, http://www.cnn.com/2003/US/03/04/sprj.irq.college.protest/

103) Judith LeBlanc, "United for Peace and Justice!," People's Weekly World, June 19, 2003, https://www.peoplesworld.org/article/united-for-peace-and-justice/

104) Tony Pecinovsky, "Protest greets Bush at fat cat banquet," People's Weekly World, July 1, 2003, https://www.peoplesworld.org/article/protest-greets-bush-at-fat-cat-banquet/

105) Judith LeBlanc, "Together a peaceful world is possible," People's Weekly World, August 7, 2003, https://www.peoplesworld.org/article/together-a-peaceful-world-is-possible/

106) "Japanese CP and CPUSA meet in Nagasaki," People's Weekly World, September 12, 2003, https://www.peoplesworld.org/article/japanese-cp-and-cpusa-meet-in-nagasaki/

107) "Peace groups vow to march," People's Weekly World, August 21, 2004, https://www.peoplesworld.org/article/peace-groups-vow-to-march/

108) Judith LeBlanc, "From Aug. 29 to Election Day: Mass action can defeat the Bush agenda," People's Weekly World, https://www.peoplesworld.org/article/from-aug-29-to-election-day-mass-action-can-defeat-the-bush-agenda/

109) Judith LeBlanc, "Peace movement at a turning point," People's Weekly World, September 23, 2005, https://www.peoplesworld.org/article/peace-movement-at-a-turning-point/

110) "Make levees, not war: 300,000 marchers say End Iraq war," People's Weekly World, September 30, 2005, https://www.peoplesworld.org/article/make-levees-not-war-300-000-marchers-say-end-iraq-war/

111) "Don't worry, well [sic] raise the money," People's Weekly World, October 28, 2005, https://www.peoplesworld.org/article/don-t-worry-we-ll-raise-the-money/

112) Jennifer Barnett and Dan Margolis, "Holiday season events raise funds and spirits," People's Weekly World, December 9, 2005, https://www.peoplesworld.org/article/holiday-season-events-raise-funds-and-spirits/

113) "Stop the war meet calls for worldwide demos," People's Weekly World, January 13, 2006, https://www.peoplesworld.org/article/stop-the-war-meet-calls-for-worldwide-demos/

114) "United For Peace and Justice Helps Organize Million Doors for Peace," People's Weekly World, August 23, 2008, https://www.peoplesworld.org/article/united-for-peace-and-justice-helps-organize-million-doors-for-peace/

115) "Cancel Talisman Sabre war games!," Guardian, July 8, 2009, https://www.cpa.org.au/guardian/2009/1418/06-cancel-telisman-sabre.html

116) "The peace movement in the USA," Guardian, July 8, 2009, https://www.cpa.org.au/guardian/2009/1418/16-peace-movement-usa.html

117) Kevin Martin, "JudithPalooza! Honoring A Long Distance Runner For Peace And Justice," Peace Action, https://www.peaceaction.org/2015/04/15/judithpalooza-honoring-a-long-distance-runner-for-peace-and-justice/

118) Judith LeBlanc, "How we won the 'no' in #NoDAPL – and what we must take on next," Nation of Change, December 6, 2016, https://www.nationofchange.org/2016/12/08/won-no-nodapl-must-take-next/

119) Maggie Astor, "A Look at Where North Dakota's Voter ID Controversy Stands," The New York Times, October 19, 2018, https://www.nytimes.com/2018/10/19/us/politics/north-dakota-voter-identification-registration.html?module=inline and Maggie Astor,

"In North Dakota, Native Americans Try to Turn an ID Law to Their Advantage," The New York Times, October 30, 2018, https://www.nytimes.com/2018/10/30/us/politics/north-dakota-voter-id.html

120) Danielle McLean, "Native Americans overcome North Dakota's restrictive voter ID laws, turn out in record numbers," Think Progress, November 8, 2018, https://thinkprogress.org/native-americans-turned-out-in-record-numbers-to-vote-despite-north-dakotas-restrictive-id-laws-35ad1d116ec9/

121) "Native Nations Rise March and Rally," C-Span, March 10, 2017, https://www.c-span.org/video/?425181-1/members-standing-rock-sioux-tribe-hold-protest-white-house&start=363

Chapter Six

1) W. J. Tettey, K. P. Puplampu and B. J. Berman, ed., *Critical Perspectives in Politics and Socio-Economic Development in Ghana* (Brill, 2003), 120

2) Dennis Laumann, *Colonial Africa: 1884-1994* (Oxford University Press, 2013), 62-65

3) George B. Murphy, Jr., "William Alphaeus Hunton: His Roots In Black America," Freedomways, Vol. 10, No. 3, 249

4) See: Horne, *White Supremacy Confronted...*, Ibid. For an analysis of Soviet and China competition to win over national liberation movements, see: Jeremy Friedman, *Shadow Cold War: The Sino-Soviet Competition for the Third World* (University of North Carolina Press, 2015)

5) Clarence G. Contee, "W.E.B. Du Bois and the Encyclopedia Africana," The Crisis, November 1970, 379

6) Horne, *Black & Red...*, Ibid, p 344 and Murphy, Jr., "William Alphaeus Hunton...," Ibid

7) Contee, "W.E.B. Du Bois and the...," Ibid, p 378

8) Herbert Aptheker, ed., *The Correspondence of W. E. B. Du Bois: Volume III Selections, 1944-1963* (University of Massachusetts Press, 1997), 458, 459

9) James T. Campbell, *Middle Passages: African American Journeys to Africa, 1787-2005* (The Penguin Group, 2007) and *William Alphaeus Hunton Papers, 1926-1967*, New York Public Library Archives & Manuscripts: Biographical / Historical Information, http://archives.nypl.org/scm/20646

10) W. Alphaeus Hunton, "Recapturing A Buried Past," Daily World, February 21, 1970, M-3

11) Campbell, *Middle Passage...*, Ibid and Contee, "W.E.B. Du Bois and the...," Ibid, 379

12) NYU, TAM 347, Box 8, Folder 5: Letter from Dorothy Hunton to Esther Cooper Jackson, no date (early 1966)

13) NYU, TAM 347, Box 8, Folder 5: Letter from Dorothy Hunton to Esther Cooper Jackson, August 28, 1966

14) NYU, TAM 347, Box 8, Folder 16: Letter from Dorothy Hunton to Esther Cooper Jackson, December 8, 1966

15) Alan S. Oser, "African Encyclopedia Still Alive, Scholar Ousted by Ghana Says," The New York Times, January 29, 1967

16) Contee, "W.E.B. Du Bois and the...," Ibid, 379

17) Dorothy Hunton, *Alphaeus Hunton: The Unsung Valiant* (self-published, 1986), 58

18) Horne, *White Supremacy Confronted...*, Ibid

19) *William Alphaeus Hunton Papers...*, Ibid, Von Eschen, *Race Against Empire...*, Ibid, 60, James Hunter Meriwether, *Proudly We Can Be Africans: Black Americans and Africa, 1935-1961* (University of North Carolina Press, 2002), 61 and Paul Finkelman, ed., *Volume 1 – Encyclopedia Of African American History, 1896 To The Present: From The Age Of Segregation To The Twenty-First Century* (Oxford University Press, 2009), 475

20) Gellman, *Death Blow to Jim Crow...*, Ibid, 115 and Doxey A. Wilkerson, "William Alphaeus Hunton: A Life That Made A Difference," Freedomways, Vol. 10, No. 3 (Third Quarter), 1970, 254

21) Solomon, *The Cry Was Unity...*, Ibid, 304 and *William Alphaeus Hunton Papers...*, Ibid

22) Naison, *Communists in Harlem...*, Ibid, 177-178

23) Jonathan Holloway, *Lecture 12 – Depression and Double V* (continued) [February 17, 2010], Open Yale courses, http://oyc.yale.edu/transcript/111/afam-162

24) Gilmore, *Defying Dixie...*, Ibid, 308 and Solomon, *The Cry Was Unity...*, Ibid, 303

25) Holloway, *Lecture 12 – Depression and Double V...*, Ibid

26) Solomon, *The Cry Was Unity...*, Ibid, 303, Naison, *Communists in Harlem...*, Ibid, 183 and Gellman, *Death Blow to Jim Crow...*, Ibid, 155

27) Lightfoot, *Chicago Slums...*, Ibid, 70

28) Naison, *Communists in Harlem...*, Ibid, 177-178

29) Von Eschen, *Race Against Empire...*, Ibid and Meriwether, *Proudly We Can Be Africans...*, Ibid

30) Naison, *Communists in Harlem...*, Ibid, 179-180

31) Horne, *Black Revolutionary...*, Ibid, 87

32) Gwendolyn Mildo Hall, ed., *A Black Communist In The Freedom Struggle: The Life Of Harry Haywood* (University of Minnesota Press, 2012), 224

33) Gunnar Myrdal, *An American Dilemma, Volume 2: The Negro Problem and Modern Democracy* (Harper & Row, Publishers / Transaction Publishers, 2009 / 1996), 817

34) Naison, *Communists in Harlem...*, Ibid, 179-180

35) Solomon, *The Cry Was Unity...*, Ibid, 304

36) *The John P. Davis Collection: The Forgotten Civil Rights Leader.* Rare Pamphlets: John P. Davis Collection: General Rare Pamphlets Collection, http://www.collection.johnpdaviscollection.org/

37) *William Alphaeus Hunton Papers...*, Ibid, Wilkerson, "William Alphaeus Hunton: A Life ...," Ibid, Finkelman, ed., *Volume 1 – Encyclopedia Of African American History...*, Ibid, 475 and Hunton, *Alphaeus Hunton...*, Ibid, 47, 49

38) Horne, *Communist Front...*, Ibid and Horne, *Black Revolutionary...*, Ibid

39) Wilkerson, "William Alphaeus Hunton: A Life ...," Ibid, 255 and Craig Simpson, "Shootings by DC Police Spark Fight Against Brutality, 1936-41," Washington Area Spark, http://washingtonspark.wordpress.com/tag/national-negro-congress/

40) Hunton, *Alphaeus Hunton...*, Ibid, 47

41) See, for example: Robeson, *The East Is Black...*, Ibid

42) Wilkerson, "William Alphaeus Hunton: A Life ...," Ibid, and Simpson, *Shootings by...*, Ibid

43) Gellman, *Death Blow to Jim Crow...*, Ibid, 130

44) Wilkerson. "William Alphaeus Hunton: A Life...," Ibid, 255

45) Myrdal, *An American Dilemma...*, Ibid, 818

46) Gilmore, *Defying Dixie...*, Ibid, 308

47) NYU, TAM 132, Box 110, Folder 19: Official Proceedings: Second National Negro Congress, October 15-17, 1937 (NNC, 1937)

48) Brenda Gayle Plummer, *Rising Wind: Black Americans and U.S. Foreign Affairs, 1935-1960* (University of North Carolina Press, 1996), 190

49) Haviland, *James and Esther Cooper Jackson...*, Ibid, Lewis, Nash, Leab, ed., *Red Activists and Black Freedom...*, Ibid

50) Lightfoot, *Chicago Slums...*, Ibid, 73

51) Elizabeth Davey and Rodney Clark, ed., *Remember My Sacrifice: The Autobiography Of Clinton Clark, Tenant Farm Organizer And Early Civil Rights Activist* (Louisiana State University Press, 2007), Introduction lvi

52) Lewis, Nash, Leab, ed., *Red Activists and Black Freedom...*, Ibid, 26

53) Robin D. G. Kelley: *Christopher Columbus Alston: Organizer, Fighter and Historian,* Marxist Internet Archive, https://www.marxists.org/history/etol/newspape/atc/2514.html

54) Lewis, Nash, Leab, ed., *Red Activists and Black freedom...*, 23-27

55) Davey and Clark, ed., *Remember My Sacrifice...*, Ibid

56) Gilmore, *Defying Dixie...*, 309

57) Waldo Martin, *"A Dream Deferred": The Southern Negro Youth Congress, The Student Nonviolent Coordinating Committee, And The Politics Of Historical Memory,* http://hutchinscenter.fas.harvard.edu/sites/all/files/Waldo%20Martin%20A%20Dream%20Deferred%20

-%20SNYC%20SNCC%20and%20the%20Politics%20of%20Historical%20Memory.pdf

58) Duberman, *Paul Robeson...*, Ibid, 258

59) Finkelman, ed., *Volume 1 – Encyclopedia Of African American History...*, Ibid, 475

60) *William Alphaeus Hunton Papers...*, Ibid

61) Holloway, *Lecture 12 – Depression and Double V...*, Ibid

62) Gilmore, *Defying Dixie...*, p 310 and Holloway, *Lecture 12 – Depression and Double V...*, Ibid

63) Andrew E. Kersten, *A. Phillip Randolph: A Life in the Vanguard* (Roman & Littlefield Publishers, Inc., 2007), 44

64) Gellman, *Death Blow to Jim Crow...*, Ibid, 151, 155, 156

65) See: Philip Yale Nicholson, *Labor's Story In The United States* (Temple University Press, 2004), Gilbert Jonas, *Freedom's Sword: The NAACP and the Struggle Against Racism in America, 1909-1969* (Routledge, 2005), Robert H. Zieger, *For Jobs And Freedom: Race And Labor In America Since 1865* (University Press of Kentucky, 2007), and Philip S. Foner, *Organized Labor & The Black Worker, 1619-1981* (International Publishers, 1981)

66) Robert L. Allen, *The Brotherhood of Sleeping Car Porters: C.L. Dellums and the Fight for Fair Treatment and Civil Rights* (Paradigm Publishers, 2015), 47-48, 58

67) For example, see: Judith Stepan-Norris and Maurice Zeitlan, *Left Out: Reds and America's Industrial Unions* (Cambridge University Press, 2002), Clarence Taylor, *Reds At The Blackboard: Communism, Civil Rights, and the New York City Teachers Union* (Columbia University Press, 2011), Bruce Nelson, *Workers on the Waterfront: Seaman, Longshoremen, and Unionism in the 1930s* (University of Illinois Press, 1990), Roger Keeran, *The Communist Party and the Auto-Workers' Union* (International Publishers, 1986), Rosemary Feurer, *Radical Unionism In The Midwest, 1900-1950* (University of Illinois Press, 2006), James L. Lorence, *The Unemployed People's Movement: Leftists, Liberals, And Labor In Georgia, 1929-1941* (University of Georgia Press, 2011), Gerald Horne, *Fighting In Paradise: Labor Unions, Racism, And Communists In The Making Of Modern Hawaii* (University of Hawaii Press, 2011), Gerald Horne, *Class Struggle In Hollywood, 1930-1950: Moguls, Mobsters, Stars, Reds, & Trade Unionists* (University of Texas Press, 2001), Michael Dennis, *Blood On Steel: Chicago Steelworkers And The Strike Of 1937* (Johns Hopkins University Press, 2014)

68) Zieger, *For Jobs And Freedom...*, Ibid, 90

69) Gerald Horne, *Red Seas: Ferdinand Smith and Radical Black Sailors in the United States and* Jamaica (New York University Press, 2009)

70) Von Eschen, *Race Against Empire...*, Ibid, 47-53, Adolf Sturmthal, "Discussions And Communications: The Crisis of the WFTU,"

ILR Review, Vol. 1, No 4 (July 1948), 630. For a brief history of the WFTU, see: *World Federation of Trade Unions, 1) The Founding Congress,* http://www.wftucentral.org/history/. Anthony Carew, *Labour under the Marshall Plan: The politics of productivity and the marketing of management science* (Manchester University Press, 1987), p 60, 70. Ironically, it would be a former communist, Jay Lovestone, who would be the "biggest contributor to the molding of postwar AFL international policy." Lovestone eventually became a paid CIA informant. See: Kevin K. Gaines, *Black Expatriates and the Civil Rights Era: American Africans in Ghana* (University of North Carolina Press, 2006), 97

71) "The International Confederations of Free Trade Unions," R.F., The World Today, Vol. 9, No. 1 (January 1953)

72) Horne, *The Rise & Fall...,* Ibid, 86

73) Von Eschen, *Race Against Empire...,* Ibid, 51-52

74) Horne, *Black Liberation / Red Scare...,* Ibid, 201

75) Gellman, Death Blow..., Ibid, 143, 144

76) Hunton, *Alphaeus Hunton...,* Ibid, 55, 82

77) Horne, *Black Revolutionary...,* Ibid, 99

78) Paul Kengor, *The Communist* (Threshold Editions/Mercury Ink, 2012), 81

79) Erik Gellman, "When Fighting Racism Meant Fighting Economic Exploitation," interview by Shawn Gude, Jacobin, March 12, 2019, https://www.jacobinmag.com/2019/03/national-negro-congress-jim-crow-gellman

80) "1941 Cabal Of Reds In Ohio Described," New York Times, July 13, 1950

81) Gilmore, *Defying Dixie...,* 314, 351

82) Hunton, *Alphaeus Hunton...,* Ibid, 51, 52

83) Frederick N. Rasmussen, "George Aloysius Meyers, 86, Communist Party member," Baltimore Sun, October 21, 1999, http://articles.baltimoresun.com/1999-10-21/news/9910210183_1_communist-party-meyers-party-members

84) Gettleman *"No Varsity Teams"...,* Ibid, 342

85) "Carver School Opens Tonight," Daily Worker, October 2, 1944, 11

86) Wilkerson. "William Alphaeus Hunton: A Life...," Ibid, 255 and Finkelman, ed., *Volume 1 – Encyclopedia Of African American History...,* Ibid, 475

87) Paul Robeson, Jr., *The Undiscovered Paul Robeson: Quest for Freedom, 1939 – 1976* (John Wiley & Sons, Inc., 2010), 10

88) Von Eschen, *Race Against Empire...,* Ibid, 17-21

89) Hunton, *Alphaeus Hunton...,* Ibid, 58

90) Duberman, *Paul Robeson...,* Ibid, 258

91) Horne, *Paul Robeson...,* Ibid, 103

92) Von Eschen, *Race Against Empire...,* Ibid, 20

93) Eric Arnesen, *Civil Rights and the Cold War At Home: Postwar Activism, Anticommunism, and the Decline of the Left,* George Washington University, January 2012, 31

94) Horne, *White Supremacy Confronted...,* Ibid

95) Paul Robeson, *Here I Stand* (Othello Associates, Inc., 1958), 127

96) Re Robeson and the CPUSA, See: Gus Hall, "Paul Robeson: An American Communist," Communist Party, USA (text of a centennial tribute speech delivered on May 31, 1998, at the Winston Unity Auditorium, CP national office, 235 W. 23rd St., New York, NY), 3, 6, 8. Later reprinted as Gus Hall, "Paul Robeson: Artist, Freedom Fighter, Hero, American Communist," Political Affairs, July, 1998. Hall writes: "My own most precious moments with Paul were when I met with him to accept his dues and renew his yearly membership in the CPUSA. I and other Communist leaders, like Henry Winston...met with Paul to brief him on politics and Party policies and to discuss his work and struggles." See, also: Vijay Prashad, "Comrade Robeson: A Centennial Tribute to an American Communist," Social Scientist, Vol. 25, No. 7/8 (Jul.-Aug. 1997), 40, 41. Prashad, however, quotes from the above. Gerald Horne wondered if Robeson had been a member of the Communist Party of Great Britain, which was "more of a likelihood than U.S. membership." See: Gerald Horne, *Paul Robeson: The Artist as Revolutionary* (Pluto Press, 2016), 6. Martin Duberman notes that Robeson offered to publicly join the CPUSA in 1951 out of solidarity with his beleaguered comrades, but that the proposal was rejected by the Party's leadership. See: Martin Duberman, *Paul Robeson: A Biography* (The New Press, 1989), 420. While Robeson's membership in the CPUSA is contested, it is apparent he did not hesitate to align himself with the CPUSA, its leadership and its policies.

97) Meriwether *Proudly We Can be Africans...,* Ibid, 61, 62 and Finkelman, ed., *Volume 1 – Encyclopedia Of African American History...,* 475, 476

98) Campbell, *Middle Passages...,* Ibid, 337 and Von Eschen, *Race Against Empire...,* 60, 122

99) Hunton, *Alphaeus Hunton...,* Ibid, 62, 65

100) Robeson, *Here I Stand,* Ibid, 127

101) Hunton, *Alphaeus Hunton...,* Ibid, 57

102) James Pope, "Exploring the Parallels Between the U.S. Civil Rights Movement and the African Liberation Movement," Poverty & Race, May/June 2010, http://www.prrac.org/full_text.php?text_id=1269&item_id=12371&newsletter_id=111&header=Race+%2F+Racism&kc=1)

103) Carol Anderson, *Eyes Off The Prize: The United Nations and the African American Struggle for Human Rights, 1944-1955* (Cambridge University Press, 2003), 163

104) Campbell, *Middle Passages...,* Ibid, 337 and Meriwether, *Proudly We Can be Africans...,* Ibid, 61

105) *The Road to Democracy Series (Book 3) International Solidarity, Part II* (Unisa Press, 2008, South African Democracy Trust), 754

106) Von Eschen, *Race Against Empire...*, Ibid, 20

107) Edward O. Erhagbe, "Assistance and Conflict: The African Diaspora and Africa's Development in the Twenty-first Century," Africa Development, Vol. XXXII, No. 2, 2007, 32

108) Hunton, *Alphaeus Hunton...*, Ibid, p 63

109) Campbell, *Middle Passage...*, Ibid, p 339

110) Horne, *Communist Front...*, Ibid

111) Zecker, *"A Road to Peace and Freedom"...*, Ibid

112) "Meeting Aids South Africans," The New York Times, January 8, 1946

113) Helen Simon, "4,000 Give Food, Urge Liberty for Africans," Daily Worker, January 9, 1946, 8

114) Alphaeus Hunton, "Today's Guest Column: Harlem Rallies to Aid Famine-Stricken Africa," Daily Worker, January 3, 1946, 7

115) Alphaeus Hunton, "Today's Guest Column: Hunger, Disease, Fascist Repression - South Africa," Daily Worker, December 6, 1945, 7

116) W.A. Hunton, "Progress in South Africa," The New York Times, May 17, 1947

117) "Colonial Empires Assailed In Rally," The New York Times, June 7, 1946

118) Francis Njubi Nesbitt, *Race for Sanctions: African Americans against Apartheid, 1946-1994* (Indiana University Press, 2004), 19, 20

119) Pope, *Exploring the Parallels...*, Ibid and Von Eschen, *Race for Sanctions...*, Ibid, 27

120) Roberta Wood's comment on manuscript; in author's possession

121) "Home from South Africa: Angela Davis, Charlene Mitchell plan national report-back tour," Daily World, September 21, 1991, 2

122) Pope, *Exploring the Parallels...*, Ibid and Nesbitt, *Race for Sanctions...*, Ibid, 27

123) Alphaeus Hunton, "Today's Guest Column: Trade Unionism in Nigeria," Daily Worker, September 28, 1944, 7

124) Robeson, *Here I Stand*, Ibid, 127

125) Alphaeus Hunton, "Today's Guest Column: Two Letters From South Africa," Daily Worker, February 8, 1945, 7

126) Pope, *Exploring the Parallels...*, Ibid

127) Von Eschen, *Race Against Empire...*, Ibid, 3

128) Horne, *Paul Robeson...*, Ibid, 150

129) Erhagbe, *Assistance and Conflict...*, Ibid

130) Alphaeus Hunton, "Today's Guest Column: Textbook for Conference On Colonial Freedom," Daily Worker, July 20, 1944, 7

131) See: Horne, *White Supremacy Confronted...*, Ibid, Von Eschen, *Race Against Empire...*, Ibid, and Nicholas Grant, *Winning Our Freedoms Together: African Americans and Apartheid, 1945–1960* (University of North Carolina Press, 2017)

132) Alphaeus Hunton, "Today's Guest Column: People of Africa Learn From the USSR," Daily Worker, August 3, 1944, 7

133) Alphaeus Hunton, "Today's Guest Column: 'Back to Africa' Cry Is Leveled Against Teheran," Daily Worker, August 17, 1944, 7

134) "Map Nonpartisan Drive For Negro Registration," Daily Worker, September 2, 1944, 5

135) Alphaeus Hunton, "Today's Guest Column: Negro People Concerned With Africa's Future," Daily Worker," August 24, 1944, 7

136) Alphaeus Hunton, "Today's Guest Column: Role of U.S. Elections In Future of Colonial Peoples," Daily Worker, September 14, 1944, 7

137) Alphaeus Hunton, "Today's Guest Column: South African Native Labor Movement Growing," Daily Worker, October 5, 1944, 7

138) Alphaeus Hunton, "Today's Guest Column: Johannesburg Riot Reflects a World Problem," Daily Worker, November 9, 1944, 9

139) Alphaeus Hunton, "Today's Guest Column: A New Deal for Colonial and Dependent Peoples," Daily Worker, November 23, 1944, 7

140) Alphaeus Hunton, "Today's Guest Column: South Africa's Residence Law And the Reprisal by India," Daily Worker, November 30, 1944, 7

141) Alphaeus Hunton, "Today's Guest Column: Negro People Going Forward With Roosevelt," Daily Worker, November 2, 1944, 7

142) Alphaeus Hunton, "Today's Guest Column: Colonial Peoples Look Forward as 1945 Opens," Daily Worker, January 4, 1945, 7

143) Alphaeus Hunton, "Today's Guest Column: British Guiana's Labor Delegate to the London Parley," Daily Worker, January 25, 1945, 7

144) Alphaeus Hunton, "Today's Guest Column: Disquieting British Views on the Colonies," Daily Worker, February 1, 1945, 7

145) Alphaeus Hunton, "Today's Guest Column: Two Letters From South Africa," Daily Worker, February 8, 1945, 7 and Kelley, *Hammer and Hoe...*, Ibid

146) Alphaeus Hunton, "Today's Guest Column: Perspectives For Africa's Development," Daily Worker, April 5, 1945, 7

147) Alphaeus Hunton, "Today's Guest Column: The Westbrook Pegler Of Negro Journalism," Daily Worker, March 8, 1945, 7

148) Alphaeus Hunton, "Today's Guest Column: Lippmann Sees Colonies Through Col. Blimp's Glasses," Daily Worker, March 29, 1945, 7

149) Alphaeus Hunton, "Today's Guest Column: Hull Defined The Solution," Daily Worker, May 24, 1945, 11

150) Alphaeus Hunton, "Today's Guest Column: The Charter and the Colonial Countries," Daily Worker, July 3, 1945, 12

151) Duberman, *Paul Robeson: A Biography,* Ibid, 296

152) Alphaeus Hunton, "Today's Guest Column: A Voice from South Africa," Daily Worker, July 6, 1945, 12

153) Alphaeus Hunton, "Today's Guest Column: Why Imperialists Get South Africa's Help," Daily Worker, December 13, 1945, 7

154) Horne, *White Supremacy Confronted...,* Ibid

155) Alphaeus Hunton, "Today's Guest Column: Dangers In U.S. Pacific Policy," Daily Worker, August 30, 1945, 7

156) Pomeroy, *The Forest...,* Ibid, Pomeroy, *Bilanggo...,* Ibid

157) Alphaeus Hunton, "Today's Guest Column: The East Is Fed Up With Promises," Daily Worker, September 27, 1945, 7

158) "Today's Gues Column: Fate of Indonesia Signpost Of Future – It's Up To The People," Daily Worker, November 15, 1945, 7

159) Hannah Beech, "U.S. Stood By as Indonesia Killed a Half-Million People, Papers Show," The New York Times, October 18, 2017, https://www.nytimes.com/2017/10/18/world/asia/indonesia-cables-communist-massacres.html

160) Hunton, *Today's Gues Column: Fate of Indonesia...,* Ibid

161) Alphaeus Hunton, "Today's Guest Column: Thanksgiving Milestones," Daily Worker, November 22, 1945, 7

162) Alphaeus Hunton, "Today's Guest Column: 11 Badges of Serfdom in South Africa," Daily Worker, December 20, 1945, 7

163) Alphaeus Hunton, *Africa fight for Freedom* (New Century Publishers, March 1950), 5, 10-15

164) "Robeson At Korea Rally," The New York Times, July 4, 1950

165) "Rally In Garden Barred," The New York Times, August 29, 1950

166) "Robeson Backers May Picket Garden In Protest Against the Ban on Meet," The New York Times, September 2, 1950

167) Hunton, *Alphaeus Hunton...,* Ibid, 82

168) Horne, *White Supremacy Confronted...,* Ibid

169) Minter, Hovey and Cobb Jr., ed., *No Easy Victories...,* Ibid, http://www.noeasyvictories.org/select/01_hunton.php

170) NYU, TAM 347, Box 13, Folder 52: Alphaeus Hunton, *Spotlight On Africa,* CAA Newsletter, February 1, 1952 (Issue 1, Vol. 1)

171) *William Alphaeus Hunton Papers...,* Ibid

172) Anderson, *Eyes Off The Prize...,* Ibid, 164, 165

173) *The Road to Democracy in South Africa...,* Ibid

174) Duberman, *Paul Robeson: A Biography,* Ibid, 330

175) Herbert Aptheker, *History and Reality* (Cameron Associates, Inc., 1955), 119 and Gilmore, *Defying Dixie...,* Ibid, 436, 437

176) "African Affairs Unit Avoids Partisanship," The New York Times, February 3, 1948

177) Duberman, *Paul Robeson: A Biography,* Ibid, 331

178) George Streator, "Rift In Negro Unit Is Laid To Leftists," The New York Times, April 6, 1948

179) Duberman, *Paul Robeson: A Biography,* Ibid, 331

180) "Hammond Balks At Rift," The New York Times, April 8, 1948

181) Duberman, *Paul Robeson: A Biography,* Ibid, 332-333

182) "Battles Left Wing For Groups Office," The New York Times, May 29, 1948 and Duberman, *Paul Robeson: A Biography,* Ibid, 333

183) Alphaeus Hunton and Louis Burnham, "'Fight for 12 Is Fight for Negroes,'" Daily Worker, August 9, 1949, 5

184) Russell Porter, "Bail of 14 Reds Voided Again; New Bonds Required Today," The New York Times, July 17, 1951, Washington, *The Other Blacklist...,* Ibid, 140, Plummer, *Rising Wind...,* Ibid, 191, Von Eschen, *Race Against Empire...,* Ibid, 137, Russell Porter, "Dashiell Hammett And Hunton Jailed In Red Bail Inquiry," The New York Times, July 10, 1951, and "Judge Revokes Bail of 14 Reds: Must Get New Money Or Go to Jail," The Pittsburgh Press, July 16, 1951, p 2, http://news.google.com/newspapers?nid=1144&dat=19510716&id=ADAbAAAAIBAJ&sjid=d00EAAAAIBAJ&pg=6156,19448

185) Horne, *Black Revolutionary...,* Ibid, 138, Russell Porter, "Judge Seizes Bail Of 4 Fugitive Reds; Its Donors Sought," The New York Times, July 4, 1951, Peter Kihss, "Red Bail Jumpers Wreck Fund, State takes Over to Liquidate," The New York Times, April 15, 1952 and "Red's Bail Fund, frozen by Court," The New York Times, May 6, 1952

186) Russell Porter, "Red Bail Trustees Also Defy State," The New York Times, August 1, 1951 and "State Ends Query Of 4 On Red Bail," The New York Times, September 12, 1951

187) Zecker, *"A Road to Peace and Freedom"...,* Ibid and Author J. Sabin, *Red Scare in Court: New York Versus the International Workers Order* (University of Pennsylvania Press, 1993)

188) "Fields Loses Appeal On Contempt term," The New York Times, December 4, 1951

189) Gil Green, *Cold War Fugitive: A Personal Story Of The McCarthy Years* (International Publishers, 1984), 97

190) "Reds' Bail Fund Will Go Back to Donors, Who Will be Disclosed Only to the F.B.I.," The New York Times, July 1, 1952

191) NYU, TAM 681, Box 1, Folder – Correspondence: Robeson, CAA: Letter from Robeson to Ben Segal, October 29, 1953 and November 10, 1953

192) Albert E. Kahn, *McCarthy On Trial* (Cameron & Kahn, 1954), 9, 11, 26, 27

193) Campbell, *Middle Passage...,* Ibid, 339 and Von Eschen, *Race Against Empire...,* Ibid, 143

194) Horne, *Black Revolutionary...,* Ibid, 138

195) Hunton, *Alphaeus Hunton...,* Ibid, 91

196) NYU, TAM 132, Box 112, Folder 4: Letter from Herman P. Osborne, April 15, 1973

197) Robeson, *Here I Stand,* Ibid, 128

198) Niebyl-Proctor Marxist Library: Spotlight on Africa, May 1955 (XIV, 5)

199) Hunton, *Alphaeus Hunton...,* Ibid, 94 and Campbell, *Middle Passage...,* Ibid, 339

200) NYU, TAM 134, Box 3, Folder 8: Letters from Hunton to Morford, February 11, 1957 and May 11, 1957

201) Alphaeus Hunton, *Decision in Africa: Sources of Current Conflict* (International Publishers, 1957), 9, Campbell, *Middle Passage...,* Ibid, 339 and Wilkerson, "William Alphaeus Hunton, A Life...," Ibid

202) P.L. Prattis, "The Angry Truth," Pittsburgh Courier, January 11, 1958

203) NYU, TAM 134, Box 3, Folder 8: Letter from Hunton to Mr. Holman, November 14, 1957

204) NYU, TAM 134, Box 3, Folder 8: Letter from Morford to Friends of the National Council, December 10, 1957

205) NYU, TAM 134, Box 3, Folder 8: Letter from Hunton to Morford, January 7, 1958

206) Hunton, *Decision in Africa...,* Ibid, 218-229

207) Campbell, *Middle Passage...,* Ibid, 339

208) Alphaeus Hunton, "Central Africa and Freedom," Political Affairs, April 1959, 48

209) Dennis Laumann, "A Soviet View on Southern African Liberation Movements," Journal of African History, Vol. 52, Issue 3 (Nov. 2011), 414

210) Hunton, *Alphaeus Hunton...,* Ibid, 96, 104, 105, 121, 122, 124

211) Alphaeus Hunton, "Upsurge In Africa," Masses & Mainstream, February 1950, 16

212) Meriwether, *Proudly We Can be Africans...,* Ibid, 227 and Emmanuel Gerard and Bruce Kuklick, *Death In The Congo: Murdering Patrice Lumumba* (Harvard University Press, 2015)

213) Mike Newberry, "A Talk With Editor Of 'Freedomways,'" The Worker, Sunday, June 18, 1961, 9

214) Hunton, *Alphaeus Hunton...,* Ibid, 114, 118, 126

215) *William Alphaeus Hunton Papers...,* Ibid

216) Hakim Adi and Marika Sherwood, *Pan-African History: Political Figures from Africa and the Diaspora Since 1787* (Routledge, 2003), 94

217) Alan S. Oser, "African Encyclopedia Still Alive, Scholar Ousted by Ghana Says," The New York Times, January 29, 1967

218) Henry Winston, *Strategy for a Black Agenda: A Critique of New theories of Liberation in the United States and Africa* (International Publishers, 1973), 11, 15

219) Adi and Sherwood, *Pan-African History...*, Ibid, 94

220) NYU, TAM 347, Box 8, Folder 5: Letter from Dorothy Hunton to Esther Cooper Jackson, February 8, 1970

221) Von Eschen, *Race Against Empire...*, Ibid, 57

222) Wilkerson, "William Alphaeus Hunton, A Life...," Ibid

223) "William Alphaeus Hunton," Daily World, Thursday, January 15, 1970, 7

224) "W. Alphaeus Hunton, fighting scholar," Daily World, Thursday, January 15, 1970, 9

225) "Dr. W.S. Hunton, Expert On Africa," The New York Times, January 16, 1970

226) Alphaeus Hunton College Teachers Club, "Discussion of the Draft Resolution," Party Affairs, Vol. 9, No. 5 (May 1975), 37

227) "Negro People Are on the Move, Eastern Seaboard Parley Showed," The Worker, April 18, 1943, 8

228) Hunton, *Alphaeus Hunton...*, Ibid, 85

229) Aptheker, ed., *The Correspondence of W. E. B. Du Bois...*, Ibid, 459

Selected Bibliography

Abt, John J. with Myerson, Michael, *Advocate and Activist: Memoirs of an American Communist Lawyer* (University of Illinois Press, 1993)

Aptheker, Bettina, *Intimate Politics: How I Grew Up Red, Fought for Free Speech, and Became A Feminist Rebel* (Seal Press, 2011)

Boyce Davies, Carole, *Left of Karl Marx: The Political Life of Black Communist Claudia Jones* (Duke University Press, 2008)

Buelna, Enrique M., *Chicano Communists And The Struggle For Social Justice* (University of Arizona Press, 2019)

Chapman, Jr., Frank Edgar, *The Damned Don't Dry* (Lulu Press, 2019)

Dennis, Michael, *Blood On Steel: Chicago Steelworkers And The Strike Of 1937* (Johns Hopkins University Press, 2014)

Duffy, Peter, *The Agitator: William Bailey and the First American Uprising against Nazism* (Public Affairs, 2019)

Feurer, Rosemary, *Radical Unionism In The Midwest, 1900-1950* (University of Illinois Press, 2006)

Foner, Philip S., ed., *The Bolshevik Revolution: Its Impact on American Radicals, Liberals, and Labor* (International Publishers, 2017)

Gellman, Erik S., *Death Blow to Jim Crow: The National Negro Congress and the Rise of Militant Civil Rights* (University of North Carolina Press, 2014)

Ghodsee, Kristen, *Second World, Second Sex: Socialist Women's Activism and Global Solidarity during the Cold War* (Duke University Press, 2018)

Gilmore, Glenda, *Defying Dixie: The Radical Roots of Civil Rights, 1919-1950* (W. W. Norton & Company, August 10, 2009)

Grant, Nicholas, *Winning Our Freedoms Together: African Americans and Apartheid, 1945–1960* (University of North Carolina Press, 2017)

Haviland, Sara Rzeszutek, *James and Esther Cooper Jackson: Love And Courage In The Black Freedom Movement* (University Press of Kentucky, 2015)

Holsaert, Noonan, Richardson, Robinson, Young and Zellner, ed., *Hands On The Freedom Plow: Personal Accounts By Women In SNCC* (University of Illinois Press, 2012)

Honey, Michael K., *Southern Labor and Black Civil Rights: Organizing Memphis Workers* (University of Illinois, 1993)

Horne, Gerald, *Black and Red: W. E. B. DuBois and the Afro-American Response to the Cold War, 1944-1963* (University of New York Press, 1986)

———. *White Supremacy Confronted: U.S. Imperialism and Anti-Communism vs. the Liberation of Southern Africa, from Rhodes to Mandela* (international Publishers, 2019)

———. *Black Liberation/Red Scare: Ben Davis and the Communist Party* (University of Delaware Press, 1994)

———. *Black Revolutionary: William Patterson and the Globalization of the African American Freedom Struggle* (University of Illinois Press, 2013)

———. *Communist Front: The Civil Rights Congress, 1946-1956* (Associated University Presses, 1988)

———. *Fighting In Paradise: Labor Unions, Racism, And Communists In The Making Of Modern Hawai'i* (University of Hawaii Press, 2011)

———. *Paul Robeson: The Artist as Revolutionary* (Pluto Press, 2016)

———. *Class Struggle In Hollywood, 1930-1950: Moguls, Mobsters, Stars, Reds, & Trade Unionists* (University of Texas Press, 2001)

———. *Red Seas: Ferdinand Smith and Radical Black Sailors in the United States and* Jamaica (New York University Press, 2009)

———. *Race Woman: The Lives Of Shirley Graham Du Bois* (New York University Press, 2000)

Isserman, Maurice, *Which Side Were You On? : The American Communist Party During the Second World War* (Wesleyan University Press, 1982)

Johanningsmeier, Edward P., *Forging American Communism: The Life of William Z. Foster* (Princeton University Press, 1994)

Johnson, Howard Eugene; Johnson, Wendy; Naison, Mark D., ed., *A Dancer in the Revolution: Stretch Johnson, Harlem Communist at the Cotton Club* (Fordham University Press, 2014)

Kaplan, Judy and Shapiro, Linn, ed., *Red Diapers: Growing Up In The Communist Left* (University of Illinois Press, 1998)

Keeran, Roger, *The Communist Party and the Auto-Workers' Union* (International Publishers, 1986)

Kelley, Robin D. G., *Hammer And Hoe: Alabama Communists During The Great Depression* (University of North Carolina Press, 1990)

Larson, Eric, ed., *Jobs With Justice: 25 Years, 25 Voices* (PM Press, 2013)

Levering Lewis, David; Nash, Michael H.; Leab, Daniel J., ed., *Red Activists and Black Freedom: James and Esther Jackson and the Long Civil Rights Revolution* (Routledge, 2010)

Lorence, James L., *The Unemployed People's Movement: Leftists, Liberals, And Labor In Georgia, 1929-1941* (University of Georgia Press, 2011)

Lumpkin, Beatrice, *Always Bring A Crowd: The Story of Frank Lumpkin Steelworker* (International Publishers, 1999)

Martelle, Scott, *The Fear Within: Spies, Commies, and American Democracy on Trial* (Rutgers University Press, 2001)

McDuffie, Erik S., *Sojourning For freedom: Black Women, American Communism, and the Making of Black Left Feminism* (Duke University Press, 2011)

Mickenberg, Julia L., *American Girls In Red Russia: Chasing the Soviet Dream* (University of Chicago Press, 2017)

Mildo Hall, Gwendolyn, ed., *A Black Communist In The Freedom Struggle: The Life Of Harry Haywood* (University of Minnesota Press, 2012)

Mortimer, Wyndham, *Organize: My Life as a Union Man* (Beacon Paperback, 1972

Murrell, Gary, *"The Most Dangerous Communist in the United States": A Biography of Herbert Aptheker* (University of Massachusetts Press, 2015)

Naison, Mark, *Communists in Harlem during the Depression* (University of Illinois Press, 2005)

Nelson, Bruce, *Workers on the Waterfront: Seaman, Longshoremen, and Unionism in the 1930s* (University of Illinois Press, 1990)

Nesbitt, Francis Njubi, *Race for Sanctions: African Americans against Apartheid, 1946-1994* (Indiana University Press, 2004)

Ottanelli, Fraser M., *The Communist Party Of The United States: From the Depression to World War II* (Rutgers University Press, 1992)

Robeson, Taj Fraizier, *The East Is Black: Cold War China in the Black Radical Imagination* (Duke University Press, 2015)

Roman, Meredith L., *Opposing Jim Crow: African Americans And The Soviet Indictment Of U.S. Racism, 1928-1937* (University of Nebraska Press, 2012)

Ryan, James G., *Earl Browder: The Failure of American Communism* (University of Alabama Press, 2005)

Sabin, Author J., *Red Scare in Court: New York Versus the International Workers Order* (University of Pennsylvania Press, 1993)

Solomon, Mark, *The Cry Was Unity: Communists and African Americans, 1917-1936* (University Press of Mississippi, 1998)

Somerville, John, *The Communist Trials and the American Tradition: Expert Testimony on Force, and Violence and Democracy* (International Publishers, 2000)

Spencer, Robyn, *Angela Davis: Radical Icon* (Westview Press, 2020)

Stepan-Norris, Judith and Zeitlan, Maurice, *Left Out: Reds and America's Industrial Unions* (Cambridge University Press, 2002)

Swerdlow, Amy, *Women Strike For Peace: Traditional Motherhood and Radical Politics in the* 1960s (University of Chicago Press, 1993)

Taylor, Clarence, *Reds At The Blackboard: Communism, Civil Rights, and the New York City Teachers Union* (Columbia University Press, 2011)

Vapnek, Lara, *Elizabeth Gurley Flynn: Modern American Revolutionary* (Westview Press, 2015)

Von Eschen, Penny M., *Race Against Empire: Black Americans and Anticolonialism, 1937-1957* (Cornell University Press, 1997)

Washington, Mary Helen, *The Other Blacklist: The African American Literary and Cultural Left of the 1950s* (Columbia University Press, 2014)

Zecker, Robert M., *"A Road to Peace and Freedom": The International Workers Order and the Struggle for Economic Justice and Civil Rights, 1930-1954* (Temple University Press, 2018)

Index